AMERICAN FOREIGN POLICY, PRESENT TO PAST

Urgent Issues in American Society Series:

American Habitat, Barbara Gutmann Rosenkrantz and
  William A. Koelsch
The Military and American Society, Stephen E. Ambrose and
  James Alden Barber, Jr.
The American Economy, Arthur M. Johnson
Shaping the American Educational State, Clarence J. Karier

AMERICAN FOREIGN POLICY, PRESENT TO PAST

A Narrative With Readings and Documents

Edited by
LLOYD C. GARDNER

THE FREE PRESS
A Division of Macmillan Publishing Co., Inc.
NEW YORK

Collier Macmillan Publishers
LONDON

For Becky, Erin, and Timmy

Copyright © 1974 by The Free Press
      A Division of Macmillan
      Publishing Co., Inc.

327.73
A512

All rights reserved. No part of this book may be reproduced or transmitted in any form or by any means, electronic or mechanical, including photocopying, recording, or by any information storage and retrieval system, without permission in writing from the Publisher.

The Free Press
A Division of Macmillan Publishing Co., Inc.
866 Third Avenue, New York, N.Y. 10022

Collier-Macmillan Canada Ltd.

Library of Congress Catalog Card Number: 74–2651

Printed in the United States of America

Printing number
1 2 3 4 5 6 7 8 9 10

Library of Congress Cataloging in Publication Data

Gardner, Lloyd C   date   comp.
   American foreign policy, present to past.

   (Urgent issues in American society series)
   Includes bibliographical references.
   1. United States--Foreign relations--1945-
I. Title.
E744.G342   327.73   74-2651
ISBN 0-02-911310-5
ISBN 0-02-911300-8 (pbk.)

The author gratefully acknowledges permission to reprint the following material:

iv

ACKNOWLEDGMENTS

"Nixon Interview" by C. L. Sulzberger of March 9, 1971. Copyright © 1971 by the New York Times Company. Reprinted by permission. See page 1.

"The Viet Nam Negotiations" by Henry A. Kissinger. Excerpted by permission from *Foreign Affairs,* January 1969. Copyright © 1968 by Council on Foreign Relations, Inc. See page 10.

"The Viet Nam Policy Reversal of 1968" by Hedrick Smith and William Beecher of March 6, 7, 1969. Copyright © 1969 by The New York Times Company. Reprinted by permission. See page 19.

Excerpt from *Truth Is the First Casualty* by Joseph C. Goulden. Copyright © 1969 by Joseph C. Goulden. Published by Rand McNally & Company. Excerpt from Frank N. Trager, "The Far East," in *National Security: Political, Military and Economic Strategies in the Decade Ahead,* eds. David W. Afshire and Richard V. Allen (New York: Praeger Publishers, Inc., 1965). See page 49.

Jerome Levinson and Juan de Onis, *The Alliance That Lost Its Way: A Critical Report on the Alliance for Progress.* © 1970 by The Twentieth Century Fund, New York. Published by Quadrangle Books. See page 74.

Abridged from pages 142, 144–145, 147–151 in *The Essence of Security* by Robert S. McNamara. Copyright © 1968 by Robert S. McNamara. By permission of Harper & Row, Publishers, Inc. See page 91.

"Economic Aspects of U.S. Imperialism" by Harry Magdoff. Copyright © 1966 by Monthly Review, Inc.; reprinted by permission of Monthly Review Press. See page 123.

The Radical Left and American Foreign Policy by Robert Tucker. Copyright © 1971 by The Johns Hopkins University Press; reprinted by permission of the Publisher. See page 132.

"Kennedy and the Strategy of Aid: The Clay Report and After" by Usha Mahajani, from *Western Political Quarterly,* vol. 19, no. 3 (September 1966), pages 656–668. Copyright © 1966 by the University of Utah; reprinted by permission of the University of Utah, copyright holder. See page 138.

The Cuban Missile Crisis: An Analysis of Soviet Calculations and Behavior, by Arnold L. Horelick, in *World Politics,* vol. XVI, no. 3 (Copyright © 1964 by Princeton University Press): an excerpt of 1600 words. Reprinted by permission of Princeton University Press. See page 154.

"The Cuban Crisis Revisited" by Leslie Dewart, in *Studies on the Left* (Spring 1966). Copyright © 1966 by Leslie Dewart. Reprinted by permission of the author. See page 162.

U.S. Business Interests in Cuba and the Rise of Castro, by Leland L. Johnson, in *World Politics,* vol. XVII, no. 3 (Copyright © 1965 by Princeton University Press): an excerpt of 5200 words. Reprinted by permission of Princeton University Press. See page 166.

ACKNOWLEDGMENTS

From pages 213–214 in *Riding The Storm, 1956–1959,* by Harold Macmillan. Copyright © 1971 by Thomson Newspapers Limited. By permission of Harper & Row, Publishers, Inc. See page 188.

From *The White House Years; Mandate for Change,* 1953–1956 by Dwight D. Eisenhower: Copyright © 1963 by Dwight D. Eisenhower. Reprinted by permission of Doubleday & Company, Inc., and of William Heinemann Ltd., Publishers. See page 201.

From *The Invisible Government* by David Wise and Thomas B. Ross. Copyright © 1964 by David Wise and Thomas B. Ross. Reprinted by permission of Random House, Inc. See page 217.

"The Failure of a Policy Rooted in Fear" by Steven E. Ambrose, from *The Progressive,* November 1970. Copyright © 1970 by *The Progressive.* Reprinted by permission of *The Progressive.* See page 253.

"The Sources of Soviet Conduct" by George F. Kennan ("X"). Excerpted by permission of *Foreign Affairs,* July 1947. Copyright 1947 by Council on Foreign Relations, Inc. See page 297.

Abridged from pages 10–17, 21–24 30–31, 33–35, 40, 46–47, 50, 51, 58–59, 60–61 in *The Cold War: A Study in U.S. Foreign Policy* by Walter Lippmann. Copyright, 1947 by Walter Lippmann. By permission of Harper & Row, Publishers, Inc. See page 309.

"The Conflict Over Trade Ideologies" by Herbert Feis. Reprinted by permission of *Foreign Affairs,* January 1947. Copyright 1946 by Council on Foreign Relations, Inc. See page 332.

"Wallace speech" by Henry A. Wallace from *Vital Speeches,* vol. XII (October 1946). Copyright 1946 by *Vital Speeches.* Reprinted by permission of *Vital Speeches,* City News Publishing Company. See page 345.

Contents

Preface   *viii*

CHAPTER ONE

America's Longest War   *1*

CHAPTER TWO

Pax Americana: The Theory and Practice   *63*

CHAPTER THREE

Cold War Crises in the Third World   *144*

CHAPTER FOUR

Frame of Reference: Korea and Before   *226*

CHAPTER FIVE

In the Beginning . . .   *296*

Index   *362*

Preface

History is very often the policy maker's chief counsellor. He looks to this aide for precedents and justifications to support his view of the world and to explain his goals to others. Whether it be Richard Nixon pondering the decline of the "Establishment's" willingness to face the problems of a post-Cold War era, Dean Rusk contrasting Ho Chi-minh's revolutionary aims with those of the American Founding Fathers, or Harry S. Truman seeing the 1931 Manchurian crisis in the Korean War, the image of the past carries great weight in policy decisions. Critics have the same need for a "usable" past, to supply themselves with answers and refutations. Both have this in common: they reach back from the present.

Those who write history, on the other hand, fill their pages from the beginning and work forward. While this process seems more logical, it may also obscure certain aspects of historical reality. When Jerry Grob suggested the idea of this book to me, therefore, I was intrigued with the possibilities for re-focusing on the events since World War II from the perspective of the present. Writing the narrative in this fashion was a lot like seeing a movie run backwards. Presumably readers will get the same feeling, yet hopefully they will also pick out important points missed in more traditional collections.

The organizing principle was determined by no rigid plan, but by where I thought an explanation for certain phenomena might be found and illustrated. Many of the documents and readings have not appeared in previous collections. Some have, of course, or there would be a danger of assuming too much about the reader's familiarity with recent American foreign policy.

PREFACE

In January 1973 an agreement was signed making it possible for President Nixon to withdraw American troops from Vietnam, said his spokesmen, without weakening American power and prestige elsewhere. Months earlier, the President and American television cameras visited China. It was the week the Cold War finally became history. And months before that trip, in February 1972, the President outlined the basic assumptions of his "new" American foreign policy, what he called "The Emerging Structure of Peace."

Today, two and a half decades after the war, new realities are reflected in a new American approach to foreign policy. The growing strength and self-confidence of others allow them to assume greater responsibilities and us to shift to a more restrained role. And with the time long past when one nation could speak for all Communist countries, we deal with individual nations on the basis of their foreign, and not their domestic policy.[*1]

For at least a decade many liberals had wanted a President to speak those words, and many conservatives had just as fervently hoped against such a moment. Neither expected to hear them from Richard Nixon, the first of the Cold Warrior politicians in the late 1940's—and still the most vigorous two decades later. Throughout those long years, moreover, the domestic change thesis was the key to American policy toward the Soviet Union, China, and finally, Cuba. It was the foundation of bi-partisanship in foreign policy, and the ideological cement which held Cold War alliances together. It was the premise for both the Truman-Acheson "Containment" policy and the Eisenhower-Dulles "Liberation" approach. According to this thesis there had to be a domestic change in Communist nations before there could be any chance for diplomatic adjustment anyplace in the world.

And here was Nixon suddenly calling it off: ". . . we deal with individual nations on the basis of their foreign, and not their

---

[*1] *U.S. Foreign Policy for the 1970's: The Emerging Structure of Peace, A Report to the Congress by Richard Nixon* . . . (Washington, D.C.: Government Printing Office, 1972), p. 27.

domestic policy." True, he had not said that the Communist nations had abandoned their goals of world revolution, the most obvious manifestation to Western leaders of Soviet Marxism. But he no longer spoke of it as a Kremlin conspiracy: ". . . with the time long past when one nation could speak for all Communist countries."

It was a remarkable speech, and a remarkable turn-about. Some were so upset that they found themselves worrying about a "new isolationism," the favorite bugaboo of liberals ever since Wilson's unsuccessful effort to push the United States into the League of Nations. Yet Nixon himself warned against isolationism in the post-Cold War era, explaining his decision to go slow in withdrawing from Vietnam precisely because he wanted to guard against a domestic and international backlash leading to an American retreat everywhere. In one speech the President even quoted Henry James, the philosopher of American pragmatism, on the need for a moral equivalent to war to stimulate the spirit of sacrifice and as a spur to greater achievements in the pursuits of peace. But perhaps the fullest expression of the President's post-Cold War vision came in a July 1971 speech to midwestern news media executives. In it he explained Vietnamization, but more than that he used the past to explain where America must go in the future:

Following are excerpts from the transcript of remarks made by President Nixon at Kansas City, Mo., on July 6 [1971] before news media executives from 13 Middle Western States attending a background briefing on domestic policy initiatives.[1]

I think perhaps for this kind of meeting what I could best do is to put all of these domestic programs into a broader context, to indicate the relationship between these programs and the problems that America has in the world.

Sometimes that seems very, very hard to do. I realize that it is quite the approach these days to suggest that we either ought to look at our foreign policy and put that as priority number one—

---

[1] For the complete transcript of President Nixon's remarks, see White House press release (Kansas City, Mo.) dated July 6.

in other words, the security of America must come first—or we must put our priority on domestic problems and turn away from the problems in the world.

The answer to that is that we must do both. It would not be any good to have clean air and water if we were not around to enjoy it. On the other side of the coin, we are not going to play an effective role in the world unless we have a healthy environment, economically and every other way.

For a few moments, I would like to discuss the world position we find ourselves in today and indicate why I believe these domestic programs—a program of reform which goes far beyond any program of reform which has been submitted to the American people in over 40 years, why that program is so essential at this particular time, why it is that America now cannot be satisfied domestically, we cannot rest on our laurels, why we have to make a critical examination of everything we are doing in this country to see whether we are doing it with the most efficiency possible.

Now, in terms of our world situation, the tendency is, and this has been the case for the last 5 to 6 years, for us to obscure our vision almost totally of the world because of Viet-Nam. That is understandable. We are always concerned about the war in which we are currently involved. That was true at the time of Korea. It is now true of Viet-Nam.

The difficulty is that as we obscure our vision with Viet-Nam, we do not see very significant changes that have occurred in the world over the past 25 years, the period since World War II, and changes that have occurred, even more dramatically perhaps, over the past 5 to 10 years and ones that may be in the offing. So I would like to take Viet-Nam very briefly.

I have nothing new to say on Viet-Nam. It seems to me, however, that since so much has been written and said in recent weeks about how we got in, it might be well to reiterate what we are doing to get out.

On Viet-Nam, what we find is that 300,000 Americans have left Viet-Nam since this administration came in. A division a month are coming home each month at this time. As far as casualties are concerned, it is interesting to note that the casualties in the month of June were less on a monthly basis than the weekly casualties we were having a year ago. When we came into office, they were 15 times as great per month or week or day, take the index, whatever it is. One is too many, but that does indicate the winding down of the war.

As far as the ending of the war is concerned, as far as American involvement, we find that we are proceeding on two tracks. We are actively pursuing the negotiating channel. We also, regardless of what happens on the negotiating front, are pursuing our program of Vietnamization in which all Americans will be withdrawn from Viet-Nam consistent with two objectives: first, of course, the release of our prisoners of war; and secondly, in a way that will contribute to a permanent and lasting peace, we hope, in Southeast Asia and in the Pacific, rather than in a way that might increase the danger of another war.

I will simply conclude this section by saying this: Viet-Nam is an issue which, of course, concerns us. It is an issue, however, to which we have an answer. The American involvement is being ended. It will be ended certainly. The question is only a matter of time and only a matter of how. So consequently, it seems to me that a group of editors, opinion makers like yourselves, should, and I think will, appreciate the opportunity to look beyond Viet-Nam.

NEW ECONOMIC POWER CENTERS

For example, a year from now, what is the world going to look like as Viet-Nam moves from our vision, or at least recedes from it, and what will America's role in the world be at that time?

As I came into the room, I noticed Martin Hayden [editor, Detroit News]. I shook hands with him. I perhaps can put my remarks on the world scene in context by pointing out that he first came to see me when I was a freshman Congressman. It was 24 years ago. I was thinking how much had happened in those 24 years. Many of you, a few of you, are old enough to remember what America was 24 years ago.

We were number one in the world militarily with no one who even challenged us, because we had a monopoly on atomic weapons. We also at that point were number one economically by all odds. In fact, the United States of America was producing more than 50 percent of all the world's goods.

That was just 25 years ago. Now, 25 years having passed, let's look at the situation today and what it may be 5 years from now or 10 years from now. I will not try to limit myself to 5 or 10 years except to say that in the next decade we are going to see changes that may be even greater than what have occurred in the last 25 years, and very great ones have occurred in that respect.

First, instead of just America being number one in the world from an economic standpoint, the preeminent world power, and instead of there being just two superpowers, when we think in economic terms and economic potentialities there are five great power centers in the world today. Let's look at them very briefly.

There is, of course, the United States of America. There is, second, Western Europe, Western Europe with Britain in the Common Market. That means 300 million of the most advanced people in the world, with all the productivity and all the capacity that those people will have and, of course, with the clout that they will have when they act together, as they certainly will. That is a new factor in the world scene that will come, and come very soon, as we all know.

Then in the Pacific, looking also at free-world countries, we have a resurgent Japan. I met with steel leaders of industry and unions this morning. I pointed out what happened to Japan in terms of their business. Twenty years ago Japan produced 5 million tons of steel; this year 100 million; 2 years from now Japan will produce more steel than the United States of America.

That is what has happened. It has happened in the case of Japan, in the case of Germany, our two major enemies in World War II, partly as a result of our help in getting them on their feet and partly because of their own energy and ability.

Now we have three power centers—the United States, Western Europe, and Japan, noting that both Western Europe and Japan are very potent competitors of the United States; friends, yes; allies, yes; but competing and competing very hard with us throughout the world for economic leadership.

NEGOTIATIONS WITH THE SOVIET UNION

Now we turn to the other two superpowers, economic superpowers, I will say for the moment. The Soviet Union, of course, first comes to mind. Looking at the Soviet Union, we are entering a period which, only time will tell, may be successful in terms of creating a very new relationship or a very different relationship than we have had previously.

I referred to the need for an era of negotiation rather than confrontation when I made my inaugural speech. We have been negotiating. We have made some progress in the negotiations. The important thing is we are negotiating rather than confronting in many areas of the world where confrontation could lead to explosion. Whether it is on limitation of nuclear arms, the issue of Europe, or negotiations on the Mideast, the negotiations are going on.

I am not suggesting that these negotiations are going to lead to instant peace and instant relationships with the Soviet Union such as we presently have with our friends in Asia who may be allied with us or who may have systems of government that are more closely aligned to ours. What we have to recognize is that even as we limit arms, if we do reach an agreement in that field, and even if we find ways to avoid confrontation in other areas and perhaps work out a negotiated settlement for mutual force reductions in Europe and the problem of Berlin and all the others that come to mind, we must recognize that the Soviet Union will continue to be a very potent, powerful, aggressive competitor of the United States of America. And ironically—and this is also true of mainland China, as I will point out in a moment—as we have more and more success on the negotiation front, as for example the Soviet Union, like the United States, may be able if we have a limitation in nuclear arms, if we are able to turn our eyes more toward our economic development and our economic problems, it simply means that the competition changes and becomes much more challenging in the economic area than it has been previously.

So what we find, in other words, is that the success, and we do want success, of a policy of negotiation rather than confrontation will lead to infinitely more economic competition from the Soviet Union.

Mainland China is, of course, a very different situation. First, in terms of its economic capacity at the present time, a pretty good indication of where it is is that Japan, with 100 million people, produces more than mainland China with 800 million people. But that should not mislead us, and it gives us and should give none of the potential competitors in the world markets, mainland China, any sense of satisfaction that it will always be that way, because when we see the Chinese as people—and I have seen them all over the world, and some of you have, too, whether in Hong Kong or Thailand or Singapore or Bangkok, any of the great cities, Manila, where Chinese are there—they are creative, they are productive, they are one of the most capable people in the world, and 800 million Chinese are going to be, inevitably, an enormous economic power, with all that means in terms of what they could be in other areas if they move in that direction.

ENDING THE ISOLATION OF MAINLAND CHINA

That is the reason why I felt that it was essential that this administration take the first steps toward ending the isolation of mainland China from the world community. We had to take those steps because the Soviet Union could not because of differences that they have that at the present time seem to be irreconcilable. We were the only other power that could take those steps.

Let me be very, shall I say, limited in what I would discuss on this particular issue, because we should not consider that more has happened than has happened. What we have done is simply open the door—open the door for travel; open the door for trade.

Now, the question is whether there will be other doors opened on their part. But at least the doors must be opened and the goal of U.S. policy must be in the long term ending the isolation of mainland China and a normalization of our relations with mainland China because, looking down the road—and let's just look ahead 15 to 20 years—the United States could have a perfectly effective agreement with the Soviet Union for limitation of arms; the danger of any confrontation there might have been almost totally removed. But mainland China outside the world community, completely isolated, with its leaders not in communication with world leaders, would be a danger to the whole world that would be unacceptable, unacceptable to us and unacceptable to others as well.

So, consequently, this step must be taken now. Others must be taken, very precisely, very deliberately, as there is reciprocation on the other side.

But now let's see how this all fits into the economic program I mentioned a moment ago, and the economic challenge. The very success of our policy of ending the isolation of mainland China will mean an immense escalation of their economic challenge, not only to us but to others in the world.

I again come back to the fundamental point: 800 million Chinese open to the world, with all the communication and the interchange of ideas that inevitably will occur as a result of that opening, will become an economic force in the world of enormous potential.

So, in sum, what do we see? What we see as we look ahead 5, 10, and perhaps 15 years, we see five great economic superpowers: the United States, Western Europe, the Soviet Union, mainland China, and, of course, Japan.

Now, I do not suggest, in mentioning these five, that Latin America is not important, that Africa is not important, that South Asia is not important. All nations are important, and all peoples in underdeveloped or less developed countries will play their role. But these are the five that will determine the economic future and, because economic power will be the key to other kinds of power, the future of the world in other ways in the last third of this century.

Now let's see what this means to the United States. It means that the United States, as compared with that position we found ourselves in immediately after World War II, has a challenge such as we did not even dream of. Then we were talking about the dollar gap; then we were talking about the necessity of, putting it in terms of a poker game, that the United States had all the chips and we had to spread a few of the chips around so that others could play.

We did it—$100 billion for Western Europe to rebuild them and billions of others to other countries, and it was the correct policy as it turned out. Now as we see the world in which we are about to move, the United States is no longer in the position of complete preeminence or predominance. That is not a bad thing. As a matter of fact, it could be a constructive thing. The United States is still the strongest nation in the world, the richest nation in the world, but now we face a situation where four other potential economic powers have the capacity, have the kind of people—if not the kind of government, at least the kind of people —who can challenge us on every front.

That brings us back home, and it brings us back home for a hard look at what America needs to do if we are going to run this race economically and run it effectively and maintain the position of world leadership, a position that can only be maintained if the United States retains its preeminent position in the economic field.

U.S. WORLD LEADERSHIP

We wonder what kind of a nation we are going to be then [the Fourth of July, 1976]. Well, I will flatly predict that 5 years from now we will still be the richest nation in the world, if we want to be—and this will depend upon the American people—and need to be. We will still be the strongest nation in the world. But the critical question is whether the United States will be a healthy nation, a healthy nation not simply with a healthy government and a healthy economy and a healthy environment and a healthy physical system insofar as we personally are concerned but healthy in terms of its moral strength.

On that, there is a question. That question is raised often in your editorial columns that I have noted, because I read many of them. It should be raised. But I would only suggest that part of the reason for raising it is that again we tend to allow the problems of the moment to obscure our vision of the future. We tend to allow our faults—and we have many—to obscure the many virtues of our society.

I will not list them. Let us simply say that world leadership— oh, I know all the criticisms: The United States can't be trusted with power; the United States should recede from the world scene and take care of its own problems and leave world leadership to somebody else, because we engage in immorality in the conduct of our foreign policy. Let's take a look.

We have been in four wars in this century, and four times young Americans have gone abroad. We have done so without any idea of conquest or domination. We have lost hundreds of thousands of lives, and we have not gotten a thing out of any of it, and we have helped each of our enemies, after each of the wars, get on his feet again.

We made our mistakes. We make them now, for example, as we made them in previous wars. Let me say this: Think for a moment. What other nation in the world would you like to have in the position of preeminent power? What other nation in the world that has what it takes would have the attitude that the United States has, as far as its foreign policy is concerned?

Here is a nation that did not seek the preeminent world position. It came to us because of what had happened in World War II. But here is a nation that has helped its former enemies, that is generous now to those who might be its opponents, a nation that, it seems to me, is one that the world is very fortunate, in a way, to have in a position of world leadership.

In terms of our domestic policies, I think we can truly say we have some problems. They are quite significant, and we like to look at those problems, not only look at them, but we must work on them and constantly see that America is revitalized and reinvigorated.

But as we look at those problems, the enormous strengths of this country can only be appreciated once you have seen other countries, great as they are and as much as they have to offer, and come back to see what we have in America. I am not speaking of wealth. I am speaking of freedom. I am speaking of opportunity. I am speaking of concern, concern that people have not only for people here but for people in other places.*2

Nixon's sense of the "historical turning point" is acute. As his domestic "Watergate" difficulties grew steadily worse, his spokesmen talked of the President's other constituency—world leaders who had confidence in his foreign policy and who depended upon him to see them through the transition to a new world order. Yet his foreign policies are as deeply concerned with American needs as when he and others developed the original Cold War world view. And before that, American foreign policy was grounded in many of the same concerns. The narrative, readings, and documents which follow are an effort to explore those concerns and interests from present to past.

LONDON, ENGLAND

*2 Department of State Bulletin, July 26, 1971, pp. 93–97.

CHAPTER ONE
★ ★ ★ ★ ★

America's Longest War

On March 9, 1971, President Richard M. Nixon granted *The New York Times* a special interview on foreign affairs. Columnist C. L. Sulzberger observed that the President "spoke easily, sitting relaxed in an armchair and more or less thinking aloud as he began to recapitulate his aims, methods and hopes." After a few preliminary remarks, the President took up the problem of how the Vietnam War had affected the nation's attitudes on foreign policy:

The irony today, for those who look at the Washington scene, is that the great internationalists of the post-World War II period have become the neoisolationists of the Vietnam war period and especially of the period accompanying the ending of that war. And it is ending.

This is also true of the attitude of those former internationalists with respect to our defense posture and defense spending. And, for some, it is even true of our foreign trade policy. . . . Why has this happened? Why have many former internationalists developed neo-isolationist tendencies, at least in some degree? Part of the answer is simply that Americans, like all idealists, are very impatient people. They feel that if a good thing is going to happen it should happen instantly.

And a great many of these people are very disillusioned with the United Nations. I am not, personally, because I never expected it could settle all problems involving major powers but could nevertheless play a useful role in development and in peacekeeping in areas where the superpowers were not directly involved.

The older a nation and a people become, the more they become conscious of history and also of what is possible. Now I will explain to you what I mean. I rate myself as a deeply committed pacifist, perhaps because of my Quaker heritage from my mother. But I must deal with how peace can be achieved and how it must be preserved.

I know that some national leaders and some countries want to expand by conquest and are committed to expansion, and this obviously creates the danger of war. Moreover, some peoples have hated each other for years and years. . . .

With this in mind, I am deeply devoted to a desire that the United States should make the greatest possible contribution it can make to developing such a peaceful world.

It is not enough just to *be* for peace. The point is, what can we *do* about it?

Through an accident of history we find ourselves today in a situation where no one who is really for peace in his country can reject an American role in the rest of the world. Of course, we had our own period of colonial expansion as typified by Theodore Roosevelt and the idea of Manifest Destiny. But that period is fortunately gone.

Since then this country has fought in four wars which we didn't start, and really what they have in common is the effort to bring about a better chance for a peaceful world.

And this applies for the Vietnam war as well as the two World Wars and Korea. Obviously it was a political temptation when I started office to state simply that we would get out right away without any responsibility for what came next.

But I knew too much about history, about Asia, about the basic feeling in the United States. If we failed to achieve our limited goal—to let a small country exercise the right to choose its own way of life, without having a Communist government imposed upon it by force—if we failed to achieve this, we would not help the cause of peace.

For a time, perhaps, we would be seen as a kind of hero. But soon it would be seen that we had left behind a legacy of even greater dangers for Southeast Asia and for the Pacific region. And, after all, we are a Pacific power.

In 1966 and 1967—culminating in 1968—the American people began to tire of playing a role in the world. We had fought four wars, selflessly and for no gain. We had provided some $100-billion in foreign aid, much of it to former enemies who are now our competitors, like Japan.

And we found ourselves committed in Vietnam, in a war where there arc no heroes, only goats. Our people became sick of Vietnam and supported our men there only in order to get them out— after this period of change in mood. Somewhere a great change had taken place.

We had used our power for peace in four wars but this new attitude gained force: "If we can't handle this one, to hell with it."

We got caught up in a vicious cross fire, and it became increasingly difficult to make people understand. I must say that without television it might have been difficult for me to get people to understand a thing.

The cross fire I referred to was this. The superdoves opposed our commitment in Vietnam and *all* world responsibilities—Korea, the Philippines, the Middle East, Europe. This was the kind of isolationism of those who felt the United States shouldn't have played any role at all in Southeast Asia from the very start. For these people Vietnam was a distant, small, foreign country in just the terms that Chamberlain mentioned concerning Czechoslovakia at the time of Munich. These were the superdoves.

But on the other side, the opposite cross fire came from the superhawks. This group stood by their Commander in Chief, the President, but became fed up with the war for their own reasons. They felt that if the United States can't handle a distant little war, why then let's just pull out and build up our strength at home. Their logic also favored isolationism, but from another angle. And they want to develop a Fortress America at home and cram it full of missiles while the superdoves want us to pull out of the world also, but reducing our strength at home.

3

In between there are those of us who stand in the middle of the cross fire. The superhawk feels it is his duty to support the President even if that same superhawk isn't sure he wants to see us do what we are doing. The superdove has a different attitude.

He is a good-hearted fellow, but when he looks around and sees the problems of the poor, the blacks, the Indians, the poor whites, the pot-smoking kids, crime in the cities, urban slums, the environment, he says: "We must get out of the war right away and concern ourselves only with our problems at home."

The fact is, however, that there has never been so great a challenge to U.S. leadership. This war is ending. In fact, I seriously doubt if we will ever have another war. This is probably the very last one.

In any theoretical question of a war on the basis of "either them or us," I am sure everyone in the country would join in behind me. But this is not the case in a small country so far away involved in a situation so difficult to explain.

I am certain a Gallup poll would show that the great majority of the people would want to pull out of Vietnam. But a Gallup poll would also show that a great majority of the people would want to pull three or more divisions out of Europe. And it would also show that a great majority of the people would cut our defense budget.

Polls are not the answer. You must look at the facts. The Soviets now have three times the missile strength (ICBM) of ourselves. By 1974 they will pass us in submarines carrying nuclear missiles.

All of these things are very directly related. For example, when Mrs. Meir, the Israeli Prime Minister, visited me, she understood me right away when I said that if America winds up the war in Vietnam in failure and an image is developed that the war was fought only by stupid scoundrels, there would be a wave of isolationism. This would embrace the U.S. role everywhere—including the Middle East. Mrs. Meir saw the point immediately.

As I see it, we have to take certain specific steps. First of all, what we now have to do is end the war—as we now are doing—in a way that gives South Vietnam a reasonable chance to survive without our help. But this doesn't mean we would withdraw all our responsibilities everywhere.

As I stated in first explaining the Nixon doctrine, our idea is to create a situation in which those lands to which we have obligations or in which we have interests, if they are ready to fight a fire, should be able to count on us to furnish the hose and water.

Meanwhile, in Europe, we can't cut down our forces until there is a mutual agreement with the other side. We must stand with our European friends if they will only do a bit more themselves in NATO—as they have indicated they will do.

And we cannot foolishly fall behind in the arms competition. In the United States, we remain ahead in the navy and in the air, but the Soviets are ahead in ICBM's and soon will pass us in modern submarine strength.

But each has a kind of sufficiency. The Soviets are a great land power opposite China as well as having far-reaching interests elsewhere. We are a great sea power and we must keep our strength. I am a strong Navy man myself. I believe in a strong conventional navy which helps us to play a peace-keeping role in such areas, for example, as Latin America. . . .

I want the American people to be able to be led by me, or by my successor, along a course that allows us to do what is needed to help keep the peace in this world.

We used to look to other nations to do this job once upon a time. But now only the United States plays a major role of this sort in the world. Our responsibilities are not limited to this great continent but include Europe, the Middle East, Southeast Asia, East Asia, many areas whose fate affects the peace of the world.

We must above all tend to our national obligations. We must not forget our alliances or our interests. Other nations must know that the United States has both the capability and the will to defend these allies and protect these interests.

Unless people understand this and understand it well, the United States will simply retreat into isolationism, both politically and diplomatically. We would, of course, continue to be an economic giant; but that is not enough.

Let us look at the world today. There are two great powers facing us, Russia and China. They are great powers and great people. Certainly neither of them wants war. But both are motivated by a philosophy which announces itself as expansionist in character. This they will admit themselves.

5

And only the United States has sufficient strength to be able to help maintain a balance in Europe and other areas that might otherwise be affected.

What I am saying is not a cold-war philosophy. I hope that we can further develop our negotiations with the Soviet Union. For, although we recognize that their ideology is expansionist, they know what it means if the genie comes out of the bottle and that their interest in survival requires that they avoid a conflict with the United States. This means that we must find a way of cooperating.

For obviously pragmatic reasons, therefore, we can see peace slowly shaping up. First, as we are doing, we must end the war in Vietnam. We must continue our Soviet negotiations and open the door of cooperation to China. And in this way there will be a chance of building a world that is relatively peaceful.

I deliberately say relatively peaceful. That doesn't mean everyone will be disarmed, safe and loving everyone else. The kind of relative peace I envision is not the dream of my Quaker youth. But it is realistic and I am convinced we can bring it about.

Yet, to do this, we can't heed either our superhawks whose policy would ultimately lead to war or to our superdoves who believe that only they are capable of achieving peace and that everyone else is a heretic. The trouble is that their policy of weakness would also quickly lead to war.

The day the United States quits playing a responsible role in the world—in Europe or Asia or the Middle East—or gives up or recedes from its efforts to maintain an adequate defense force—on that day this will become a very unsafe world to live in.

I can assure you that my words are those of a devoted pacifist. My very hardest job is to give out posthumous Medals of Honor. . . .

The big question to my mind is: Will our Establishment and our people meet their responsibilities? Frankly, I have far more confidence in our people than in the Establishment. The people seem to see the problem in simple terms: "By golly, we have to do the right thing."

But the real problem, what worries me most, is: Will our Establishment see it that way? I am not talking about my critics but about a basic, strange sickness that appears to have spread

6

among those who usually, in this country, can be expected to see clearly ahead into the future.

These are the people who, after World War II, supported the Greek-Turkish aid program, the Marshall Plan, NATO. But today they are in disarray because of two things. They are terribly disillusioned about Vietnam, which is so hard a problem to understand. And they have an enormous concern with home problems of a sort and a degree that did not face us a generation earlier.

I understand these factors. There is a vast need for reforms, for improvements in health, education and environment. But we have to assume our responsibilities both abroad and at home. We have to do both. After all, if we manage to improve the environment and living conditions in this country we must also assure that we will be around to enjoy those improvements.[1]

As the President re-affirmed his confidence in the people and in their understanding that the nation must do the "right thing" in Vietnam, the war was entering its seventh year. Soon it would be the nation's longest conflict, longer even than the War of Independence from 1776 to 1783. And the questions it raised reopened controversies from the time of the American Revolution—the issue of the executive's war-making powers under the Constitution, as well as the problem of dissent in a democratic society. Not since World War II had a foreign policy matter so troubled the American mind and physically disrupted the country.

How had the nation become so deeply committed in Southeast Asia? What possible relationship did little Vietnam have to American security? A recent sampling of public opinion had indicated that 73 percent of the people favored pulling out all American troops by December 31, 1971; another 59 percent thought it had been a mistake to send them in the first place. Polls also indicated a decline in the people's confidence in Nixon's handling of the war.

Individual opinion samplings were hardly Mr. Nixon's most serious concern. They went up and down like elevators. In January 1973, after his re-election and the signing of a Vietnam truce, the

[1] *The New York Times,* March 10, 1971, p. 14.

polls reflected tremendous confidence in the President. What did worry him—as it had worried his predecessor—was that "strange sickness" spreading through the "Establishment." His task was to see it through in Vietnam, yes, but in such a way as to maintain the government's prestige at home as well as abroad. Impatience with Cold War rhetoric was no longer confined to "intellectuals," but was spreading to other groups who began to see Vietnam as a positive danger to national interests. The absurdity of arguing that Vietnam constituted a strategic interest worth all it had cost—and would yet cost—suddenly cast in doubt twenty-five years of foreign policy. Convictions held and certainties felt since the end of World War II rapidly gave way to disbelief and disillusion.

Troubled by many of the same questions, an angry, peevish President Lyndon Baines Johnson had snapped in 1966: "I am going to tell you how we got in Vietnam. We have always been in Vietnam." In that remark, barely below the surface, was the source of both Johnson's and Nixon's difficulties in holding the lid on the nation. If we had always been in Vietnam, declared protestors, what was left of the original Cold War premise which posited a mortal struggle between Communism and the Free World?

Throughout his first term in office, Nixon was hard put to salvage something from the Vietnamese situation which might be useful to a new era. The word was out that all the Administration wanted was a decent interval to justify all that America had put into the war. Direct military expenditures for Vietnam had surpassed $100 billion. More than 44,000 Americans had been killed. A Senate Committee estimated civilian casualties in South Vietnam alone at more than one million. It also calculated that there were five million war refugees in South Vietnam, an additional one million in Laos, and yet another million and a half in Cambodia. The Defense Department estimated that nearly three-quarters of a million enemy soldiers had been killed, a not unreasonable figure for all Vietnamese combat deaths.

To fight this kind of war, the United States had sent a 500,000 man army, plus 250,000 more in support roles. Yet the real nature of the war was better measured by relating bombing tonnage used in Indochina to World War II totals. The United States dropped two million-plus tons of explosives on the Axis; by mid-1971 the total delivered against enemy targets in Indochina had surpassed 5,500,000 tons. It was saturation bombing against a guerilla force whose offense and defense was elusiveness, the weapon of the country against the city. More than anything else, the bombing stirred the consciences of those who opposed the war.

Nor did it ever bring victory, or even the promise of a decent interval. Bombing alternated with ground offensives into Laos and Cambodia in an effort to compel the North Vietnamese and the National Liberation Front to negotiate on American terms, i.e., without the U.S. yielding to the demand that the Saigon government be dissolved and replaced with a provisional coalition government. On February 8, 1971, South Vietnam launched a ground attack against the so-called Ho Chi-minh trail in Laos, the supply route North Vietnam had used so effectively throughout the war. Nixon asserted that the enemy would "have to fight here or give up the struggle to conquer South Vietnam." A year earlier, Secretary of Defense Melvin Laird justified new bombing raids on North Vietnam on the grounds that Hanoi had broken an understanding by refusing to engage in meaningful peace talks. "They understood," he told a skeptical Senate Foreign Relations Committee, "that we expected them to sit down for serious negotiations in Paris."

The rhythm of American policy speeded up and slowed down, but still there seemed no way to end the war. In April 1970 the President had told the nation that Vietnamization was going so well that regardless of the lack of progress in the Paris peace talks, he was withdrawing an additional 150,000 men from combat assignments. Then ten days later came a television broadcast from the White House with Nixon announcing to a surprised nation that he had ordered an attack on enemy sanctuaries in Cambodia. His military advisers had determined that the enemy was about to launch a massive attack against American troops; there could be no other choice but to preempt that design by combined South Vietnamese–American operations against the "headquarters for the entire Communist military operation in South Vietnam."

There was good reason for the nation's surprise, aside from the claims that Vietnamization was working so well that 150,000 troops could be withdrawn. Secretary of State William P. Rogers had just gone out of his way to assure Congress that American troops were not going to be sent into Cambodia for any reason. If they did, he said, "our whole program is defeated."

Nixon had other advisers, most especially National Security Adviser Henry Kissinger. He may or may not have urged the Cambodian "incursion" on the President, but it followed the general outlines of a policy the Harvard Professor had recommended in his book, *Nuclear Weapons and Foreign Policy*, which closed with an appeal to run risks in Cold War situations. Otherwise the initiative would always be with the other side. Preservation of the *status quo* was not enough; indeed, it was the most dangerous policy of all:

The advantage of initiative is that each move opens the possibility of several further steps. If carried far enough, it will force the opponent to protect itself against an ever growing number of contingencies and, therefore, to concentrate on purely defensive measures.

These ideas were compatible with the President's own intense dislike of the postwar "containment" policy adopted by President Truman. He preferred Secretary Dulles's word, "Liberation." And he had always understood it to mean something very close to Kissinger's proposal to confront an opponent with an "ever growing number of contingencies" and thereby force him "to concentrate on purely defensive measures." Here again, however, circumstances had changed. When Kissinger made those suggestions originally, in the 1950's there was still much talk of Cold War offensives in the Third World. Nixon sought to apply the policy to save a deteriorating situation in Southeast Asia. Before joining the President's inner circle, Kissinger had said as much in a magazine article which appeared in *Foreign Affairs Quarterly*. Above all, he insisted, the new Administration must not impose a solution on others or "bug-out" in a way that might unloose the forces of disorder around the world.

Here is an extract from his January 1969 article in *Foreign Affairs:*

The peace negotiations in Paris have been marked by the classic Vietnamese syndrome: optimism alternating with bewilderment; euphoria giving way to frustration. The halt to the bombing produced another wave of high hope. Yet it was followed almost immediately by the dispute with Saigon over its participation in the talks. The merits of this issue aside, we must realize that a civil war which has torn a society for twenty years and which has involved the great powers is unlikely to be settled in a single dramatic stroke. Even if there were mutual trust—a commodity not in excessive supply—the complexity of the issues and the difficulty of grasping their interrelationship would make for complicated negotiations. Throughout the war, criteria by which to measure progress have been hard to come by; this problem has continued during the negotiations. The dilemma is that almost any statement about Viet Nam is likely to be true; unfortunately, truth does not guarantee relevance. . . .

American "victories" were empty unless they laid the basis for an eventual withdrawal. The North Vietnamese and Viet Cong, fighting in their own country, needed merely to keep in being forces sufficiently strong to dominate the population after the United States tired of the war. We fought a military war; our opponents fought a political one. We sought physical attrition; our opponents aimed for our psychological exhaustion. In the process, we lost sight of one of the cardinal maxims of guerrilla war: the guerrilla wins if he does not lose. The conventional army loses if it does not win. The North Vietnamese used their main forces the way a bullfighter uses his cape—to keep us lunging in areas of marginal political importance. . . .

All this caused our military operations to have little relationship to our declared political objectives. Progress in establishing a political base was excruciatingly slow; our diplomacy and our strategy were conducted in isolation from each other. President Johnson had announced repeatedly that we would be ready to negotiate, unconditionally, at any moment, anywhere. This, in effect, left the timing of negotiations to the other side. But short of a complete collapse of the opponent, our military deployment was not well designed to support negotiations. For purposes of negotiating, we would have been better off with 100 percent control over 60 percent of the country than with 60 percent control of 100 percent of the country. . . .

   • Much of the bitter debate in the United States about the war has been conducted in terms of 1961 and 1962. Unquestionably, the failure at that time to analyze adequately the geopolitical importance of Viet Nam contributed to the current dilemma. But the commitment of 500,000 Americans has settled the issue of the importance of Viet Nam. For what is involved now is confidence in American promises. However fashionable it is to ridicule the terms "credibility" or "prestige," they are not empty phrases; other nations can gear their actions to ours only if they can count on our steadiness. The collapse of the American effort in Viet Nam would not mollify many critics; most of them would simply add the charge of unreliability to the accusation of bad judgment. Those whose safety or national goals depend on American commitments could only be dismayed. In many parts of the world— the Middle East, Europe, Latin America, even Japan—stability depends on confidence in American promises. Unilateral withdrawal, or a settlement which unintentionally amounts to the same thing, could therefore lead to the erosion of restraints and to an even more dangerous international situation. No American policymaker can simply dismiss these dangers. . . .

   Coalition government is perhaps the most emotionally charged issue in Viet Nam, where it tends to be identified with . . . a joint Saigon-NLF administration of the entire country. There can be no American objection, of course, to direct negotiations between Saigon and the NLF. The issue is whether the United States should be party to an attempt to *impose* a coalition government. We must be clear that our involvement in such an effort may well destroy the existing political structure of South Viet Nam and thus lead to a communist takeover.

   Some urge negotiations on a coalition government for precisely this reason: as a face-saving formula for arranging the communist political victory which they consider inevitable. But those who believe that the political evolution of South Viet Nam should not be foreclosed by an American decision must realize that the subject of a coalition government is the most thankless and tricky area for negotiation *by outsiders.*

   The notion that a coalition government represents a "compromise" which will permit a new political evolution hardly does justice to Vietnamese conditions. Even the non-communist groups have demonstrated the difficulty Vietnamese have in compromising differences. It is beyond imagination that parties that have been murdering and betraying each other for 25 years could work together as a team giving joint instructions to the entire country. The image of a line of command extending from Saigon into the countryside is hardly true of the non-communist government in Saigon. It would be absurd in the case of a coalition government. Such a government would possess no authority other than that of each minister over the forces he controlled either through personal or party loyalty.

To take just one example of the difficulties: Communist ministers would be foolhardy in the extreme if they entered Saigon without bringing along sufficient military force for their protection. But the introduction of communist military forces into the chief bastion of governmental strength would change the balance of political forces in South Viet Nam. The danger of a coalition government is that it would decouple the non-communist elements from effective control over their armed forces and police, leaving them unable to defend themselves adequately.

In short, negotiations seeking to impose a coalition from the outside are likely to change markedly and irreversibly the political process in South Viet Nam—as Vietnamese who believe that a coalition government cannot work quickly choose sides. We would, in effect, be settling the war on an issue least amenable to outside influence, with respect to which we have the least grasp of conditions and the long-term implications of which are most problematical.

This is not to say that the United States should resist an outcome freely negotiated among the Vietnamese. It does suggest that any negotiation on this point by the United States is likely to lead either to an impasse or to the collapse of Saigon. . . .

The limits of the American commitment can be expressed in two propositions: first, the United States cannot accept a military defeat, or a change in the political structure of South Viet Nam brought about by external military force; second, once North Vietnamese forces and pressures are removed, the United States has no obligation to maintain a government in Saigon by force.

13

American objectives should therefore be (1) to bring about a staged withdrawal of external forces, North Vietnamese and American, (2) thereby to create a maximum incentive for the contending forces in South Viet Nam to work out a political agreement. The structure and content of such an agreement must be left to the South Vietnamese. It could take place formally on the national level. Or, it could occur locally on the provincial level where even now tacit accommodations are not unusual in many areas such as the Mekong Delta.

The details of a phased, mutual withdrawal are not decisive for our present purposes and, in any case, would have to be left to negotiations. It is possible, however, to list some principles: the withdrawal should be over a sufficiently long period so that a genuine indigenous political process has a chance to become established; the contending sides in South Viet Nam should commit themselves not to pursue their objectives by force while the withdrawal of external forces is going on; in so far as possible, the definition of what constitutes a suitable political process or structure should be left to the South Vietnamese, with the schedule for mutual withdrawal creating the time frame for an agreement.

The United States, then, should concentrate on the subject of the mutual withdrawal of external forces and avoid negotiating about the internal structure of South Viet Nam for as long as possible. The primary responsibility for negotiating the internal structure of South Viet Nam should be left for direct negotiations among the South Vietnamese. If we involve ourselves deeply in the issue of South Viet Nam's internal arrangements, we shall find ourselves in a morass of complexities subject to two major disadvantages. First, we will be the party in the negotiation least attuned to the subtleties of Vietnamese politics. Second, we are likely to wind up applying the greater part of our pressure against Saigon as the seeming obstacle to an accommodation. The result may be the complete demoralization of Saigon, profound domestic tensions within the United States and a prolonged stalemate or a resumption of the war. . . .

A negotiating procedure and a definition of objectives cannot guarantee a settlement, of course. If Hanoi proves intransigent and the war goes on, we should seek to achieve as many of our objectives as possible unilaterally. We should adopt a strategy which reduces casualties and concentrates on protecting the population. We should continue to strengthen the Vietnamese army to permit a gradual withdrawal of some American forces, and we should encourage Saigon to broaden its base so that it is stronger for the political contest with the communists which sooner or later it must undertake.

No war in a century has aroused the passions of the conflict in Viet Nam. By turning Viet Nam into a symbol of deeper resentments, many groups have defeated the objective they profess to seek. However we got into Viet Nam, whatever the judgment of our actions, ending the war honorably is essential for the peace of the world. Any other solution may unloose forces that would complicate prospects of international order. A new Administration must be given the benefit of the doubt and a chance to move toward a peace which grants the people of Viet Nam what they have so long struggled to achieve: an opportunity to work out their own destiny in their own way.[1]

Kissinger's prestige and credibility were enhanced in Nixon's eyes by his self-assured presence among the foreign policy elite. Nixon disliked many things about the "Establishment," but he accepted its authority and counted upon its support. Formerly Nelson Rockefeller's own private adviser on foreign policy questions, the Harvard professor brought the new Administration instant status among those who had been concerned that the new President might not know how to run the shop he had inherited from Kennedy and Johnson. But having said that, it must also be said that "Vietnamization" as practiced by Nixon was a compound of several elements, not the least of which was its appeal as a revitalized "liberation" policy to deal with similar problems in a different era.

During the 1968 campaign, Nixon promised that he had a plan to end the war. "If the war is still going on next January," the Republican candidate declared, "it can best be ended by a new Administration . . . neither defending old errors nor bound by

[1] Henry A. Kissinger, "The Viet Nam Negotiations," *Foreign Affairs Quarterly*, XLVII (January, 1969), pp. 211–234.

the old record." The Democrat, Vice-President Hubert Humphrey, actually made it easier for his opponent to leave it at that. Never emerging from the shadows of Lyndon Johnson's policy, the Vice-President had been selected by party professionals who wanted him as the standard bearer only to protect their fiefdoms from the likes of a Senator Eugene McCarthy. Win or lose, Humphrey was an organization man; win or lose, McCarthy was an irregular who could do permanent damage to the Democratic Party.

In a last minute effort to save Humphrey, Johnson ordered a total suspension of the bombing of North Vietnam. It was too late, at least for Humphrey. Nixon really had no firm plan for ending the war when he entered office, however, except those vague thoughts about updating "liberation." Johnson had gotten preliminary peace talks under way with the North Vietnamese by a partial suspension of the bombing earlier in the year. But as a secret cable he sent to American Ambassadors in Asian countries indicated, that move was largely a gambit to give himself—and his successor—more time to work out a plan which would avoid concessions to the enemy and yet not call for a continuing presence of 500,000 American soldiers in the swamps of Southeast Asia. Excerpts from the cable were printed in the "Pentagon Papers," which Nixon later tried to prevent from being published.

Excerpts from cablegram from State Department to United States Ambassadors in Australia, New Zealand, Thailand, Laos, the Philippines and South Korea, March 31, 1968, as provided in the body of the Pentagon study. The message announced provisions of the major speech President Lyndon B. Johnson was to make hours later. Paragraph in italics is the study's paraphrase or explanation.

a. Major stress on importance of GVN and ARVN increased effectiveness with our equipment and other support as first priority in our own actions..

b. 13,500 support forces to be called up at once in order to round out the 10,500 combat units sent in February.

c. Replenishment of strategic reserve by calling up 48,500 additional reserves, stating that these would be designed to strategic reserve.

d. Related tax increases and budget cuts already largely needed for non-Vietnam reasons.

3. In addition, after similar consultation and concurrence, President proposes to announce that bombing will be restricted to targets most directly engaged in the battlefield area and that this meant that there would be no bombing norh of the 20th parallel. Announcement would leave open how Hanoi might respond, and would be open-ended as to time. However, it would indicate that Hanoi's response could be helpful in determining whether we were justified in assumption that Hanoi would not take advantage if we stop the bombing altogether. Thus, it would to this extent foreshadow possibility of full bombing stoppage at a later point.

This cable offered the Ambassadors some additional rationale for this new policy for their discretionary use in conversations with their respective heads of government. This rationale represents the only available statement by the Administration of some of its underlying reasons and purposes for and expectations from this policy decision.

a. You should call attention to force increases that would be announced at the same time and would make clear our continued resolve. Also our top priority to re-equipping ARVN forces.

b. You should make clear that Hanoi is most likely to denounce the project and thus free our hand after a short period. Nonetheless, we might wish to continue the limitation even after a formal denunciation, in order to reinforce its sincerity and put the monkey firmly on Hanoi's back for whatever follows. Of course, any major military change could compel full-scale resumption at any time.

c. With or without denunciation, Hanoi might well feel limited in conducting any major offensives at least in the northern areas. If they did so, this could ease the pressure where it is most potentially serious. If they did not, then this would give us a clear field for whatever actions were then required.

d. In view of weather limitations, bombing north of the 20th parallel will in any event be limited at least for the next four weeks or so—which we tentatively envisage as a maximum testing period in any event. Hence, we are not giving up anything really serious in this time frame. Moreover, air power now used north of 20th can probably be used in Laos (where no policy change planned) and in SVN.

e. Insofar as our announcement foreshadows any possibility of a complete bombing stoppage, in the event Hanoi really exercises reciprocal restraints, we regard this as unlikely. But in any case, the period of demonstrated restraint would probably have to continue for a period of several weeks, and we would have time to appraise the situation and to consult carefully with them before we undertook any such action.[*1]

In effect, therefore, the decision for some kind of Vietnamization policy had already been made for Nixon when he came to office. It had been made over the course of several weeks' discussion after the North Vietnamese "Tet Offensive" in early 1968. Two conclusions emerged from those reevaluations: First, it was decided that the war could not be won in a traditional military sense by following present tactics, nor perhaps by any other means. Second, Vietnam simply was not worth the risk of political bankruptcy at home and financial instability abroad. Johnson's cable to American representatives in Asia did not indicate how far-reaching those deliberations had been. Perhaps Johnson did not want to admit their import (even to himself); perhaps he and others still thought something would happen to reverse opinion trends among his advisers.

However that may be Johnson left Nixon an ambiguous Vietnamization policy which could go either way. In part, this was then reflected in the alternating swing of the new President's efforts to end the war. But the "Establishment" had seemingly set upper limits on what could be expended either for victory or an honorable withdrawal. The most comprehensive account of these 1968 discussions was pieced together by Hedrick Smith

*1 Neil Sheehan et al., *The Pentagon Papers, as Published by the New York Times* (New York: Bantam Books, 1971), pp. 622–623.

and William Beecher in articles which appeared in March 1969, entitled, "The Vietnam Policy Reversal of 1968."

On the cold and cheerless early morning of Feb. 28, 1968, the Chairman of the Joint Chiefs of Staff, Gen. Earle G. Wheeler, landed at Andrews Air Force Base after an urgent mission to Saigon. Pausing only to change into a fresh uniform, he hurried through the rain to the White House to deliver a report and make a request.

The report was designed to encourage an anxious President and his beleaguered advisers, but it served only to shock them into extended debate.

The request—for more troops—was designed to bring military victory at last in the eight-year American military effort, but it led instead to a fateful series of decisions that stand in retrospect as one of the most remarkable turnabouts in United States foreign policy. . . .

On that day at the end of February, President Johnson and his closest aides assembled for breakfast around the Chippendale table in the elegant family dining room on the second floor of the Executive Mansion. Before rising from the table, they had set in motion the most intensive policy review of the Johnson Presidency—and one of the most agonizing of any Presidency. . . .

At the time of that breakfast meeting, President Johnson had been thinking for about two months about not seeking re-election. His principal advisers had little inkling of his thoughts, and the President himself had no expectation that the tensions in the Government would shatter the consensus of his inner circle. . . .

The catalytic event in the policy reappraisal—and the centerpiece of General Wheeler's vivid report—was the enemy's Lunar New Year offensive, which began Jan. 30, 1968, and swelled into coordinated assaults on 36 South Vietnamese cities and included, in Saigon, a bold penetration of the United States Embassy compound. . . .

"It was a hell of a serious breakfast," one participant recalled. "It was rough as a cob!"

Some of the participants believed that a substantial troop increase could well revive arguments for widening the war—for giving General Westmoreland permission to go after enemy sanctuaries on the ground in Cambodia and Laos, and perhaps even in North Vietnam.

The President was wary about a massive new commitment. Had he not gone to extraordinary lengths to send half a million men to Vietnam without calling up reserves or imposing economic controls? Every year the generals had come to him—sometimes more than once a year—with the plea for "a little bit more to get the job done." Now, with the nation sharply divided over the war, they were asking for mobilization. . . .

No one at the breakfast table that day advocated lowering objectives. It was a time, however, when many pressures for a change of course were converging on the White House. . . .

If tolerance of the war had worn thin, so had the nation's military resources—so thin, indeed, that there was almost nothing more to send to Vietnam without either mobilizing, enlarging draft calls, lengthening the 12-month combat tour or sending Vietnam veterans back for second tours of duty—all extremely unappealing.

Congress was in such ferment that the process of legislation was partly paralyzed. The dollar was being battered by the gold crisis in Europe and inflation at home.

More fundamentally, the nation was seriously divided. The fabric of public civility had begun to unravel as opinion on the war polarized.

President Johnson chose his long-time friend, Clark Clifford, to head a task force to advise him on the troop request. It quickly became a forum for debating the entire rationale for the war.

At 10:30 A.M. on Friday, March 1, in the East room of the White House, Mr. Clifford took the oath of office as the successor to Robert S. McNamara. Three hours later he gathered the task force around the oval oak table in the private Pentagon dining room of the Secretary of Defense. . . .

The exponents of continuity were Mr. Rusk and Mr. Rostow and Generals Wheeler and Taylor. Mr. Rusk, by then the stanchest defender of the war in public, patiently bore the heat of criticism. Tall, unbending, composed, he was, in his own words, "the iceman."

Mr. Rostow and General Taylor, who had gone to Vietnam

early in 1961 as President Kennedy's personal envoys and who came back advocating intervention, were even more opposed to "letting up the pressure." Mr. Rostow, athletic and ebullient, funneled the news from Saigon to the President.

The advocates of change . . . called into question military judgments, past strategy and the quest for victory implicit in so many earlier decisions.

Although Mr. Clifford was never alone, his eventual role was remarkable because it was wholly unexpected. . . . One man acquainted with the circumstances of the Clifford appointment said later: "I am sure the President felt, 'Here is a good, strong, sturdy supporter of the war, and that's what I need.' McNamara was wobbling—particularly on the bombing issue. I think the President felt Clifford was strong and sturdy."

But Mr. Clifford had begun to have doubts during a trip in August, 1967, to Vietnam and allied countries contributing troops to the war. On his return he confided to the President that he was deeply uneasy at having discovered that the American view of the war was not fully shared by Australia, New Zealand, Thailand and the Philippines.

Disturbed he was, but he remained a supporter of Administration policy. He was encouraged by secret diplomatic efforts in August, 1967, and again in January, 1968, to get negotiations with Hanoi started on the basis of the so-called San Antonio formula.

That proposal, made public by President Johnson in a speech in the Texas city on September 30, 1967, offered to halt the bombing of North Vietnam provided it would lead promptly to productive talks and "assuming" that Hanoi would not take military advantage of the cessation.

At Mr. Clifford's Senate confirmation hearings on Jan. 25, 1968, he had added the important interpretation that this meant that the President would tolerate "normal" levels of infiltration from North to South Vietnam.

The President had not cleared Mr. Clifford's remarks in advance and, as a result, according to one informed source, "all hell broke loose at the White House and the State Department."

Secretary Rusk was said to have argued for two days with President Johnson against giving Administration endorsement to the interpretation. He was overruled. On Jan. 29 the State Department said Mr. Clifford's remarks represented United States policy. . . .

When the Clifford task force got under way, a number of officials took the troop request as evidence of panic on General Westmoreland's part. But ranking officers who were in Saigon headquarters during and after the Tet offensive assert that there was no thought of asking for many more troops until shortly before General Wheeler's visit late in February. . . .

The Joint Chiefs of Staff had their own reasons for favoring a massive increase and a reserve call-up. For months they had been deeply concerned that the strategic reserve had been dangerously depleted and they had been looking for a chance to reconstitute it by persuading the President to mobilize National Guard units. . . .

In the view of the Joint Chiefs, only the full number would assure victory. The implication was that with 206,000 more men, the war would "not be terribly long," as one Pentagon civilian put it—but there was no precise forecast.

At this point [Assistant Secretary of Defense Paul] Warnke, in his nasal Massachusetts accent, read a paper that challenegd the military thesis head on. Hanoi, he said, would match American reinforcements as it had in the past, and the result would simply be escalation and "a lot more killing" on both sides.

Besides, the task force was told, the financial costs would be immense. The proposed scale of reinforcements would add nearly $10-billion to a war already costing $30-billion a year.

As an alternative, Mr. Warnke urged a turn toward de-escalation—a pullback from General Westmoreland's aggressive search-and-destroy tactics and the abandonment of isolated outposts like the besieged Marine garrison at Khesanh. He said that American forces should be used as a mobile shield in and around population centers and that more should be demanded from the South Vietnamese Army.

The sheer complexity of the troop issue began to raise doubts in Mr. Clifford's mind. "Part of it was Clark's intelligent questioning and part of it was his naiveté," a colleague recalled. "He asked about things that others more familiar with the details would not have asked.

"He just couldn't get the figures straight on troops. He drove

Bus Wheeler mad. He would say, 'Now I understand you wanted 22,000 men for such and such,' and Wheeler would point out this didn't include the support elements, and if you added them, it would be 35,000 in all."

"This happened again and again every time Clark wanted to get the numbers down as low as possible, and it had a psychological impact on him," the source added. . . .

Word was passed to President Johnson that the review "wasn't going well" and had hit a "discordant note." But Mr. Clifford's doubts had not hardened into convictions by the time he handed the President his first report on March 5.

A short, unsigned, four- or five-page memorandum, it recommended giving General Westmoreland 50,000 more troops in the next three months and set out a schedule for readying the rest of the 206,000 men for dispatch over the next 15 months.

Characteristically, the President's advisers disagreed on the recommendation's significance. The Pentagon saw it as a move "to get the pipeline going"—general approval of the troop request; State Department officials viewed it as part of a process of "whittling down" the 206,000 figure.

Although Mr. Clifford had passed along the report, he was uneasy about it. He was worried that if the President approved the first batch of troops, that action would move him irrevocably toward the whole 206,000. But the Secretary did not challenge the report directly; he tried to stall, suggesting that the task force check General Westmoreland's reaction to be sure the "mix" of forces was right.

General Wheeler wanted to move ahead, but others, including Mr. Rusk and Mr. Rostow, were willing to have the issue studied further, so the task force carried on for several more days.

This seemed to suit Mr. Johnson's mood, too. His instinct, a White House aide explained later, was to delay implementing the plan. "He kept putting off making an initial decision," the aide said. . . .

As the task force persisted, Secretary Clifford himself was putting more pointed questions. "What is our military plan for victory?" he asked. "How will we end the war?" He was not satisfied.

Then the bombing came under his scrutiny. Mr. [Townsend]

Hoopes wrote him a memorandum urging a halt, arguing that the bombing was not having significant results and that, because of Soviet and Chinese Communist aid, North Vietnam had become "on balance a stronger military power today than before the bombing began."

Mr. Hoopes contended that it was "a military fiction" that American combat casualties would rise if the bombing were halted. American losses, he said, were primarily a result of the aggressive ground strategy in the South.

Under the impact of such arguments, Mr. Clifford's doubts became convictions. . . . The debate, by now in the White House, seesawed through the middle of March. At this time Mr. Clifford began to state his case for a fundamental change in American policy: It was time to emphasize peace, not a larger war.

He now challenged the task-force recommendation for more troops. "This isn't the way to go at all," he told the President. "This is all wrong."

With the nation bitterly divided over the war and in desperate need at home, he maintained, it would be immoral to consider enormous added investment in Vietnam—a "military sinkhole.". . .

Secretary Rusk apparently did not disagree with Mr. Clifford so sharply on troop numbers, but he was opposed to the long-run implications of Mr. Clifford's arguments—that in the end, the United States would have to settle for less. Mr. Rostow felt that the new Defense Secretary had fallen under the influence of "the professional pessimists" in the Defense Department. . . .

At the Pentagon, morale was rising among civilian advocates of a new policy. "We used to ask," a former Pentagon civilian said of the Secretary, "is he one of us? Well, there was 'one of us' at the White House." He was Harry McPherson, the President's speech drafter, who, unknown to the Pentagon or the State Department, was already at work on a major Vietnam speech. . . .

The speech was originally conceived late in February on the basis of Mr. Rostow's analysis that the Tet offensive had not been a real setback and that the allies should pull up their socks and hang on until the enemy came to his senses. While the discussions of troop strength were proceeding, Mr. McPherson was developing his draft.

Initially, it included an open-ended commitment to the war—a willingness to carry on at whatever the cost. But as the internal debate over troop figures raged on and the numbers dwindled, the tone softened. But the President would not commit himself to any draft or any figure.

Then came a series of signal events: Senator Eugene J. McCarthy scored a stunning upset in the New Hampshire Democratic primary on March 1. American dead and wounded in Vietnam reached 139,801—exceeding over-all Korean-war losses. American and Western European bankers held an emergency meeting in Washington to stem the run of gold as the price soared. Senator Robert F. Kennedy announced on March 16 that he would seek the Democratic Presidential nomination.

All this formed the backdrop for the most delicate argument of all—that about the bombing.

On March 15, Arthur J. Goldberg, the American representative at the United Nations, sent an eight-page memo to the President urging him to halt the bombing to get negotiations started. . . .

A day after the Goldberg memo arrived, the subject came up in Mr. Johnson's inner circle. The President, his patience sorely tested, sat up in his chair and said:

"Let's get one thing clear! I'm telling you now I am not going to stop the bombing. Now I don't want to hear any more about it. Goldberg has written me about the whole thing, and I've heard every argument. I'm not going to stop it. Now is there anybody here who doesn't understand that?"

There was dead silence.

The bombing issue was dropped at that meeting, but it was not dead. Mr. Clifford, the lawyer, had noticed a loophole. . . . He proposed that the bombing be restricted to the Panhandle region of North Vietnam south of the 20th Parallel.

No one knew where Mr. Johnson stood on that issue. It was still two weeks before he would announce a major shift in the direction of his Vietnam policy—a shift toward de-escalation that is still having its impact on the daily decisions of the Nixon Administration.

At that time the pressures for change—political and economic—

were mounting. The public was increasingly impatient with the war.

"Something had to be done to extend the lease on public support for the war," a high State Department official remarked. "We were focused on what we could do without significant military drawbacks to make clear to people we were serious about peace."

Secretary Clifford pleaded skillfully for the proposal that the bombing be restricted to the region south of the 20th Parallel. A cutback, he said, would not violate the President's insistence that there be no halt without matching restraint from Hanoi. He added that it would not, as the military feared in the case of a halt, jeopardize American troops in outposts just south of the demilitarized zone—Khesanh, Camp Carroll, the Rockpile and others.

The region south of the 20th Parallel contains many of the "meatiest" targets. All North Vietnamese troops and most of the supplies heading into South Vietnam have to pass through this region.

The proposal was also thought to offer a diplomatic opening: If Hanoi and Washington were not able to walk directly to the negotiating table, Mr. Clifford suggested, perhaps they could begin to "crawl."

This was not a new idea. In the spring of 1967, Mr. Clifford's predecessor as Defense Secretary, Robert S. McNamara, had his aides draft a similar proposal for cutting back to the 19th or 20th Parallel as a means of starting the process of tacit de-escalation. For many months, too, Secretary of State Dean Rusk had been developing a variety of plans for cutbacks.

The theory was that if Washington made the first move, Hanoi might match it and, step by step, they could begin scaling down the war even without negotiations.

President Johnson refused to accept the plan after it ran into heavy opposition from the Joint Chiefs of Staff. There were reports at the time that some senior generals would have resigned if it had been carried out.

Nonetheless, gingerly and indirect soundings of Hanoi were made at the time through what one diplomatic source called a "quasi-disavowable channel." The reaction from Hanoi, as read in Washington, was negative: Only a halt could produce talks. Now, in March, 1968, the diplomatic experts thought that this was still a problem. Privately, the President had made no decision on the plan but publicly he was as stern as ever.

With Senator Robert F. Kennedy now in the race for the Democratic Presidential nomination and with the political tide apparently running against Mr. Johnson, he lashed back at his critics. In one of his pet phrases, he was "hunkering down like a Texas jackrabbit in a hailstorm."

On March 18 in Minneapolis, the President derided critics who would "tuck our tails and violate our commitments" in Vietnam. He raised the specter of appeasement in the Munich style. The Clifford camp took this as a counterattack aimed at them by the hawkish faction of the Administration led by Walt W. Rostow, the President's adviser on national security affairs.

President Johnson ridiculed proposals for shifting to a less ambitious ground strategy in Vietnam, as the doves wanted. "Those of you who think you can save lives by moving the battlefield in from the mountains to the cities where the people live have another think coming," he said acidly. . . .

The bombing cutback seemed to have been brushed aside. The only hopeful sign, Mr. Clifford thought, was the fact that Mr. Johnson had still not approved the troop reinforcements for Gen. William C. Westmoreland. The request by the American commander in Vietnam, which amounted to 206,000 men, had precipitated the reappraisal when presented by Gen. Earle G. Wheeler, Chairman of the Joint Chiefs of Staff, on Feb. 28.

It was clear in the middle of March that despite his public declarations, President Johnson was deeply uneasy and undecided.

Late in the afternoon of March 20 he met in his oval office with Arthur J. Goldberg, the United States representative at the United Nations. It was their first meeting since Ambassador Goldberg, in a secret memo to the President on March 15, had proposed a bombing halt.

It was this proposal that had provoked the President's angry outburst at the White House meeting a day later. Mr. Goldberg had not been there and was unaware of Mr. Johnson's reaction. Now the two men met alone, and the President seemed interested in Ambassador Goldberg's position. He asked him to go through his arguments again, listening carefully and putting questions now and then. There were no angry words.

Before they parted, Mr. Johnson invited the silver-haired envoy to take part in a secret council of "wise men" that was to meet in Washington March 25. "I hope you'll put these same views to them there," he said.

The next hint of the President's thinking—though its significance was denied at the time—came on March 22. He announced that he was making General Westmoreland Army Chief of Staff, effective in July. He insisted that this did not necessarily foreshadow a change in strategy. . . .

President Johnson was upset over the immediate speculation that, as an aide put it, he was "sacking Westy because of Tet," the costly Lunar New Year offensive the enemy had sprung in Vietnam on Jan. 30. To this day Mr. Johnson says privately as well as publicly that in his own heart that was not his motive. But some who know Mr. Lyndon Johnson extremely well believe that the shift came at this time—subconsciously, at least—as part of a gradual transition to a new policy. . . .

By March 22, the inner circle in Washington had been informed that the President was going to give a Vietnam speech and they gathered in the family dining room of the White House to discuss it. . . .

The speech, conceived in the combative spirit after the Tet offensive, was still militant in tone. It deeply disturbed Mr. Clifford and others, who yearned to include some gesture of peace along with the scheduled reinforcements.

Once again Mr. Clifford urged the President to consider a bombing cutback on the ground that it would improve the Administration's position, internationally and domestically. Just two weeks before the crucial Democratic primary in Wisconsin, on April 2, most of the President's aides thought he needed a political shot in the arm. Vice President Humphrey believed that the bombing should be halted, not curtailed, if there was to be a change. . . .

After seven hours, Secretary Rusk gave a lucid summary. Mr. Rusk, who had himself raised the possibility of a bombing halt as early as March 3, said that there seemed to be a consensus that some step toward negotiations was desirable. But, according to one account, he cast doubt on whether a curtailment would satisfy the North Vietnamese. . . .

The next morning Mr. McPherson, a bright, boyish-looking man, sent the President a memo that sought to strike a compromise between the general desire to make a peace gesture and the fear of rejection by Hanoi. The memo urged the President to stop the bombing north of the 20th Parallel and, simultaneously, to offer to stop the rest if Hanoi showed restraint at the demilitarized zone and left Saigon and other cities free from major attack.

The President sent the memo to Secretary Rusk, who later returned it with the comment that these were ideas that he had been working on and that they should be developed further. His reaction was favorable but, according to one account, he did not make any specific recommendation. . . .

President Johnson, canvassing more opinion, was reaching outside the administration to summon to Washington the secret council of trusted advisers he mentioned to Ambassador Goldberg. They had a special and surprising impact on the President. . . .

They gathered at the State Department on Monday, March 25, with the President's address to the nation six days away. They constituted a "who's who" of the American foreign-policy establishment:

Dean Acheson, Secretary of State under President Truman; George W. Ball, Under Secretary of State in the Kennedy and Johnson Administrations; Gen. Omar N. Bradley, retired World War II commander; McGeorge Bundy, special assistant for national security affairs to Presidents Kennedy and Johnson; Arthur H. Dean, President Eisenhower's Korean war negotiator; Douglas Dillon, Secretary of the Treasury under President Kennedy.

Also Associate Justice Abe Fortas of the Supreme Court; Mr. Goldberg; Henry Cabot Lodge, twice Ambassador to Saigon; John J. McCloy, United States High Commissioner in West Germany under President Truman; Robert D. Murphy, ranking diplomat in the Truman-Eisenhower era; Gen. Matthew B. Ridgway, retired Korean war commander; Gen. Maxwell D. Taylor, former Chairman of the Joint Chiefs of Staff and a constant Presidential adviser on Vietnam, and Cyrus R. Vance, former Deputy Defense Secretary and President Johnson's trouble-shooter.

The wise men heard candid briefings, some of which bordered on pessimism, and then questioned Messrs. Rusk, Clifford and Rostow and others about the extent of the Tet disaster and the plans for the future. The discussion continued late that night and resumed the next morning at the White House.

For the first time President Johnson got the trend of their views. He was "deeply shaken," one aide said, by the change of temper of the wise men, who were deeply discouraged over the war after the exalted hopes of the previous fall.

The President was especially impressed by the fact that Mr. Acheson, McGeorge Bundy and to a lesser degree Mr. Vance had joined Mr. Ball and Mr. Goldberg in opposing further military commitments and advocating some way of getting out of the war. He was jolted when Mr. Bundy, one of the architects of intervention in the early sixties and of the bombing of North Vietnam in 1965, now took an opposite tack.

There was, to be sure, a faction that held firm in defense of the harder line—Justice Fortas, General Taylor and Mr. Murphy. Mr. Murphy wanted more bombing, not less. . . .

There was no consensus on the bombing issue. Mr. Goldberg and Mr. Ball advocated a halt as a way to negotiations. The others were uncertain but the impression left with Government sources was that the wise men as a group were saying: "We had better start looking for another way to get this war settled."

To the President and his senior advisers, one close observer said later, such shifts carried "more weight than something like the new Hampshire primary." Someone suggested that Mr. Johnson consider the impact of his Vietnam decisions on the coming election; he replied testily that the campaign was the least of his concerns.

Two days later, on March 28, Messrs. Rusk, Clifford, Rostow, McPherson and William Bundy met in Mr. Rusk's mahogany-paneled office on the seventh floor of the State Department to polish the President's speech.

It was still, in the words of one participant, a "teeth-clenched, see-it-through" speech, announcing that about 15,000 more troops would be sent to Vietnam. It made a pro-forma plea for peace at the negotiating table and said nothing about cutting back the bombing.

Secretary Clifford launched an impassioned plea against taking this approach.

"I can't do it—I can't go along with it," he said. "I can't be in the position of trying to polish a speech of this kind. This speech can't be polished. What's needed is a new speech. This one is irrevocably setting the President down the wrong road."

. . . It would tear the country apart, the Defense Secretary argued, to hear a speech that promised only more war. What was needed, he said, was not a "war speech, but a peace speech—the issue is as sharp as the edge of an ax."

To Mr. Clifford's surprise, Mr. Rusk did not cut him short. The others chimed in. Mr. Rusk sent out for sandwiches. Mr. Clifford appealed for some compromise, and once again they debated the 20th Parallel idea.

By this time the military commanders were no longer raising strong objections. Some, like Adm. U.S. Grant Sharp, the Pacific Fleet commander, who had overall charge of the bombing, thought the cutback would fail. He fully expected that if it were tried, the President would order full bombing again in a month or so. Some officials thought this was Mr. Rostow's view also.

Secretary Rusk, eager to find some way to the negotiating table, still did not think the cutback would satisfy Hanoi. The month's arguments had had a cumulative effect on him.

At the end of the day—the meeting lasted until 5 P.M.—Mr. Rusk had agreed with Mr. Clifford that Mr. McPherson should prepare "an alternate draft." That night, while the President was showing Senator Mike Mansfield, the Democratic majority leader, a draft of the original hawkish speech, Mr. McPherson began writing alternate draft No. 1. Working through the night, he had it ready by morning.

He sent the draft, the first one containing the proposal for a bombing cutback to the 20th Parallel, to Mr. Johnson with a note saying that it seemed to reflect the sentiments of some of the President's leading advisers. He also offered to go back to the original version if that was Mr. Johnson's wish.

Later in the day the President called Mr. McPherson in to discuss changes in an item on "Page 3." He did not specify which draft, but it was clear that he was now working with the new speech. That was how he signaled a major break in the debate.

He had been deeply influenced by the shift in the public mood, as reflected in the wise men's meetings and his contacts on Capitol Hill. The country was in turmoil and the dollar was in danger.

He had been shaken by the change in his friend, Mr. Clifford, and was finally persuaded to try a new tack by Mr. Clifford's sheer persistence. The mood of others had softened in the crucible of debate, too.

From then until 9 P.M. on the 31st, the speech went through five more drafts. The speech had become progressively more dovish until, one official said, "it ended up 180 degrees from where it started."

Late the previous day Mr. Clifford had been concerned that the peroration, left over from original drafts, was still too militant, so Mr. McPherson was to draft a substitute.

When the Saturday session ended Mr. Johnson asked for the revised peroration. Mr. McPherson said he had not had time to rewrite it but would do so promptly.

The President, his shirt open and his tie down, muttered, "No need to—I may have one of my own." He winked at Mr. McPherson, who turned to Mr. Clifford and said: "My God? Do you think he is going to say sayonara?" Mr. Clifford responded with a strange and unbelieving grimace. . . .

Initially Mr. Johnson hesitated to make his withdrawal announcement with the policy declaration. But some time near the end of March, as he became convinced of the need for a bombing cutback, he evidently concluded that it would be more effective if he made it clear that he was not just appealing for votes or pacifying domestic critics or serving some other personal interest.

The approach of the Wisconsin primary also served as a deadline for action, in the view of some of his political advisers. They thought his withdrawal would be more dignified and more effective if made before the primary rather than after the expected victory for Senator Eugene J. McCarthy of Minnesota.

By the eve of the speech the President's mind was made up.

He did not sleep particularly well that night, and he was up before dawn. In the afternoon, he began rehearsing the Vietnam portion of the speech. About 4 P.M. Mr. Busby gave him the revised ending on not seeking re-election. The President made a few final adjustments to insure that his motives would be understood. . . .

Secretary Clifford and his wife were invited to the Executive Mansion half an hour before the President was to go on nationwide television. Mr. Clifford already knew of the Vietnam decision—the bombing cutback to the 20th Parallel, 13,500 more troops for General Westmoreland and more equipment for the South Vietnamese Army at a cost of $2.5-billion a year.

After the wrenching tensions of the policy debate and the chill that had crept into their personal relations, the Secretary was warmed to learn that the President wanted to see him before delivering the speech. Upstairs in the family quarters, the Cliffords joined Mrs. Johnson and Jack Valenti, the President's former aide and an old Texas friend.

Mr. Johnson motioned Mr. Clifford into his bedroom and without a word handed him the last two paragraphs of the speech.

"With America's sons in the fields far away, with America's future under challenge right here at home, with our hopes and the world's hopes for peace in the balance every day," the President told the nation later, "I do not believe that I should devote an hour or a day of my time to any personal, partisan causes or to any duties other than the awesome duties of this office—the Presidency of your country.

"Accordingly, I shall not seek, and I will not accept, the nomination of my party for another term as your President."[*1]

Johnson had installed Clark Clifford in Robert McNamara's place at the head of the Pentagon, presuming the former was still an unruffled hawk. "Don't see Bob," President Johnson had remarked to one senator—"he's gone dovish on me." McNamara's miraculous transformation into a late-feathering dove was a post-Tet phenomenon, but ambivalences had appeared in his 1967 testimony before the Stennis Committee, a subcommittee of the redoubtable Mississippian's Armed Services Committee. It was

[*1] *The New York Times,* March 6, 1969, pp. 1, 14; March 7, 1969, pp. 1, 14.

the favorite roosting place for the remaining Senate "hawks." On this occasion John Stennis demanded the reason for the Administration's continued refusal to attack several "strategic" targets regarded by air power enthusiasts as the only way to bring Hanoi to its knees, to force it to crawl to the peace table.

There was simply no way, began the Defense Secretary in the rimless eyeglasses, that the United States could prevent North Vietnam from sustaining combat operations in the South by a stepped-up bombing campaign. "To pursue this objective would not only be futile, but would involve risks to our personnel and to our nation that I am unable to recommend." But he would not explain himself, and the response infuriated Stennis and his fellow hawks. Filled with unhappy memories of "privileged sanctuaries" and "no win" strategies in Korea, their discontent at the war took the form of personal attacks on the defense "intellectual" Kennedy had hired in 1961.

The Tet Offensive in February 1968 allowed other doubters to reveal themselves to one another. Suddenly it seemed there was a whole flock of doves in the Pentagon. During the Tet attacks, the NLF and its allies all but erased the highly-touted "pacification" program in the countryside, and shattered the illusion that the cities were secure. Hue, the cultural capital of Vietnam, was captured and held by the enemy for more than three weeks. In its recapture, 80 per cent of the buildings were destroyed, 75 per cent of the people left homeless. Perhaps, as General William Westmoreland contended, Tet was the enemy's "last desperate push" to stave off ultimate defeat. But earlier predictions of victory had so often proved false that there was no reason to believe the American commander, despite his report that "bodycount" ratios were still holding firm—33,000 enemy dead to only 3400 Americans and South Vietnamese.

McNamara had originated the bodycount ratio as a means of quantifying progress in counterinsurgency campaigns. According to the new textbooks on guerilla warfare, a government had to maintain a 10:1 kill ratio to win. If the enemy-to-allies bodycount reached or approached that magic figure, success could only be a matter of time. So every day the Pentagon released figures supplied by field commanders which demonstrated a better than 10:1 ratio; yet every day "victory" seemed more remote.

A reporter who attended a frontline briefing with the Defense Secretary was so depressed by all this "objective" analysis that he commented to McNamara afterwards that Vietnam was a bottomless pit. "Mr. Vanocur," came the reply, "every pit has its bottom." Under McNamara were those fledgling doves, the Assistant Secretaries, who still kept quiet publicly but who harbored growing doubts even within earshot of the Pentagon's droning computers. One of these, John McNaughton, returned from a 1967 White House conference appalled by what had transpired. "We seem to be proceeding," he confided to a colleague, "on the assumption that the way to eradicate the Viet Cong is to destroy all the village structures, defoliate the jungles, and then cover the entire surface of South Vietnam with asphalt."[1]

Outside the Administration, protests against the war had passed beyond the 1965-66 "teach-in" phase on college campuses to a semi-permanent (and growing) national movement enlisting the support of former advisers to John F. Kennedy as well as Congressional "doves" of both parties. A "Republican White Paper," prepared by the research staff of the Senate Republican Policy Committee, also appeared in 1967, though its critical conclusions were accepted only in part by most party members, who, while they might favor a strong stand in Asia, wanted to absolve Eisenhower of any responsibility for the way Democrats were conducting Asian policy. Against these criticisms, the Administration defended its policies as a middle ground between unacceptable extremes, and issued strongly worded warnings about Chinese expansionism. In speeches that would come back to haunt him in the 1968 campaign, Vice-President Hubert Humphrey went the full distance with this argument. "Make no mistake about it," he warned three thousand listeners in Doylestown, Pennsylvania. "Make no mistake about it. Communist China has failed in its attempt to overrun Southeast Asia because we are there resisting aggression. North Vietnam has failed in its objective to absorb South Vietnam in the swamp of Communism. North Vietnam has failed because we are there resisting aggression."[2]

During a press conference on October 12, 1967, Secretary of State Dean Rusk raised the spectre of "a billion Chinese . . . armed with nuclear weapons" threatening to "overrun" the "free nations of Asia," and then asked how it was possible that some senators could vote for the Gulf of Tonkin Resolution declaring Southeast Asia vital to American security and two years later "brush that aside as having no validity." For two long days, January 28 and February 18, 1966, the Secretary had faced his critics in nationally televised hearings before the Senate Foreign Relations Committee. On the first day, the United States was still completing a diplomatic offensive which included a thirty-nine-day bombing pause. Early in his testimony Rusk asserted that it was "the policy of Peiping that has greatly stimulated Hanoi and has apparently blocked the path toward a conference." China's militancy, he noted, had caused great problems within the Communist world, quite apart from the difficulties it had caused in countries of the "free world." It was that premise which the critics disputed. Rusk's answers elaborated on the argument and established the Administration's worldview—in which Vietnam occupied the foreground for the time being:

SECRETARY RUSK: The present effort was decided upon in 1959 in Hanoi. It was publicly organized and announced in Hanoi during 1960, and it has been followed up ever since.

Then there is . . . I think a very special case here in these divided countries. We could not accept the argument that, because West Germans and East Germans are both Germans, if they went after each other, that would be simply an indigenous affair. I can assure you the Russians wouldn't accept it on that basis.

When the North Koreans went after the South Koreans with many organized divisions we couldn't accept that as an indigenous affair, a civil war among Koreans. There have been agreements, there have been settlements, there have been demarcation lines that are as important as frontiers. If we are going to organize the peace, we had better insist in the case of these divided countries that, if there are any problems, those problems should be settled by peaceful means and not by force. Otherwise this world is going to go up in smoke. . . .

I think what China considers to be a national interest of theirs is very much engaged here; that is, the application of the technique

of a militant "war of liberation," as they call it. . . . I don't subscribe to the view that I have heard expressed by some, that the
Soviet Union is very glad that we are all mixed up in this problem, and that China is very glad to see us all mixed up in this
problem. I think that they would prefer that we not come there
at all. They would prefer to have seen their world revolution move
ahead. I don't think that they are getting what they want in this
present situation—nor are we, yet. . . .

During the past 35 days there has been a major effort to enlist
the assistance of other governments, including Communist governments, to bring this matter to a peaceful conclusion. Those
efforts have been harshly and peremptorily rejected by the other
side. The infiltration continues. This is Ho Chi Minh's war. . . .

SENATOR [FRANK] CHURCH: If it is Ho Chi Minh's war, is it not
true that Ho Chi Minh was the chief architect in securing Vietnamese independence against the French?

SECRETARY RUSK: He was the leader of a nationalist movement
that had in it many elements, and many of the elements of that
nationalist movement are now in South Vietnam supporting and
trying to build a system in South Vietnam that is not Communist.

SENATOR CHURCH: Is it not true that at the time the war was
fought and the French were driven out, that Ho Chi Minh was
generally regarded as the leader of the revolutionary effort?

SECRETARY RUSK: That is correct, sir.

SENATOR CHURCH: So if this now is Ho Chi Minh's war, that
may be one of the reasons why so many Vietnamese are willing
to die in it.

SECRETARY RUSK: Well, they may—

SENATOR CHURCH: It seems to me that there is a difference between guerilla war or revolution and the kind of aggression that
we faced in Korea and in Europe, and, further, that the underdeveloped world is going to be beset with guerilla wars, regardless
of the outcome in Vietnam, and that we will have to live in a
world afflicted with such revolutions for a long time to come.

That is why it is so important to try to determine what our

basic foreign policy attitude is going to be in dealing with these revolutionary wars in many parts of the underdeveloped world in the future; and, as I have listened to your explanations this morning, I gather that wherever a revolution occurs against an established government, and that revolution, as most will doubtlessly be, is infiltrated by Communists, that the United States will intervene, if necessary, to prevent a Communist success. . . .

SECRETARY RUSK: Senator, I think it is very important that the different kinds of revolutions be distinguished. We are in no sense committed against change. As a matter of fact, we are stimulating, ourselves, very sweeping revolutions in a good many places. The whole weight and effort of the Alliance for Progress [in Latin America] is to bring about far-reaching social, economic changes.

SENATOR CHURCH: That is change sought, Mr. Secretary, without violence. History shows that the most significant change has been accompanied by violence.

Do you think that with our foreign aid program we are going to be able, with our money, to avert serious uprisings in all of these destitute countries in future years?

SECRETARY RUSK: Not necessarily avert all of them, but I do believe there is a fundamental difference between the kind of revolution the Communists call their wars of national liberation, and the kind of revolution which is congenial to our own experience, and fits into the aspirations of ordinary men and women around the world.

There is nothing liberal about that revolution that they are trying to push from Peiping. This is a harsh, totalitarian regime. It has nothing in common with the great American revolutionary tradition, nothing in common with it.

SENATOR CHURCH: The objectives of Communist revolution are clearly very different indeed from the earlier objectives of our own. But objectives of revolutions have varied through the centuries.

The question that I think faces this country is how we can best cope with the likelihood of revolt in the underdeveloped world in the years ahead, and I have very serious doubts that American military intervention will often be the proper decision.

I think too much intervention on our part may well spread Communism throughout the ex-colonial world rather than thwart it.

Now, the distinction you draw between the Communist type of guerilla war and other kinds of revolution, if I have understood it correctly, has been based upon the premise that in Vietnam the North Vietnamese have been meddling in the revolution in the South, and, therefore, it is a form of aggression on the part of the North against the South.

But I cannot remember many revolutions that have been fought in splendid isolation. There were as many Frenchmen at Yorktown when Cornwallis surrendered as there were American Continentals.

Senator [Claiborne] Pell tells me more. I accept the correction.

In any case, it seems to me that the Communists have not changed the rules of revolution by meddling in them, regardless of how much we disapprove of their goals.

When we were an infant nation we stood up for the right of revolution, and I am afraid . . . that if we intervene too much in wars of this type, our policy may well turn out to be self-defeating. . . . I think that the most significant thing about the underdeveloped countries in recent years is the conspicuous lack of progress that the Communists have made in taking them over and where they have had success it has usually been in places where Communism has been able to catch hold of nationalist aspirations, as in Vietnam, where the Communist leader happened to be the authentic architect of Vietnamese independence. . . . I think that in these areas where the sensitivity toward Western imperialism, born of three centuries of colonialism, is so very great that Mao Tse-tung might want us to move in with a massive importation of Western troops from the opposite side of the world believing that this intervention serves the larger interests of China in Asia, and tends to spread Communism by identifying it with Asian nationalism, and our own policy with the hated old Western imperialism.

To be sure this is not how we regard our policy nor how we define our objectives. But the important thing is how Asians look at it, and in that respect Mao Tse-tung may have a better basis for judgment than we do.

SECRETARY RUSK: Senator, I cannot for a moment find a way to identify the purposes of the Liberation Front organized in Hanoi in 1960 with the purposes of the American Revolution or the purposes of the national revolutions which we associate with decolonization.

We are prepared, and have said so over and over again publicly and privately, to let the South Vietnamese themselves decide that question. The other side is not willing to do that. They are not prepared to let the South Vietnamese choose their government.

They said as late as this morning in a Hanoi broadcast—or at least in a letter to the chiefs of the other Communist countries—that the Liberation Front must be accepted as the sole spokesman for the South Vietnamese people.

Now, we know very well from our many, many contacts with the South Vietnamese people and their leaders, and not just those in government but outside, that that is exactly what the South Vietnamese people do not want. This can be tested in a free election.

The 325th Division that moved from North Vietnam to South Vietnam did not come in there to provide the South Vietnamese with a liberal democratic revolution in keeping with the modern trend of the sort of revolutions that we should welcome—not at all.[1]

Several members of the Senate Foreign Relations Committee disagreed with Secretary Rusk (and also among themselves) about the 1964 Gulf of Tonkin Resolution, frequently cited by the Administration as its authority for sending more than the already large number (200,000) of troops to Vietnam. The Chairman, Senator J. William Fulbright, insisted that he "did not at that time visualize or contemplate that this was going to take the turn that it now appears about to take." Fulbright was in an especially awkward position, since he had led the floor fight to secure the resolution's passage. Secretary Rusk countered with the

[1] U.S. Senate, Foreign Relations Committee, *Hearings: Supplemental Foreign Assistance Fiscal Year 1966—Vietnam*, 89th Cong., 2d Sess. (Washington, 1966), pp. 30, 32, 74–76.

argument that Congress had been fully consulted in August 1964 when President Johnson requested authority; he hoped the Senators would not now seek to rescind their action simply because the going had gotten tough.

Chairman Fulbright's new role as the leading senatorial war critic brought him into opposition with his long-time friend and colleague, Lyndon Johnson. His decision to hold these hearings marked the point of no return in relations between the two, although their disagreement had not begun over Vietnam, but over the President's decision to intervene in the 1965 Dominican Republic revolution.[3] Only later did he see the Vietnam War as part of the pattern he was to describe in *The Arrogance of Power.* In fact, Fullbright praised the "affirmative tone" of President Johnson's April 7, 1965 Vietnam speech at Johns Hopkins, though he expressed the hope that the Administration would seek a temporary ceasefire to prove it wanted a peaceful settlement in Vietnam.

Almost simultaneously with the President's Johns Hopkins speech appeared Hanoi's "four points" for settling the issue by returning to the 1954 Geneva Agreements. According to those agreements, said North Vietnamese Premier Pham Van Dong, the United States "must withdraw from South Vietnam U.S. troops, military personnel, and weapons of all kinds," although this might wait until after negotiations were concluded. The second and fourth proposals referred back to 1954 stipulations on military neutralization and peaceful reunification without foreign interference. The Johnson Administration objected most vigorously, however, to the third point, which translated: "The internal affairs of South Vietnam must be settled by the South Vietnamese people themselves, in accordance with the program of the National Front for the Liberation of South Vietnam, without any foreign interference."[4] It was this point Secretary of State Dean Rusk had referred to in the 1966 hearings when he charged that the other side was demanding "that the Liberation Front must be accepted as the sole spokesman for the South Vietnamese people." That interpretation of Hanoi's Point Three was never really tested—it might well have meant that a settlement made without foreign interference was in accordance with the program of the NFL—because Johnson's Johns Hopkins speech

**seemed to exclude the Front from *any* peace talks, and to rule
out any compromise.⁵ On that occasion the President began:**

I have come here to review once again with my own people
the views of the American Government.

Tonight Americans and Asians are dying for a world where each
people may choose its own path to change. This is the principle
for which our ancestors fought in the valleys of Pennsylvania. It is
a principle for which our sons fight tonight in the jungles of Viet-
Nam. . . .

Why must we take this painful road? Why must this nation
hazard its ease, its interest, and its power for the sake of a people
so far away?

We fight because we must fight if we are to live in a world
where every country can shape its own destiny, and only in such
a world will our own freedom be finally secure.

This kind of world will never be built by bombs or bullets. Yet
the infirmities of man are such that force must often precede
reason, and waste of war, the works of peace. We wish that this
were not so. But we must deal with the world as it is, if it is ever
to be as we wish.

The world as it is in Asia is not a serene or peaceful place.

The first reality is that North-Viet-Nam has attacked the independent nation of South Viet-Nam. Its object is total conquest.
Of course, some of the people of South Viet-Nam are participating
in attack on their own government. But trained men and supplies,
orders and arms, flow in a constant stream from North to South.

This support is the heartbeat of the war.

And it is a war of unparalleled brutality. Simple farmers are the
targets of assassination and kidnapping. Women and children
are strangled in the night because their men are loyal to their
government. And helpless villages are ravaged by sneak attacks.
Large-scale raids are conducted on towns, and terror strikes in the
heart of cities.

The confused nature of this conflict cannot mask the fact that
it is the new face of an old enemy.

Over this war—and all Asia—is another reality: the deepening shadow of Communist China. The rulers in Hanoi are urged on by Peiping. This is a regime which has destroyed freedom in Tibet, which has attacked India, and has been condemned by the United Nations for aggression in Korea. It is a nation which is helping the forces of violence in almost every continent. The contest in Viet-Nam is part of a wider pattern of aggressive purposes.

Why are these realities our concern? Why are we in South Vietnam?

We are there because we have a promise to keep. Since 1954 every American President has offered support to the people of South Viet-Nam. We have helped to build, and we have helped to defend. Thus, over many years, we have made a national pledge to help South Viet-Nam defend its independence.

And I intend to keep that promise. . . .

We are also there to strengthen world order. Around the globe, from Berlin to Thailand, are people whose well-being rests in part on the belief that they can count on us if they are attacked. To leave Viet-Nam to its fate would shake the confidence of all these people in the value of an American commitment and in the value of America's word. The result would be increased unrest and instability, and even wider war.

We are also there because there are great stakes in the balance. Let no one think for moment that retreat from Viet-Nam would bring an end to conflict. The battle would be renewed in one country and then another. The central lesson of our time is that the appetite of aggression is never satisfied. To withdraw from one battlefield means only to prepare for the next. We must say in Southeast Asia—as we did in Europe—in the words of the Bible: "Hitherto shalt thou come, but no further."

There are those who say that all our effort there will be futile— that China's power is such that it is bound to dominate all Southeast Asia. But there is no end to that argument until all of the nations of Asia are swallowed up.

There are those who wonder why we have a responsibility there. Well, we have it there for the same reason that we have a responsibility for the defense of Europe. World War II was fought in both Europe and Asia, and when it ended we found ourselves with continued responsibility for the defense of freedom.

Our objective is the independence of South Viet-Nam and its freedom from attack. We want nothing for ourselves—only that the people of South Viet-Nam be allowed to guide their own country in their own way. We will do everything necessary to reach that objective, and we will do only what is absolutely necessary.

In recent months attacks on South Viet-Nam were stepped up. Thus it became necessary for us to increase our response and to make attacks by air. This is not a change of purpose. It is a change in what we believe that purpose requires.

We do this in order to slow down aggression.

We do this to increase the confidence of the brave people of South Viet-Nam who have bravely borne this brutal battle for so many years with so many casualties.

And we do this to convince the leaders of North Viet-Nam—and all who seek to share their conquest—of a simple fact:

We will not be defeated.

We will not grow tired.

We will not withdraw, either openly or under the cloak of a meaningless agreement.

We know that air attacks alone will not accomplish all of these purposes. But it is our best and prayerful judgment that they are a necessary part of the surest road to peace.

We hope that peace will come swiftly. But that is in the hands of others besides ourselves. And we must be prepared for a long continued conflict. It will require patience as well as bravery—the will to endure as well as the will to resist.

I wish it were possible to convince others with words of what we now find it necessary to say with guns and planes: armed hostility is futile—our resources are equal to any challenge—because we fight for values and we fight for principle, rather than territory or colonies, our patience and our determination are unending.

Once this is clear, then it should also be clear that the only path for reasonable men is the path of peaceful settlement. Such peace demands an independent South Viet-Nam—securely guaranteed and able to shape its own relationships to all others—free from outside interference—tied to no alliance—a military base for no other country.

These are the essentials of any final settlement.

We will never be second in the search for such a peaceful settlement in Viet-Nam.

There may be many ways to this kind of peace: in discussion or negotiation with the governments concerned; in large groups or in small ones; in the reaffirmation of old agreements or their strengthening with new ones.

We have stated that this position over and over again 50 times and more to friend and foe alike. And we remain ready with this purpose for unconditional discussions.*1

And until that bright and necessary day of peace we will try to keep conflict from spreading. We have no desire to see thousands die in battle—Asians or Americans. We have no desire to devastate that which the people of North Viet-Nam have built with toil and sacrifice. We will use our power with restraint and with all the wisdom that we can command.

But we will use it.

This war, like most wars, is filled with terrible irony. For what do the people of North Viet-Nam want? They want what their neighbors also desire—food for their hunger, health for their bodies, a chance to learn, progress for their country, and an end to the bondage of material misery. And they would find all these things far more readily in peaceful association with others than in the endless course of battle. . . .

The first step is for the countries of Southeast Asia to associate themselves in a greatly expanded cooperative effort for development. We would hope that North Viet-Nam would take its place in the common effort just as soon as peaceful cooperation is possible.

The United Nations is already actively engaged in development in this area, and as far back as 1961 I conferred with our authorities in Viet-Nam in connection with their work there. And I would hope tonight that the Secretary-General of the United Nations could use the presige of his great office and his deep knowledge of

*1 In a commentary, dated Apr. 1, 1965, on President Johnson's speech, the South Vietnamese Government said that it would negotiate only after the withdrawal of Communist troops and cadres from South Viet-Nam and that it would not negotiate with the National Front for the Liberation of South Viet-Nam. This commentary was dropped in leaflet form over North Viet-Nam (text in George M. Kahin and John W. Lewis, *The United States in Vietnam* [Dell Publishing Co., 1967], pp. 430–431).

Asia to initiate, as soon as possible, with the countries of that area, a plan for cooperation in increased development.

For our part I will ask the Congress to join in a billion-dollar American investment in this effort as soon as it is underway. And I would hope that all other industrialized countries, including the Soviet Union, will join in this effort to replace despair with hope and terror with progress. . . .

The vast Mekong River can provide food and water and power on a scale to dwarf even our own TVA. The wonders of modern medicine can be spread through villages where thousands die every year from lack of care. Schools can be established to train people in the skills needed to manage the process of development. And these objectives, and more, are within reach of a cooperative and determined effort.

I also intend to expand and speed up a program to make available our farm surpluses to assist in feeding and clothing the needy in Asia. We should not allow people to go hungry and wear rags while our own warehouses overflow with an abundance of wheat and corn and rice and cotton. . . .

This will be a disorderly planet for a long time. In Asia, and elsewhere, the forces of the modern world are shaking old ways and uprooting ancient civilizations. There will be turbulence and struggle and even violence. Great social change—as we see in our own country—does not always come without conflict.

We must also expect that nations will on occasion be in dispute with us. It may be because we are rich, or powerful, or because we have made some mistakes, or because they honestly fear our intentions. However, no nation need ever fear that we desire their land, or to impose our will, or to dictate their institutions.

But we will always oppose the effort of one nation to conquer another nation.

We will do this because our own security is at stake.

But there is more to it than that. For our generation has a dream. It is a very old dream. But we have the power, and now we have the opportunity to make that dream come true.

For centuries nations have struggled among each other. But we dream of a world where disputes are settled by law and reason. And we will try to make it so.

For most of history men have hated and killed one another

in battle. But we dream of an end to war. And we will try to make it so.

For all existence most men have lived in poverty, threatened by hunger. But we dream of a world where all are fed and charged with hope. And we will help to make it so. . . .

Man now has the knowledge—always before denied—to make this planet serve the real needs of the people who live on it.

I know this will not be easy. I know how difficult it is for reason to guide passion, and love to master hate. The complexities of this world do not bow easily to pure and consistent answers.

But the simple truths are there just the same. We must all try to follow them as best we can.

We often say how impressive power is. But I do not find it impressive at all. The guns and the bombs, the rockets and the warships, are all symbols of human failure. They are necessary symbols. They protect what we cherish. But they are witness to human folly.

A dam built across a great river is impressive.

In the countryside where I was born, and where I live, I have seen the night illuminated, and the kitchen warmed, and the home heated, where once the cheerless night and the ceaseless cold held sway. And all this happened because electricty came to our area along the humming wires of the REA. Electrification of the countryside—yes, that, too, is impressive.

A rich harvest in a hungry land is impressive.

The sight of healthy children in a classroom is impressive.

These—not mighty arms—are the achievements which the American nation believes to be impressive. And if we are steadfast, the time may come when all other nations will also find it so.

Every night before I turn out the lights to sleep I ask myself this question: Have I done everything that I can do to unite this country? Have I done everything I can to help unite the world, to try to bring peace and hope to all the peoples of the world? Have I done enough?

Ask yourselves that question in your homes—and in this hall tonight. Have we, each of us, all done all we can do? Have we done enough?

We may well be living in the time foretold many years ago when it was said: "I call heaven and earth to record this day

47

against you, that I have set before you life and death, blessing and cursing: therefore choose life, that both thou and thy seed may live."

This generation of the world must choose: destroy or build, kill or aid, hate or understand. We can do all these things on a scale that has never been dreamed of before.

Well, we will choose life. And so doing, we will prevail over the enemies within man, and over the natural enemies of all mankind.*2

The April 7, 1965 speech was directed to two audiences: (1) the Vietnamese, both North and South, and (2) academic critics who spoke at and supported the growing "teach-in" movement on college campuses. The first of these was held at the University of Michigan on March 24, 1965, in the wake of the first systematic bombing raids against North Vietnam. Officially described as retaliation for Vietcong raids on the big air base at Pleiku, which left eight Americans dead and 126 wounded, the bombing raids grew more numerous until at last there was no need to keep up the pretense that each strike was in retaliation for specific Vietcong acts of terrorism. "Pleikus are streetcars," Presidential Adviser McGeorge Bundy later told a newsman— meaning, if one waits long enough, they come along.[6]

When the first U.S. Marine Corps battalions landed at Danang, South Vietnam, on March 7, 1965, Secretary of State Dean Rusk assured a national television audience that "It is not their mission to engage in the pacification operations." Saigon had not asked for "combat personnel," he continued. "They have very substantial armed forces that are fighting with effectiveness and with gallantry."[7] Both campaigns, the air war against the North and the initiation of large-scale "search and destroy" missions in the South, had their genesis in contingency plans drawn up months before the 1964 Gulf of Tonkin crisis by a special "Vietnam Working Group," composed of representatives from the State Department, the Central Intelligence Agency, and the Pentagon. That "crisis" remains shrouded in layers of speculation and con-

---

*2 U.S. Department of State, *American Foreign Policy: Current Documents, 1965* (Washington, D.C., 1968), pp. 848–852.

fusion. At the time, Administration leaders testified before the Senate Foreign Relations Committee that the North Vietnamese had carried out two attacks on American vessels operating in international waters in the Gulf of Tonkin. Later hearings in 1968 produced considerable evidence that the American vessels were engaged in electronic reconnaissance measures (which involved feints against the mainland), were in the vicinity of South Vietnam operations against North Vietnamese island outposts, and that there was considerable doubt as to whether the second attack ever took place. But when President Johnson announced that he had ordered a retaliatory raid against North Vietnamese PT-boat bases, and asked Congress for authority to undertake "all necessary action to protect our armed forces and to assist nations covered by the SEATO Treaty," the response was nearly unanimous. The Resolution that resulted empowered the President to "take all necessary steps, including the use of armed force, to assist any member or protocol state of the Southeast Asia Collective Defense Treaty requesting assistance in defense of its freedom." Only two Senators dissented, Wayne Morse and Ernest Gruening. Many Democrats later implied that they had voted for the resolution for domestic political reasons, i.e., to strengthen Johnson's hand against the Republican hard-liner candidate Barry Goldwater. But no one, Democrats, Republicans, or President Johnson, anticipated it would take more than a half-million soldiers to underwrite the Gulf of Tonkin Resolution of August 7, 1964.

As Joseph C. Goulden explains, the proposals of the "Vietnam Working Group" envisioned a very different ending:

Prior to 1964, the special operations in the North had an *ad hoc* quality, their object random harassment rather than accomplishment of long-range war goals. One Operation Haylift mission was directed against a municipal waterworks in a town just north of the demilitarized zone—scarcely the type of destruction to diminish North Vietnam's war-making potential. The Laotian activities against the Ho Chi Minh Trail were hit-and-miss (usually the latter) and did not materially reduce traffic. Moving arguments were advanced to fit the special operations into a formal war structure. Frank N. Trager, professor of international affairs at New York University and prominent among the outside consultants relied upon by the Pentagon and CIA for national strategic planning, summarized the case for punishing the North in a 1963 talk at the Center for Strategic Studies in Washington:

> If the past fifteen years, that is, since George Kennan first advocated a policy of containment for Europe . . . have demonstrated any one fact, it is that Communist ideology, power policy, and advancing strategy have not been contained, even when we had nuclear monopoly. It should be evident in terms of . . . past and recent East, South and Southeast Asian experience that even to maintain the *current* defensive perimeter we shall sooner or later have to make an effort at penetrating, undermining, threatening and possibly attacking the enemy at bases on his terrain. Americans will not be willing to suffer casualties over a long period of time in Vietnam for want of stopping Vietminh (sic) at the source. Sooner or later we shall have to face up to the strategy of defending 'Saigon' by seriously threatening or attacking Hanoi.

The intensification of special operations had its genesis in Johnson's appointment, in December 1963, of a "Vietnam Working Group" to help guide day-to-day conduct of the war and to plan strategy. Its leader was William H. Sullivan, a 41-year-old foreign service officer whom Ambassador Averell Harriman plucked from obscurity and made his principal deputy. . . .

After six weeks' research the Sullivan group began writing a paper whose thrust . . . was to develop a plan to "win" the war, or to stabilize it, without resorting to negotiation in the near future. . . . Even Harriman is reliably reported to have expressed shock at the product (although his close relationship with Sullivan was not affected).

Sullivan's paper, sent to the White House in an unbound loose-leaf folder to expedite revisions and updatings, began with the premise that nothing short of direct United States force would halt or even delay the Viet Cong. The strength of the VC infrastructure in both the cities and the countryside gave the National Liberation Front a "government" far more viable than that of Saigon. Further, despite Pentagon gripes that the VC flourished only because of the North Vietnamese "sanctuary" and supplies flowing from it, Sullivan argued that the VC for the immediate future could be considered a self-sustaining force.

What, then, should be done?

Sullivan's paper tacitly accepted the thesis that Hanoi guided the NLF; were North Vietnam to be held accountable for its "aggression" and punished, it would likely order the NLF to lessen the tempo of battle (and also slow its supply of men and arms). Sullivan addressed himself to possible methods of persuading Hanoi to cease-and-desist, within the format of a plan of gradually increasing pressures, beginning with psychological techniques and ranging upward into conventional warfare.

Certain of the lower-rung proposals appear at first consideration too childish to be a part of international strategic maneuvering. One suggestion was to have unmarked United States jets, manned by South Vietnamese pilots, sweep low over Hanoi, Haiphong, and other major cities, rocking them with sonic booms.[*1] [Premier Nguyen] Khanh would be encouraged to talk belligerently about an invasion of North Vietnam, and the United States would comment so ambiguously that no one could be certain of its intentions. United States advisers would make themselves conspicuous during reconnaissance patrols along the southern fringe of the DMZ.

Through diplomatic contacts the United States would bluntly tell the North Vietnamese that she intended to get tough and would continue to do so, in ever-hardening gradations, unless Hanoi stopped supporting the National Liberation Front. Make a public fuss, the United States would say, and we'll reply that you don't know what you are talking about. We are going to be careful enough that you can't obtain any physical evidence of our participation in the sonic boom 'raids' and no one outside the Communist world would ever believe that the United States, with its arsenal of missiles, nuclear warheads, and supersonic bombers,

---

[*1] Author's note—No one in government has ever admitted publicly that the United States indeed did try to frighten Hanoi out of the war by rattling its windows and disturbing Ho Chi Minh's sleep. But in the late spring and early summer of 1964, Hanoi radio did complain frequently of violations of its air space.

is "fighting" a fourth-rate Asian nation with noisemakers. The flights would demonstrate to Hanoi that the United States was capable of unrestricted air operations over North Vietnam, and that the next noise well could be the sounds of bombs, rather than sonic booms. The private boastings and public denials of responsibility for violations of Communist air space would convey the notion that the United States was ready to play dirty.

The next phase called for massing United States warships off the coast of North Vietnam, in international waters (that is, beyond a three-mile limit) but close enough to the mainland to be unnerving. Destroyers would make frequent feints at the shore. Powerful ship-based jamming transmitters would attempt to disrupt domestic Vietnamese broadcasts and communications between Hanoi and NLF military units in the South. A South Vietnamese "Saigon Rose"—the American answer to Hanoi Rose —would make propaganda broadcasts to the North Vietnamese military and civilian population, denouncing the Communist government, sympathizing with the economic and political misery of persons living under Ho Chi Minh, extolling the joys of non-Communist life in the South, and asking that Vietnamese not be forced to fight against Vietnamese.

Should sonic booms, verbal bombast, and the sight of warships fail to dissuade Hanoi, the United States would blockade the port of Haiphong and use force, if necessary, to halt shipping—even if it meant firing upon Soviet vessels. South Vietnamese torpedo boats and other small patrol craft would be permitted to raid North Vietnamese islands and coastal installations. . . . The CIA's active program of parachuting saboteurs and small guerilla teams into the North would be expanded, and United States military personnel . . . would be permitted to accompany South Vietnamese across the border.

The United States would not actively seek combat—but pilots would be authorized to shoot back if they were fired upon during reconnaissance missions over Laos, or if the North Vietnamese attempted to break the proposed blockade of Haiphong. Finally, if all else failed, the United States would commence a "tit for tat" bombing of North Vietnam, striking first for military bases directly involved in the support of the NLF, next at war-connected industrial installations, finally at Hanoi and Haiphong. . . .

Should this extreme be reached, the Sullivan group warned, the United States should be prepared for the eventuality of a massive open intervention by the North Vietnamese army, and substantially increased aid from the Soviet Union and Communist China. It was argued that the Sino-Soviet split had the Communist nations in such turmoil that neither Moscow nor Peking wanted involvement in the war; however, the Sullivan group's conclusion was that the rivalry for party leadership would compel both factions to send aid lest they be disgraced as traitors to the revolutionary cause. Were this to happen, Sullivan warned, the investment of a "substantial" number of United States troops could be required—as many as six divisions, meaning 100,000 men when support troops are included.

In conclusion, Sullivan said the United States should make abundantly clear to the world that it had no intention of destroying or occupying North Vietnam, and that any pressures would promptly end once Hanoi ceased its support of the NLF. But unless the United States gave North Vietnam painful incentive for doing so, he said, that support would continue.

Thus given the potential United States price for "saving" South Vietnam, Johnson wouldn't accept the package. Persons who watched him that spring [1964] concluded that he was stalling; that when suddenly brought against the hard decisions required to implement his broad policy goal, he was not so confident it was worth the effort. In the view of subordinates, Johnson raised procrastination to the level of an art form. "He wouldn't say No to any part of the plan; he said Maybe to others, and we'd go ahead with it. But mostly it was a matter of sending back pieces bit by bit and asking for proof for the conclusion that Phase X wouldn't bring the Chinese down on us," one man recollects. "I can certainly appreciate presidential caution, because we were talking about the possibility, even the likelihood, that the United States would go to war. But someone said one day, 'He's filibustering so that he won't have to make up his mind one way or another.' That seemed like a fair assessment."

However, Johnson did approve the expansion of special operations against the North—although in doing so he made plain to the White House national security staff that they shouldn't consider the Sullivan plan a firm blueprint for what he intended to do in the future. But the changes of tactics in the war were soon felt by the men in the field.*²

Goulden's reconstruction of pre-Tonkin Gulf events lacked documentation which became available with the publication of the "Pentagon Papers" in 1971. These documents revealed that a draft resolution empowering the President to commit American forces to the war had been drawn up on May 25, 1964, and that other contingency plans preceded even that draft:

U.S. Order for Preparations
For Some Retaliatory Action

Excerpts from National Security Action Memorandum 288, "U.S. Objectives in South Vietnam," March 17, 1964, as provided in the body of the Pentagon study. The words in brackets are the study's. The paragraph in italics is the paraphrase by a writer of the study.

[The United States' policy is] to prepare immediately to be in a position on 72 hours' notice to initiate the full range of Laotian and Cambodian "Border Control actions" . . . and the "Retaliatory Actions" against North Vietnam, and to be in a position on 30 days' notice to initiate the program of "Graduated Overt Military Pressure" against North Vietnam . . . .

We seek an independent non-Communist South Vietnam. We do not require that it serve as a Western base or as a member of a Western Alliance. South Vietnam must be free, however, to accept outside assistance as required to maintain its security. This assistance should be able to take the form not only of economic and social measures but also police and military help to root out and control insurgent elements.

Unless we can achieve this objective in South Vietnam, almost all of Southeast Asia will probably fall under Communist

*² Joseph C. Goulden, *Truth Is the First Casualty: The Gulf of Tonkin Affair—Illusion and Reality* (Chicago: Rand McNally & Co., 1969), pp. 86–91.

dominance (all of Vietnam, Laos, and Cambodia), accommodate to Communism so as to remove effective U.S. and anti-Communist influence (Burma), or fall under the domination of forces not now explicitly Communist but likely then to become so (Indonesia taking over Malaysia). Thailand might hold for a period without help, but would be under grave pressure. Even the Philippines would become shaky, and the threat to India on the West, Australia and New Zealand to the South, and Taiwan, Korea, and Japan to the North and East would be greatly increased.

All of these consequences would probably have been true even if the U.S. had not since 1954, and especially since 1961, become so heavily engaged in South Vietnam. However, that fact accentuates the impact of a Communist South Vietnam not only in Asia but in the rest of the world, where the South Vietnam conflict is regarded as a test case of U.S. capacity to help a nation to meet the Communist "war of liberation."

Thus, purely in terms of foreign policy, the stakes are high. . . .

We are now trying to help South Vietnam defeat the Viet Cong, supported from the North, by means short of the unqualified use of U.S. combat forces. We are not acting against North Vietnam except by a modest "covert" program operated by South Vietnamese (and a few Chinese Nationalists)—a program so limited that it is unlikely to have any significant effect. . . .

There were and are some sound reasons for the limits imposed by the present policy—the South Vietnamese must win their own fight; U.S. intervention on a larger scale, and/or GVN actions against the North, would disturb key allies and other nations; etc. In any case, it is vital that we continue to take every reasonable measure to assure success in South Vietnam. The policy choice is not an "either/or" between this course of action and possible pressure against the North; the former is essential and without regard to our decision with respect to the latter. The latter can, at best, only reinforce the former. . . .

Many of the actions described in the succeeding paragraphs fit right into the framework of the [pacification] plan as announced by Khanh. Wherever possible, we should tie our urgings of such actions to Khanh's own formulation of them, so that he will be carrying out a Vietnamese plan and not one imposed by the United States. . . .

Among the alternatives considered, but rejected for the time being . . . were overt military pressure on North Vietnam, neutralization, return of U.S. dependents, furnishing of a U.S. combat unit to secure the Saigon area, and a full takeover of the command in South Vietnam by the U.S. With respect to this last proposal, it was said that

. . . the judgment of all senior people in Saigon, with which we concur, was that the possible military advantages of such action would be far outweighed by adverse psychological impact. It would cut across the whole basic picture of the Vietnamese winning their own war and lay us wide open to hostile propaganda both within South Vietnam and outside.*[1]

Lyndon Johnson took charge of the Vietnamese policy and the presidency by accident. Henry Cabot Lodge, the patrician Republican who had lost the Vice-Presidency to Johnson in 1960, had been scheduled to report to President John F. Kennedy on developments in South Vietnam since the overthrow of Ngo Dinh Diem by dissident generals. He was still in San Francisco when he heard the news of Kennedy's assassination, but was told to come to the White House since Johnson would need his information and advice even more now. Lodge's report was a bleak survey, filled with references to an impending time of hard decisions. "Unfortunately, Mr. President," the Ambassador concluded, "you will have to make them." Despite the turmoil and emotional drain of that assassination weekend, Johnson was full of conviction. "I am not going to lose Vietnam," he said. "I am not going to be the President who saw Southeast Asia go the way China went."[8] Ambassador Lodge was told to return to Saigon to inform the new government there that Washington would stand by its commitments.

For a thousand days Lyndon Johnson had stood in John F. Kennedy's shadow; now he stepped forth determined to prove himself every bit as qualified to face the challenge of world revo-

*[1] Neil Sheehan, et al., *The Pentagon Papers, as Published by the New York Times* (New York: Bantam Books, 1971), pp. 283–284.

lution as his predecessor at the time of the 1962 Cuban missile crisis. Paradoxically, notes Walter LaFeber, the Cuban missile crisis intensified the situation in Vietnam. It was here that the United States chose to refute the supposed Communist thesis on "wars of liberation."[9] In the last days before his assassination, Kennedy may have had doubts about this choice—and even thoughts of re-evaluating the general policy behind the still pivotal commitment to whoever ruled in Saigon. Johnson, honestly and deeply moved by Kennedy's death, had no chance seriously to re-examine either his predecessor's policy assumptions or his own. Like Harry Truman in 1945, he succeeded a President whose style had captured the nation's imagination. To fail here out of indecision or over-cautiousness would end any chance to begin, let alone carry out, a successful presidency. Hence Johnson reaffirmed the position he had taken in May 1961, when he returned from Southeast Asia after completing a special mission for President Kennedy. From Johnson's report and those of other special advisers, Kennedy had decided Vietnam was the key to Southeast Asia, and, therefore, the place to put counter-insurgency theories to the test.

MEMORANDUM

TO: The President

FROM: The Vice-President

RE: Mission to Southeast Asia, India and Pakistan

May 23, 1961

The mission undertaken May 9, 1961, at your request, was informative and illuminating far beyond my expectations. Unusual candor—as well as unusual length—marked exchanges in each country. The purpose of this brief memorandum is to convey concisely such of my own impressions and evaluations as seem most pertinent to decisions now under your consideration. It would be wholly unrealistic to assume that such valid visits afford any basis for substantive policy judgments. It would be equally unrealistic not to recognize that the circumstances and timing of this mission elicited a depth and substance of expression not normally present in exchanges through usual channels. My purpose is to offer perspective—not, I wish to emphasize, to propose policy.

Beyond question, your judgment about the timing of our mission was correct. Each leader—except Nehru—publicly congratulated you on the "timing" of this mission. Chiang said—and all others privately concurred—that the mission had the effect of "stabilizing" the situation in the Southeast Asian nations.

Our mission arrested the decline of confidence in the United States. It did not—in my judgment—restore any confidence already lost. The leaders were as explicit and courteous as courtly men could be in making it clear that deeds must follow words—soon.

We didn't buy time—we were given it.

If these men I saw at your request were bankers, I would know—without bothering to ask—that there would be no further extension on my note.

Starting with President Diem at Saigon, it was my conclusion that the interests of the United States would be served—and protected—by the issuance of joint communiqués. My purpose was this: To attach the signature and the name of each of the leaders to a joint public statement embodying acceptance of each and agreement with the details of your letters which I delivered in your behalf. Without such statements in writing, it was clear that the United States could be victimized later by self-serving statements that you—and the Administration—had offered "nothing" or "too little," etc. . . .

I should make these two points clear: Assurances I gave were those you sent me to convey, and no commitments were asked and none were given beyond those authorized in your letters. In some instances, for various reasons, I did not express all the commitments or proposals authorized in the State position papers.

I cannot stress too strongly the extreme importance of following up this mission with other measures, other actions, and other efforts. . . .

I have reached certain other conclusions which I believe may be of value as guidance for those responsible in formulating policies. These conclusions are as follows:

The battle against Communism must be joined in Southeast Asia with strength and determination to achieve success there—or the United States, inevitably, must surrender the Pacific and take up our defenses on our own shores. Asian Communism is compromised and contained by the maintenance of free nations on the subcontinent. Without this inhibitory influence, the island outposts—Philippines, Japan, Taiwan—have no security and the vast Pacific becomes a Red Sea.

The struggle is far from lost in Southeast Asia and it is by no means inevitable that it must be lost. In each country it is possible to build a sound structure capable of withstanding and turning the Communist surge. The will to resist—while now the target of subversive attack—is there. The key to what is done by Asians in defense of Southeast Asian freedom is confidence in the United States.

There is no alternative to United States leadership in Southeast Asia. Leadership in individual countries—or the regional leadership and cooperation so appealing to Asians—rests on knowledge and faith in United States power, will and understanding.

SEATO is not now and probably never will be the answer because of British and French unwillingness to support decisive action.

We should consider an alliance of all the free nations of the Pacific and Asia who are willing to join forces in defense of their freedom. Such an organization should:

a. Have a clear-cut command authority.

b. Should also devote attention to measures and programs of social justice, housing, land reform, etc.

Any help—economic as well as military—we give less developed nations to secure and maintain their freedom must be a mutual effort. These nations cannot be saved by United States help alone. To the extent the Southeast Asian nations are prepared to take the necessary measures to make our aid effective, we can be—and must be—unstinting in our assistance. It would be useful to enunciate more clearly than we have—for the guidance of these young and unsophisticated nations—what we expect or require of them.

In large measure, the greatest danger Southeast Asia offers to nations like the United States is not the momentary threat of Communism itself. Rather, that danger stems from hunger, ignorance, poverty and disease. We must—whatever strategies we evolve—keep these enemies at the point of our attack, and make imaginative use of our scientific and technological capability in such enterprises.

The basic decision in Southeast Asia is here. We must decide whether to help these countries to the best of our ability or throw in the towel in the area and pull back our defenses to San Francisco and a "Fortress America" concept. More important, we would say to the world in this case that we don't live up to treaties and don't stand by our friends. This is not my concept. I recommend that we move forward promptly with a major effort to help these countries defend themselves. I consider the key here is to get our best people to control, plan, direct and exact results from our military aid program. In Vietnam and Thailand, we must move forward together.

In Vietnam, Diem is a complex figure beset by many problems. He has admirable qualities, but he is remote from the people, is surrounded by persons less admirable and capable than he. The country can be saved—if we move quickly and wisely. We must have coordination of purpose in our country team, diplomatic and military. The most important thing is imaginative, creative American management of our military aid program.

The Republic of China on Taiwan was a pleasant surprise to me. I had long been aware of the criticisms against Chiang Kaishek and his government and cognizant of the deep emotional American feelings in some quarters against him. I know these feelings influence our U S policy. Whatever the cause, a progressive attitude is emerging there. Our conversations with Chiang and Mme. Chiang were dominated by discussions of measures of social progress, to my gratified surprise. As with the Republic of Germany in Western Europe, so I believe we might profitably and wisely encourage the Republic of China in Asia to export talents, skills, and resources to other Asian lands to assist in programs of progress. . . .

To recapitulate, these are the main impressions I have brought back from my trip.

The fundamental decision required of the United States—and time is of the greatest importance—is whether we are to attempt to meet the challenge of Communist expansion now in Southeast Asia by a major effort to support of the forces of freedom in the area or throw in the towel. This decision must be made in a full realization of the very heavy and continuing costs involved in terms of money, of effort and of United States prestige. It must be made with the knowledge that at some point we may be faced with the further decision of whether we commit major United States forces to the area or cut our losses and withdraw should our other efforts fail. We must remain master of this decision. What we do in Southeast Asia should be part of a rational program to meet the threat we face in the region as a whole. It should include a clear-cut pattern of the specific contributions to be expected by each partner according to his ability and resources.

I believe that the mission—as you conceived it—was a success. I am grateful to the many who labored to make it so.

LYNDON B. JOHNSON[1]

A decade of deepening involvement in South Vietnam thus began with Lyndon Johnson's conclusion that America must develop a rational program to meet the Communist threat in Asia, and must apply it without flinching, or retreat to a "Fortress America" concept. Policymakers never considered the Vietnam involvement an aberration—at least not until it became a quagmire. It rested upon assumptions and historical analogies that everyone thought valid. And these, in turn, were rooted (as we shall see in later chapters) in even older conclusions about America's needs and interests in the world.

Johnson had warned in his 1961 memorandum that America had to remain master of the decisions on troop commitments. As President he was unable to carry out his own advice. And

[1] William S. White, The Professional: Lyndon B. Johnson (Boston: Houghton Mifflin, 1964), pp. 238–244.

that was where the trouble really began. At Kennedy's death there were 16,000 advisers there. In early 1964 the number rose to 21,000. Six months later it reached 50,000. Then 110,000 in December 1965. And finally 540,000 in 1968.

The shortlived 1973 truce that ended the war for American troops and bomber pilots was based on the 1954 Geneva Agreements which ended the first Vietnam War between the French and the Vietminh. Administration spokesmen stoutly denied it, but the provisions for new elections and an interim provisional government of all factions looked backward to those earlier agreements. What had changed? The war raged on with both sides still being supplied by powerful allies, but in the middle of the war the weight of historical advice began to shift against Cold War assumptions. What had not changed? Those older conclusions about America's needs and interests which had helped to produce the Cold War view in one era and the post-Cold War view in the time of Nixon's presidency.

NOTES

[1] Townsend Hoopes, *The Limits of Intervention* (New York: David McKay & Co., 1969), p. 51.
[2] *The New York Times*, October 12, 1967, p. 53.
[3] See Chapter II.
[4] The fullest discussion of the larger context of Hanoi's "four points" is in George McTurnan Kahin and John W. Lewis, *The United States in Vietnam* (New York: Dell Publishing Co., 1967), chap. IX.
[5] *Ibid.*, pp. 210–211.
[6] Hoopes, *The Limits of Intervention*, p. 30.
[7] U.S. Department of State, *American Foreign Policy: Current Documents,* 1965 (Washington, D.C., 1968) pp. 842–843.
[8] Tom Wicker, *LBJ and JFK* (Baltimore: Penguin Books Inc., 1969), pp. 204–205.
[9] Walter LaFeber, *America, Russia, and the Cold War, 1945–1967* (New York: John Wiley & Sons, 1968), pp. 237–238.

CHAPTER TWO
★★★★★

Pax Americana:
The Theory
and Practice

Deeply troubled by what he knew must follow his speech, Senator J. William Fulbright, the Chairman of the Senate Foreign Relations Committee, rose to address his colleagues on September 15, 1965.

I was in doubt about the advisability of making a statement on the Dominican affair [he began] until some of my colleagues made public statements on the floor. Their views . . . on the Dominican crisis as a whole are so diametrically opposed to my own that I now consider it my duty to express my personal conclusions drawn from the hearings held by the Committee on Foreign Relations. . . .

U.S. policy in the Dominican crisis was characterized initially by overtimidity and subsequently by overreaction. Throughout the whole affair it has also been characterized by a lack of candor. . . .

I am frankly puzzled as to the current attitude of the U.S. Government toward reformist movements in Latin America. On the one hand, President Johnson's deep personal commitment to the philosophy and aims of the Alliance for Progress is clear; it was convincingly expressed, for example, in his speech to the Latin American ambassadors on the fourth anniversary of the Alliance for Progress—a statement in which the President compared the Alliance for Progress with his own enlightened program for a Great Society at home. On the other hand, one notes a general tendency on the part of our policy makers not to look beyond a Latin American politician's anticommunism. One also notes in certain Government agencies, particularly the Department of Defense, a preoccupation with counterinsurgency, which is to say, with the prospect of revolutions and means of suppressing them. . . .

It is of great importance that the uncertainty as to U.S. aims in Latin America be resolved. We cannot successfully advance the cause of popular democracy and at the same time align ourselves with corrupt and reactionary oligarchies; yet that is what we seem to be trying to do. The direction of the Alliance for Progress is toward social revolution in Latin America; the direction of our Dominican intervention is toward the suppression of revolutionary movements which are supported by Communists or suspected of being influenced by Communists. The prospect of an election in nine months which may conceivably produce a strong democratic government is certainly reassuring on this score, but the fact remains that the reaction of the United States at the time of acute crisis was to intervene forcibly and illegally against a revolution which, had we sought to influence it instead of suppressing it, might have produced a strong popular government without foreign military intervention. Since just about every revolutionary movement is likely to attract Communist support, at least in the beginning, the approach followed in the Dominican Republic, if consistently pursued, must inevitably make us the enemy of all revolutions and therefore the ally of all the unpopular and corrupt oligarchies of the hemisphere. . . .

It is not surprising that we Americans are not drawn toward

the uncouth revolutions of the non-Communist left. We are not, as we like to claim in Fourth of July speeches, the most truly revolutionary nation on earth; we are, on the contrary, much closer to being the most unrevolutionary nation on earth. We are sober and satisfied and comfortable and rich; our institutions are stable and old and even venerable; and our Revolution of 1776, for that matter, was not much of an upheaval compared to the French and Russian revolutions and to current and impending revolutions in Latin America, Asia, and Africa. . . .

We must try to understand social revolution and the injustices that give it rise because they are the heart and core of the experience of the great majority of people now living in the world. . . .

I think that in the case of the Dominican Republic we did close our minds to the causes and to the essential legitimacy of revolution in a country in which democratic procedures had failed. That, I think, is the central fact concerning the participation of the United States in the Dominican revolution and, possibly as well, its major lesson for the future. . . .

The United States intervened in the Dominican Republic for the purpose of preventing the victory of a revolutionary force which was judged to be Communist dominated. On the basis of Ambassador Bennett's messages to Washington, there is no doubt that the threat of communism rather than danger to American lives was his primary reason for recommending military intervention. . . .

. . . The evidence does not establish that the Communists at any time actually had control of the revolution. There is little doubt that they had influence within the revolutionary movement, but the degree of that influence remains a matter of speculation.

The Administration, however, assumed almost from the beginning that the revolution was Communist-dominated, or would certainly become so, and that nothing short of forcible opposition could prevent a Communist takeover. In their apprehension lest the Dominican Republic become another Cuba, some of our officials seem to have forgotten that virtually all reform movements attract some Communist support, that there is an important difference between Communist support and Communist control of a political movement, that it is quite possible to compete with the

Communists for influence in a reform movement rather than abandon it to them, and, most important of all, that economic development and social justice are themselves the primary and most reliable security against Communist subversion. . . .

Intervention on the basis of Communist participation as distinguished from control of the Dominican revolution was a mistake in my opinion which also reflects a grievous misreading of the temper of contemporary Latin American politics. Communists are present in all Latin American countries, and they are going to inject themselves into almost any Latin American revolution and try to seize control of it. If any group or any movement with which the Communists associate themselves is going to be automatically condemned in the eyes of the United States, then we have indeed given up all hope of guiding or influencing even to a marginal degree the revolutionary movements and the demands for social change which are sweeping Latin America. Worse, if that is our view, then we have made ourselves the prisoners of the Latin American oligarchs who are engaged in a vain attempt to preserve the status quo—reactionaries who habitually use the term "Communist" very loosely, in part out of emotional predilection and in part in a calculated effort to scare the United States into supporting their selfish and discredited aims. . . .

In the eyes of educated, energetic and patriotic young Latin Americans—which is to say, the generation that will make or break the Alliance for Progress—the United States committed a worse offense in the Dominican Republic than just intervention; it intervened against social revolution and in support, at least temporarily, of a corrupt, reactionary military oligarchy.

It is not possible at present to assess the depth and extent of disillusion with the United States on the part of democrats and reformers in Latin America. I myself think that it is deep and widespread. . . .

The tragedy of Santo Domingo is that a policy that purported to defeat communism in the short run is more likely to have the effect of promoting it in the long run. Intervention in the Dominican Republic has alienated—temporarily or permanently, depending on our future policies—our real friends in Latin America. These, broadly, are the people of the democratic left. . . . By our intervention on the side of a corrupt military oligarchy in the

Dominican Republic, we have embarrassed before their own people the democratic reformers who have counseled trust and partnership with the United States. We have lent credence to the idea that the United States is the enemy of social revolution in Latin America and that the only choice Latin Americans have is between communism and reaction. . . .

The Foreign Relations Committee's study of the Dominican crisis leads me to draw certain specific conclusions regarding American policy in the Dominican Republic and also suggests some broader considerations regarding relations between the United States and Latin America. . . .

FIRST. The United States intervened forcibly in the Dominican Republic in the last week of April 1965 not primarily to save American lives, as was then contended, but to prevent the victory of a revolutionary movement which was judged to be Communist-dominated. The decision to land thousands of marines on April 28 was based primarily on the fear of "another Cuba" in Santo Domingo.

SECOND. This fear was based on fragmentary and inadequate evidence. There is no doubt that Communists participated in the Dominican revolution on the rebel side, probably to a greater extent after than before the landing of U.S. Marines on April 28, but just as it cannot be proved that the Communists would not have taken over the revolution neither can it be proved that they would have. . . .

THIRD. The United States let pass its best opportunities to influence the course of events. The best opportunities were on April 25, when Juan Bosch's party, the PRD, requested a "United States presence," and on April 27, when the rebels, believing themselves defeated, requested United States mediation for a negotiated settlement. Both requests were rejected, in the first instance for reasons that are not entirely clear, but probably because of United States hostility to the PRD, in the second instance because the U.S. Government anticipated and desired a victory of the anti-rebel forces.

FOURTH. U.S. policy toward the Dominican Republic shifted markedly to the right between September 1963 and April 1965. In 1963, the United States strongly supported Bosch and the PRD as enlightened reformers; in 1965 the United States opposed their return to power on the unsubstantiated ground that a Bosch or PRD government would certainly, or almost certainly, become Communist-dominated. Thus the United States turned its back on social revolution in Santo Domingo and associated itself with a corrupt and reactionary military oligarchy.

FIFTH. U.S. policy was marred by a lack of candor and by misinformation. The former is illustrated by official assertions that U.S. military intervention was primarily for the purpose of saving American lives; the latter is illustrated by exaggerated reports of massacres and atrocities by the rebels—reports which no one has been able to verify. . . . A sobor examination of such evidence as is available indicates that the Imbert junta was guilty of at least as many atrocities as the rebels.

SIXTH. Responsibility for the failure of American policy in Santo Domingo lies primarily with those who advised the President. In the critical days between April 25 and April 28, these officials sent the President exaggerated reports of the danger of a Communist takeover in Santo Domingo and, on the basis of these, recommended U.S. massive military intervention. It is not at all difficult to understand why, on the basis of such advice, the President made the decisions he made.

SEVENTH. Underlying the bad advice and unwise actions of the United States was the fear of another Cuba. The specter of a second Communist state in the Western Hemisphere—and its probable repercussions within the United States and possible effects on the careers of those who might be held responsible—seems to have been the most important single factor in distorting the judgment of otherwise sensible and competent men. . . .

In the eyes of educated, energetic and patriotic young Latin Americans—which is to say, the generation that will make or break the Alliance for progress—the United States committed a worse offense in the Dominican Republic than just intervention; it intervened against social revolution and in support, at least temporarily, of a corrupt, reactionary military oligarchy. . . . The tragedy of Santo Domingo is that a policy that purported to defeat communism in the short run is more likely to have the effect of promoting it in the long run.[1]

---

[1] *Congressional Record*, 89th Congress, 2d Sess., September 15, 1965.

Not since the 1920's when Senator William E. Borah had criticized a Republican President for sending the marines to Nicaragua had the chairman of the Foreign Relations Committee challenged his own party's administration. With Borah, moreover, dissent was a business-as-usual practice; Fulbright was uncomfortable in the role. A close friend of President Lyndon B. Johnson, Fulbright had demonstrated his loyalty only a few months before in a speech praising the former for his commitment to the goal of ending the war in Vietnam by negotiation. And it had been Fulbright who guided the Gulf of Tonkin resolution through the Senate, assuring his colleagues that the President would use this authority responsibly.

The Dominican crisis raised doubts, first about Johnson's personal capabilities in the foreign affairs area, but more seriously about the nation's Cold War policies in general. For many, including Fulbright, the Dominican crisis put Vietnam into new perspective. The Administration's defense of its Caribbean actions only strengthened the link. At a meeting of Congressional leaders in the White House, Johnson asked for $700 million for the military to carry out American policy in Vietnam. "We would hope that you could thoroughly and carefully consider it and, with a minimum of difficulty and discord, say to the rest of the world that we are going to spend every dollar, we are going to take every action, we are going to walk the last mile, in order to see that peace is restored, that the people of not only the Dominican Republic but South Viet-Nam have the right of self-determination and that they cannot be gobbled up in the 20th Century and swallowed just because they happen to be smaller than some of those whose boundaries adjoin them."[1]

The President's choice of language at this conference (and at other times during the Dominican intervention) left him open to criticism. Was not the closest big country to the Dominican Republic the United States? And did not the President's remarks suggest a comparison between China's policy in Southeast Asia, as interpreted by the Administration's experts, and our own dominance in the Caribbean area? McGeorge Bundy's absence from the National Teach-In on May 15, 1965, further pointed up the connection. For several weeks the Administration's critics had been seeking a confrontation with Bundy, the President's National Security Adviser, on the origins and conduct of America's Vietnam policy. At the last minute Bundy was called away "because of other duties." These duties were in the Dominican Republic, where it had become necessary to supplement the landing of Marines with some political expertise. Throughout the day his empty chair reminded the participants, both for and against the Government's policy, that it was impossible to consider Vietnam in isolation.

Bundy's letter to the organizers of the meeting concluded with a plea for unity on general goals: "The Administration which now bears the responsibility for the conduct of our foreign affairs does not admire force for its own sake or brinkmanship of any sort. The purpose of its foreign policy in Vietnam, as elsewhere, is that diplomacy and power and progress and hope shall be held together in the service of the freedom of us all. So I trust that the discussion this afternoon will not turn upon charge and countercharge against the motives of those with whom we disagree. Let it turn, instead, upon analysis of the situation as it is and of choices for the future which can serve the purposes we share."[2]

Diplomacy, power, progress, and hope were, in Bundy's words, the basis of America's position in the Cold War. The critics asserted, on the other hand, that "analysis of the situation as it is" and was would produce a different view of the postwar *Pax Americana.*

Two weeks before the National Teach-In, President Johnson had told the American people that in "the dark mist of conflict and violence, revolution and confusion, it is not easy to find clear and unclouded truths." But certain things were clear, according to the President:

The revolutionary movement [in the Dominican Republic] took a tragic turn. Communist leaders, many of them trained in Cuba, seeing a chance to increase disorder, to gain a foothold, joined the revolution. They took increasing control. And what began as a popular democratic revolution, committed to democracy and social justice, very shortly moved and was taken over and really seized and placed into the hands of a band of Communist conspirators.*1

Johnson's task, however difficult his later efforts to justify unpopular policies might become, was easier than that assigned to Adlai Stevenson, America's Ambassador to the United Nations Security Council. It was Stevenson's job to defend the intervention before an audience made up, increasingly, of the representatives of newly independent and revolutionary nations:

In the Dominican Republic there are three Communist political organizations. They are the Partido Socialista Popular Dominicano . . . , which follows Moscow's direction; the Movimiento . . . , a small but aggressive Marxist-Leninist revolutionary party which follows the Chinese Communist ideological line; and the largest of the three, the Agrupacion Politica Catorce de Junio . . . , which is Castro-oriented and with connections to Soviet and Communist Chinese regimes as well. . . .

Direct involvement of Castro in Dominican affairs is also of long standing. As long ago as 1959 Castro organized, trained, and equipped an expedition which invaded the Dominican Republic, whose leadership included a Cuban army officer, and which was escorted to Dominican shores by the Cuban navy. . . .

In 1963 also the Castro and the Chinese-oriented Communist parties of the Dominican Republic launched an open guerilla warfare movement in the hinterland of the Dominican Republic. Dominicans known to have received training in Cuba took part in that abortive effort. The bulk of the captured rebels were deported in May 1964, and most of them became political exiles in France. From there, many have since traveled in the Soviet bloc countries, including Cuba and Communist China.

Last year Dominican Communists published the Marxists' justification for their revolution in terms of national liberation, a handbook entitled *Seven Themes of Study*. Later, in September,

*1 U.S. Department of State, *American Foreign Policy: Current Documents*, 1965 (Washington, 1968), pp. 961–965.

they issued a call for unity of the "forces of the left under the leadership of the Dominican Communist Party."

And in November the Havana Conference of the Communist Parties of Latin America, to which I have already referred, called for "active aid" to the so-called freedom fighters in Latin America.

Beginning in late 1964, various of the exiled Castro and Chinese party leaders began to infiltrate back into the Dominican Republic, some clandestinely, to rejoin their respective political organizations.

Then on the very evening of the army officers' revolt inspired by the PRD—the party of Juan Bosch—April 24, these top-level Communist leaders, especially those of the Moscow-oriented old-line Communist Party, the PSPD, seized upon the unstable situation as ripe for subversive exploitation. Word was issued to party members and to other extremist groups calling for agitation and the staging of "spot rallies and demonstrations" in the streets.

Within one or two hours of the first rebel moves, members of the Castroist movement were busy in the streets of Santo Domingo.

Communist and Castroist leaders shortly thereafter got quantities of arms and ammunition from the armory at the "27 February" camp outside Santo Domingo, where rebelling army officers had seized control as the opening act of the coup. A sizable quantity of arms and ammunition thus fell into the hands of leaders of the PSPD (the Moscow party), and the members of this party were quickly formed into armed paramilitary teams which fanned out in the downtown and *barrio* (slum) areas, taking control of secondary targets and organizing the inhabitants. At the same time a party military headquarters was established, and arms collected from loyalist police and military personnel were stored there.

With relatively tight discipline and effective organization, the extreme leftist groups, particularly the PSPD but also, prominently, the MPD and the Castro movement, were soon providing a significant portion of the rebel forces and were decisively influencing the political leadership of the rebellion, which in the beginning had been in the hands of the democratic leaders of the Bosch party. . . .

[Ambassador Stevenson then listed nine men "who have sought to turn this rebellion into a Communist takeover."]

It may, of course, be said—I think accurately—that the bulk of the participants in the rebellion are not Communist and that even in the present leadership non-Communists are active. I do not purport to predict the future.

But I would remind you that only twelve men went to the hills with Castro in 1956 and that only a handful of Castro's own supporters were Communists. I would also remind you that Castro, too, came into power under cover of constitutionalism, moderation, and cooperation with others. But within months the true complexion appeared, and the list of leaders imprisoned, expelled, or forced to flee once control was achieved is well-known. It is an impressive list. . . .*1

Stevenson's indictment of the Dominican revolutionaries as likely imitators of Fidel Castro once they gained power was not universally well received by an audience containing many admirers of the Cuban Revolution. More significant than the unpopularity of the American intervention among Third World nations, however, was the Ambassador's inability to pinpoint control by any one of the three movements he had listed at the outset. All through the speech he had been forced to qualify statement after statement to include the complex interaction of revolutionary parties. For dedicated Cold Warriors it was enough that they could all be called "Communist," but for skeptics the speech was a highly revealing instance in which America had not caught up to changed world conditions.

During the Kennedy–Johnson era a great deal of effort went into the writing of so-called "White Papers" to justify American intervention in different crises around the globe. Events in the Dominican Republic had outrun even the fastest pens in the State Department, but Stevenson's speech served as a substitute.

At one time the Dominican Republic was the showcase of Kennedy's Alliance for Progress. On May 30, 1961, long-time dictator Rafael Trujillo had been assassinated. After consulting with his aides, President Kennedy outlined the situation as he saw it: "There are three possibilities in descending order of preference:

*1 *Current Documents*, 1965, pp. 970–972.

a decent democratic regime, a continuation of the Trujillo regime, or a Castro regime. We ought to aim at the first, but we really can't renounce the second until we are sure that we can avoid the third."[3] Fortunately, Kennedy thought he could avoid the third by supporting Juan Bosch, a man "strongly in the progressive democratic tradition." But in 1965, Johnson chose differently.

In both instances, the underlying assumption was the same: lurking behind almost every revolutionary movement were agents of the International Communist Conspiracy. The task for toughminded liberals like Kennedy, and the "crisis managers" in second-level positions, was to apply all their talents to measures which would contain the thrust of immediate revolutionary challenges, while, at the same time, devising long range solutions: for example, the "Alliance for Progress." Kennedy announced this plan on March 13, 1961, pledging a ten-year commitment of $20 billion; in return, Latin American countries were supposed to supply $80 billion, and social reform measures such as land and tax laws designed to aid the middle class and peasants. It was hoped that these combined efforts would produce a 5.5 per cent increase in Latin America's economic growth rate.

The Dominican intervention was a serious setback to the political goals of the *Alianza*, but it was already suffering graver illnesses in Brazil:

At the beginning of 1962, foreign ownership of public utilities had become a major issue in Brazil. The Goulart government, seeking to halt inflation, was reluctant to grant rate increases to the power and telephone companies, both of which were in large part owned by American investors. Without rate increases, maintenance and new investment declined, and as service deteriorated, public dissatisfaction mounted. The companies became an easy target for demagogic politicians.

The International Telephone and Telegraph Company, a major provider of telephone services in Brazil, owned an old local company valued at about $6 million in Pôrto Alegre, the capital of Rio Grande do Sul, the southernmost state of Brazil. The governor of the state, Leonel Brizola, who was President Goulart's brother-in-law and an influential member of the ruling Brazilian Labor Party, expropriated . . . [an] IT&T [International Telephone and Telegraph] subsidiary. The ensuing controversy triggered a national campaign by the left for expropriation of all foreign-owned utilities. To some U.S. investors it appeared that all American companies in Brazil were under attack.

To protect the interests of American companies abroad, Senator Bourke B. Hickenlooper, urged on by Harold Geneen, the president of IT&T, introduced an amendment to the Foreign Assistance Act of 1962. This amendment required the president to suspend all economic assistance to any country that expropriated the property of a U.S. company, repudiated a contract with a U.S. company, or made a U.S. company subject to discriminatory taxation or administration. Suspension of all forms of economic assistance included not just foreign aid, but such legislation as that allotting sugar quotas to favored nations. A country had six months in which to take "effective steps" to provide compensation for expropriated property in "convertible foreign exchange." Thereafter the president was allowed no discretion to waive enforcement of the amendment.

President Kennedy opposed the proposed legislation because it would invade his right to make foreign policy and embroil the U.S. government in quarrels between U.S. companies and foreign governments regardless of the merits of each case, but he was not prepared to make a public fight about it.

In a feverish attempt to head off passage, Lincoln Gordon, then ambassador to Brazil, pressed Goulart to settle the IT&T issue promptly. Goulart, however, feared that settlement would alienate the left, which he saw as his defense against the military coup d'état being organized by Carlos Lacerda, the powerful governor of the state of Guanabara. While Goulart vacillated, Harold Geneen, supported by other U.S. companies with interests in the hemisphere, pressed for passage of the amendment. The amendment was a statement of congressional policy, tying the foreign assistance program to the protection of United States overseas investments.

Goulart finally settled the IT&T case. The company agreed to reinvest 75 percent of its compensation in diversified investments outside the utility field in Brazil. But the mere availability of the Hickenlooper Amendment became a powerful factor in the dispute between the American and Foreign Power Company (AMFORP) and the Brazilian government.

In April 1963, during an official visit to Washington, Goulart suggested to President Kennedy that it was politically undesirable for United States companies to control Brazilian industries that were in effect public utilities. He proposed that Brazil buy out these interests. Kennedy was enthusiastic about the idea as long as the companies agreed. He commented, [Richard N.] Goodwin recalls, that every month, when the electric bill came due, thousands of Brazilians were bound to think, "It's that damned U.S. company." Late in April 1963, AMFORP and the Brazilian government announced an agreement by which the government would purchase the company's holdings, valued at $135 million; the company would reinvest 75 percent of this price in non-utility enterprises in Brazil; and the government would pay the remaining 25 percent in dollars over twenty-two years, with interest. The Kennedy administration greeted this agreement with relief. Governor Brizola attacked it as a betrayal by Goulart of the nationalist left (now supported by the Communists). Carlos Lacerda attacked it from the right, claiming that the equipment to be purchased was obsolete and overvalued. Goulart again procrastinated. His two key ministers, for war and economy, who had approved the purchase terms, were forced to resign. The agreement was never consummated.

In 1964, immediately following Goulart's overthrow, the United States offered the new Brazilian government a $50 million program loan, future capital assistance, and debt renegotiation, contingent on, among other things, fulfillment of the AMFORP contract. President Castelo Branco, unlike Goulart, favored increased foreign enterprise. The new authorities felt that Brazil's resources could be better utilized in productive enterprises than in paying for expropriated properties, and therefore requested AMFORP to reconsider the contract. The government promised to set electric service rates that would assure the company an adequate return on its investment. (And it ultimately kept this promise.) The AMFORP management, however, insisted that the Castelo Branco government honor the contract signed by the

Goulart government, invoking U.S. government assistance as a bargaining weapon. . . .

The AMFORP affair also convinced many Brazilians that although the U.S. government was not above twisting the arm of the Castelo Branco government, it would do so for the benefit of U.S. companies rather than for the social objectives of the Alliance for Progress.

In an interview in August 1968, Rafael de Almeida Magãlhaes . . . , one of Brazil's leading young politicians and hardly a radical leftist, declared, "U.S. aid in Brazil simply reinforced the existing inequities of Brazilian society. . . . Since you intervened here so extensively, why didn't you at least do so for the right reasons?"

. . . Since World War II the United States has provided 75 percent of foreign private investment in Latin America. But in 1961 U.S. businessmen were undertaking few new ventures in the region. Cuba's seizure of nearly $1 billion in U.S.-owned sugar mills, hotels, banks, nickel mines, factories, and other assets had been a psychological as well as a financial blow. Brazil, Chile, Colombia, and Argentina, suffering from inflation accompanied by high debt payments and low export earnings, generated additional apprehension. During the first few years of the Alliance, although reinvestment of profits by subsidiaries remained relatively steady, new investments were sharply curtailed. But after 1964, with Cuba well isolated from the hemisphere by a collective and economic blockade and Brazil under a military regime friendly to the United States, a new mood of optimism arose in the U.S. business community, producing an upsurge of investment in Latin America. . . .

As of 1969, the level of direct U.S. private investment in Latin America was $12 billion. The March 1969 issue of the U.S. Department of Commerce *Survey of Current Business* reports a gradual shift in investment emphasis from Canada and western Europe to Latin America and other countries. With substantial gains in all industries, capital investment in Latin America showed the largest increase of all major areas for 1968, easily surpassing the 16 percent gain in 1967. . . .

During most of the Alliance, U.S. business interests, and in several cases the interests of a particular corporation, have taken precedence over the U.S. national interest in Latin America . . . . Initially as the Business Group for Latin America, some twenty to thirty executives of corporations involved in Latin America, headed by David Rockefeller, advised U.S. government policy-makers on the views of the business community with respect to the Alliance for Progress. In 1965 the Business Group expanded into the Council for Latin America (CLA), again led by Rockefeller and representing some 224 corporations, approximately 85 percent of all U.S. companies doing business in Latin America. Its membership list includes such giants as Du Pont, Caterpillar, Standard Oil of New Jersey, and the Chase Manhattan Bank. CLA holds regular meetings with State, AID, IBRD, IDB, CIAP, and other government agencies whose work may affect U.S. business interests in Latin America. Its board of trustees meets two to three times a year for consultation with U.S. government officials in Washington. . . .

The relationship is important to both sides. The business community depends heavily on the official assessment of a region's and an individual country's economic and political prospects in planning its immediate and long-term investments. And because it has a permanent stake in the area and benefits directly from AID-financed orders for the sale of goods, business can be an effective ally for the AID program in the Congress or a powerful enemy if offended.

It is easy to condemn the State Department for identifying uncritically with United States business. But business is the only interest group that consistently presents its viewpoint on Latin American affairs to U.S. government policymakers.[*1]

Lest one conclude too easily that the Alliance for Progress was, reversing Lyndon Johnson's description of the Communist infiltration of the Dominican revolution, "very shortly moved and was taken over and really seized and placed into the hands of a band of . . . [business] conspirators," it would be wise to consider

[*1] Jerome Levinson and Juan de Onis, *The Alliance That Lost Its Way: A Critical Report on the Alliance for Progress* (Chicago: Quandrangle Books, 1970), pp. 135–136, 143–146, 159–160.

the comments of the President of the World Bank, Eugene Black, on how the foreign aid programs, including the Alliance for Progress, were designed: "Our foreign aid program constitutes a distinct benefit to American business. The three major benefits are: (1) foreign aid provides a substantial and immediate market for U.S. goods and services; (2) foreign aid stimulates the development of new overseas markets for U.S. companies; (3) foreign aid orients national economies toward a free enterprise system in which U.S. firms can prosper."

While the last-named benefit is perhaps the least quantifiable of the three, it, and the value system associated with making the world safe for American-style institutions generally, has been the most pervasive theme in U.S. diplomacy throughout the Cold War. Interestingly enough, no interest group has pursued that theme with greater vigor than the American labor movement. When disillusionment set in during the darkest days of the Vietnam War, labor leaders found themselves under attack from critics who called into question the close relationship between official agencies of the government and the private efforts of organized labor abroad. On August 1, 1969, George F. Meany, president of the American Federation of Labor-Congress of Industrial Organizations, replied to those charges in testimony before the Senate Foreign Relations Committee. Chairman Fulbright opened the session with this statement:

Since 1962, the American Institute for Free Labor Development, which is under the direction of the AFL–CIO, has received a little over $28 million in foreign-aid funds for its operations in Latin America. Similar AFL–CIO-directed institutes have been established for work on a more modest scale in Africa and Asia. Members of the Committee will be interested in having an explanation of the purposes of this program, how it operates, and how it relates to the overall objectives of our foreign policy.

Mr. Meany, will you come forward please, sir?

MR. MEANY: Yes, Sir.

THE CHAIRMAN: Do you have a prepared statement, Mr. Meany?

MR. MEANY: Yes, I have, Mr. Chairman.

THE CHAIRMAN: Will you proceed, sir?

MR. MEANY: . . . Our involvement with Latin America stems from 1916 when the American Federation of Labor joined with Latin America labor leaders to found the Pan American Federation of Labor. After World War II we expanded significantly our activities throughout the world, including Latin America where we helped to establish the first Inter-American Conference of Workers. In 1951 we also helped to establish the Inter-American Regional Organization of Workers which exists actively to this day, and is known as the ORIT.

In August 1960, when we came to a full realization as to what happened to the Cuban workers and the entire Cuban people under Castro, the AFL–CIO appropriated $20,000 for the purpose of making a feasibility study of the establishment of a mechanism through which we could help to strengthen the free labor unions of Latin America and develop trade union leadership. This led to the creation of the AIFLD, during the Eisenhower administration and before the establishment of the Alliance for Progress.

We did not then and do not want our Latin American trade union brothers to pattern their unions after our organizations in the United States.

We do expect and hope, however, that they will build unions which are strong, independent, representative of the workers and capable, through their own efforts, of improving the conditions of the workers, and making a contribution to the economic development of their own countries.

Throughout the years we had always wanted to see Latin American trade unionists and workers build a more effective labor movement. We hoped we could assist them to make significant contributions of their own to the economic and social development of their own countries.

Now, you might ask, "Why do we have this interest? Why should American unions have an interest in the situations in Latin America, in the workers of Latin America?"

The AFL–CIO has always had an interest in workers in every part of the world. That is fraternal solidarity, humanitarianism in the best sense of the word. We have a stake in the freedom of workers everywhere. We have learned from experience that when workers in other countries lose their freedom, where they are forced to submit to the yoke of a dictatorship or tyrannical government of any kind, their repression and enslavement constitutes a grave threat to our own freedom. And of course, we have learned from the history of recent years that the very first to lose their freedoms in these circumstances are the workers. For these reasons the AFL–CIO international activities have always been extensive so that in addition to the AIFLD in Latin America, we sponsor institutes conducting a broad range of similar assistance in Africa and Asia. I would like to emphasize, Mr. Chairman, that we are not looking for or trying to recruit members for the AFL–CIO in any country of any of these continents.

In view of our extensive international activities, on which we spend about 20 percent of our income, it was only natural when we looked at Latin America, our closest neighbors in the trade union field, we felt that we had a responsibility as workers to workers—yes; a great humanitarian responsibility—to be of help. We also felt, as American citizens, that it was certainly in the interest of our country that free governments be achieved and maintained in the Western Hemisphere. Now I'm not going to tell you that we have never made mistakes nor that we have performed miracles. Latin America still has its great problems. For example, there is still too much money being spent for unnecessary military hardware in many countries and too little being spent on the welfare of the people. But we are trying to make a contribution to help the working people of these lands play a constructive role in building democratic societies through free trade unions.

The AFL–CIO Executive Council decided unanimously that we should bring enlightened American business into this institution on the theory that they should also have an interest in developing a friendly attitude toward the building of free societies in Latin America. They naturally want to do business there, and they certainly want to do business with countries that have viable economies. We feel that you cannot have a viable economy unless you have the positive participation of all segments of the society, especially the workers who are the most important element of production and consumption. So we went to American business, and we told them why we thought they should cooperate. We got a most encouraging response.

The result is that we have some outstanding American businessmen contributing to the work of the AIFLD including Peter Grace, Chairman of the AIFLD, who is president of the W. R. Grace Co.; Mr. William Hickey, president of the United Corp.; Mr. U. W. Balgooyen, director of EBASCO Industries; Mr. Brent Friele, senior vice president, American International Association for Economic and Social Development; Mr. Juan Trippe, founder and for many years head of Pan American airways; Mr. Henry Woodbridge of the True Temper Corp., among others. We have several outstanding businessmen sitting on the board of trustees, headed by our chairman, J. Peter Grace. It should be noted that in going to these businessmen, we told them quite frankly what we wanted to do; namely, to help strengthen free trade unions in Latin America.

At this point I would like to submit for the record a list of the American corporations and individual businessmen who have contributed to the AIFLD. This list contains approximately 50 or 60 names and it includes practically every large corporation in America. Can I submit that, Mr. Chairman?

THE CHAIRMAN: Yes; it will be received.

MR. MEANY: The AFL–CIO feels that in our democratic society the voluntary organizations have a great role to play in influencing and molding the foreign relations of our country. This is our responsibility as citizens and trade unionists. While we welcome and appreciate the assistance AIFLD has received from our Government through the AID in order to carry out our programs, we would also like to point out that contributions in excess of $2,-300,000 have been made to our work in Latin America from the AFL–CIO, and the corporations I have listed, submitted. In addition, the AFL–CIO and U.S. private investors have themselves committed $31 million for low-cost worker housing sponsored by AIFLD.

Now, let me get to the actual work of the AIFLD which falls into two categories. One is workers' education. The second is social projects whose objectives is to improve workers' standards of living under the Alliance for Progress.

Let me first go into the educational phases of the institute. Small groups of trade unionists from Latin American countries, carefully selected by unions in these countries and covering every country in Latin America except Cuba, Haiti, and Paraguay, are brought to the United States for an 8- to 12-week intensive training course. Our high level course in the United States is designed to train trade union teachers and technicians who can take their skills back to their respective countries to train unionists. As a result, thousands of workers have benefited from this training.

A typical advanced course begins with U.S. university professors teaching modern adult education—the psychology of training adults, how to use visual aids, classroom techniques, and so forth. I would like to say at this point, Mr. Chairman, that quite a number of major universities are represented in our program as instructors in some form or other.

The students then move into specialized subjects such as the history of the labor movement, collective bargaining, labor legislation and social security. Just about every subject of basic interest to a modern, dynamic labor movement is covered. The students also travel around the United States to get a look at our free economy at work, to learn how American workers live, and to understand better how our trade unions operate. The wages and expenses of these students are paid for by the AIFLD here in the United States. . . .

Now, on the social projects, keep this in mind, this social projects department came into being when this country decided they were going to help Latin America through the Alliance for Progress, and we said to President Kennedy, "If you give all this money to the established institutions in these countries you will not change the situation." We said we think that we can help in channeling this money into projects that are beneficial for workers.

Now, you take a housing project, Senator, you have all sorts of people. It takes 10 months or 11 months or sometimes 12 months, to finish a feasibility study for a housing project. All of these technical people, architects, land experts, water experts, experts in design and maintenance and so on and so forth, these people are sent down there, and they are paid by the U.S. Government, through contract with AIFLD.

This is where this money goes. This is money that the Alliance for Progress has to spend for these purposes. We actually, in effect, introduced to the Alliance for Progress the labor people who have these projects.

Now, we certainly agree or at least we find agreement in AID that all of this money used for the Alliance for Progress should not go to governments, that it should go to the private institutions, and to say that we spent it as we pleased is complete nonsense. Everyone of these people is subject to Government checks. Their salaries and their expenses are all audited by government, and they are not all labor people, Mr. Chairman. These are technicians, these are architects, land experts, water experts, tax experts, experts in the field of housing.

Now, in the educational side of this program, I could be wrong in the figures, but my judgment is that this is a tripartite proposition, as far as the money that the AFL–CIO puts in, that private business puts in, and to which the Federal Government makes a contribution. I would say that goes three ways.

Now, in addition to that we have this impacts project program which we have put about a half a million dollars in, and this is something I would judge to be along the lines of the Peace Corps. In other words, you go right into communities, you help them help themselves. We buy machines with which you can very economically make cement blocks. So we believe these machines and these people with very little quantities of cement and the materials that are available help them help themselves.

In Honduras we built low cost houses, I think we built about a hundred houses, costing $500,000 for the banana workers, but it represents the first possession these people ever had in their lives in the way of housing.

So this project, this impact project program, this is entirely AFL–CIO money or it was at the start. Now I understand that the ambassadors in the different countries are forwarded some money by the State Department for the same type of project.

But the Social Projects Department money is used to pay these technicians whose job it is to channel this money to the various projects. We act as the inbetween agency that lets the State Department know here is a union that wants to build a housing project for its members, here they are and we tell them who they are. From that point of this feasibility study goes into everything and it is just the same as if we were not in the picture because if the U.S. Government wants to send this money down there and help these people and decided to go into the housing field they would have to make this sort of feasibility study.

What happens when the housing is built? We finance it out of trade union funds, we hold the mortgage. . . .

SENATOR CASE: What kind of instruction is given to these people and how independent is it?

MR. MEANY: Regarding that I can take a lot of time. Let me say the first instruction they get is something to acquaint them with the U.S. economy as to how our economy works. We teach communications, and the learning process—this is the advanced teacher course at Front Royal—labor educational programs in the participating countries; theory and practice automation in developed and developing nations; inflation and unemployment in Latin America; the teacher's role and class participation; population growth and education; communism and economic development; international labor movement; totalitarianism, democracy, and the role of the free trade unions; methods and techniques in adult education; planning conferences and meetings; evaluation of educational programs; planning conferences and workshop; educational workshop; union structure and finances in the union structures; and civil rights and equality of opportunity in Washington.

Then in addition to that we take these people around, let them see something of the country on their way back and forth so they can see what America looks like, and surely there is nothing subversive in our courses.

SENATOR CASE: I don't think anybody, even our Chairman, has suggested you were subversive. It is just a question as to whether it was Government-controlled or a fairly—

MR. MEANY: The Government agencies know what we are doing. I would not say that they lay out the program. I really could not tell you but they do not disapprove of it I am sure.

Now, here we have got the Georgetown University class which is now in session, which will graduate in October. This is the higher educational group. This is a group of people who had a college background or equivalent in Latin America, and we felt that we could make these people what we in this country call labor economists. These are the 9-month courses. This is apart from this other series. Industrial relations, economics, statistics, collective bargaining, history and problems of the Latin American labor movement, and all of the research and technical services that we supply to our unions are made available so that they can, when they go back to their own country, serve their unions in that same capacity.

SENATOR CASE: The question really is not so much the objective of it, because I am sure we all share this objective of trying to increase democratic activities in all of these countries where we are operating. Rather, it is whether it is an effective way to do it, and whether your organization and its affiliated institutions are made less effective because you are Government-supported. That is the real question.

MR. MEANY: Could I, Senator, without reading the names, just read the different universities that supply the teachers for this course I just mentioned? Louisiana State, University of Wisconsin, Ohio State, Tulane, Howard, Loyola, Houston, Columbia, Syracuse, Duke, Vanderbilt, University of Barcelona, Catholic University, Georgetown University. This is where these people come from.

So surely I do not think we are trying to make revolutionaries out of these people but you can never tell what happens to them after they leave. . . .

SENATOR CHURCH: . . . When it is known in Latin America that your activities are financed to this degree by the Government, don't you think that this tends to impair the influence that you might otherwise have if you were financing it entirely on your own?

MR. MEANY: No; I don't think so. I think the people of Latin America know there is an Alliance for Progress. I think they know that the U.S. Government is committed to help down there.

SENATOR CHURCH: I am not talking about the social projects. I am talking about the educational work you do in the development of a labor movement.

MR. MEANY: Well, Senator, let me say that when we went to the business people, this was the unanimous decision of our executive council, to bring business in, we did not need business in here. The amount of money that business puts in we could very well put in ourselves; it is not beyond our resources to put this money in. But we felt that the businessmen should have the same interests in Latin America as we have, that they should want to see safe, sound, free societies there, especially if they were businesses that had some business to do in Latin America.

So there is no secret in this, that we have Government money and Government assistance in this field. In fact, the amount of Government assistance we get in the educational field, we could get along without that too, we could carry that, too. We felt it was a proper partnership of labor, business, and Government in this country and, of course, we were criticized by the Communists, but we cannot worry about our image with the Communist unions because whether we use Government help or not they would criticize us for something else, so we are not concerned with that. But we have no problem with the Latin American unions, none at all. . . .

We think the development of free trade unions in itself acts as a guarantee that there will be a free society, because if there isn't a free society there can't be any free trade unions, and we feel that all of these things are in the interests of our country, and we come to this conclusion, Senator, because of our experience over the past.

I think the Communists realize the importance of trade unions. I never heard of the Communists trying to get control of the great business institutions; they don't bother with the business institutions, but they do spend great efforts to get control of worker organizations. They did in Italy in 1948, tried desperately to get control of the worker organizations in Italy, and they did not succeed because the American trade unions, without any government participation, helped in seeing that that free trade union movement was preserved.

The same thing happened in France when they captured the old French trade union movement. When liberation came, a new group was set up, and the A.F. of L. at that time helped finance that group, and, this was done because of our experience.

Just think of what happened in Czechoslovakia 22 years ago. The Communists didn't have control of any of the great industries of Czechoslovakia, they didn't have any control of the great banking institutions of Czechoslovakia, they didn't have any control of any votes of any substance in the Czech Parliament, but they managed to achieve control of the trade union movement. They didn't turn the members into Communists. They didn't become Communists. They are not Communists today.

SENATOR MCGEE: You mean the trade union movement in Czechoslovakia?

MR. MEANY: Czechoslovakia. But the Communists took control of this organization in 1947, and they tied up the city of Prague. There wasn't a loaf of bread baked, there wasn't a quart of milk delivered, there wasn't a telephone in operation, there wasn't a radio in operation, there wasn't a wheel turned. It was a dead city, and then they went to Edward Benes and those in charge of the Government and they said, "We have proved that we have the people of this country with us. We have tied up this city."

And let me tell you what happened. Within 7 days after they got a compromise out of Benes and got one Cabinet post, Minister of Internal Security, within 7 days the Czech people lost their freedom.

They didn't bother with the banks. But the banks went down the drain with the business institutions. They had done this because they had secured control of the means of production by controlling the trade union movement, and they proved that they had control by shutting down the city of Prague. And within 7 days they had control, and the Czech people lost their freedom and they haven't got their freedom back.

And let me tell you, I knew some of the Czech trade unionists back in those days. I was active in those days, and let me say to you they were just as devoted to freedom and just as patriotic as were the citizens of any country on earth but still they lost their freedom because the Communists got control of the workers' trade union movement, and this is what we want to prevent.

We feel that we have a selfish interest in this. We want to maintain a free society here in the United States, and we have every good reason to have a stake in a free society because under a free society we have managed through a free trade union movement to bring to workers the highest standard of living that prevails in the entire world right here in the United States.

So we have a stake in this.

There are people in Government who believe that the development of free trade unions in other parts of the world is in the interests of the United States of America, and that is why, that is how we are into this particular thing. We don't get any members in Latin America. We spend our money in Latin America. We spend the money of American trade unions in Latin America. We spend over 20 percent of our national income of the AFL–CIO, we spend it outside the country, spend it in Asia, in Africa.

I didn't testify on it but we have a going program in Africa where we have a different situation, where we are not really at the stage where we can say we can develop a viable trade union movement. We are devoting most of our money there to vocational training, to train the workers who never had any training. They were just the source of common labor under colonial rule. Now in these countries we are developing some skills.

We have a tailoring institute project that we started in Nairobi about 8 or 9 years ago that we financed without any Government assistance whatsoever, and now we have an industry employing many workers in that city making dresses and things like that.

We have a motor drivers and mechanics school in Nigeria. We have got all sorts of activities going on there which have nothing to do with AID or the AIFLD.

So the whole basic idea is that we believe that development of free trade unions is in the interest of the whole future security of the United States of America.

I say to you it is very interesting, very interesting that we were able to get the large corporations of America, and they are large:

Rockefeller Brothers Fund, International T. & T., United Corp., David Rockefeller personally, Kennecott Copper Co., Standard Oil, Koppers, Gillette, Shell Petroleum, Crown Zellerbach, Anaconda, Sterling Drug; even the Readers Digest made a contribution; [laughter] Monsanto Chemical, Merck Co., Pfizer Co., Otis Elevator, all these great corporations some of whom have no relation with unions in the United States, but they agreed with us that it was in the interests of the United States of America to see free trade unions developed in Latin America and they put their money in. . . .

THE CHAIRMAN: Well, Mr. Meany, the hour is getting late. There are a few articles raising some of the questions upon which the questions that I have given you have been based. I want to put them in the record but I would like to read part of them to you and have you comment on them. Here is a recent one from a local newspaper, the Washington Post of April 21, 1969. It is by Mr. William Greider. Since headlines can often be misleading, as you know, I won't read the headline. The article says: "Blessed with new subsidies from the Government's foreign aid program, the AFL–CIO is putting extra muscle into its worldwide operations to create counterrevolutionary labor movements in underdeveloped countries."

That is the first paragraph. It is a rather long article.

MR. MEANY: That is the Commie line; that is what the Communists say about us every day.

THE CHAIRMAN: It is.

MR. MEANY: Oh, yes.

THE CHAIRMAN: Well, are you suggesting that either the Washington Post or Mr. William Greider are Communists?

MR. MEANY: No. No; I am just suggesting that they are parading the Commie line.

THE CHAIRMAN: Well, if not Communists you say that they approve of Communists.

MR. MEANY: What is that?

THE CHAIRMAN: If they are not Communists then are you suggesting that they approve of communism?

MR. MEANY: No, I do not. I am just suggesting that they are following the Communist line. The Communist line is that we interfere the minute we go outside of our own country.

Of course, the best financed labor movements in the world are those that are financed by Moscow. The Italian CGIL and the French CGT, they are financed directly by Moscow; they have no worry. They don't even collect dues from their members.

THE CHAIRMAN: Well, Mr. Meany, I have never considered that what Moscow does should be a model for what we do. This is the very question at issue: if they do it whether or not it is a justification for us to do it.

MR. MEANY: I didn't say it should be a model.*1

Meany's well-organized conception of the close partnership of labor, business and government in the achievement of key foreign policy goals was not new for labor or to the Cold War. In 1898 Samual Gompers had taken a strong stand in favor of war with Spain to free Cuba, on much the same ground, i.e., that unfree labor in a Spanish colony harmed the cause of free labor and free institutions everywhere. Gompers' thought, again like Meany's, was that while far from perfect, American-style capitalism and its expansion was the best security for American laboring classes. Meany himself noted that close involvement with Latin America began in 1916, during World War I when American supremacy in the hemisphere seemed threatened by external force, Germany, and internal subversion, the Mexican Revolution.

Equally interesting was Robert McNamara's conception of the responsibilities the Department of Defense had, or should have, for waging "peacefare" around the world. These went far beyond traditional military responsibilities, even during the unorthodox Cold War. Yet, in a speech delivered in Montreal, McNamara called them, "The Essence of Security":

*1 U.S. Senate, Committee on Foreign Relations, *Hearings: American Institute for Free Labor Development*, 91st Cong., 1st Sess. (Washington, 1969), pp. 1, 5–7, 48–49, 50, 54–55, 68–71.

There is among us an almost ineradicable tendency to think of our security problem as being exclusively a military problem, and to think of the military problem as being exclusively a weapons or manpower problem. The truth is that contemporary man still conceives of war and peace in much the same stereotyped terms that his ancestors did. The fact that these ancestors, both recent and remote, were conspicuously unsuccessful at avoiding war and enlarging peace doesn't seem to reduce our capacity for clichés. We still tend to conceive of national security almost solely as a state of armed readiness, a vast, awesome arsenal of weaponry. We still tend to assume that it is primarily this purely military ingredient that creates security. We are haunted by this concept of military hardware. . . .

Roughly one hundred countries today are caught up in the difficult transition from traditional to modern societies. There is no uniform rate of progress among them, and they range from primitive societies, fractured by tribalism held feebly together by the slenderest of political sinews, to relatively sophisticated countries well on the road to agricultural sufficiency and industrial competence. This sweeping surge of development, particularly across the southern half of the globe, has no parallel in history. It has turned traditionally listless areas of the world into seething caldrons of change. On the whole it has not been a very peaceful process.

In the eight years through late 1966 alone there were no less than 164 internationally significant outbreaks of violence, each of them specifically designed as a serious challenge to the authority or the very existence of the government in question. Eighty-two different governments were directly involved, and what is striking is that only 15 of these 164 significant resorts to violence were military conflicts between two states, and not a single one of the 164 conflicts was a formally declared war. Indeed, there has not been a formal declaration of war anywhere in the world since World War II.

The planet is becoming a more dangerous place to live on not merely because of a potential nuclear holocaust but also because of the large number of *de facto* conflicts and because the trend of such conflicts is growing rather than diminishing. At the beginning of 1958 there were 23 prolonged insurgencies going on around the world. As of February, 1966, there were 40. Further, the total number of outbreaks of violence has increased each year: in 1958 there were 34; in 1965 there were 58. . . .

[McNamara then traced out the relationship between economic conditions and violence, and the gap between rich nations and poor.]

The conclusion to all of this is inescapable. Given the certain connection between economic stagnation and the incidence of violence, the years that lie ahead for the nations in the southern half of the globe look ominous. This would be true even if no threat of Communist subversion existed, as it clearly does. Both Moscow and Peking, however harsh their internal differences, regard the modernization process as an ideal environment for the growth of Communism. Their experience with subversive internal war is extensive, and they have developed a considerable array of both doctrine and practical measures in the art of political violence.

It is clearly understood that certain Communist nations are capable of subverting, manipulating, and finally directing for their own ends the wholly legitimate grievances of a developing society. But it would be a gross oversimplification to regard Communism as the central factor in every conflict throughout the underdeveloped world. Of the 149 serious internal insurgencies in those eight years under discussion, Communists were involved in only 58 of them, 38 percent of the total, and this includes seven instances in which a Communist regime was itself the target of the uprising. Whether Communists are involved or not, violence anywhere in a taut world threatens security and stability of nations half a globe away.

But neither conscience nor sanity itself suggests that the United States is, should or could be, the Global Gendarme. Quite the contrary, experience confirms what human nature suggests, that in most instances of internal violence the local people themselves are best able to deal directly with the situation within the framework of their own traditions. The United States has no mandate from on high to police the world and no inclination to do so. There have been classic cases in which our own deliberate nonaction was the wisest action of all. Where our help is not sought, it is seldom prudent to volunteer.

Certainly we have no charter to rescue floundering regimes which have brought violence on themselves by deliberately refusing to meet legitimate expectations of their citizenry. Further, throughout the next decade technology will reduce the requirement for bases and staging rights at particular locations abroad, and the whole pattern of forward deployment will gradually change. Though all these caveats are clear enough, the irreducible fact remains that our security is related directly to the security of the newly developing world, and our role must be precisely this, to help provide security to those developing nations which genuinely need and request our help and which demonstrably are willing and able to help themselves. The rub is that we do not always grasp the meaning of security in this context.

In a modernizing society security means development. Security is not military hardware, though it may include it; security is not military force, though it may involve it; security is not traditional military activity, though it may encompass it. Security is development, and without development there can be no security. A developing nation that does not, in fact, develop simply cannot remain secure for the intractable reason that its own citizenry cannot shed its human nature.

If security implies anything, it implies a minimal measure of order and stability. Without internal development of at least a minimal degree, order and stability are impossible. They are impossible because human nature cannot be frustrated indefinitely. It reacts because it must; that is what we do not always understand and what governments of modernizing nations do not always understand.

But by emphasizing that security arises from development I do not deny that an underdeveloped nation can be subverted from within or be the victim of a combination of the two. This can happen, and to prevent any or all of these conditions a nation does require appropriate military capabilities to deal with the specific problem.

The specific military problem, however, is only a narrow facet of the broader security problem. Military force can help provide law and order, but only to the degree that a basis for law and order already exists in the developing society, a basic willingness on the part of the people to cooperate. Law and order is the shield behind which development, the central fact of security, can be achieved. . . .

What should our help be? Clearly it should help toward development. In the military sphere that involves two broad categories of assistance. We must help the developing nation with such training and equipment as are necessary to maintain the protective shield behind which development can go forward. The dimensions of that shield must vary from country to country. What is essential, though, is that it be a shield and not a capacity for external aggression.

The second and perhaps less understood category of military assistance in a modernizing nation is training in civic action, another one of those semantic puzzles. Too few Americans and too few officials in developing nations really comprehend what military civic action means. Essentially, it means using indigenous military forces for non-traditional military projects, projects that are useful to the local population in fields such as education, public works, health, sanitation and agriculture—indeed, anything connected with economic or social progress.[*1]

Even as Secretary McNamara delivered this speech, his efforts to broaden the Defense Department's research capabilities to include the social and behavorial sciences had come under sharp criticism both inside and outside the walls of the Pentagon. Dr. John S. Foster, Director of Defense Research and Engineering, defended the expenditures for studies done for the Pentagon in the social science area by explaining that "We see the responsibility and challenge to match our enormous technical and military capabilities with comparable economic, social, and political insight." To that end, the Defense Department planned to spend $50.6 million in 1969 for projects ranging from studies of witchcraft among Asian natives to the behavior of Latin American college students. Senator Fulbright was skeptical:

[*1] Robert S. McNamara, *The Essence of Security, Reflections in Office* (New York: Harper & Row, 1968), pp. 142, 144–145, 147–151.

I think we had better study the university students in this country before we go to Latin America.

Why don't you have one on Columbia University to find out what motivates those students? Maybe you have one.

DR. FOSTER: No, sir. We haven't one, but you can imagine we are quite concerned.

THE CHAIRMAN: You think you might do one?

DR. FOSTER: No, sir.*1

This exchange was only a prelude to the testimony of Admiral Hyman Rickover, the developer of techniques which paved the way to the nuclear submarine. McNamara's speech had left open key issues: on the one hand, he disavowed any future role for the United States as global gendarme, yet he also seemed to be suggesting that in the future the United States would have to be involved not only in traditional counter-subversive measures, even when Communists were *not* involved, but also in efforts to use the military in foreign countries to promote development. Rickover saw this ambiguity, and reviewed the checkered history of Defense Department ventures into "peacefare" since World War II:

It all began with the Rand Corp. which was set up by the Air Force shortly after World War II. Since that time the "think tanks," so-called, have proliferated. Currently, the Department of Defense contracts out research to 16 of them. . . .

There is now virtually no subject that the DOD might not wish to "research" on its own, and virtually no one to gainsay its right to do so. To use an analogy with nuclear science and technology: As you know, one has to get a "critical mass" before a nuclear bomb "takes off." What has happened to the DOD, I think, is that it has attained that "critical mass" and "taken off."

*1 U.S. Senate Committee on Foreign Relations, Hearings: Defense Department Sponsored Foreign Affairs Research, 90th Cong., 2d Sess. (Washington, 1968), p. 33.

It may be difficult to regain control of the DOD. Yet, if its empire building is not restrained, it may become the most powerful branch of the National Government. This certainly was not intended by the Founding Fathers; nor, I feel sure, is it the will of the American people.

The DOD has been able to involve itself in research having only the remotest relevance to the problems encountered by the armed services—matters at no previous time, nor anywhere else in the world, deemed to lie within the province of the defense function—just because it has the money; it has more money than any other public agency. It gets more money because the word "defense" has in itself an element of urgency. Whatever is asked in its name somehow acquires the connotation of a life and death matter for the Nation. . . .

Already the State Department is, to all intents and purposes, but a junior partner. In its own area of responsibility—foreign affairs—it receives but a tenth as much for research as the DOD. From the testimony given at your last hearing, it is evident that the DOD considers itself—together with the State Department—the chief adviser to the President on policies concerning the use of our military resources. Although Congress alone has the constitutional authority to declare war, other branches of the Government may confront it with situations that make war inevitable. This could lose us the protection against war which Jefferson deemed one of the best features of the Constitution. In a letter to Madison from Paris (September 6, 1789), where he was our envoy at the time the Constitution was being drafted, Jefferson wrote jubilantly that we have "given in example one effectual check to the dog of war by transferring the power of letting him loose from the executive to the legislative body, from those who are to spend to those who are to pay."

. . . President Eisenhower in his last speech in office warned of the military-industrial complex; others have warned of the industrial-political complex; but potentially the most dangerous is the close inner circle composed of researchers within the Department of Defense and those working for the Department of Defense under contract. . . .

Now, take Project Themis: According to the Department of

Defense the social sciences are not yet fully developed. It expects that it will take a number of decades before they will be adequately developed; that more social scientists must be trained. Now, it seems to be the most farfetched reasoning to conclude that it is the Department of Defense that must help develop these sciences and train these scientists. The result of a project like Themis is that there will be university professors who get additional money besides their university salaries—money given to them by the Department of Defense. These professors will be "contractors" of the Department of Defense and therefore to some extent beholden to the military. This strikes me as most undesirable. . . .

I think the Camelot affair is most instructive as to what we ought not to do. It angered the Chileans and did us no good in the rest of Latin America. You will remember that it was to be a study, in the words of the Chief of Army Research and Development, "that would use the systems analysis approach to studying internal war," that is, "the internal cultural, economic, and political conditions that generate conflict between national groups."

The project was "sold," as it were, to Chilean scientists and university people by a Chilean-born professor of anthropology at the University of Pittsburgh. He was later accused of having submitted copies of the project in which all references to the Army were carefully made illegible. He was severely castigated for having violated his moral and professional obligation to inform his Chilean colleagues that the study was financed by the armed forces of a foreign power, and was to be utilized in formulating foreign policy of that foreign power. Ultimately, he was declared persona non grata and banned from returning to Chile: the project had been declared "a grave threat to our sovereignty" by the Secretary-general of the University of Chile. . . . The whole affair seems incredibly gauche and amateurish and raises the gravest misgiving of any DOD research in foreign countries. This had really better be left to other departments if the Government is to be involved at all. . . .

SENATOR MUNDT: I was wondering, Admiral, if you are by any chance familiar with the research project which was one time called Pax Americana?

ADMIRAL RICKOVER: I am generally familiar with it, yes, sir.

SENATOR MUNDT: It was done I believe by the Douglas Aircraft Corp.

ADMIRAL RICKOVER: Yes, sir.

SENATOR MUNDT: At a cost to the taxpayers of $84,000. What interests me is that it was a report classified secret. Efforts by our Committee to have a look at it and study it, and to have the study declassified, were rejected by the Department of Defense. The staff tells me that quite by accident they discovered that the Pax Americana study has been declassified at the request of Douglas Aircraft. Indeed, I note that the unclassified version is dated January 1966, prior to the date of February 28, 1966 on the classified version. Since both documents are substantially the same, this raises some interesting questions. In any event, a number of the declassified copies were circulated among political and social scientists. In other words, while this Committee, citing the Moss Act, was unable to have the studies declassified, the Defense Department had declassified it for the purpose of Douglas.

I have two of the volumes before me of the unclassified version. The title of the study was changed to "Projected World Patterns, 1985" which I also have before me.

From this unclassified version, I would like to read to you a paragraph or two and see what you have to say about them, because it is virtually identical with the classified study which I also have before me.

From the unclassified version let me read a couple of their conclusions to see whether you think this is a wise use of the taxpayers' money. It is under the heading of "General Conclusions."

While the United States is not an imperialistic nation she exhibits many of the characteristics of past imperiums and in fact has acquired imperial responsibilities.

First, I would like to know this—you are an expert at this business of research—what would Douglas Aircraft Corp. know about diplomatic imperialistic policies? Do they have specialists in this area?

ADMIRAL RICKOVER: If my memory is correct, wasn't it the Douglas Aircraft Corporation that was responsible for starting the Rand Corporation for the Air Force? I believe there is a connection there.

SENATOR MUNDT: ... I can't for the life of me see how an aircraft company is going to have a specialist in diplomacy and foreign relations and crystall ball gazing so they could project what our diplomatic posture is going to be in 1985.

ADMIRAL RICKOVER: Senator, I think their competence in these areas is about as great as that of any of the think factories; I wouldn't run them down for that reason.

SENATOR AIKEN: I think Pan Am is as effective in many fields as the State Department.

SENATOR MUNDT: I think I would rather take a chance on Jean Dixon.

ADMIRAL RICKOVER: I think it is simply the fact that the money is available. I simply can't imagine why such a study was DOD-sponsored.

SENATOR MUNDT: Now, the second conclusion is:

> Probabilities are relatively high that the world situation in 10 or 20 years in the future will be as good from the American point of view as in 1965 and very possibly would be moving toward a genuine Pax Americana. This world configuration might take either a U.S. imperial form or a U.N. international posture.

I wondered whether they classified this just to keep the taxpayer from knowing how they were wasting the money. I can't see where they would qualify in wisdom or prophetic advice.

ADMIRAL RICKOVER: I think you could get as profound and meaningful a statement from an average high school graduating class.

SENATOR MUNDT: Yes; I just got through visiting with the salutatarian and valedictorian at a high school commencement who had comments just as good as these.

Third, "the Army will be the major military instrument in the continuation of U.S. leadership." I thought you people in the Navy would like to know about that. I will reread it.

"The Army will be the major military instrument in the continuation of U.S. leadership whether at home or abroad."

ADMIRAL RICKOVER: It may be that the Army sponsored the study. Of course, if you conduct a study for the Army, this is a very fine thing to say—to prove that the Army is our major military instrument. If the Senate had a study conducted which said, "We believe that the Senate is going to be the leading force in the world from now on," I am sure you probably would give them another research contract. . . . The conclusions you have read so far are plain nonsense. The words sound good but they have no meaning.

SENATOR MUNDT: They have a whole series of them, I am on the 37th conclusion now. The 37th conclusion reads:

> Probably the most important future role of the Army will be the role of nation-building and keeping secure the frontiers of the U.S. imperium. Relevant here is the Army's past and present role in the Philippines, Taiwan, Europe, South Korea, Thailand and now South Vietnam.

ADMIRAL RICKOVER: Well, maybe that is the reason why the Army did not want these conclusions published. It might create a bad "image" of the Army because this description limited its nation-building activities to but a single part of the world instead of the entire world. Maybe that is why they wouldn't let it be shown to Congress.

As to refusing a request of Congress to see these studies, it seems to me that wherever Government money is spent Congress has a right to find out how that money is spent. If you can't do that, where then is your responsibility?*[1]

Congress, especially the Senate Foreign Relations Committee, had been trying to rediscover and reassert its responsibility in

---

*[1] U.S. Senate, Foreign Relations Committee, *Hearings: Defense Sponsored Foreign Affairs Research*, Part II, 90th Cong., 2d Sess. (Washington, 1968), pp. 12–13, 15, 17, 28, 32–35.

the foreign affairs area for some time. Two decades had gone by since the last serious debate on foreign policy. Since then the advocates of bipartisan support for the Executive had prevailed, although there were a few exceptions, most notably the Republican dissent from the Truman Administration's Far Eastern policy. Many legislators, moreover, conceded the point that in the nuclear era Congress was simply incapable of making the necessary split-second decisions on war and peace which had been possible in a less dangerous time. Finally, throughout much of the Cold War, the men who made policy in both the executive and legislative branches of government were influenced by a "Pearl Harbor" psychology, the fear of sudden attack without warning. Together, these components formed a powerful bond which fastened the Cold War view on liberals and conservatives alike.

But when it began to dissolve, liberals and conservatives both found it easy to take out their frustrations on the Department of Defense. A "hawk" on Vietnam, Senator Karl Mundt raised all the crucial questions about the Pax Americana project; a "dove," Senator Albert Gore, took on the Defense Department's military aid program. Gore and others charged that American weapons were being used for purposes directly at odds with foreign policy goals. In the case of the India-Pakistan clash, both sides were armed with U.S. equipment. Even worse, jet aircraft supplied to Iran were acquired by the Pakistanis in a roundabout fashion, making a mockery of the claim that these planes were essential to prevent Russian aggression. "This is a pattern that is occurring about the world," declared Gore. "The United States seems to be arming one little country after another, one against the other." Assistant Secretary of Defense Paul Warnke tried to explain the rationale for aid to "forward-defense countries" such as Iran, Turkey, and South Korea. The last-named was a classic example, said Warnke. American aid had enabled South Korea to develop a considerable military capacity. Without it, the American people would have been faced "with the prospect of putting more American troops into South Korea to hold back the aggressive intentions of the North Koreans." Iran, too, was more stable because of the military aid it had received from the United States, he said.

Senator John Sparkman was troubled about this: Why was

it considered necessary to send the Shah sophisticated American weapons when Iran was also buying military equipment from the Soviet Union? He also noted that the Russians were building a $280 million steel plant for the Iranians, and participating in the construction of a $40 million natural gas pipeline.

Warnke replied that once the Soviet Union had been a real threat to Iran; therefore, the fact that Moscow was making such friendly overtures to Teheran proved American military aid had had a stabilizing influence. The aid it got from Russia was not of the same order as that coming from the United States. "Now, Iran has continued to purchase from us its major items, the items which require technicians and which give us a continuing degree of influence in the Iranian military establishment."

When Senator Gore pressed Warnke on this point, the Assistant Secretary was much less inclined to affirm that the major reason for the arms sales was to perpetuate American influence. Gore began by asking, "Mr. Secretary, who threatens Iran?"

MR. WARNKE: . . . I would say that the Soviet Union in the past has been a potential aggressor against Iran. I would say that it is not an immediate threat to Iran's independence, because of the fact that Iran is militarily strong. I would say if Iran did not remain militarily strong the Soviet Union again would be an immediate threat to Iran's independence. As a consequence, I think it is important that we keep Iran militarily strong.

SENATOR GORE: The Soviet Union must think that is important too, because they are supplying them with a great deal of equipment.

MR. WARNKE: They are supplying them, Senator, I believe, with something like $150 million worth of equipment.

SENATOR GORE: Isn't that a great deal?

MR. WARNKE: It is less in scale and in degree and also it is different in kind from the equipment that the Iranians buy from the United States. It is for the most part——

SENATOR GORE: It is complementary to what they buy from the United States?

MR. WARNKE: It certainly is complementary in the sense that it fills up their overall stock of military equipment; that is correct.

SENATOR GORE: If we supply the guns and the Soviets supply the ammunition, it would be rather strained logic to conclude that the Soviets were supplying the ammunition to a potential victim of their aggression. I don't know why you are selling all this to Iran. You have identified the Soviet Union as a potential aggressor against Iran if Iran were weak, which the Soviet Union is trying to correct and see that they don't remain weak or become weak. Let's look again.

MR. WARNKE: Senator, if I could respond to that, the military equipment provided by the Soviet Union does not make the difference between Iran being weak and Iran being strong, militarily. The equipment that Iran purchases from us is sufficient to keep her strong militarily. The Soviet Union knows that. As a result they recognize that they aren't increasing Iran's ability to preserve its independence by supplying these relatively minor items of military equipment. And as I have said earlier, I think that the only reason that the Soviet Union is willing to enter into this kind of a transaction is because they recognize that Iran is strong and Iran is not a country that they could readily take over. So that it doesn't alter that situation for them to provide this $150 million worth of vehicles and items of that sort.

SENATOR GORE: I don't happen to believe that you are supplying, and you don't convince me that you are supplying, military equipment to Iran because of a threat, real or potential, from the Soviet Union. I think it is some other cause. Will you identify some other cause if you can?

MR. WARNKE: Well, respectfully, Senator, I would have to say we do have a difference of opinion with respect to the situation *vis à vis* the Soviet Union.

SENATOR GORE: I understand.

MR. WARNKE: In addition to that, as I have explained earlier, I believe that Iran's military strength prevents any aggressive designs by the radical Arab States against Iran.

SENATOR GORE: Who would that be?

MR. WARNKE: That would be the countries that are the recipients of aid from the Soviet Union.

SENATOR GORE: Which countries?

MR. WARNKE: Primarily they would include the United Arab Republic, Syria, and Iraq.

SENATOR GORE: You think there is a threat that Egypt might invade Iran? They seem to have had their hands full with Israel.

MR. WARNKE: I certainly agree that they have had their hands full. I think they do, however, present a possible threat to Iran and that if Iran were weak, this would encourage aggressiveness on the part of those radical Arab States.

SENATOR GORE: Is that the real reason you are supplying such vast amounts of arms?

MR. WARNKE: That is one of the real reasons; yes, Senator.

SENATOR GORE: What is another real reason?

MR. WARNKE: I gave the other real reason earlier, which is, I think, that Iran's military strength prevents the Soviet Union from constituting an immediate threat to Iran.

SENATOR GORE: The number of nations on the globe has increased in a few years from 50 to some 120-odd, now. All of them seem to want more and more military equipment. Their reasons run from a desire to defend their independence to a desire to preserve internal order, and then the next step seems to be, as the basis of a request, a defense against aggression, potential aggression, by a neighbor.

I was in Latin America in January and found politicians, particularly the military leaders, in Peru wanting jet fighter planes because of an imagined potential threat from Chile. It seemed to me fantastic. This is a pattern that is occurring all about the world. The United States seems to be arming one little country after another, one against the other. You have just cited an instance, Iran against Egypt. I think it is a fantasy in many instances.

MR. WARNKE: Senator, I find a distinct difference between the situation between Peru and Chile and the situation that exists in the Middle East. Just a year ago we found that the war could break out very rapidly in the Middle East. I don't think, and I certainly agree with you in this respect, that Peru should apprehend any attack on the part of Chile. And certainly we make every effort that we can to avoid arming small nations so that they can attack one another. I don't think we have done it and I don't think we are about to do it.

SENATOR GORE: It is interesting that you say you don't think we have done it. I seem to recall that every coup in Latin America by a military dictator has been accomplished with weapons supplied by the United States.

MR. WARNKE: Senator, I would disagree that these coups were in any respect stimulated by our military assistance or sales programs.

SENATOR GORE: I didn't say stimulated; I said accomplished by.

MR. WARNKE: I am sure, Senator, they used whatever arms were available. I think for the most part these coups have been bloodless and what they have reflected is the fact that there are unstable societies which can be taken over by military groups. I think it is the instability that should concern us.

SENATOR GORE: It would be interesting to examine your use of the word "stimulating." Stimulation usually stems from capacity to accomplish, doesn't it?

MR. WARNKE: I would suppose that that is a partial definition, yes.

SENATOR GORE: What is an additional definition?

MR. WARNKE: Well, you have to have also the motivation and you would also have to have the conditions which would make that kind of attack possible, which gets us back to the question of insecurity.

SENATOR GORE: All right.

I seem to detect in humanity rather widespread motivation for power. This is particularly acute in military leaders in Latin America. So given the motivation and given in hand the military equipment with which to accomplish the coup, it seems to me you have the stimulation.

MR. WARNKE: Senator, I would say that where the formula in my opinion, very respectfully, breaks down is that this would assume that if we were not furnishing military equipment to these countries that these coups could not take place because the military capability would not be there. It doesn't take much in the way of military equipment to support a coup. It doesn't take the kind of sophisticated weapons system about which we have been talking. It takes relatively unsophisticated military equipment which is readily available from a number of sources other than the sources to which Senator Symington referred as being the only sources of sophisticated military weapons. So that really in these instances the question is should we remove or should we eliminate any attempt on our part to continue to exercise influence? Should we allow other foreign countries to become the sole suppliers to these Latin American republics, so that they are the influential factor rather than the United States of America? I think it is certainly desirable, if not essential, that we retain these degrees of influence.

SENATOR GORE: Now this may be, and this comes to the bare bones of the policy. You just stated it. It is a policy to acquire, to hold, influence, which is the principal motivation of our arms sales and our military assistance program. You have just stated it. Thank you, sir.

MR. WARNKE: No, I didn't say that, sir. If you take a look at the distribution of our military assistance, it goes for the most part, and in very major share, to the countries that are faced with a threat of Communist aggression.

Now, what I have said is that with respect to Latin America there are instances in which military coups have taken place. These military coups, I submit, would have taken place whoever had supplied military equipment, and that, therefore, our military assistance was not the stimulating factor.

I have also said that I think it is important, and I do think it is important, that the United States try to maintain some influence in these areas.

SENATOR GORE: I think influence is very important. I would hope that we could have more of it. I am not sure that our military sales are very effective in obtaining influence despite being—

MR. WARNKE: I agree with you it is not the major factor.

SENATOR GORE (continuing): Despite being the major supplier of military equipment in the world, we seem to be losing rather than gaining influence. I am not sure that the formula is very successful.

MR. WARNKE: I am not sure I would agree with your conclusion, Senator.

SENATOR GORE: Well, I respectfully make no such requirement.

MR. WARNKE: Thank you, Senator. [Laughter.]*1

More than a year before these hearings, the staff of the Senate Foreign Relations Committee had completed a survey of the entire military aid and sales program. Their findings pointed up yet another aspect of Secretary McNamara's implementation of "cost effectiveness" accounting in the Pentagon, the effort to bolster the American economy by increased arms sales. He had also argued that it would be cheaper for underdeveloped nations to acquire their weapons from the United States. The staff study found a contradiction, however, in Washington's desire to promote economic growth abroad, and its own arms sales program:

Since the Second World War the United States has recognized that it is in the national interest to give military support to friendly countries to enable them to defend themselves against the threat of aggression. The military assistance programs beginning in 1949

*1 U.S. Senate, Foreign Relations Committee, *Hearings: Foreign Military Sales*, 90th Cong., 2d Sess. (Washington, 1968), pp. 10–13, 20–24.

with congressional approval of the Mutual Defense Assistance Act have provided various kinds of military grant aid to countries unable to pay for their own defense needs. Over the years the Congress has paid particularly close attention to the military assistance programs with an eye to withdrawing such aid from countries having sufficient resources to maintain their own forces and preventing U.S. military aid from either being misused or overburdening struggling economies.

In recent years both the President and the Congress have become increasingly aware of another responsibility directly related to the use of military assistance. This is the question of conventional arms control in the developing regions of the world. In his message of last January to the Eighteen Nation Disarmament Conference, President Johnson reminded the delegates:

> As we focus on nuclear arms, let us not forget that resources are being devoted to nonnuclear arms races all around the world. These resources might be better spent on feeding the hungry, healing the sick, and teaching the uneducated. The cost of acquiring and maintaining one squadron of supersonic aircraft diverts resources that would build and maintain a university. We suggest therefore that countries, on a regional basis, explore ways to limit competition among themselves for costly weapons often sought for reasons of illusory prestige.

Despite President Johnson's concern, the pursuit of "illusory prestige" has recently quickened throughout the developing regions of the world. For example, the United States has agreed to sell to Iran a squadron of F-4 Phantoms, its most sophisticated operational supersonic aircraft. Morocco has purchased 12 F-5's, among the United States' most modern fighter-interceptors. The international record of such sales is long: American F-104 interceptors to Jordan, British Hawker Hunter jet fighters to Chile, American A-4B tactical attack aircraft to Argentina, Soviet Mig 21's to Iraq, Czechoslovakian armored cars and bazookas to Cyprus—to cite some recent examples.

What is clearly in process is a competition among the industrial nations to sell arms to the developing nations of the world.

In the Indian subcontinent and the Middle East these sales have contributed to an intense arms race; while in North Africa, sub-Saharan Africa and most of Latin America the situation is still, in Lincoln Bloomfield's words, that of an "arms walk." But the arms pace, even where it still remains a "walk," shows every sign of accelerating unless the major powers take a stronger interest in slowing the pace.

This growing problem of arms competition in the underdeveloped world and the diversion of scarce resources is directly related to a dramatic shift in the composition of U.S. military assistance and sales programs. It seems that at a moment of increasing congressional oversight of the military grant assistance, emphasis has shifted from these programs to a concentration on military sales. In the fiscal years 1952 to 1961 the U.S. military grant aid programs and military sales amounted to a total value of $22 billion—$17 billion in grant aid and $5 billion in sales. According to the Defense Department, the comparative amounts will be radically altered in the 1962-71 period—that is $15 billion in military sales, and $7 billion in grant aid. (In fiscal year 1961, for example, sales were 43.4 percent of grant aid; in fiscal year 1966, sales stood at 235.1 percent of aid.) Since 1962 the Defense Department has already obtained $11.1 billion in foreign military orders and commitments. The average of all military export sales in the 1952-61 period was around $300 million annually. In fiscal year 1961 military export sales rose to $600 million; they were $1.3 billion in fiscal year 1963; $1.26 billion in fiscal year 1964; $1.97 billion in fiscal year 1965; and were around $1.93 billion in fiscal year 1966. That is a total of some $6 to $7 billion in the past 4 years.

Of the $9 billion in orders and commitments the United States received between 1962 and 1965, almost $5 billion has been received in cash receipts, an amount offsetting almost 40 percent of the dollar costs of maintaining U.S. forces abroad during that period. Furthermore, these sales offsets have risen from 10 percent of overseas expenditures in 1961 to 44 percent in 1965.

Secretary of Defense McNamara made it very clear in 1965 that he considered military grants and the increasing military sales as an important instrument of American foreign policy:

I think it is extremely important to understand that in our military assistance program and in our military sales program we face two extremes.

In the one case we face nations, our allies, who for a variety of reasons may not have developed their defense program to a level commensurate with their economic strength, their obligations to their own people, and their obligations to the alliance of which we are a part. Nations that fall in that category are the developed countries, the countries which have had a remarkable economic growth, in the last decade or two, economic growth in many cases stimulated by Marshall plan aid.

In these instances it is very much in our interest to work with those nations to expand their defense program, to increase their military personnel strength, to add to their equipment, and where it can be done to our mutual advantage to insure that they buy their equipment from U.S. producers. This we do.

The result has been very substantial increases in the defense budgets of many of the Western nations, Australia, the Federal Republic, to name two. This is ultimately in their interest. It is very much in our interest. In no way does it conflict with economic development and economic strength which, I want to emphasize as Secretary of Defense, I consider to be the foundation ultimately of national security. In any case, that is one extreme.

The other extreme is represented by those underdeveloped nations which have not yet met the minimum needs of their people for social and economic progress but who nonetheless are inclined to divert an unreasonable share of their scarce human and material resources to defense.

In those cases our first objective is to use the influence that we gain through the military assistance programs and occasionally through the military export sales programs to work with them to reduce the share of their resources devoted to defense and to increase the portion of their human and material capital that is allocated to economic and social programs.*[1]

*[1] News conference, Sept. 16, 1965.

It is difficult to fault the objectives and the logic of such an approach to the military assistance and sales programs. But the developing nature of the arms competition seems to defy the best intentions of Mr. McNamara's reasonable explanation of how the United States conducts its arms sales. The question that must be addressed is whether the governmental machinery designed for the management of our military sales program is adequate to the task of bringing the U.S. actions in line with Secretary McNamara's intentions.

There is evidence to suggest that it is not.

Since its establishment in October of 1961 a Defense Department office called International Logistic Negotiations (ILN) has been the center of U.S. military sales. In 1964 the Director of ILN, Henry J. Kuss, was promoted to the rank of Deputy Assistant Secretary of Defense as the result of his success in boosting military sales. ILN's sales force of some 21 professional officers is organized into four teams—red, grey, blue, and white—each charged with particular functional and regional responsibilities. The white team, for example, devotes almost its entire efforts to selling military equipment to West Germany in an effort to offset by military sales the approximately $775 million it costs the United States in dollars to keep our troops in the Federal Republic (West Germany has bought some $3 billion worth of military equipment in the last 4 years). The measure of ILN's success is the 600-percent increase in annual military sales over the levels of the 1950's.

The Defense Department's approach to the arms sales field has been dynamic and aggressive. The Department through the Military Export Committee of the Defense Industry Advisory Council has sought the cooperation of industry and the financial community in an effort to further overseas military sales. Defense is also supporting plans to organize symposia throughout the United States aimed at convincing the smaller arms manufacturers, the "non-bigs" as they are called, of the advantages of entering the military export market.

In fostering these commercial ties, the Department of Defense is appreciative of the fact that there are a number of ways by which arms can be sold abroad: private firms selling to a foreign government, private firms selling through an agency of the U.S. Government, and government to government sales. There are other possibilities as well, such as a U.S. manufacturer licensing a foreign firm to produce his products. Because of the variety of ways that arms are sold and distributed it is difficult to know the extent of just how much equipment is being purchased. For example, the F-86's Venezuela recently bought from West Germany were manufactured in Italy under a U.S. licensing arrangement. The F-86's West Germany "sold" to Iran but which mysteriously seem to actually belong to Pakistan (despite U.S. efforts to halt the flow of arms into Pakistan) were manufactured in Canada.

In other words, neither the sales figures given by International Logistics Negotiations—which do not include commercial military sales with the exception of those to West Germany—nor even customs statistics would be able to give the full story of the extent of arms traffic for which the United States is responsible.

The Defense Department's interest in the potential of the export market has prompted a number of appeals to the American armament industry to go "international." In a speech before the American Ordinance Association in October of 1966, Mr. Kuss had this comment about the companies who were reluctant to "go international."

This tendency of American companies to refrain from entering into the international arms market is a serious one and affects our entire international posture in a military, economic, and political way.

From the military point of view we stand to lose all of the major international relationships paid for with grant aid money unless we can establish professional military relationships through the sales media. . . .

From the economic point of view the stability of the dollar in the world market is dependent on our ability to resolve balance of payments problems. Failure to resolve these balance of payments problems creates economic pressures in the international and in the domestic spheres. The solution to balance of payments is principally in more trade. All other solutions merely temporize the problem.

From the political point of view international trade is the "staff of life" of a peaceful world. With it comes understanding; the lack of it eliminates communications and creates misunderstandings.*2

Of particular interest to the Defense Department as a means of furthering its international sales is the eventual creation of a NATO Defense Common Market. Secretary McNamara first proposed the Defense Common Market in May of 1965. Such a common market for defense materials in NATO is also appealing because of the stimulus it would give to the standardization of military weapons and the development of common production facilities. The Department seems most impressed, however, with arms sales potential in such a common market area. Mr. Kuss has said that "the highly competitive approach that has been taken here in the United States, particularly as a result of Secretary McNamara's cost reduction programs, places U.S. industries in fit condition for competition throughout the world." ILN estimates that over the next 10 years U.S. allies "may purchase a minimum of $10 to $15 billion of their requirements from the United States by sheer virtue of the fact that most of these items will be a minimum of 30 percent to 40 percent cheaper and will be highly competitive from a technical point of view. . . ."*3 An important objective of American military export policies is to break down what ILN has termed "protectionist interests in Europe." For as Mr. Kuss has put it:

We must establish by our actions in Government and industry that there is merit in an orientation toward the United States. We must sell the benefits of collaboration in defense matters with competition. We must demonstrate that the free world has more to gain from the U.S. model of defense competition than it has from the temptation to allocate the market and build little, safe, high-cost arrangements across national borders.

As an example of this temptation, Mr. Kuss cites the recommendations of the Plowden report on the British aircraft industry

---

*2 Speech before the American Ordinance Association on Oct. 20, 1966.
*3 Remarks of Henry J. Kuss before the National Security Industrial Association on Oct. 8, 1965.

as "indicative of the frustrations and consequent protectionism that is arising in Europe."[*4]

For all the excitement generated in the American press over arms sales to Latin America and other developing regions of the world, the fact is that only a small percentage of total U.S. arms sales is involved. During the period fiscal years 1962–66, $9.85 billion of $11.1 billion in orders and commitments went to developed countries in Europe and Asia. This is 88 percent of the total, with $8.7 of the $9.85 billion going to Europe alone. (How much of this equipment is eventually transshipped as surplus to the underdeveloped world is another matter.) By way of contrast, during the same period the United States sold some $45 million to Africa and $162.7 million to Latin America (mainly to Argentina, Brazil, and Venezuela). In the Middle East and south Asia the 1962–66 total was some $972 million or 8 percent of the grand total. (Half of this amount went to Iran alone.)

Again, these figures do not include grant aid shipments or sales to which the U.S. Government was not a party.

In the case of Latin America, for example, total sales of U.S. military equipment, including commercial sales, may be 10 or 15 percent higher than the $162 million. The problem of compilation of total sales is complicated, if not made impossible, by the absence of any public or even government sources that give totals of all U.S. military exports to countries or regions.

The fact that sales to underdeveloped countries amount to only 12 percent of the total military sales handled by the Department of Defense is important for a number of reasons. These figures on sales to underdeveloped countries lead to the conclusion that the U.S. motives in arranging such sales simply cannot be rooted in balance of payments considerations. If the United States were to lose its entire arms market to the underdeveloped world the impact on our overall balance-of-payments accounts would be small. Therefore, our justification for such sales must be based on the other considerations, such as influencing the development of the local military elites or helping a country resist the threat of external aggressions. Preventing the influx of military equipment of other nations, a sort of preemptive selling, has also been a strong U.S. motive in the underdeveloped areas of the world.

[*4] Speech before the Los Angeles World Affairs Council on Mar. 24, 1966.

Almost two-thirds of all military sales abroad over the past few years have been for cash. The largest such customer is West Germany, although other industrial nations such as Australia, Canada, and United Kingdom (with the major exception of the billion dollar F-111 deal) have also normally paid cash. Conversely, sales to the underdeveloped regions of the world have been mainly credit financed. For example, of the roughly $56 million in arms sold to Latin America through the Department of Defense in fiscal year 1966 only $8 million was for cash. This 7-to-1 ratio of credit to cash probably is common throughout the underdeveloped world.

The International Logistics Negotiations Office, not AID or the Export-Import Bank, has acquired the responsibility of negotiating the terms of the credit extended for military purchases. The sources of this credit are the Eximbank, private banking facilities, and a military assistance account available for the use of the Defense Department under the authority of section 508 of the Foreign Assistance Act.

EXPORT-IMPORT BANK

The Eximbank has taken an active interest in the financing of military export sales only since 1963, when the Defense Department was given authority to insure credits.

The Eximbank role is one of providing a service function for the Department of Defense and bringing to military sales on credit the advantages of the Bank's experience in the international credit field. These loans are usually on a medium-term basis, or 5 to 7 years, at an interest rate that now stands around 5½ percent. Eximbank makes direct loans for military equipment only to industrial nations such as Great Britain, Australia, etc.

In addition, Eximbank makes so-called "country-x loans." Such loans are the result of Eximbank establishing what amounts to an accounts receivable fund for the use of the Department of Defense in arranging loans to underdeveloped countries. The Eximbank does not know or want to know where this money goes. The Department of Defense guarantees these funds through the military assistance account described below. The bank therefore avoids the problem of directly financing military sales to underdeveloped countries.

PRIVATE BANKING FACILITIES

It is not clear how large a role private banking facilities play in the financing of U.S. military exports. According to the Military Export Reporter, a trade journal for U.S. contractors in the arms business, during the period of fiscal years 1962–65 approximately $2 billion, or 40 percent of total arms sales, were financed by private banks or the Export-Import Bank. Since the Eximbank only entered the field in 1963 and carried only a very small amount of direct credit until fiscal year 1966, it can be roughly estimated that private banks extended some 90 percent or $1.8 billion of the funds during that period. But these figures are most tentative. It is safe to say, however, that private banks do not participate in such loans, particularly to underdeveloped countries, without a full guarantee of repayment. In the case of underdeveloped countries, the military assistance credit account serves as the primary source of credit guarantees.

THE MILITARY ASSISTANCE CREDIT ACCOUNT

The military assistance credit account is the most useful instrument at the disposal of the International Logistics Negotiations (ILN) office for use in providing credit for arms sales to areas where commercial and direct Eximport credits are unavailable.

The idea that the Department of Defense should have funds available to arrange credit terms for arms sales was initiated with the Mutual Security Act of 1957, when a fund of $15 million was authorized for this purpose. This account officially became a "revolving account" to finance additional sales when the Foreign Assistance Act of 1961 (sec. 508) authorized that repayments from such sales were to "be available until expended solely for the purpose of furnishing military assistance on cash or credit terms." Consequently, this fund, through yearly appropriations ranging from $21 to $83 million, has grown to over $300 million. An important amendment to the Foreign Assistance Act came in 1964, when the Defense Department asked for, and received from the Congress, the authority to allow the Department of Defense to guarantee 100 percent of the credit extended by U.S. banks for arms sales while only obligating 25 percent of the amount from the military assistance credit account as a reserve to back up the guarantees in the event of a default. In other words, the $300 million in the ever-increasing "revolving account" now allows the Department of Defense to put the full guarantee of the U.S. Government behind over a billion dollars in military credits.

This provision permits ILN to guarantee loans the Export-Import Bank might make available through the "country-x" accounts or to back a loan made by a private bank.

Another option provided for ILN by the Foreign Assistance Act is the use of the military assistance credit account to extend direct credit for foreign purchases. The terms of such credit are at the discretion of the Defense Department and range from commercial rates to as low as a zero interest charge. A low interest charge from the military assistance credit account would normally be used in a package loan, which might include credit funds from a commercial bank and the Export-Import Bank, in order to bring down the overall interest charge to the customer. If the extension of credit were to underdeveloped countries, ILN would probably guarantee the other pieces of the loan package as well. . . .

The burgeoning arms sales program raises a number of major and intertwined policy concerns: First, what is the effect of U.S. current military export policy on our European Alliance relationships; second, what is the effect of these arms exports on the external indebtedness and general financial circumstances of the underdeveloped countries; and third, what are the prospects for arms control in the developing regions of the world given the present pace and pattern of the international traffic in arms?

On the question of the arms sales and U.S. relations with its European allies, the central fact is that while the financial success of the U.S. military sales is beyond dispute, there is ample reason for concern as to the side effects of the vigorous sales campaigns.

American sales efforts have become a source of great irritation in Europe, particularly in West Germany and Great Britain, and may also be a major cause of the increasing interest of Europeans in competing for arms markets in developing regions of the world. . . .

Total U.S. arms sales have now reached something over the $2 billion per year level—not including grant aid. The problem of the disposal of surplus military equipment is certain to grow with this increase in sales. The surplus arms of the industrial nations may provide the ingredients of an arms race in the underdeveloped regions of the world. It should also be noted that some of the arms used by Latin American guerrillas today were exported by the U.S. —for quite different reasons—yesterday.

The question of what effect American arms sales have on the debt servicing difficulties of underdeveloped nations cannot be answered here. According to the Development Assistance Committee (the DAC) of the OECD, external debt of the most underdeveloped nations "has increased at a considerably higher percentage rate than exports of goods and services, gross national product, or savings."

In Latin America, for example, the Inter-American Committee on the Alliance for Progress (CIAP) estimates suggest that two-thirds of Latin America's foreign exchange deficit is caused by external debt service payments.

Credits for military purchases are usually hard loans with high interest rates and a short repayment period. Development loans are normally just the opposite. Unless all credits to a particular country—both development and military sales—are subject to a comprehensive review how can we know enough about the total economic circumstances of a country to make the right decisions? At the moment there seems to be very little coordination between the right hand of military export credit policy and the left hand of development loans.

Finally, there is the question of the compatibility of our present arms sales policies with the United States' expressed desire to control arms races in the developing regions of the world. The Congress has fully supported the efforts of the executive agencies to administer military assistance and sales with the goal of arms control in mind at all times. The Foreign Assistance Act of 1966, for example, states:

Programs for the sale or exchange of defense articles shall be administered so as to encourage regional arms control and disarmament agreements and so as to discourage arms races.

In addition, there has been growing concern by individual Senators over the role U.S. arms are playing in a series of international crises—Kashmir, the Middle East, and in time, perhaps in Latin America. Senator Bourke Hickenlooper expressed such a concern before the American Management Association when he remarked:

> The United States did not cause the Indian-Pakistan war but we did supply most of the rocks and brickbats. I hope we have learned from this experience that foreign military aid must be appraised in the widest possible context with particular emphasis on what effect this aid will have on regional problems.

What seems to be lacking in the U.S. approach to the arms sales issue is a boldness of policy often demanded of a great power. It is a commonplace to hear discussions on whether the United States should or should not sell military equipment to this or that country end with "but if we don't sell it to them the Russians (or the British, or the French, etc.) will." Fully aware of this flaw in the U.S. armor, many countries have exploited it in order to acquire equipment we don't really want to sell them. Consequently, the United States often ends up selling, say, the Iranians supersonic F-4 aircraft for defense primarily because the Shah says he will go to the Russians if we don't give him the equipment he wants. When this sort of compelling argument is added to the glint of a balance-of-payments success, a momentum is created which tends to divorce the process from its appropriate overall policy context.[5]

To the authors of the Staff Study—and to Admiral Rickover— the trouble was located in the momentum of burgeoning arms

[5] Staff study, *Arms Sales and Foreign Policy*, prepared for the use of the Senate Foreign Relations Committee, 90th Cong., 1st Sess. (Washington, 1967), pp. 1–7, 10–11.

sales and an overgrown Pentagon which divorced the "process" from an appropriate "foreign policy context." Rickover, citing President Dwight D. Eisenhower's words, referred to the scientific-military-industrial complex. Eisenhower's famous "Farewell Message" was quoted many times by critics in the latter part of the decade. It is doubtful that Eisenhower intended his speech as anything more than a reply to the "missile gap" enthusiasts who found an ally in John F. Kennedy. McNamara's reign in the Pentagon, nonetheless, seemed to critics to demonstrate the former President's powers of prophecy.

. . . We now stand ten years past the midpoint of a century that has witnessed four major wars among great nations; three of these involved our own country. Despite these holocausts America is today the strongest, the most influential and most productive nation in the world. Understandably proud of this pre-eminence, we yet realize that America's leadership and prestige depend not merely upon our unmatched material progress, riches, and military strength, but on how we use our power in the interests of world peace and human betterment. . . .

Progress toward these noble goals is persistently threatened by the conflict now engulfing the world. It commands our whole attention, absorbs our very beings.

We face a hostile ideology—global in scope, atheistic in character, ruthless in purpose, and insidious in method. Unhappily the danger it poses promises to be of indefinite duration. To meet it successfully there is called for not so much the emotional and transitory sacrifices of crisis, but rather those which enable us to carry forward steadily, surely, and without complaint the burdens of a prolonged and complex struggle—with liberty the stake.

Only thus shall we remain, despite every provocation, on our charted course toward permanent peace and human betterment.

Crises there will continue to be. In meeting them, whether foreign or domestic, great or small, there is a recurring temptation to feel that some spectacular and costly action could become the miraculous solution to all current difficulties. A huge increase in newer elements of our defenses; development of unrealistic programs to cure every ill in agriculture; a dramatic expansion in basic and applied research—these and many other possibilities, each possibly promising in itself, may be suggested as the only way to the road we wish to travel.

But each proposal must be weighed in the light of a broader consideration: the need to maintain balance in and among national programs—balance between the private and the public economy, balance between the cost and hoped for advantages—balance between the clearly necessary and the comfortably desirable; balance between our essential requirements as a nation and the duties imposed by the nation upon the individual; balance between actions of the moment and the national welfare of the future. Good judgment seeks balance and progress; lack of it eventually finds imbalance and frustration.

The record of many decades stands as proof that our people and their Government have, in the main, understood these truths and have responded to them well in the face of threat and stress.

But threats, new in kind or degree, constantly arise. . . .

A vital element in keeping the peace is our military establishment. Our arms must be mighty, ready for instant action, so that no potential aggressor may be tempted to risk his own destruction.

Our military organization today bears little relation to that known of any of my predecessors in peacetime—or, indeed, by the fighting men of World War II or Korea.

Until the latest of our world conflicts, the United States had no armaments industry. American makers of plowshares could, with time and as required, make swords as well.

But we can no longer risk emergency improvisation of national defense. We have been compelled to create a permanent armaments industry of vast proportions. Added to this, three and a half million men and women are directly engaged in the defense establishment. We annually spend on military security alone more than the net income of all United States corporations.

Now this conjunction of an immense military establishment and a large arms industry is new in the American experience. The total influence—economic, political, even spiritual—is felt in every city, every state house, every office of the Federal Government. We recognize the imperative need for this development. Yet we must not fail to comprehend its grave implications. Our toil, resources and livelihood are all involved; so is the very structure of our society.

In the councils of Government, we must guard against the acquisition of unwarranted influence, whether sought or unsought, by the military-industrial complex. The potential for the disastrous rise of misplaced power exists and will persist.

We must never let the weight of this combination endanger our liberties or democratic processes. We should take nothing for granted. Only an alert and knowledgeable citizenry can compel the proper meshing of the huge industrial and military machinery of defense with our peaceful methods and goals, so that security and liberty may prosper together. . . .[1]

The term "military-industrial complex" conveyed a conspiratorial tone whenever it was used. It was like "merchants of death," a term used in the 1920's by World War I "revisionists." As an explanation of *Pax Americana*, moreover, it had a limited usefulness. The point was, argued a New Left group of analysts, that the "military-industrial complex," so-called, was neither a thing apart from the overall context of foreign policy nor a special part of the American economy. Liberals who thought they could cut the Pentagon down to size were mistaken. The trouble was the system itself. Eisenhower himself had put ideological considerations at the heart of the matter: "We face a hostile ideology—global in scope, atheistic in character, ruthless in purpose, and insidious in method." It was essential to understand American ideology, and the economic foundations which produce its political attitudes. That task was undertaken by, among others, Harry Magdoff, an editor of the Socialist journal, *Monthly Review*.

. . . One of the reasons frequently given for believing that economic imperialism is an unimportant influence in foreign and

---

[1] *Public Papers of the Presidents of the United States . . . Dwight D. Eisenhower, 1960–1961* (Washington, D.C.: Government Printing Office, 1961), pp. 1036–1039.

military policy is that only a small segment of American business is vitally concerned with foreign or military economic activities. This might be a meaningful observation if economic resources were widely distributed and the majority of domestic-minded business firms could conceivably be mobilized against policies fostered by the small minority of foreign-oriented businesses. But the realities of economic concentration suggest quite the opposite. In manufacturing industries, 5 corporations own over 15 percent of total net capital assets (as of 1962). The 100 largest corporations own 55 percent of total net capital assets. This means that a small number of firms—with their own strength and that of their allies in finance and mass communication media—can wield an overwhelming amount of economic and political power, especially if there is a community of interest within this relatively small group.

And it is precisely among the giant corporations that we find the main centers of foreign and military economic operations. Just a cursory examination of the 50 largest industrial concerns shows the following types of firms heavily involved in international economic operations and the supply of military goods: 12 in oil, 5 in aviation, 3 in chemicals, 3 in steel, 3 in autos, 8 in electrical equipment and electronics, and 3 in rubber. These 37 companies account for over 90 percent of the assets of the top 50 industrial firms.

The community of interest among the industrial giants in foreign and military operations stems from relations that are not always obvious in terms of the customary statistical categories. First, there is the interrelationship among the firms via the financial centers of power. Second, there are the direct economic ties of business. While only five firms get one-fourth of the volume of military contracts and 25 firms account for more than half of such contracts, a large part of this business is distributed to other businesses that supply these chief contractors. Thus . . . the primary nonferrous metal manufacturers who receive very few direct military contracts nevertheless get over 22 percent of their business from military demand. And, third, because of the rich growth potential and other advantages of the military and foreign-oriented businesses, the postwar merger movement among industrial giants has intermingled the typically domestic with the typically outer-market-directed business organizations. The most unlikely-seeming business organizations are today planted with both feet in foreign and military business. We see, for example, traditional producers of grain mill products and of plumbing and heating equipment acquiring plants that make scientific instruments; meat packing firms buying up companies in the general industrial machinery field, and many other cross-industry mergers.

The concentration of economic power, so much part of the domestic scene, shows up in even stronger fashion in the field of foreign investment. The basic available data on this are taken from the 1957 census of foreign investments. These data refer only to direct investments and do not include portfolio investments or

U.S. Direct Foreign Investment by Size of Investment (1957)

Value of Direct Investment by Size Classes	Number of Firms	Percent of Total U.S. Investment
$100 million and over	45	57
$ 50–100 million	51	14
$ 25– 50 million	67	9
$ 10– 25 million	126	8
$ 5– 10 million	166	5
Total	455	93

Source: *United States Business Investments in Foreign Countries*, U.S. Dept. of Commerce, 1960, p. 144.

such economic ties as are created by the licensing of patents, processes, and trademarks. We note from this table that only 45 firms account for almost three fifths of all direct foreign investment. Eighty percent of all such investment is held by 163 firms. The evidence is still more striking when we examine the concentration of investment by industry:

Industry	No. of Firms	Percent of Total Assets Held
Mining	20	95
Oil	24	93
Manufacturing	143	81
Public Utilities	12	89
Trade	18	83
Finance and Insurance	23	76
Agriculture	6	83

These data are shown from the viewpoint of total United States foreign investment. If we examined the situation from the angle of the recipient countries, we would find an even higher degree of concentration of United States business activities. But from either perspective, the concentration of foreign investment is but an extension of domestic monopolistic trends. The latter provide the opportunity to accumulate the wealth needed for extensive foreign investment as well as the impetus for such investment.

The question of control is central to an understanding of the strategic factors that determine the pattern of foreign investment. In its starkest form, this control is most obvious in the economic relations with the underdeveloped countries—in the role of these countries as suppliers of raw materials for mass-production industries and as a source of what can properly be termed financial tribute.

Let us look first at the distribution of foreign investment. We see here two distinct patterns. In Latin America, Asia, and Africa, the majority of the investment is in the extractive industries. Although Canada is an important source of minerals and oil, only 35 percent of United States investment is in these extractive industries, with 45 percent going into manufactures. The investment in extractive industries in Europe is minimal: the data on petroleum represent refineries and distribution, not oil wells.

The economic control, and hence the political control when dealing with foreign sources of raw material supplies, is of paramount importance to the monopoly-organized mass production industries in the home country. In industries such as steel, aluminum, and oil, the ability to control the source of raw material is essential to the control over the markets and prices of the final products, and serves as an effective safety factor in protecting the large investment in the manufacture and distribution of the final product. The resulting frustration of competition takes on two forms. First, when price and distribution of the raw material are controlled, the competitor's freedom of action is restricted; he cannot live very long without a dependable source of raw materials at a practical cost. Second, by gobbling up as much of the world's resources of this material as is feasible, a power group can forestall a weaker competitor from becoming more independent as well as discourage possible new competition. How convenient that a limited number of United States oil companies control two thirds of the "free world's" oil!

At this level of monopoly, the involvement of business interests with United States foreign policy becomes ever more close. The assurance of control over raw materials in most areas involves not just another business matter but is high on the agenda of maintaining industrial and financial power. And the wielders of this power, if they are to remain in the saddle, must use every effort to make sure that these sources of supply are always available on the most favorable terms: these foreign supplies are not merely an avenue to great profits but are the insurance policy on the monopolistic position at home.

The pressure to obtain external sources of raw materials has taken on a new dimension during the past two decades, and promises to become increasingly severe. Even though United States business has always had to rely on foreign sources for a number of important metals (e.g., bauxite, chrome, nickel, manganese, tungsten, tin), it has nevertheless been self-reliant and an exporter of a wide range of raw materials until quite recently. This generalization has been a mainstay of those who argued that U.S. capitalism had no need to be imperialistic. But even this argument, weak as it may have been in the past, can no longer be relied on. The developing pressure on natural resources, especially evident since the 1940's, stirred President Truman to establish a Materials Policy Commission to define the magnitude of the problem. The ensuing commission report, *Resources for Freedom* (Washington, D.C.,

1952), graphically summarized the dramatic change in the following comparison for all raw materials other than food and gold: at the turn of the century, the U.S. produced on the whole some 15 percent more of these raw materials than was domestically consumed; this surplus had by 1950 turned into a deficit, with U.S. industry consuming 10 percent more than domestic production; extending the trends to 1975 showed that by then the overall deficit of raw materials for industry will be about 20 percent.

Perhaps the awareness of this development was a contributing factor to President Eisenhower's alerting the nation to the unity of political and economic interests in his first inaugural address (January 20, 1953): "We know . . . that we are linked to all free peoples not merely by a noble idea but by a simple need. No free people can for long cling to any privilege or enjoy any safety in economic solitude. For all our own material might, even we need markets in the world for the surpluses of our farms and our factories. Equally, we need for these same farms and factories vital materials and products of distant lands. This basic law of interdependence, so manifest in the commerce of peace, applies with thousand-fold intensity in the event of war."

As is so often the case, economic interests harmonize comfortably with political and security goals, since so many of the basic raw materials are considered essential to effective war preparedness. Quite understandably the government makes its contribution to the security of the nation as well as to the security of business via diplomatic maneuvers, maintenance of convenient military bases in various parts of the world, military aid to help maintain stable governments, and last but not least a foreign aid program which is a fine blend of declared humanitarian aims about industrialization and a realistic appreciation that such progress should not interfere with the ability of supplying countries to maintain a proper flow of raw materials. To do a real job of assuring an adequate supply of raw materials in the light of possible exhaustion of already exploited deposits, and in view of possible needs for missiles and space programs, the government can make its greatest contribution by keeping as much of the world as possible "free" and safe for mineral development. Clarence B. Randall, president of Inland Steel Co. and adviser on foreign aid in Washington, comments on the fortunate availability of uranium deposits in the Belgian Congo as the atom bomb was developed: "What a break it was for us that the mother country was on our side! And who can possibly foresee today which of the vast unexplored areas of the world may likewise possess some unique deposit of a rare raw material which in the fullness of time our industry or our defense program may most urgently need?"

The integration of less developed capitalisms into the world market as reliable and continuous suppliers of their natural resources results, with rare exceptions, in a continuous dependency on the centers of monopoly control that is sanctified and cemented by the market structure which evolves from this very dependency. Integration into world capitalist markets has almost uniform effects on the supplying countries: (1) they depart from, or never enter, the paths of development that require independence and self-reliance; (2) they lose their economic self-sufficiency and become dependent on exports for their economic viability; (3) their industrial structure becomes adapted to the needs of supplying specialized exports at prices acceptable to the buyers, reducing thereby such flexibility of productive resources as is needed for a diversified and growing economic productivity. The familiar symptom of this process is still seen in Latin America where, despite industrialization efforts and the stimulus of two world wars, well over 90 percent of most countries' total exports consists of the export of agricultural and mineral products. The extreme dependence on exports, and on a severely restricted number of export products at that, keeps such economies off balance in their international economic relations and creates frequent need for borrowing. Debt engenders increasing debt, for the servicing of the debt adds additional balance of payments difficulties. And in all such relations of borrowing and lending, the channels of international finance are in the hands of the foreign investors, their business associates, and their government agencies.

The chains of dependence may be manipulated by the political, financial, and military arms of the centers of empire, with the help of the Marines, military bases, bribery, CIA operations, financial maneuvers, and the like. But the material basis of this dependence is an industrial and financial structure which through the so-called normal operations of the marketplace reproduces the conditions of economic dependence.

A critical element of the market patterns which helps perpetuate the underdeveloped countries as dependable suppliers of raw materials is the financial tribute to the foreign owners who extract not only natural resources but handsome profits as well. The following comparison for the years 1950–1965 is a clear illustration of the process and refers to only one kind of financial drain, the income from direct investments which is transferred to the United States:

| | (Billions of Dollars) | | | |
	Europe	Canada	Latin America	All other Areas
Flow of direct investments from U.S.	$8.1	$6.8	$ 3.8	$ 5.2
Income on this capital transferred to U.S.	5.5	5.9	11.3	14.3
Net	+$2.6	+$ .9	−$ 7.5	−$ 9.1

In the underdeveloped regions almost three times as much money was taken out as was put in. And note well that besides drawing out almost three times as much as they put in, investors were able to increase the value of the assets owned in these regions manyfold: in Latin America, direct investments owned by United States business during this period increased from $4.5 to $10.3 billion; in Asia and Africa, from $1.3 to $4.7 billion. . . .

The postwar foreign economic expansion of United States manufacturing firms has resulted in the transformation of many of the giants of United States business into a new form of multinational organizations. The typical international business firm is no longer limited to the giant oil company. It is as likely to be a General Motors or a General Electric—with 15 to 20 percent of its operations involved in foreign business, and exercising all efforts to increase this share. It is the professed goal of these international firms to obtain the lowest unit production costs on a world-wide basis. It is also their aim, though not necessarily openly stated, to come out on top in the merger movement in the European Common Market and to control as large a share of the world market as they do of the United States market. To the directors of such organizations the "oneness" of economic and national interests is quite apparent. The president of General Electric put it succinctly: "I suggest we will perceive that overriding both the common purposes and cross-purposes of business and government, there is a broader pattern—a 'consensus' if you will, where public and private interest come together, cooperate, interact and become the national interest."

Needless to stress, the term "private interest" refers to private enterprise. Another officer of this corporation grapples with the identity of the private and national interest: "Thus, our search for profits places us squarely in line with the national policy of stepping up international trade as a means of strengthening the free world in the Cold War confrontation with Communism."

Just as the fight against Communism helps the search for profits so the search for profits helps the fight against Communism. What more perfect harmony of interests could be imagined?[*1]

The "missing link" in Magdoff's analysis of *Pax Americana* becomes apparent at the point of decision-making: do policymakers calculate the net effect on the American economy of all major decisions? Would their expansionist inclinations be any different if they did not share a capitalist world view? And so on. In regard to the recent past, the historian can count on only the most restricted access to policy documents to help him determine such matters. But even after the documents do become available, as in the case of the Pentagon Papers concerning Vietnam, disputes over the intention and motives of a given policymaker, or group of policymakers, continue unabated. One is never really satisfied that one has *all* the truth. While some observers speak of evidence of American "interests" and "influence," others use the same evidence to document a case for "obligations" and "responsibilities" as the basis for foreign-policy decisions. Truth, says a third group, floats elusively somewhere in the middle.

[*1] Harry Magdoff, "Economic Aspects of U.S. Imperialism," *Monthly Review* (November, 1966), pp. 10–41.

Once again from the Pentagon Papers we learn that authors of key policy papers usually put the alternative they favored in between two extreme courses of action, each obviously unacceptable upon a first reading by the decisionmaker. Historians do the same thing. Not all of them, of course; not Magdoff, and not Robert W. Tucker, who replied to the specifics of the economic argument. "In the case of investment," begins Tucker's assessment of that part of the radical critique:

the sheer magnitude of America's foreign economic involvement gives the radical argument . . . an apparent plausibility. In 1969, American investments abroad, official and private, were valued at $158 billion, with private investments ($110 billion) making up approximately two-thirds of the total. Direct investment in branches and subsidiaries of U.S. enterprises abroad, the critical category of private foreign investment, was valued at $70.8 billion. Moreover, the figures on private investment represent book value, which is substantially below true market value.

American investment abroad is not only impressive in its sheer magnitude, it also reveals a dramatic rate of growth. From 1960 to 1969 direct investment increased 122%. In 1968, total new assets, which includes net reinvested earnings of business abroad, was $11.4 billion, an increase of 60.4% over 1966. In 1969, new private direct investment was $7.6 billion, an increase of 48% over 1966. Whether the growth of recent years may be expected to continue in the future is a matter of some debate and uncertainty. There is no question, though, of the very considerable impact of American direct investments both in the world economy and in the economies of individual countries. One indication of this impact may be seen in the gross value of the output of American firms operating abroad. Calculated at over $120 billion in 1967, this output ranked ahead of all but the two largest national economies.

However large American investment abroad appears when measured in absolute terms, and however great the impact of this investment on others, its significance for the domestic economy must of course be understood primarily in terms relative to this economy. In 1968, gross private domestic investment was $127.7

billion, on a base of $1.6 trillion in total corporate assets. Direct investment abroad as a percentage of total investment was roughly 6%. Viewed in another way, the value of private investment abroad (direct and portfolio) in 1968 represented 8% of total corporate assets for that year. Again, in 1968, the return on total private investment abroad was $8.6 billion. When compared with domestic corporate profits of $92.3 billion, the return on foreign investment was 9.3% of domestic corporate profits. Viewed simply in absolute terms, the magnitude of American private investment may prove very misleading as an indication of its significance for the domestic economy.

It may, of course, be argued that these percentages, while seemingly modest, are nevertheless crucial, in that without the outlet provided by foreign investment (though only 6%) and the earnings obtained from abroad (9.3% of total corporate profits) the American economy could not function at anywhere near its present levels. If the argument is impossible to substantiate, it may be conceded that it is also difficult to disprove. Is it necessary, however, to make the effort to disprove it? It would not seem so, if for no other reason than the geographical location of American investments.

It is not in the Third World, the low-income states, that the bulk of American assets and investments are to be found, but in Western Europe (30%), Canada (29%), Australia, New Zealand, and South Africa (6%), and Japan (2%). These states are the home of $47.7 billion in direct investment, with only $20 billion invested in all of the low investment states (with $13 billion of the $20 billion in Latin America). In 1969, the developed—and Capitalist—countries accounted for $4.2 billion of the $5.8 billion growth in the book value of direct investment. In contrast, direct investment rose only $1.2 billion in the lesser developed areas. These figures continue a trend observable throughout the 1960s of a steady decline in the percentage of direct investments in poor states. Whereas in 1960 the latter had 40% of American direct investment, in 1969 the percentage had shrunk to 30.

It is true that returns on investments from the underdeveloped states are proportionately higher than returns from investments located in developed states. For the most part, this disparity is to be explained by the high concentration of investment in petroleum. In 1969, 41% of American private investment in low-income countries was in petroleum. At the same time, the earnings from investment in petroleum ($2.4 billion) represented 61% of the earnings from all investment in these countries ($4 billion). The special case of oil excluded, in 1969 the rates of return on manufacturing investments between industrial and nonindustrial areas were about the same. Even if the high returns on oil are included, the earnings on investments from the nonindustrial areas have in recent years formed a slightly decreasing percentage of earnings on private foreign investment as a whole.

The October 1970 issue of *Survey of Current Business* states: "With the rise in the rate of return on manufacturing investments abroad to 12.8% in 1969, the rate of return of 12.6% on comparable domestic investments was exceeded for the first time in a number of years. Over the past ten years yields on domestic investment averaged 12.4%, only slightly higher than the 11.8% average on direct investments abroad. These percentages included all manufacturing investments abroad. The *Survey* goes on to note that rates of return on manufacturing investments between industrial and nonindustrial areas "are about the same." Inasmuch, then, as the charge of exploitation held to attend investment in undeveloped areas rests on the presumed marked disparity in rates of return on domestic and foreign investment, it must concentrate largely on oil (and to a much lesser degree on mining and smelting). The case of oil is of course a very special one not only because it accounts for so much of the earnings from undeveloped areas and enjoys a rate of return that is inordinately higher than manufactures (and minerals), but also because of the industry's evident dependence on overseas profits. Concentrated in the Middle East, the book value alone of the American investment in this area is between $2 and $3 billion and its net benefit to the United States balance of payments is $1.5 billion. Given the radical view, one would expect that here, if anywhere, American policy would faithfully reflect economic interests. The reality, as is well known, is otherwise. Apart from the increasing and successful pressures oil countries have employed to increase their royalty and tax income (pressures which have not provoked any notable countermeasures), the American government has contributed to the steady deterioration of the favorable position American oil companies once enjoyed in the Middle East. A *New York Times* correspondent, John M. Lee, writes: "The remarkable thing to many observers is that the oil companies have had such little influence in American foreign policy toward Israel."

. . . Can the need for exports explain what the need for imports (raw materials) and foreign investments fails to explain? Is it plausible to find in the search for foreign markets the roots of an interventionist and counterrevolutionary policy? . . . It is not enough simply to point out that the export of goods was valued at $34.7 billion for 1968 and that this figure more than tripled in the period from 1950 to 1968. What is relevant here is the significance of exports when taken in relation to the domestic economy. One indication of their significance is that in 1968 they represented 4% of a GNP of $860 billion. Radical critics have argued that this percentage is misleading when used to indicate the significance of exports to the domestic economy, since it compares the value of goods as exports with the domestic value of both goods and services. Whereas the value of exports in relation to GNP is 4%, in relation to the value of goods sold domestically it is 8%. Even if the latter percentage is taken as a more meaningful indication of the significance of exports to the domestic economy, it scarcely bears out the argument of a dependence on exports. Moreover, unless it can be demonstrated that the economy as a whole remains critically dependent upon the goods-producing sector, there is no persuasive reason for accepting the latter percentage as the more meaningful one.

Let us assume, however, that the export of goods is critical to the domestic economy as it presently functions and, further, that [exports] were to be cut off. Although neither assumption is plausible, the consequences would still not be those suggested by the radical argument, and for the most apparent of reasons. Against $34.7 billion in exports, 80 percent of which are made up of five product groups—transportation (mainly aircraft), chemicals, electrical machinery (computers and highly spohisticated office machinery), nonelectrical machinery, and scientific instruments— the United States imported $33.3 billion [of goods] in 1968, 70% of which comprised manufactures. Assuming that foreign markets were cut off, we may also assume that the domestic market would be—or, at least, could be—closed to foreign manufactures (we leave aside the problem of raw-material imports). The hardship imposed on particular industries apart, the resultant blow to the economy as a whole would be something considerably short of mortal. At a more serious level of analysis, a comparsion of exports as a percentage of total output of goods indicates the relatively small amounts involved. Using government input-output tables for 1958 and 1963, we find that only two industries (iron and ferroalloy-ore mining, and scientific instruments) show significant increases for the five-year period, while several industries show a decline. . . .

Given the structure of American exports, it follows that our trade is predominantly with rich competitors and not with the developing States of the Third World. In 1968, 67% of American exports went to Western Europe, Canada, and Japan. These countries continue to take an ever-increasing percentage of American exports while sharing an ever-increasing percentage of American imports. By contrast, the percentage of American exports to the developing states declined from 37% to 31.3% between 1955 and 1968. With respect to the Third World, then, the parallel between exports and investments (or, for that matter, imports) is clear. It is in the developed nations that America's economic involvement abroad is increasingly concentrated. . . .

Whereas the radical critic clearly sees—indeed, too clearly sees —the calculation and self-interest that have marked American foreign policy, he persistently ignores the deeper sources of collective self-aggrandizement. Even if it were true that America's security in this century has been totally unconditioned by events occurring beyond our frontiers, it would not follow that our expansion must be attributed to forces generated by a particular socio-economic structure. There may be few reliable lessons that the study of state relations reveals. But one is surely that the identification of the collective self with something greater than the self is so endemic a trait in the case of great states that it may be considered to form part of their natural history. The radical attempt to find the roots of America's expansion primarily in her institutional forms dismisses this lesson. It necessarily denies that it is power itself, more than a particular form of power, which prompts expansion.

Thus radical criticism will not confront the eternal and insoluble problems inordinate power creates, just as it will not acknowledge that men possessed of this power are always ready to use it if only in order to rule over others. In the radical *Weltanschauung* there is little, if any, appreciation that dominion is its own reward and that men may sacrifice material interest in order to rule (or, for that matter, to be emulated). There is also little, if any, appreciation that expansion may be rooted in an insecurity that is not simply self-generated. It is no doubt true that America's expansion is in large measure the result of an expansive concept of security and that this concept is, in part, related to the nature of America's institutions. It is not true that America's security in this century has been unconditioned by events occurring beyond our frontiers and that, in consequence, to the extent our security has been compromised it has been the result of our own persistent expansionism and aggressiveness. The issue of physical security apart, the radical case proceeds from the assumption that whatever threat there has been to American security in its greater than physical dimensions, such threat has followed either from the way we have mistakenly defined our security (that is, as a function of what were supposedly our institutional needs) or from the objective needs of America's institutions. In neither form, however, does this assumption rest upon a persuasive showing that given different institutions a hostile world would have posed no threat to us. The radical critique takes for granted what must instead be plausibly demonstrated.*[1]

Professor Tucker's assertion that "it is power itself more than a particular form of power, which prompts expansion" rests upon the view that men and nations are as mechanistic as the outlook he criticizes, and perhaps even more abstract. The exercise of power is carried out by men operating in concrete circumstances, and upon assumptions they presume will improve and enlarge their institutions. Thus Under Secretary of State George Ball, a typical spokesman for the Kennedy-Johnson Administration on foreign economic policy and a corporation lawyer, explained to

*[1] Robert W. Tucker, *The Radical Left and American Foreign Policy* (Baltimore: Johns Hopkins Press, 1971), pp. 126–131, 133–136, 151–152.

a Senate Committee that exports were concentrated "in the dynamic, high-wage segment of the economy. . . . What is more, they have made it possible to produce in volume, in industries where volume is especially critical for cutting costs. For these are the industries in which heavy sums must be spent in research and in capital [investment]. And such investments can only be justified if, at the very outset, there is the promise of a large international market."[4]

Ball may have been exaggerating, or simply mistaken, in his efforts to achieve passage of a new foreign trade act; but there is no reason to assume he was not speaking his mind, and for the Administration. It is equally true that different interest groups within the nation struggle for supremacy in the foreign policy area, and see such measures as foreign aid from separate, if related, perspectives. The adoption by the Kennedy Administration of a strategy of foreign aid indicates how one issue was decided:

The appointment of the Citizens' Committee in December 1962 went largely unnoticed outside the United States; but its relative anonymity was shattered when its report on American aid policy was published on March 25, 1963. Its major recommendations were given world-wide publicity both by the press and by United States government agencies. The Citizens' Committee primarily dwelt on regions peripheral to the Communist area. Its starkly frank views couched in equally unconventional language seemed calculated to shake off complaceny both within the United States and among recipient countries. The Clay Report proposed a Draconic formula to give a face-lift to American aid programs: trimmed costs; gradual but steady cuts in existing aid projects, especially those under the Point 4 program; emphasis on loans as against grants; transformation of aid programs from alleged distribution of wealth into a sound business transaction; withdrawal of aid programs from certain areas—particularly Africa (which should be a special responsibility of ex-Colonial powers); and a ceiling on American contribution to UN projects. On the promotional side of aid policies, the formula prescribed that the United States should prod Western allies to augment their aid programs, vigorously promote foreign investment abroad, and withhold aid to those state enterprises which compete with existing private enterprises; finally, stringent self-reliance and self-help should be demanded of the recipients.

Subsequent developments indicate that the Clay Committee and its findings were not a perfunctory step taken by President Kennedy and that its views exercised greater influence on his aid policies than previous reports by experts. In an aid message to the Congress President Kennedy deferentially referred to the Clay Report seven times, setting forth in detail how the new aid program was based on the application of standards "affirmed by the Clay Committee." . . .

The Kennedy administration had been subjected to considerable stresses in its attempts to fashion new economic aid strategies. Influential critics in the Congress had accused it of schizophrenia' in its claim that aid is both a most potent weapon against communism (element of national security) and a device to raise living standards of poorer nations (element of idealism). President Kennedy had had to resolve a dichotomy inherent in the making of foreign policy in a democratic system of checks and balances: an obligation to prune costs without losing continuity of aid programs; a need to invoke vital security interests to win internal public support and a desire to project abroad an idealistic image of generosity; Congressional pressure to divulge policy objectives as against dictates of diplomacy [or] window-dressing.

In 1961, President Kennedy and his advisors advocated a long-term aid program on grounds of vital security arising from growing competition with the Communist powers, and those of moral obligation.

In his view, the "struggle in the area of new and poorer nations will be a continuing crisis of this decade." He expressed concern "about waste of national security that might flow from too small an appropriation" and warned that the dangers of spending too little and too late were greater than those of spending too much too often. Secretary of State Dean Rusk noted that adequate aid funds and flexibility to work with nations willing to plan for progress was necessary for "continued life of the United States and the Free World." To administer the new "bold and enlightened aid program" the Kennedy administration at the outset decided to recruit "social welfare professionals, scientists, agricultural and labor specialists and educators."

In 1962, President Kennedy restated that economic aid was "small in cost compared to our military outlays for the defense of freedom. Yet all our armies and atoms combined will be of little avail if these nations fall." Dean Rusk added, "In the continuing effort toward economic development the stakes are the security of the world today and the shape of the world tomorrow."

The realistic "security" approach had not been regarded by President Kennedy as incompatible with the teleological philosophy of aid programs. He had maintained that there had been a "turn around" ever since his aid policies had been geared to specific needs of each nation "to strengthen [its] capacity to master the inherent stress of rapid change and to repel Communist efforts to exploit such stress from within and without." American aid programs, while "giving hope where hope was lacking" were also "helping to serve the deep American urge to extend a generous hand to those working toward a better life. . . ."

The tersely critical tone of the Clay Report accusing the government of attempting "too much for too many too soon" was out of tune with the recurring note of confident idealism struck in the authoritative statements of the American Government quoted above. . . .

In the external strategy of aid, the Clay Report served to herald a shift in President Kennedy's policies: the growing stress on the role of private investment and free enterprise in foreign aid policy.

In 1962 President Kennedy had stated, "We must reject oversimplified theories of international life—the theory . . . that the American mission is to remake the world in the American image." The Mansfield Report similarly did not ask the United States Government either to promote free enterprise and American investment abroad or to withhold American funds from state-owned projects in recipient countries. The Clay Report, by contrast, cast the questions of private investment and free enterprise in an ideological mold. Referring to too many instances of American aid to countries which do not foster a free enterprise system, it categorically demanded that the "United States should not aid a foreign government in projects establishing government-owned industrial and commercial enterprises which compete with existing private endeavors." Realizing that the United States "cannot insist on molding others in its own image," the Clay Committee nevertheless emphasized that it "should not extend aid which is inconsistent with our beliefs, democratic traditions, and knowledge of economic organization and consequence." Reiterating this opinion, General Clay explained that the criterion for judgment could be whether a country was seriously trying to foster a free enterprise system or was deliberately trying to establish something other than that.

The importance of the Clay Committee's views on private investment was enhanced by the fact that they were incorporated into President Kennedy's administrative and legislative policies. The "primary new initiative" in the 1963 aid program was related to increased efforts by the United States to encourage the investment of private capital in the underdeveloped countries. The United States missions in underdeveloped countries were "directed to urge more forcefully the importance of making full use of private resources and improving the climate for private investment, both domestic and foreign," and to insist on full implementation of investment guarantee programs. President Kennedy welcomed "effective participation of an enlightened United States businessman, especially in partnership with private interests in the developing country. . . ." Legislatively, two new measures to stimulate American investment in developing countries have been adopted: (1) on the recommendation of the U.S. businessmen's committee for the Alliance for Progress, U.S. taxpayers are granted a tax credit for new investments in underdeveloped countries for a trial period; (2) the investment guarantee provisions of the Foreign Assistance Act have been amended to enlarge and clarify the guarantee program.

In a news briefing, General Clay left little doubt that India was the object of his dictum on public versus private enterprise. In fact the Clay Report submits advice on policy towards India: the United States should give aid to India because of her "determination to resist Communism"; but it should not extend a loan for India's state-owned steel mill at Bokaro as it presumably competes with the existing private steel enterprise in India. President Kennedy, rejecting the Clay Committee's reasoning, warned, "It would be a great mistake not to build [the projected steel plant]. India needs that steel." American proponents of the scheme voiced concern that a failure in this test case might lose for the United States distinction achieved in other difficult ones and Indian frustration might fray Indo-American understanding. However, in the ensuing debate over the basic question of the use of American funds to fortify a socialistic economy the Indian Government is understood to have withdrawn its request for an American loan.

The Clay Committee's counsel of retreat in Africa did not win approval either of the Congress or of President Kennedy who, in order to forestall or counteract Communist penetration, and in keeping with his concept of "moral obligation of the rich to the poor," reaffirmed the sympathy of the people of America with African aspirations.

The self-help criterion, which the Clay Committee wished to uphold even at the cost of political popularity, if necessary, being increasingly applied by the United States. In August 1963, it withdrew aid from the Congolese Government in two categories to impel it to make long-overdue reforms. An Inter-American Committee for Development has been set up to allocate U.S. aid on the basis of self-help measures by recipient Latin American countries. While official sources in Malaya envisage a need of American assistance for Malaysia, the United States has not offered any. . . .

In the total perspective of a diplomacy of foreign aid, the Clay Report has raised a crucial question of foreign aid as a means to foster an economic ideology. Hitherto many an underdeveloped country has pursued a non-alignment policy not only *vis à vis* military blocs or political ideologies but concepts of industrial organization as well. Cambodia believes in Buddhist Socialism; the U.A.R. has evolved Arab Socialism; India is committed to a Socialist society founded on *Sarvodaya*—universal uplift. In recognition of this, the Soviet Union and the United States have evolved a new technique—persuasive presentation of models of their respective economic systems—in which a donor tries to show through foreign aid that its own "model" is best suited to development needs of a recipient. The adoption of the Clay recommendation would abolish this "competition through models" and introduce new elements of "superimposition" and "strings" into the American aid program. But its precise impact upon the total American strategy of foreign aid is yet to be determined.*1

The ongoing debate over a proper foreign aid strategy for the United States illustrated the complexities of Cold War policy and the unresolved tensions within the *Pax Americana*. Often during the postwar years an administration was called upon by Congress to demonstrate its commitment to fostering "Free Enterprise" systems through its aid programs. Just as often administrations felt the need to take into account other factors in deciding how to distribute aid most advantageously. Soviet leaders labeled the competitive model system described above, "Peaceful Co-Existence." But neither term allieviated the anxiety felt by American policy makers about Cold War crises in the Third World.

The Clay Report, for example, reflected concern about recent developments in Cuba and Latin America. Already nearly three years old, the Cuban crisis was the most dramatic and certainly the closest of the increasing examples that the Cold War had become a struggle for and within the underdeveloped world.

NOTES

1 U.S. Department of State, *American Foreign Policy: Current Documents, 1965* (Washington, 1968), pp. 968–970.
2 Louis Menashe and Ronald Radosh, eds., *Teach-Ins: U.S.A., Reports, Opinions, Documents* (New York: Vintage Books, 1967), pp. 153–155.
3 Arthur Schlesinger, Jr., *A Thousand Days: John F. Kennedy in the White House* (Boston: Houghton Mifflin Co., 1965), p. 769.
4 U.S. Congress, Joint Economic Committee, *Hearings: Foreign Economic Policy of the United States*, 2d Cong., 1st Sess. (Washington, 1961), p. 350.

*1 Usha Mahajani, "Kennedy and the Strategy of Aid: The Clay Report and After," *Western Political Quarterly*, November, 1966, pp. 656–668.

CHAPTER THREE
★ ★ ★ ★ ★

Cold War Crises
in the
Third World

In the foreword to the 1962 volume of his public messages
and speeches, President John F. Kennedy wrote:

Future historians, looking back at 1962, may well mark this
year as the time when the tide of international politics began at
last to flow strongly toward the world of diversity and freedom.
Following the launching of Sputnik in 1957, the Soviet Union began to intensify its pressures against the non-communist world—
especially in Southeast Asia, in Central Africa, in Latin America,
and around Berlin. The notable Soviet successes in space were
taken as evidence that communism held the key to the scientific
and technological future. People in many countries began to accept the notion that communism was mankind's inevitable destiny.

Nineteen sixty-two stopped this process—and nothing was
more important in deflating the notion of communist invincibility
than the American response to Soviet provocations in Cuba. The
combination of firmness and restraint in the face of the gravest

challenge to world peace since 1939 did much to reassure the rest of the world both about the strength of our national will and the prudence of our national judgment.[*1]

During the decade which ended with the Cuban missile crisis of October 1962, the Cold War had spread around the world. Journalists used the phrase "brinkmanship" to describe Secretary of State John Foster Dulles's willingness to risk confrontation with Moscow or Peking in a series of Far Eastern crisis during the 1950's. Yet when Senator Kennedy ran for the presidency in 1960, his principal charge against the Eisenhower Administration was that it lacked boldness and determination in foreign policy! In the era of Cold War orthodoxy, politics demanded that candidates outdo one another in getting tough with the Soviet Union. But there were difficulties with this view of world events, as Kennedy's impromptu review of the Cuban crisis during a December 1962 television interview suggested:

MR. [SANDER] VANOCUR: Mr. President, have you noted since you have been in office that this terrible responsibility for the fate of mankind has—notwithstanding the differences that divide you— has drawn you and Mr. Khrushchev somewhat closer in this joint sense of responsibility? He seems to betray it, especially in his speech to the Supreme Soviet earlier.

THE PRESIDENT: I think in that speech this week he showed his awareness of the nuclear age. But of course, the Cuban effort has made it more difficult for us to carry out any successful negotiations, because this was an effort to materially change the balance of power, it was done in secret, steps were taken really to deceive us by every means they could, and they were planning in November to open to the world the fact that they had these missiles so close to the United States; not that they were intending to fire them, because if they were going to get into a nuclear struggle, especially in Southeast Asia, in Central Africa, in Latin America,

---

[*1] *Public Papers of the Presidents of the United States . . . John F. Kennedy,* 1962 (Washington, D.C.: Government Printing Office, 1963), p. v.

they have their own missiles in the Soviet Union. But it would have politically changed the balance of power. It would have appeared to, and appearances contribute to reality. So it is going to be some time before it is possible for us to come to any real understandings with Mr. Khrushchev. But I do think his speech shows that he realizes how dangerous a world we live in.

The real problem is the Soviet desire to expand their power and influence. If Mr. Khrushchev would concern himself with the real interests of the people of the Soviet Union, that they have a higher standard of living, to protect his own security, there is no real reason why the United States and the Soviet Union, separated by so many thousands of miles of land and water, both rich countries, both with very energetic people, should not be able to live in peace. But it is this constant determination which the Chinese show in the most militant form, and which the Soviets also have shown, that they will not settle for that kind of a peaceful world, but must settle for a Communist world. That is what makes the real danger, the combination of these two systems in conflict around the world in a nuclear age is what makes the 'sixties so dangerous.'[*1]

To a man, Kennedy's biographers agree that the "Thirteen Days" of the missile crisis were the President's finest: under his direction the nation's political and military policymakers mounted a coordinated effort which exposed Russia's duplicity before the world, and forced Khrushchev into a public confession that the Soviet Union had placed Intermediate Range Ballistic Missiles (IRBMs), Medium Range Ballistic Missiles (MRBMs) and light bombers (IL-28s) on the island. The Soviet Premier had been thoroughly out-maneuvered by the young American President, and left no other course but to dismantle the weapons for a hasty return shipment to Russia. "The tide of international politics," Kennedy would say, "began at last to flow strongly toward the world of diversity and freedom."

Reinterpretations of the Cuban missile crisis (and its origins) began almost at once. On one level there were attacks from

[*1] *Ibid.*, pp. 897–898.

conservative critics who challenged the notion of a brilliant Kennedy performance as "crisis manager," with the retort that all that happened could be put down to "dumb luck." Former Secretary of State Dean Acheson, himself a noted crisis manager in the early days of the Cold War, advanced this view. He added, "I felt we were too eager to liquidate this thing. So long as we had the thumbscrew on Khrushchev, we should have given it another turn every day. We were too eager to make an agreement with the Russians. They had no business there in the first place." According to the informal settlement reached between Kennedy and Khrushchev, the United States agreed that in exchange for removal of offensive weapons systems it would "give assurances against an invasion of Cuba." Such an understanding, of course, would leave Fidel Castro in power, an avowed Marxist who had invited the Russians into Cuba in the first place.

For two years the Kennedy Administration had insisted that communism in the Western Hemisphere was not a negotiable issue. On October 8, 1962, for example, American Ambassador to the United Nations Adlai Stevenson had said to newspaper reporters: "The maintenance of communism in the Americas is not negotiable. Furthermore, the problem of Cuba is not a simple problem of United States–Cuban relations. It is a collective problem for all the States of this Hemisphere." A few days earlier, Secretary of State Dean Rusk had told an interviewer, "the penetration of this hemisphere by Castro communism is something which cannot be accepted in the hemisphere and by the United States." But by the terms of the Kennedy–Khrushchev agreement, new military steps against the Castro regime had been ruled out. So communism in the hemisphere was, after all, negotiable.

Another missile crisis question concerned the President's assertion that Russian placement of "offensive" weapons in Cuba "was an effort to materially change the balance of power." In his post-crisis television interview, the President had amended that statement twice, first to say, "it would have politically changed the balance of power," and then even more radically, "it would have appeared to, and appearances contribute to reality." No such ambiguity had characterized Kennedy's dramatic address to the nation on the evening of October 22, 1962. Then the President talked only of the military threat. Newspaper headlines carried the same message, quoting "high administration sources" as saying that Russian missiles in Cuba threatened to tip the balance of military power in favor of the Soviets. Delivered to the nation from the President's office, with a chart behind him illustrating the range of the missiles, Kennedy's words filled in a somber picture of a world on the edge of nuclear war:

Good evening, my fellow citizens. This Government, as promised, has maintained the closest surveillance of the Soviet military build-up on the island of Cuba. Within the past week unmistakable evidence has established the fact that a series of offensive missile sites is now in preparation on that imprisoned island. The purposes of these bases can be none other than to provide a nuclear strike capability against the Western Hemisphere.

Upon receiving the first preliminary hard information of this nature last Tuesday morning (October 16) at 9:00 A.M., I directed that our surveillance be stepped up. And having now confirmed and completed our evaluation of the evidence and our decision on a course of action, this Government feels obliged to report this new crisis to you in fullest detail.

The characteristics of these new missile sites indicate two distinct types of installations. Several of them include medium-range ballistic missiles capable of carrying a nuclear warhead for a distance of more than 1,000 nautical miles. Each of these missiles, in short, is capable of striking Washington, D.C., the Panama Canal, Cape Canaveral, Mexico City, or any other city in the southeastern part of the United States, in Central America, or in the Caribbean area.

Additional sites not yet completed appear to be designed for intermediate-range ballistic missiles capable of traveling more than twice as far—and thus capable of striking most of the major cities in the Western Hemisphere, ranging as far north as Hudson Bay, Canada, and as far south as Lima, Peru. In addition, jet bombers, capable of carrying nuclear weapons, are now being uncrated and assembled in Cuba, while the necessary air bases are being prepared.

This urgent transformation of Cuba into an important strategic base—by the presence of these large, long-range, and clearly offensive weapons of sudden mass destruction—constitutes an explicit threat to the peace and security of all the Americas, in flagrant and deliberate defiance of the Rio Pact of 1947, the traditions of this nation and Hemisphere, the Joint Resolution of the 87th Congress, the Charter of the United Nations, and my own public warnings to the Soviets on September 4 and 13.

This action also contradicts the repeated assurances of Soviet spokesmen, both publicly and privately delivered, that the arms build-up in Cuba would retain its original defensive character and that the Soviet Union had no need or desire to station strategic missiles on the territory of any other nation.

The size of this undertaking makes clear that it has been planned for some months. Yet only last month, after I had made clear the distinction between any introduction of ground-to-ground missiles and the existence of defensive antiaircraft missiles, the Soviet Government publicly stated on September 11 that, and I quote, "The armaments and military equipment sent to Cuba are designed exclusively for defensive purposes," and, I quote the Soviet Government, "There is no need for the Soviet Government to shift its weapons for a retaliatory blow to any other country, for instance Cuba," and that, and I quote the Government, "The Soviet Union has so powerful rockets to carry these nuclear warheads that there is no need to search for sites for them beyond the boundaries of the Soviet Union." That statement was false.

Only last Thursday, as evidence of this rapid offensive build-up was already in my hand, Soviet Foreign Minister Gromyko told me in my office that he was instructed to make it clear once again, as he said his Government had already done, that Soviet assistance to Cuba, and I quote, "pursued solely the purpose of contributing to the defense capabilities of Cuba," that, and I quote him, "training by Soviet specialists of Cuban nationals in handling defensive armaments was by no means offensive," and that "if it were otherwise," Mr. Gromyko went on, "the Soviet Government would never become involved in rendering such assistance." That statement also was false.

Neither the United States of America nor the world community of nations can tolerate deliberate deception and offensive threats on the part of any nation, large or small. We no longer live in a world where only the actual firing of weapons represents a sufficient challenge to a nation's security to constitute maximum peril. Nuclear weapons are so destructive and ballistic missiles are so swift that any substantially increased possibility of their use or any sudden change in their deployment may well be regarded as a definite threat to peace.

For many years both the Soviet Union and the United/States, recognizing this fact, have deployed strategic nuclear weapons with great care, never upsetting the precarious status quo which insured that these weapons would not be used in the absence of some vital challenge. Our own strategic missiles have never been transferred to the territory of any other nation under a cloak of secrecy and deception; and our history, unlike that of the Soviets since the end of World War II, demonstrates that we have no desire to dominate or conquer any other nation or impose our system upon its people. Nevertheless, American citizens have become adjusted to living daily on the bull's eye of Soviet missiles located in side the U.S.S.R. or in submarines.

In that sense missiles in Cuba add to an already clear and present danger—although it should be noted the nations of Latin America have never previously been subjected to a potential nuclear threat.

But this secret, swift, and extraordinary build-up of Communist missiles—in an area well known to have a special and historical relationship to the United States and the nations of the Western Hemisphere, in violation of Soviet assurances, and in defiance of American and hemispheric policy—this sudden, clandestine decision to station strategic weapons for the first time outside of Soviet soil—is a deliberately provocative and unjustified change in the status quo which cannot be accepted by this country if our courage and our commitments are ever to be trusted again by either friend or foe.

The 1930's taught us a clear lesson: Aggressive conduct, if allowed to grow unchecked and unchallenged, ultimately leads to war. This nation is opposed to war. We are also true to our word. Our unswerving objective, therefore, must be to prevent the use of these missiles against this or any other country and to secure their withdrawal or elimination from the Western Hemisphere.

Our policy has been one of patience and restraint, as befits a peaceful and powerful nation, which leads a worldwide alliance.

We have been determined not to be diverted from our central concerns by mere irritants and fanatics. But now further action is required—and it is underway; and these actions may only be the beginning. We will not prematurely or unnecessarily risk the costs of worldwide nuclear war in which even the fruits of victory would be ashes in our mouth—but neither will we shrink from that risk at any time it must be faced.

Acting, therefore, in the defense of our own security and of the entire Western Hemisphere, and under the authority entrusted to me by the Constitution as endorsed by the resolution of the Congress, I have directed that the following initial steps be taken immediately:

First: To halt this offensive build-up, a strict quarantine on all offensive military equipment under shipment to Cuba is being initiated. All ships of any kind bound for Cuba from whatever nation or port will, if found to contain cargoes of offensive weapons, be turned back. This quarantine will be extended, if needed, to other types of cargo and carriers. We are not at this time, however, denying the necessities of life as the Soviets attempted to do in their Berlin blockade of 1948.

Second: I have directed the continued and increased close surveillance of Cuba and its military build-up. The Foreign Ministers of the Organization of American States in their communiqué of October 3 rejected secrecy on such matters in this Hemisphere. Should these offensive military preparations continue, thus increasing the threat to the Hemisphere, further action will be justified. I have directed the Armed Forces to prepare for any eventualities; and I trust that in the interests of both the Cuban people and the Soviet technicians at the sites, the hazards to all concerned of continuing this threat will be recognized.

Third: It shall be the policy of this nation to regard any nuclear missile launched from Cuba against any nation in the Western Hemisphere as an attack by the Soviet Union on the United States, requiring a full retaliatory response upon the Soviet Union.

Fourth: As a necessary military precaution I have reinforced our base at Guantanamo, evacuated today the dependents of our personnel there, and ordered additional military units to be on a standby alert basis.

Fifth: We are calling tonight for an immediate meeting of the

Organ of Consultation, under the Organization of American States, to consider this threat to hemispheric security and to invoke articles six and eight of the Rio Treaty in support of all necessary action. The United Nations Charter allows for regional security arrangements—and the nations of this Hemisphere decided long ago against the military presence of outside powers. Our other allies around the world have also been alerted.

Sixth: Under the Charter of the United Nations, we are asking tonight that an emergency meeting of the Security Council be convoked without delay to take action against this latest Soviet threat to world peace. Our resolution will call for the prompt dismantling and withdrawal of all offensive weapons in Cuba, under the supervision of United Nations observers, before the quarantine can be lifted.

Seventh and finally: I call upon Chairman Khrushchev to halt and eliminate this clandestine, reckless, and provocative threat to world peace and to stable relations between our two nations. I call upon him further to abandon this course of world domination and to join in an historic effort to end the perilous arms race and transform the history of man. He has an opportunity now to move the world back from the abyss of destruction—by returning to his Government's own words that it had no need to station missiles outside its own territory, and withdrawing these weapons from Cuba—by refraining from any action which will widen or deepen the present crisis—and then by participating in a search for peaceful and permanent solutions.

This nation is prepared to present its case against the Soviet threat to peace, and our own proposals for a peaceful world, at any time and in any forum in the Organization of American States, in the United Nations, or in any other meeting that could be useful —without limiting our freedom of action.

We have in the past made strenuous efforts to limit the spread of nuclear weapons. We have proposed the elimination of all arms and military bases in a fair and effective disarmament treaty. We are prepared to discuss new proposals for the removal of tensions on both sides—including the possibilities of a genuinely independent Cuba, free to determine its own destiny. We have no wish to war with the Soviet Union, for we are a peaceful people who desire to live in peace with all other peoples.

But it is difficult to settle or even discuss these problems in an atmosphere of intimidation. That is why this latest Soviet threat— or any other threat which is made either independently or in response to our actions this week—must and will be met with determination. Any hostile move anywhere in the world against the safety and freedom of peoples to whom we are committed—including in particular the brave people of West Berlin—will be met by whatever action is needed.

Finally, I want to say a few words to the captive people of Cuba, to whom this speech is being directly carried by special radio facilities. I speak to you as a friend, as one who knows of your deep attachment to your fatherland, as one who shares your aspirations for liberty and justice for all. And I have watched and the American people have watched with deep sorrow how your nationalist revolution was betrayed and how your fatherland fell under foreign domination. Now your leaders are no longer Cuban leaders inspired by Cuban ideals. They are puppets and agents of an international conspiracy which has turned Cuba against your friends and neighbors in the Americas—and turned it into the first Latin American country to become a target for nuclear war, the first Latin American country to have these weapons on its soil.

These new weapons are not in your interest. They contribute nothing to your peace and well being. They can only undermine it. But this country has no wish to cause you to suffer or to impose any system upon you. We know that your lives and land are being used as pawns by those who deny you freedom.

Many times in the past Cuban people have risen to throw out tyrants who destroyed their liberty. And I have no doubt that most Cubans today look forward to the time when they will be truly free—free from foreign domination, free to choose their own leaders, free to select their own system, free to own their own land, free to speak and write and worship without fear or degradation. And then shall Cuba be welcomed back to the society of free nations and to the association of this Hemisphere.

My fellow citizens, let no one doubt that this is a difficult and dangerous effort on which we have set out. No one can foresee precisely what course it will take or what costs or casualties will be incurred. Many months of sacrifice and self-discipline lie ahead—

months in which both our patience and our will will be tested, months in which many threats and denunciations will keep us aware of our dangers. But the greatest danger of all would be to do nothing.

The path we have chosen for the present is full of hazards, as all paths are; but it is the one most consistent with our character and courage as a nation and our commitments around the world. The cost of freedom is always high—but Americans have always paid it. And one path we shall never choose, and that is the path of surrender or submission.

Our goal is not the victory of might but the vindication of right—not peace at the expense of freedom, but both peace and freedom, here in this Hemisphere and, we hope, around the world. God willing, that goal will be achieved.[*1]

American analysts speculated at length on Khrushchev's motives for putting the missiles in Cuba. Some concluded he had wanted to trade off the weapons for a favorable political settlement of the long-time Cold War issue over Berlin; others argued that the principle reason was his need for a "quick fix" to close the missile gap in reverse which had been revealed by the U-2 flights over Russian territory. What was most interesting about these speculations, however, was the lack of concern shown about supposed Russian intentions to convert Cuba into a spearhead of revolution. Arnold L. Horelick, a senior staff member of the RAND Corporation (the private organization most deeply involved in research on defense issues for the government) wrote the closest thing to an official explanation of Soviet intentions:

It is questionable, . . . whether deterrence of a local U.S. attack on Cuba was ever regarded by the Soviet leaders as more than a subsidiary and derivative effect of a venture intended primarily to serve other ends. Certainly the size and character of the intended deployment indicate that it was meant to achieve

---

[*1] U.S. Department of State, *Bulletin*, Volume XLVII, No. 1220 (November 12, 1962), pp. 715–720.

some broader purpose.*¹ Castro has been quoted by a friendly source, the correspondent for *Le Monde*, Claude Julien, as having said that the Cuban leaders had considered among themselves the possibility of requesting that the USSR furnish Cuba missiles, but had not come to any decision when Moscow proposed to emplace them: "They explained to us that in accepting them we would be reinforcing the socialist camp the world over, and because we had received important aid from the socialist camp we estimated that we could not decline. This is why we accepted them. It was not in order to assure our own defense, but first of all to reinforce socialism on the international scale. Such is the truth even if other explanations are furnished elsewhere."

Although Castro subsequently issued a refutation of an American press agency version of the Julien interview (not of the original *Le Monde* article),*² this quotation has the ring of truth. Of course,

*¹ For example, while the threat posed by MRBM's to cities, including Washington, D.C., in the southeastern part of the United States would, if credible, have been adequate to deter a U.S. attack on Cuba, most U.S. strategic bomber and missile bases would have been beyond the range of those weapons. These bases could have been covered by IRBM's.

*² Havana, *Prensa Latina*, March 22, 1963. Specifically, Castro denied only that "I expressed myself in an unfriendly way at any time about Soviet Prime Minister Nikita Khrushchev." Castro's general refutation pointedly referred only to the UPI version of *Le Monde's* article: "I do not believe that Julien, whom we consider a friend of Cuba, can be guilty of untruths like *some* of the statements the UPI attributes to him." (Emphasis supplied.) The March 22 TASS version of Castro's denial *omitted* both of the statements quoted above.

After this article was written, Castro was questioned by two other journalists regarding the origination of the plan to deploy Soviet missiles in Cuba. According to Herbert L. Matthews (*Return to Cuba*, Stanford University *Hispanic American Report* series [1964], 16), Castro stated flatly on October 23, 1963, that "the idea of installing the nuclear weapons was his, not the Russians'." However, three weeks later, according to Jean Daniel's account of his interview with the Cuban Premier, Castro appeared to confirm the account given earlier in the Julien interview: "We thought of a proclamation, an alliance, conventional military aid. . . . They [the Russians] reasoned that if conventional military assistance was the extent of their assistance, the United States might not hesitate to instigate an invasion, in which case Russia would retaliate and this would inevitably touch off a world war. . . . Under these circumstances, how could we Cubans refuse to share the risks taken to save us?" (Jean Daniel, "Unofficial Envoy: An Historic Report from Two Capitals," *New Republic*, December 14, 1963, 18–19.) Matthews writes that he telephoned Castro after Daniel's account was published and was again told: "We were the ones who put forward the idea of the missiles." (*Return to Cuba*, 16.)

the deployment of Soviet missiles in Cuba, to the extent that it would have strengthened the Soviet position in its "world-wide" confrontation with the United States, would also have added credibility to Soviet strategic threats, including the threat to defend Cuba against U.S. attack. In fact, the implication of the official Soviet rationale for deploying strategic weapons in Cuba— namely, that the threat posed to the United States by Soviet weapons *based in the* USSR lacked sufficient credibility to deter a U.S. attack on "socialist" Cuba—is one of the troublesome embarrassments with which Khrushchev has had to deal since the Cuban missile crisis.[*3]

Before the crisis, Khrushchev's expression of strategic support for Cuba were framed in notably cautious and equivocal terms: the USSR's capability to defend Cuba with Soviet-based missiles was affirmed, but a commitment to do so was carefully avoided. Cuban leaders, however, consistently interpreted Khrushchev's words as if they represented a firm, though tacit, commitment. For example, according to Guevara, in January 1961 it was already "well known that the Soviet Union and all the socialist states *are ready to go to war* to defend our sovereignty and that *a tacit agreement* has been reached between our peoples."

It may be assumed that the Cuban leaders had pressed Khrushchev for an explicit and unequivocal commitment to defend Cuba with Soviet-based weapons in the event of a U.S. attack. It was presumably to secure such a commitment, which the Soviet Union was evidently reluctant to give, that Castro in effect volunteered Cuba for membership in the "socialist camp" in 1961. As between an explicit and unequivocal Soviet guarantee, on the one

---

[*3] Khrushchev handled this question gingerly in defending his Cuban policy against Chinese and Albanian criticism in his speech at the Congress of the SED in Berlin on January 16, 1963: "One may object that, under the influence of the most unrestrained incitement, the U.S. imperialists will not keep their promise and will again turn their arms against Cuba. But the forces which protected Cuba now exist and are *growing in strength every day*. It does not matter where the rockets are located, in Cuba, or elsewhere. They can be used with equal success against any particular aggression." (*Pravda*, January 17, 1963; emphasis supplied.) The implicit question is: If so, why were Soviet missiles deployed in Cuba in the first place? The implicit answer is: Soviet-based strategic power was not *then* great enough to deter a U.S. attack, but it is "growing in strength every day" and soon will be (or will appear to be).

hand, and the stationing of Soviet strategic weapons on Cuban soil, on the other, Castro might well have preferred the former under certain circumstances. To the extent that Castro (1) could have had confidence that the Soviet Union would honor such a commitment; or (2) believed that it would be credited to some serious extent in the United States; or (3) believed that a U.S. attack was unlikely in any case, he might not have deemed it necessary to request the Soviet Union to establish strategic missile bases in Cuba and might have been wary of the political consequences of such a move at home, throughout Latin America, and in the United States.

For the *Soviet Union* to propose that its strategic weapons be deployed in Cuba, however, may have been another matter. Let us assume that, regardless of the real intentions of the U.S. Government, Castro believed the probability of a U.S. attack was not negligible. He may have agreed to the Soviet proposal not only because of his dependence on the Soviet Union, but also because, from the Cuban point of view, if the Soviet leaders believed their "world-wide" position *vis à vis* the United States was such that it required reinforcement by drastic means, the reliability of Soviet pledges to defend Cuba with Soviet-based weapons—equivocal pledges to begin with— must have seemed seriously compromised.[*4]

What was the "world-wide" position of the Soviet Union that needed to be reinforced by the emplacement of strategic weapons in Cuba? Despite boastful Soviet efforts to conceal it, the fact is that throughout the cold war the Soviet Union's capacity to strike the United States with nuclear weapons has been very much smaller than the U.S. capacity to strike the USSR. From the start, the bulk of the USSR's strategic nuclear capability has been effective only out to ranges of about 2,000–2,500 miles. The Soviet Union acquired a very potent nuclear capability against Western Europe, first with medium bombers and then with medium- and

---

[*4] In the immediate aftermath of the crisis, the pre-crisis positions of the Soviet Union and Cuba on the firmness of Soviet pledges to defend Cuba were sharply reversed. Whereas the Soviet leaders, presumably to placate Castro, offered increasingly strong pledges to defend Cuba, Cuban leaders ignored them and vowed to resist any U.S. attack with their own resources. Later, however, as Soviet-Cuban relations recovered from the estrangement of the fall of 1962, Cuban leaders began to welcome Soviet pledges with great public enthusiasm.

intermediate-range ballistic missiles of the type it tried to emplace in Cuba. But the Soviet heavy bomber and ICBM forces—that is, the long-range weapons required to reach the United States—did not attain the strength levels that Western observers anticipated they would reach in the 1960's. Inflated beliefs in the West, actively promoted by misleading and deceptive Soviet claims, that the Soviet Union was rapidly acquiring a large intercontinental strike force tended, until the fall of 1961, to deprive continued and even growing U.S. strategic superiority of much of its *political* value. But, in the second half of 1961, the "missile gap" was found, in Secretary McNamara's words, to be "a myth." Confidence in U.S. strategic superiority was restored in the West; moreover, it became apparent, both from Soviet behavior and from the modification of Soviet strategic claims, that the Soviet leaders knew that the West had been undeceived about the strategic balance.

The deployment of strategic weapons in Cuba may have recommended itself to the Soviet leaders as a "quick fix" measure to achieve a substantial, though far from optimal, improvement in Soviet strike capabilities against the United States. Of course, a large increase in the programmed Soviet-based ICBM force would have provided the Soviet leaders with a military capability far more effective (certainly for second-strike purposes) than could be achieved by the emplacement of highly vulnerable MRBM's, IRBM's, and light bombers in Cuba. But such an expansion of the ICBM (and missile-launching nuclear submarine) force could be achieved only gradually and at far greater cost. The Cuban deployment may not have been undertaken as a substitute for such a build-up, but as a stopgap measure, pending its completion.

Certainly the deployment of limited numbers of MRBM's and IRBM's in Cuba would not have solved the Soviet Union's strategic problem. The evident deficiencies of such a force have led some observers to conclude that military considerations were of little importance in the Soviet decision to emplace strategic weapons in Cuba. It is true that the missile sites were soft, very close to the United States, and, after detection, under close and constant surveillance. They would presumably have been highly vulnerable to a U.S. first strike, even with conventional bombs. As a

Soviet first-strike force, the Cuba-based force deployed or being readied as of October 1962 was in itself too small to destroy the U.S. strategic nuclear strike force. Even together with the larger long-range strategic force based in the USSR, it seems most unlikely that the force would have been adequate in the fall of 1962; moreover, there would have been a problem, though perhaps not an insurmountable one, of coordinating salvoes from close-in and distant bases so as to avoid a ragged attack. By the same token, however, the installation of Soviet strategic missiles in Cuba would have complicated a U.S. first strike, improved Soviet capabilities to launch a preemptive attack, and hence reduced the credibility of U.S. strategic deterrence of local aggression, say, in Europe. As to the first-strike potential of Cuba-based Soviet missiles, they could have brought a substantial portion of U.S. nuclear striking power under an attack essentially without warning; moreover, there is no assurance that the build-up would have stopped with the sites already completed or under construction when the Soviets were compelled to abandon the operation.

Whatever their strategic shortcomings, the additional capabilities with which Cuba-based missiles would have provided the Soviet leaders were not insignificant. It is difficult to conceive of any other measure that promised to produce so large an improvement in the Soviet strategic position as quickly or as cheaply. That the Cuban missile deployment would not in itself have provided the Soviet Union with a retaliation-proof first-strike capability against the United States is hardly a reason for dismissing it as of limited strategic importance, as some observers have attempted to do. As the President subsequently said, the Soviet leaders tried materially to change the balance of power. Certainly, the deployment of Soviet missiles in Cuba, in his words, "would have politically changed the balance of power; it would have appeared to [change it] and appearances contribute to reality."

The "world-wide" position of the Soviet Union that needed to be reinforced in the fall of 1962 was not only its strategic position vis-à-vis the United States, but also its position in a range of political issues upon which the strategic imbalance in favor of the United States was having some important bearing. It had become evident, since at least the second half of 1961, that the forward momentum of the Soviet Union in international affairs had largely exhausted itself without yielding the gains which the Soviet leaders had anticipated and the West had feared since the mid-1950's.

These expectations had been fed by mounting evidence of the growing military, scientific, technological, and economic power of the Soviet Union vis-à-vis the West. Some of this evidence was real enough, but much of it, particularly in the realm of strategic power, was illusory. In the framework of the cold war, precisely this realm was central. The effects of other striking achievements, as, for example, in space exploration, were amplified, sometimes out of all proportion to their intrinsic political and military worth, by their presumed bearing on the strategic balance. With the discovery that the "missile gap" had failed to materialize, or had actually materialized in reverse, there was a perceptible change in the world political climate. Western self-confidence was restored and Soviet anxieties must have grown.

Moreover, confident Soviet expectations of a few years earlier in regard to dividends from Soviet military and economic aid to the underdeveloped countries failed to materialize. Western European prosperity had reached a new peak, and despite de Gaulle's intransigence the prospects for growing European economic and political unity must (then, at least) have looked distressingly good to Moscow. At the same time, the unity of the Communist camp was being shattered by the escalating conflict between its two most powerful members. Indeed, the Chinese Communist attack on Khrushchev centered precisely on the unfavorable trend in the cold war which the Chinese attributed to Khrushchev's faulty and overcautious leadership.

Finally, there was the long-smoldering, still unresolved problem of Berlin. After almost four years of threats and retreats, Khrushchev had still not succeeded in compelling the West to accept a Berlin settlement on Soviet terms. Khrushchev may therefore have sought some quick and dramatic means for achieving a breakthrough that would strengthen the USSR's position— militarily, diplomatically, and psychologically—on a whole range of outstanding issues, and particularly on Berlin.*5

*5 A link between the Cuban missile deployment and Khrushchev's Berlin strategy was suggested by the Soviet Government's statement of September 11, 1962 in which the USSR acknowledged that it was providing military

Rarely, if ever, are such fateful ventures as the Soviet strategic deployment in Cuba undertaken to achieve narrow or isolated objectives. Where nuclear weapons are involved, even small risks are acceptable only if important interests can be advanced by assuming them. It is most unlikely that the Soviet leaders drew up a precise blueprint or detailed timetable for exploitation of the improved military-political position they would have attained had the Cuban venture been successful. But they probably anticipated that the emplacement of strategic missiles in Cuba and their acceptance by the United States would contribute in some degree to the solution of a whole range of military-political problems confronting the Soviet Union and would alter the environment of the cold war in such a manner as to promote new opportunities for political gain whose nature could not be precisely foreseen.*6

Horelick's account, complained critics on the left, ignored Cuba. The Kennedy Administration's dedication to the overthrow of Fidel Castro and Cuban socialism was the reason for the missile crisis. And it came about this way: The decisive event "that started everything," according to Castro, occurred when Kennedy conveyed certain exploratory hints to the Kremlin through Khrushchev's son-in-law, Aleksei Adzhubei, in January 1962. Reminding Adzhebei of American restraint in the 1957 Hungarian crisis, the President seemed to be asking for similar Soviet behavior in the event of an invasion of Cuba. The new situation in Cuba, Kennedy supposedly told Adzhubei, was "intolerable."

Informed of this conversation by Adzhubei, the Cuban leader immediately asked the Soviet Union to do whatever was necessary

---

assistance—though of a strictly defensive type—to Cuba, and warned that a U.S. attack on Cuba might unleash the beginning of a thermonuclear war, but at the same time declared a moratorium on new moves in Berlin until after the U.S. Congressional elections. (*Pravda*, September 11, 1962.) Khrushchev may have hoped to discourage any new U.S. action in regard to Cuba until after the elections (i.e., until after MRBM's, at least, became operational) by offering, in return, to desist from fomenting a new crisis in Berlin, and then, after establishing a strategic base in Cuba, to use this new leverage to press for a favorable settlement in Berlin.

*6 "The Cuban Missile Crisis: An Analysis of Soviet Calculations and Behavior," *World Politics* 16 (April, 1964): 363–89.

to deter an American attack. The decision to put missiles into Cuba was a result of this appeal. There may have been other motives for Khrushchev's specific response; indeed, he may have regarded this solution as less provocative than sending a large contingent of troops, given the presence of American IRBMs and MRBMs in Greece and Turkey. Nonetheless, whatever the reason missiles were chosen, the defense of Cuba against American aggression was, said the left, the primary thing on the minds of both Castro and Khrushchev. Professor Leslie Dewart of the University of Toronto has written a lengthy reply to Horelick which also stressed Russian desires to negotiate Cold War issues in a package arrangement. The heart of his argument can be extracted without doing too much damage to the author's purpose:

. . . Castro seems to have granted to the Soviet Union a single-mindedness which may have been his own. This may have been the origin of later difficulties. Castro's uncooperativeness with the subsequent Soviet-American agreement to withdraw the missiles, may have sprung from the fear that Khrushchev had worked out a deal with Kennedy "betraying" Cuba for Berlin, and from the fact that the withdrawal reduced Cuba's defenses against U.S. attack. But some such "betrayal" had been a real possibility ever since Cuba began to rely upon the Soviet Union for support. Castro's behavior since late 1960 through 1962 (e.g. his sometimes exaggerated protestations of Communist belief) becomes intelligible if we remember that abandonment by the Soviet Union had been Cuba's second greatest danger, after the danger of American attack, between February 5, 1960, and October 22, 1962.*[1]

I know of no evidence that the Soviet Union ever intended a simple trade of Cuba for Berlin, or for any other simple strategic advantage such as U.S. bases elsewhere. (I argue solely from in-

---

*[1] Horelick admits that "before the crisis, Khrushchev's expressions of strategic support for Cuba were formed in notably cautious and equivocal terms," and that "it may be assumed that the Cuban leaders had pressed Khrushchev for an explicit and unequivocal commitment to defend Cuba with Soviet-based weapons in the event of a U.S. attack. It was presumably to secure such a commitment, which the Soviet Union was evidently reluctant to give, that Castro in effect volunteered Cuba for membership in the 'socialist camp' in 1961."

dications, not from any supposed Soviet incapability to betray an ally.) On the other hand, there are indications that the objective was both to deter an invasion without a guarantee and to press, from a position of strength, for advantageous settlement of the cold war. Early in October, 1962, and at least once again before mid-month—that is, just before the crisis—the Soviet Union approached the U.S. informally through the UN, suggesting negotiations to "link the questions" of Cuba and Germany. Specific reference was made to the deployment of missiles to Cuba.[*2] The overtures were rejected by the U.S. (We shall see below why.) I do not interpret this offer to mean (as Castro for a time seemed to think) that in exchange for advantages elsewhere the Soviet Union would abandon Cuba to U.S. attack. Not only did the Soviet Union protect Cuba at a late date and despite disadvantages to its prior commitment to peaceful coexistence, but the political disadvantages of such a betrayal would hardly have been overcome by mere concessions in Turkey or Berlin.

Besides, Horelick has rightly pointed out that deterrence of U.S. attack did not require the deployment of the weapons actually sent. By the same token, the Soviet abandonment of Cuba in trade for valuable consideration could have been achieved, if at all, without deploying weapons that exceeded the requirements of deterrence alone. The idea of "linking" the questions of Cuba and Germany makes sense only if the objective was to *solve* the German question and, hence, to settle a—if not *the*—fundamental problem of the cold war. Thus, in the final analysis the hypothesis here suggested is that the objective was to wrap up a "package deal" on Germany and Cuba. For the reasons here explained, it must have appeared to Khrushchev that, paradoxically, it would be easier to negotiate on both questions together rather than separately: the U.S. did not want to negotiate on either, but it might be forced to negotiate on both. The U.S., evidently, would have considered the attainment of this Soviet objective a major defeat for itself.

It is one thing to say with Castro that the missile policy went back to February, 1962, but it is another to suppose that the decision to ship them was made at that time. It was only towards the

*2 Toronto *Globe and Mail*, October 15, 1962.

end of June that Raúl Castro, Cuba's Defense Minister, went to Moscow to initiate talks of stepped-up military aid. In the meantime a general relaxation of Soviet-American tensions did not seem at all impossible in March, 1962. Discussions at Geneva on the conjoined questions of Berlin, a nuclear test ban, and disarmament were proceeding apace.

To the U.S. administration it appeared that the Cuban question could be pursued apart from the Geneva talks. After the "disappointment" of Punta del Este the U.S. had tried to rally NATO support for its Cuban policy, but to no avail. Economic and diplomatic sanctions against Cuba had hurt her, but were obviously not bringing her to her knees. So, on April 10th, Attorney General Robert Kennedy arranged an interview between his brother and José Miró Cardona, the leader of the anti-Castro Cuban exiles. Miró's later contention, that "six divisions" were mentioned during the interview, was never denied; the same figures had been bandied about in other circles at the time. Kennedy did later deny (in 1963, when it became clear that he had given up the overthrow of Castro, and Miró, in protest, revealed his dealings with Kennedy) that he had given his assent to an actual undertaking to Miró. This is, of course, entirely credible. It is intrinsically improbable that a concrete decision to invade would have been taken even at this time. The outcome of Geneva was surely the least that Kennedy would have waited for.

On the other hand, it cannot be doubted that the overthrow of Castro remained Kennedy's objective. Even as public opinion against Castro began to subside in the months after the failure of the U.S. invasion, the same purpose was periodically restated by the administration. Its words were backed by its actions: continuation of a $2,400,000 per year subsidy to the Cuban Revolutionary Council, the maintenance and use of CIA-operated facilities in the Miami area for training exiles in subversive activities, the segregation of Cuban soldiers volunteering for enlistment in the U.S. Army, and the continuation of sabotage, infiltration, coastal raids, air-supply of guerrillas, both by the CIA's own units and by independently operating (but CIA-supplied and supervised) exile groups. The conclusion that armed intervention was being actively though hypothetically considered at this time is the most plausible one.

Ironically, Kennedy's wishes to deal separately with Russia and Cuba began to be frustrated soon. By May 4th, the "package deal" for a settlement of the Berlin question (proposed by the U.S. with British and French support) on the basis of which a detente had seemed almost certain, had completely collapsed. The terms, apparently, had been acceptable to the Soviet Union, but the Bonn government became intransigently opposed. The disarmament conference immediately became deadlocked. The Cold War was on again, and the U.S. was freer to pursue a more decisive Cuban policy—but so was the Soviet Union. Towards the end of June Raúl Castro arrived in Moscow and talked with Marshal Rodion Malinovsky, his Soviet counterpart; on July 3rd he was received by Khrushchev himself. The curtain had been raised on the drama's first act. . . .*3

At certain points the Kennedy-Horelick version of the missile crisis converges with the Castro-Dewart view. Both theories agree that much more than Cuba was at stake. For some years the Russians had lived with American missiles in Greece and Turkey; perhaps Khrushchev simply wanted to bring home some unpleasant facts about the Cold War arms race. If so, however, he could not have chosen a more sensitive spot or one where an American President would have less maneuverability with domestic opinion. But was the Cuban adventure of Nikita Khrushchev part of an ideological offensive as well? Americans thought it was, just as revolutionary insurrectionism was in Southeast Asia. The more dangerous that insurrectionism seemed, the more determined policy makers became to find "Free World" solutions to every crisis. And in the process America became the most counter-revolutionary nation in the world. The more counter-revolutionary America became, moreover, the more Third World leaders saw U.S. policy in Marxist terms. It was a vicious, and, in the nuclear age, highly dangerous circle.

The 1962 crisis had more ancient origins, however, and Kennedy's obsession with Cuba was not unique to him. Other political leaders back to Jefferson's time had pondered the Cuban prob-

*3 "The Cuban Crisis Revisited," *Studies on the Left* 5 (Spring, 1966): 15–41.

lem. What was unique about John F. Kennedy's situation was that he had attempted an intervention, in April 1961, and failed. Before the Bay of Pigs disaster, the new President had looked forward to a meeting with the Russian leader, Nikita Khrushchev, at Vienna. In the wake of the destruction of the 1700-man Brigade by Castro's armed forces, Kennedy felt that he must "prove" himself. Vienna turned out badly. The Russian Premier had tried to bully him, Kennedy told aides. "If Khrushchev wants to rub my nose in the dirt," the President confided to a newspaperman, "it's all over." Khrushchev had wanted to talk about a solution to the Berlin problem, but Kennedy kept coming back to Soviet responsibility for the world revolution. Finally the Russian declared that it would be impossible to work out anything "when the United States regarded revolution anywhere as the result of communist machinations."

Cuba was especially sensitive in this regard. Since 1898 the United States had taken on itself the responsibility for the political and economic welfare of the island. Over the years it had carried out that responsibility by sending in troops to restore order. (The most recent time, in 1933, when American intervention brought to power Fulgencio Batista, no troops were sent; other methods proved sufficient.) For twenty years Batista could count on American economic support. Then in the late 1950s, things began to change. Batista could no longer count on his American supporters; and without them he could no longer hold the lid on. Pressure was put on Batista to hold "honest" elections in 1958; and in the final months of that year an effort was made to persuade him to step down in favor of a "caretaker government unfriendly to him, but satisfactory to us, whom we could immediately recognize and give military assistance to in order that Fidel Castro not come to power."[1]

Batista resisted all these pressures, but had to flee the country when Castro's men threatened Havana itself. What followed has been written about from several points of view, but never more clearly than by another RAND expert, Leland L. Johnson.

When Castro came to power in 1959, the *total* book value of U.S. business enterprises in Cuba was greater than in any other

Latin American country except Venezuela. Table 1 indicates that on a *per capita* basis, the book value of U.S. enterprises in Cuba was over three times the value for the rest of Latin America as a whole. With respect to direct investment flows and undistributed earnings*[1] during the 10-year period 1950–1959, Cuba received well over twice as much per capita as the average for the other countries, as shown in Table 2.

TABLE 1.
Book Value—U.S. Direct Investment Enterprises in Cuba and Other Latin American Countries, 1959

Industry	Cuba (million $)	($ per capita[b])	Other Latin America[a] (million $)	($ per capita[b])
Petroleum	147	22	2,715	15
Manufacturing	111	17	1,285	7
Trade	44	7	592	3
Public utilities	313	47	790	4
Mining and smelting	—[c]	—[c]	1,254	7
Other (primarily agriculture)	341	51	527	3
Total	956	143	7,163	39

[a] Excludes Western Hemisphere dependencies.
[b] Population figures for 1959 used in per capita computations.
[c] Not available separately; included in "other" industries.

Sources: U.S. Department of Commerce, *U.S. Balance of Payments, Statistical Supplement* (rev. edn., Washington, D.C., 1963), 207; and United Nations, *Boletín Economico de América Latina* (New York, November 1960), 8.

*[1] Direct investment flow is loosely defined to include the flow of equity and loan investments from U.S. residents to foreign firms controlled by U.S. interests. The book value of direct investment enterprises includes the U.S. ownership of equity capital, loan capital, branch accounts, and intercompany accounts in foreign firms controlled by U.S. interests. For more precise definitions and a treatment of methodology, see U.S. Department of Commerce, *U.S. Business Investments in Foreign Countries* (Washington, D.C., 1960), 76–85.

TABLE 2.

Cumulative Net Direct Investment and Undistributed Corporate Earnings, Cuba and Other Latin American Countries, 1950–1959

Industry	Cuba (million $)	($ per capita[b])	Other Latin America[a] (million $)	($ per capita[b])
Petroleum	115	19	1,720	10
Manufacturing	56	9	1,250	7
Trade	26	4	494	3
Mining and smelting	—[c]	—[c]	759	4
Other (primarily agriculture)	202	33	359	2
Total	339	65	4,582	26

[a] Excludes Western Hemisphere dependencies.
[b] Population figures for 1950 used in per capita computations.
[c] Not available separtely; included in "other', industries.

Sources: U.S. Department of Commerce, *U.S. Balance of Payments, Statistical Supplement* (rev. edn., Washington, D.C., 1963), 178–207; and United Nations, *Boletín Economico de América Latina* (New York, November 1960), 8.

Moreover, U.S.-owned firms were especially prominent in certain industries. According to a Department of Commerce survey in 1956: "The only foreign investments of importance are those of the United States. American participation exceeds 90 per cent of telephone and electric services, about 50 per cent in public service railways, and roughly 40 per cent in raw sugar production. The Cuban branches of United States banks are entrusted with almost one-fourth of all bank deposits. This intimate economic relationship is so much the outgrowth of mutually helpful association that many of the problems that have plagued less close relationships in others areas have largely been avoided in Cuba."[*2]

U.S. investment in Cuba was far greater, both in total dollar and per capita terms, than was typical in the rest of Latin America. Moreover, Cuba enjoyed one of the highest per capita incomes in Latin America. Yet Cuba is today a member of the Soviet Bloc.

[*2] U.S. Department of Commerce, Bureau of Foreign Commerce, *Investment in Cuba* (Washington, D.C., 1956), 10.

Questions immediately arise about the relationships between U.S. investment and this turn of events. What was Castro's professed attitude toward U.S. business enterprise in Cuba before he came to power? What was the role of U.S. business enterprise in shaping events after he assumed power? How did the presence of U.S. business enterprise affect the bargaining positions of Cuba and the United States during the crucial days of 1959 and 1960 when Cuba was moving rapidly toward the Soviet Bloc?

CUBA AND THE UNITED STATES: 1959–1960

At the time that Castro came to power, after Batista fled Cuba on New Year's Day, 1959, the U.S. business community had little basis for regarding the turn of events with grave misgivings. Castro had not expressed open hostility either to the United States government or to private business interests. On the contrary, during the preceding two years, while he was leading the rebel forces against the Batista regime, he had gone to great lengths to gain sympathy and support from the United States. The considerate treatment of Americans who came into contact with the rebels, the frequent disclaimers of Communist association, and the public pronouncements about democracy, social justice, and economic reform couched in terms of Western tradition, all served to demonstrate a friendly attitude toward the United States. According to one press account of January 8, 1959: "American Ambassador Earl Smith describes the rebels as 'friendly and courteous,' surprisingly capable in preserving order among the populace and exhibiting not the slightest anti-American sentiment. An American banker confesses: 'The way their troops have behaved so far certainly throws dust on the fear that they are a bunch of Communists.' Another Yankee businessman exclaims, 'They're just nice kids.' "[*3]

At the same time, the business community did have some reason to feel uneasy and annoyed. Among other things, Castro had proclaimed in 1953 that under "revolutionary law" (1) workers would have "the right to share in thirty per cent of the profits of all the large industrial, commercial, and mining companies, including sugar mills," and (2) the telephone and electric utilities

[*3] *Wall Street Journal,* January 8, 1959.

would be nationalized with "return to the people of the unlawful excess that they have been charged in their rates."[4] The manifesto of the July 26th movement had condemned the colonial mentality and domination of Cuba by foreign economic interests.[5] Moreover, the rioting, sabotage, and labor strikes during the campaign against Batista had worked to the detriment, at least in the short run, of some business interests. Ruby Hart Phillips reported in 1957: "American businessmen told me that I was contributing to the ruin of the economy by stories of the rebellion. Both American and Cuban businessmen were annoyed. With Cuba as prosperous and money so plentiful, they couldn't understand why anyone would support a revolution. They wanted Batista to crush the Fidel Castro rebellion so they could 'get on with business.' "[6]

In any event, U.S. investors perceived no compelling reason to retrench or pull out of Cuba. Although Castro had left-wing leanings, to be sure, it was not clear that they posed any serious threat to the conduct of business as usual. During 1959, companies went ahead with their investment plans: ironically, U.S. net direct investment of $63 million during that year was even larger than it had been in most of the years since World War II.

Even before the end of 1959 it became apparent that Castro was more hostile towards private investment than was believed earlier. The Cuban government installed "intervenors" to oversee the operations of several large U.S.-owned companies, including the Cuban Telephone Company and the Compañía Cubana de Electricidad.[7] Reductions in telephone and electricity rates and extensions of service were quickly ordered. After passing the Agrarian Reform Law, the government seized lands producing tobacco, rice, and coffee—including large plantations owned by Americans and Cubans. The 20-year 4½ per cent bonds offered in payment came under protest by the U.S. government as not

---

[4] These statements are from Castro's "History Will Absolve Me" speech (October 6, 1953), as quoted in Jules Dubois, *Fidel Castro, Rebel— Liberator or Dictator?* (Indianapolis, 1959), 70–71.

[5] The manifesto is reproduced in Enrique Gonzalez Pedrero, *La Revolución Cubana* (Mexico City, Escuela Nacional de Ciencias Politicas y Sociales, 1959). See p. 89 for the relevant passage.

[6] R. Hart Phillips, *Cuba, Island of Paradox* (New York, 1959), 335–36.

[7] The government intervenors exercised management functions, while ownership remained unchanged.

being "prompt, adequate, and effective compensation."*8 Under new mining and petroleum laws, most of the existing claims were canceled, additional taxes were imposed, and foreign companies began closing down.

Castro's public statements became increasingly bitter about "foreign vested interests" that, being injured by the turn of events, allegedly were trying to destroy the revolution.

> The Premier declared the Revolutionary Government was being accused of communism as a pretext, because foreign vested interests do not like the revolutionary law.
>
> "All the things we do, like reducing rent, distributing land to the peasants and growing rice injure foreign vested interests," he said.*9

In February 1960, Ernesto Guevara, one of Castro's closest associates, challenged the worth of foreign investments: "We maintain the point of view that foreign investments in Cuba, as in all countries of Latin America, under the conditions on which they are made, constitute a great business for the investor, but a bad business for the country." Only a month later he charged: "Our hardest fight is against the North American monopolies. . . . Private foreign capital comes here only for profit and does nothing for the people of Cuba."*10

In February, Anastas Mikoyan arrived in Cuba to negotiate a trade pact covering the sale of Cuban sugar to the Soviet Union for industrial credits and crude oil. This was followed by establishment of diplomatic relations with the Soviet Union and Communist China. At the same time that the Cuban propaganda line was taking on an increasingly Marxist flavor—defending the Soviet Union and condemning the United States at every turn—Soviet technicians began pouring in.

In the face of verbal attack directed at the United States, closer ties with the Soviet Bloc, and expropriation of property, agitation increased in Washington to cut Cuba's sugar quota for the Ameri-

---

*8 *New York Times,* January 13, 1960, 49.
*9 *Ibid.,* October 27, 1959, 3.
*10 *Ibid.,* February 6, 1960, 1, and March 21, 1, respectively.

can market. The 1960 quota had been set, a year earlier, at 3,119,655 tons—59,180 tons *more* than for 1959. According to long-standing agreements with Cuba, the United States paid about two cents a pound above the world market price for sugar coming in under quota—a premium of well over $100 million per year. Castro, bitterly assailing the prospect of a quota reduction as "economic aggression," vowed stern retaliation: "We'll take and take until not even the nails of their shoes are left. We will take American investments penny by penny until nothing is left."[*11]

But before either country acted, a new crisis erupted in mid-1960: the three foreign-owned oil refineries in Cuba (two owned by American interests, one by European interests) refused to refine incoming Soviet crude oil being traded for Cuban sugar. Their refusal immediately led to take-over by Cuban authorities. This was the last straw. The Eisenhower Administration promptly cut the sugar quota by 95 per cent for the remainder of the year—a move resulting in a loss to Cuba of about $92 million in sales to the United States.

Castro lost no time in again assailing the United States for attempting to destroy the Cuban revolution. He complained that when "Cubans were being murdered in great numbers" and when the country was being "sacked" during the Batista era, it never occurred to the "Yankee Oligarchy . . . to have its press write of the horrors in which Cuba lived" or to demand a cut in Batista's sugar quota. The Yankee Oligarchy failed to do these things, Castro asserted, because it "was owner of our lands, our mines, our factories, our commerce, most of our banks, our public services, and withdrew millions of dollars from our economy yearly."[*12]

A month later, in early August, Castro made good his earlier counterthreat when he announced a new expropriation decree covering the telephone and electric utilities, oil refining and marketing facilities, and all U.S.-owned sugar mills on the island. The properties, valued at about $750 million, represented about two-thirds of the total value of U.S. private investment in Cuba. The announcement marked the beginning of the "Week of Jubilation." Immediately the Cuban press and radio hailed the nationalization

---

[*11] *Ibid.*, August 21, 1960, Section III, 1. See also June 24, 1960, 1.
[*12] *Ibid.*, July 8, 1960, 1.

as marking the "final independence of Cuba": "In Havana, repair trucks of the Cuban Telephone Company, . . . one of the concerns nationalized, raced through the streets filled with celebrating employes. The workers blew the horns of the vehicles, beat on the sides of the trucks with sticks and kept up a shout of, 'Cuba yes! Yankees no!' "*13

At the close of the "Week of Jubilation," the Confederation of Cuban Workers called for the enlistment of workers' and peasants' milita against any aggressor who, by means of direct intervention or counterrevolution, sought to destroy or subvert the Revolutionary Government. The meeting called for renewed vigilance against counterrevolutionaries, propagandists, saboteurs, and conspirators, and promised "to silence them with our reply or deliver them to revolutionary authorities."*14 Simultaneously, the Popular Socialist Party (the Cuban Communist Party) announced the first national assembly since it had been forced underground by the Batista regime. Foreign observers from around the world were invited to attend.

A few weeks later, while foreign ministers of the Organization of American States were meeting in Costa Rica to consider the threat of the Soviet presence in the Western Hemisphere, Castro affirmed his friendship with the Soviet Union and the Chinese People's Republic. In a lengthy speech, broadcast by radio and television, he again assailed the OAS and the United States, declaring that the strength of the revolution would carry the nation to final victory over its enemies. Among other factors of strength, Castro pointed out that the revolution "took away the lands of the big property owners and the American companies."*15 Addressing the United States, he declared that the people of Cuba ". . . no longer believe in your philosophy of exploitation and privilege, or in the philosophy of gold, the gold that you rob from the work of other people; no longer are we disposed to follow the orders of your ambassador. . . . [Nor] do we believe in your false Pan Americanism with which you cloak the system of oppression and abuse, the system of domination that you have introduced

*13 *Ibid.*, August 9, 1960, 3.
*14 *Ibid.*, August 14, 1960, 1.
*15 *Ibid.*, August 25, 1960, 12.

among our divided peoples of America. . . . [No longer will Cuba be] an appendage of your economy nor will Cuba ever again vote in the United Nations as you indicate but will vote as our dignity and conscience indicate."*16

Facing the increasing hostility of the Cuban regime, with its closer ties to the Soviet Bloc, the U.S. government contemplated new measures to reduce the threat of a Communist-oriented Cuba in the Western Hemisphere. In late August, the Senate voted to cut off foreign aid funds to any nation supplying arms or economic assistance to Cuba. In October, the United States imposed an embargo on exports to Cuba, covering everything except food and medicine.

The Cuban government then seized most of the remaining large private properties on the island. These included banks, and commercial, industrial, and transportation enterprises—about 20 of which were owned by U.S. interests. Only about 200 small U.S. enterprises were left in the hands of their owners.

In short, the year 1960 saw a rapid deterioration in relations between the United States and Cuba. Threat was met by counter-threat, punitive action by counteraction, and all the while Cuba drew closer to the Soviet Bloc. In the words of Tad Szulc: "From the time the Cuban sugar quota was cut, a physical clash between the United States and Cuba, directly or indirectly, was unavoidable. As it began to run out of its patience and tolerance toward Castro, the Eisenhower Administration, in the late spring, 1960, set up training camps in Guatemala for a rebel Cuban force to be used in a contingency of one sort or another. Soon, it was tacitly accepted on both sides that an invasion was inevitable sooner or later, and that it was only a question of time before it came."*17

U.S. BUSINESS ENTERPRISE AND THE EVENTS OF 1960

A critical aspect of the revolution involved Castro's ability to transfer the hatred his followers felt for Batista to hatred of the U.S. government and its business interests. In the beginning, the

*16 *Ibid.*
*17 Tad Szulc, *The Winds of Revolution* (New York 1963), 135.

revolution was directed against the brutal suppression and terrorism of the Batista regime. Although the rebels resented U.S. support of that regime, they did not wage a strong anti-American campaign. On the contrary, they vied with Batista for sympathy and aid from the United States. Castro's early support among Cuban intellectuals and professional classes was not predicated on the notion that Cuba must follow the Soviet economic pattern or that the United States was an implacable enemy. It was their hope of freeing Cuba from Batista and achieving a measure of political democracy, social justice, and sound economic reform within the framework of Western ideology that served as a primary source of revolutionary strength.

When Castro mounted his anti-American campaign in late 1959 and 1960, he lost support among the intellectual and professional groups, as the flight of thousands to Miami would suggest. But he was able to maintain influence, especially among the poorer classes, during that critical period within which the character of the revolution was radically transformed. In depicting the United States as the "aggressor," as the "rapacious and exploiting imperialist" in league with Batista, he was able to keep his hold over the masses through 1960, consolidate his power, and move firmly into the Soviet Bloc.

For our purposes, a fundamental question relates to the role that U.S. business enterprise may have played in the anti-American campaign. To what extent did the composition and level of U.S. business investment make it vulnerable to Castro's assaults? More specifically, what was it about the character of U.S. enterprise, if anything, that made its interests easily identifiable with those of the Batista regime? In 1960, to what extent did the apparent hostility of the U.S. government to the revolution seem (to Castro's supporters) to be motivated by the desire to defend U.S. private business interests? To what extent was U.S. enterprise vulnerable to the charge that it contributed to foreign economic domination of Cuba?

Investment in Public Utilities

An examination of the composition of U.S. investments in Cuba may provide some clues to the answers. In the first place, note in Table 1 above that the book value of U.S. public utilities investments comprised about one-third the total value of U.S.-owned Cuban investments in 1959; on a per capita basis, U.S. investments in public utilities were over ten times larger in Cuba than in other Latin American countries. The concentration of U.S. investment in public utilities may have been unfortunate from the standpoint of U.S. national interests, insofar as investment in public utilities industries became intimately associated in the minds of Castro's supporters with the Batista regime. These industries by their very nature are ones of large, noncompeting firms that must operate essentially as monopolies if they are to be economically efficient. Because competition cannot be relied upon to ensure performance in the public interest, governments typically step in to regulate the industries directly. In some cases, especially in the United States, governments establish regulatory agencies to supervise privately owned utilities. In other cases, governments both own and operate the utilities. In Cuba, the role of the Batista government as regulator of the foreign privately owned utilities made the industry vulnerable to accusations that it was in league with the Batista regime, and that it was an enemy of the revolution. Purely by matter of coincidence, a regulated public utility can appear to be embroiled in local politics and scandal, through no fault of its own, simply because of its special relationship with the host government.

A specific case in point involves the rate increase granted in 1957 by Batista to the Cuban Telephone Company. On economic grounds the rate increase may have been long overdue and entirely justified in terms of promoting new investment in the industry.*18 Yet, certain evidence suggests that the environment in which the increase was granted created an unfavorable pyscho-

*18 Many economists have observed that rates of return to public utilities are typically held to very low levels by Latin American governments. On the on hand, these enterprises face criticism for the poor service they render; on the other hand, they cannot render better service because the rates they are allowed to charge consumers are too low to cover an expansion of investment. (See D. F. Cavers and J. R. Nelson, *Electric Power Regulation in Latin America*, Baltimore 1959.) According to one source, the rate of return of the Cuban Telephone Company over a 38-year period was only about 4 per cent—far below the rate generally allowed in the United States. (*New York Times*, October 13, 1960, 34.)

logical effect that was conveniently exploited by Castro in later years.

On March 13, 1957, a poorly planned and coordinated attack was made by Cuban rebels on the presidential palace in an unsuccessful assassination attempt against Batista. The president escaped, reinforcements of loyal troops were rushed to the scene, and by the time the firing had ceased, 25 rebels were dead. A few hours later an opposition leader, Pelayo Cuervo, was brutally murdered. According to some writers, the order for the murder had come from Batista himself on the heels of the palace attack.[19] Cuervo had been "an honest, respected, and courageous lawyer."[20] He had achieved widespread recognition in filing a brief against former President Grau, alleging that he had stolen over a hundred million pesos from the public treasury. And not long before he was murdered, Cuervo had declared that he was about to start similar proceedings against Batista. Moreover, about a year before his assassination, Cuervo had filed another suit "to block a proposed increase in the rates of the American-owned Cuban Telephone Company. . . ."[21] According to one account:

> The murder of Cuervo shocked the people of Havana. There was no statement from the palace or from any government official condemning it. . . .
>
> On the morning of March 14, hours after the attack on the palace and the reprisal murder of Pelayo Cuervo, American Ambassador Arthur Gardner entered the still bullet-marked palace with officers of the economic staff of the embassy, to be present at Batista's signing of a new contract with the Cuban Telephone Company. The effort of Gardner to help Batista convey an impression both at home and abroad that things were normal in Cuba at that moment neither ingratiated him and the State Department with the people of the country nor enhanced the popularity of the Cuban Telephone Company. . . .[22]

[19] Robert Taber, M-26: *The Biography of a Revolution* (New York 1961), 124; Dubois, 154.
[20] Dubois, 153.
[21] Taber, 125.
[22] Dubois, 155–56.

In all likelihood, the new telephone contract had been negotiated long before the palace attack. It was undoubtedly a coincidence that the formal signing came just after the time of the attack and Cuervo's murder. But that is the point—simply by being closely associated with a host government, as is necessary with regulated public utilities, the company can become a victim of circumstances.

When Castro accused the United States and its vested economic interests of supporting Batista, the association between the public utilities and the Batista government lent plausibility to the argument. And when he accused the United States and its business interests of trying to destroy the revolution, this was also a plausible argument; since the companies were presuambly being hurt by Castro's early decrees, it was only natural (so Castro's supporters easily could be led to believe) for these business interests and the United States government to be hostile toward the revolution.

Besides their special association with the Cuban government, the public utilities were in a sensitive position simply because the services they supplied *were* so basic both to the industrial development of the economy and to the direct satisfaction of consumer needs. Being vital in both urban and rural areas alike, they were a conspicuous, though perhaps unjust, target for consumer complaint about services and rates. The political sensitivity of the utilities and the vital character of their services made them convenient focal points for attack during the revolution itself. It is notable that even as early as 1953 Castro had called for nationalization of the telephone and electric companies and a reduction of rates. After he came to power, his first actions against U.S. companies included intervention in the Cuban Telephone Company (in March 1959), cancellation of the telephone rate increase that had been granted by Batista, and reduction of electric utility rates.*[23]

The Sugar Economy

Table 1 also discloses that a large proportion of U.S. investment in Cuba was also concentrated in agriculture—primarily sugar

*[23] For a discussion of these events, see Freeman Lincoln, "What Has Happened to Cuban Business?" *Fortune* (September 1959), 110ff.

production. Although U.S. participation in Cuban raw-sugar production had declined from the levels of the 1930's, it still amounted to about 40 per cent of the total in the mid-1950's. Moreover, seven of the ten largest *latifundias* were owned by U.S. interests.*24 In 1955, the total sales of U.S.-owned agricultural enterprises in Cuba were responsible for nearly one-half the total sales of *all* U.S.-owned agricultural enterprises in Latin America.*25

From the standpoint of comparative advantage in international trade, Cuba's advantage may very well have been in sugar. By exporting sugar, which could be produced cheaply, and importing goods that other countries could produce more cheaply, Cuba may have been able to enjoy a higher aggregate national income than would otherwise have been forthcoming. If so, it was only natural for U.S. capital to be attracted to sugar, as the operations of the market mechanism, presumably reflecting national comparative advantages, would make sugar production relatively profitable in Cuba.*26

Of course, the major difficulty with this point of view is that aggregate national income is only one measure, and frequently a poor one at that, of a nation's economic welfare, and it may have little to do with the nation's political welfare. Long-run *growth* rates of income, income distribution, unemployment levels, and the level of perceived social justice are just a few of the factors that cannot be disregarded in any meaningful appraisal of the Cuban revolution. Although concentration on sugar production may have been a wise choice from the standpoint of Cuba's aggregate national income, it also generated a serious employment problem because of the seasonal nature of the crop, and it made Cuba's prosperity greatly dependent on its export trade. The U.S. Depart-

---

*24 Samuel Shapiro, "Cuba: A Dissenting Report," *New Republic*, September 12, 1960, 12.

*25 U.S. Department of Commerce, Office of Business Economics, *U.S. Investments in the Latin American Economy* (Washington, D.C., 1957), 47.

*26 One might argue that in terms of dynamic comparative advantage, as distinguished from the static case, perhaps Cuba's advantage was not so clearly in sugar. But we need not treat the possibility here. Rather the point made below is that even if concentration in sugar *was* in Cuba's economic interests (measured in terms of aggregate gross national income), it raised political problems and may have worked to the detriment of the United States during the revolution.

ment of Commerce reports that in 1953, for example, Cuban unemployment fell to a minimum of 8.4 per cent of the labor force during the height of the sugar harvesting season, but then rose to 20 per cent of the labor force during the rainy or dead season—as compared with the U.S. unemployment rate of 2.4 per cent in that year.[*27] Cuba's exports, of which sugar products comprised almost 90 per cent in 1952, contributed between 30 and 39 per cent of its national income in 1952–1954: ". . . almost all the activities of the island are geared to the rise and fall in the volume and value of export crops. When demand and prices abroad are favorable, all sectors of the Cuban economy are prosperous, but when conditions abroad are unfavorable, the economy has very little to cushion the effects."[*28]

Moreover, Cuba was highly dependent on the United States both for her export markets and for imports into Cuba of other products. In 1951–1953 about 59 per cent of the value of Cuban exports went to the United States, and about 76 per cent of the value of its imports came from the United States.

When Castro complained about the domination of the Cuban economy by the United States, and when he declared that Cuba would no longer be an "appendage" of the U.S. economy, the existing pattern of economic activity gave his argument an air of plausibility in the eyes of his followers. The economic dependence of Cuba on the United States, the one-crop seasonal nature of the Cuban economy, the discontent and misery of the unemployed, all contributed to a frustration and resentment exploited by Castro in his battle with the United States.

To take a case in point, the theme of land reform appears throughout the literature of the revolution. Constant reference is made to the alleged maldistribution of land in Batista's day and the plight of the landless peasant. One writer observes: "Seventy-five per cent of an agricultural country the size of England, with a population half again that of Ireland, was owned by eight per cent of the property holders, a few dozen rich Cuban families and the

---

[*27] U.S. Department of Commerce, Bureau of Foreign Commerce, *Investment in Cuba* (Washington, D.C., 1956), 5.
[*28] *Ibid.*, 7 and 139.

giant U.S. and Cuban sugar and cattle companies. Tens of thousands of rural Cubans lived in misery on marginal lands, in swamps and in the trackless mountains where their fathers and grandfathers had been driven by the ruthless expansion of the sugar monoculture, which produced sugar to rigid quotas and let millions of acres of land lie fallow to become overrun by brush and weeds."*29

During Castro's expropriation program, it may have been politically disadvantageous to the United States to have so much of Cuba's sugar production in the hands of U.S.-owned firms. Inasmuch as the land reform did injure U.S. agricultural interests in Cuba, and inasmuch as the U.S. government did seek to protect these interests (by protesting the inadequate measures of compensation), it was not difficult for Castro to make a plausible and (superficially) convincing case that the "State Department" and "Wall Street" were in league to defeat the revolution. The problem here, as in the case of public utilities, is that a good deal of U.S. investment was concentrated in an area that would be especially affected by the basic reforms being preached even before Castro came to power in 1959. When the time came for the anti-American campaign, it fitted in nicely with Castro's purposes to argue that the agricultural interests owned by foreign "monopolists" stood in the way of reform—if reforms were instituted, these interests would be hurt and, naturally, they would fight back. All the more reason, he argued, to seek help and friendship from the sympathetic Soviet Bloc in struggling against these "enemies of the revolution."

Even the favorable price and tariff treatment accorded Cuban sugar was attacked. Besides paying the price premium of two cents a pound, the United States accorded preferential tariff treatment to imports of Cuban sugar. Altogether the sugar premium and the preferential tariff were worth about $150 million a year to Cuba. At the same time, Ernesto Guevara condemned the sugar price and quota system as "economic enslavement" because these benefits were allegedly offset by reciprocal demands by the United States for preferential Cuban tariff treatment towards U.S. manu-

*29 Taber, 303.

factured products, "making it impossible for native products of the manufacturers of other countries to compete."*30

Investment and U.S. Foreign Policy

In conclusion, the foregoing discussion suggests that the presence and character of U.S. investment in Cuba did play a role in Castro's ability to maintain a measure of popular support while simultaneously waging his propaganda campaign against the United States and moving toward the Soviet camp. But we should note that there were many sources of friction between Cuba and the United States that are not obviously related in a direct way to the presence and composition of U.S. investment. And these sources, too, Castro sought to exploit. For example, the following are notable as factors that generated resentment and distrust toward the United States:

1. The sale of arms by the United States to Batista until 1958 and maintenance by the United States of a military training mission in Cuba until Batista fled the island.

2. The U.S. denial of the sales of arms to Castro and attempts to prevail upon European governments to do likewise.

3. The apparent friendliness of U.S. ambassadors to Batista that lent an "official" stamp of approval to the Batista regime.

4. The shock expressed by the American press toward the political executions carried out by Castro during his early months in power, while the press had paid little attention to the countless murders committed during the Batista period. Why were these executions any different, many Cubans reasoned, from the executions of German war criminals after the Nuremberg war trials?

5. The haven given to numerous "Batistiano" refugees by the United States, and the alleged freedom they were given to plot counterrevolutionary activities.

6. The scattered bombings of Cuban properties by small private planes flying out of Florida, and various covert counterrevolu-

*30 *New York Times*, March 5, 1960, 1.

tionary activities that were alleged to have the approval of the U.S. government.

One could maintain that these sources of friction existed quite apart from U.S. private investment activity and that they also contributed to Castro's propaganda campaign. While private investment may also have played a role, it was only one of many factors —and it is impossible to weigh the importance of each factor in the whole chain of cause-and-effect relationships.

At the same time, we could ask why, in the minds of Castro's followers, the United States seemed to be motivated to undertake these measuers that appeard so hostile to the revolution. For Castro, the answer was easy: the motivation stemmed from the desire to protect U.S. business interests that were being hurt by the revolution, and to protect the dependent colonial status of Cuba that allegedly had worked to the economic benefit of the United States at the expense of Cuba. In this sense, the factors listed above *were* related to the presence and nature of U.S. business activity in Cuba. *Quite apart from the question as to whether this explanation was actually the basis for U.S. government policy at that time,* the critical point to remember is that the objective nature of relations between the United States and Cuba made it easier for Castro's followers, at his prodding, to *believe* that the motivation of the United States stemmed from a desire to protect its economic interests. . . .*[31]

Johnson's very careful distinction between what Castro's followers *believed* was the basis for American policy, and what may *actually* have been the policy leaves open the question of motivation. Perhaps, on the other hand, it poses the wrong question. On April 8, 1961—just a few days before the American-sponsored Bay of Pigs invasion attempt—Dr. Jose Miro Cardona, the spokesman for the anti-Castro Cuban Revolutionary Council, accused Fidel of destroying the "free-enterprise system." "We emphatically assure those who have been unjustly dispossessed that all their assets shall be returned. . . . We shall encourage investment in

*[31] Leland L. Johnson, "U.S. Business Interests in Cuba and the Rise of Castro," *World Politics*, XVII (April 1965): 440–459.

private property, both national and foreign, and we shall give complete guarantees to private enterprise and to private property."

Kennedy insisted in his first State of the Union message, on January 30, 1961, that "Our objection with Cuba is not over the people's drive for a better life. Our objection is to their domination by foreign and domestic tyrannies. Cuban social and economic reform should be encouraged. Questions of economic and trade policy can always be negotiated. But Communist domination in this Hemisphere can never be negotiated." Efforts by other Latin American countries to mediate the disputes over economic and trade issues met a chilly reception in the United States. President Kennedy and his advisers took the position that Castro and communism were problems for all the hemisphere. On Cuba, however, there were two choices by 1961: Castro or Cardona, the revolution or the restoration of private enterprise. In effect what Kennedy demanded was that Castro give up the revolution; then the United States would negotiate questions of economic and trade policy.

History was indeed "repeating itself" in Cuban-American relations. In 1898 the United States promised Cubans the opportunity to determine their own future, but the restrictions imposed by the Platt Amendment reduced that freedom to a point where Cuban political growth was badly stunted. Politics on the island became primarily a question of "ins" and "outs," with the latter only too willing to blame the United States for all the ills which soon beset the new nation. Serious political discussion, moreover, had to begin with Cuba's relationship to the United States. And that, of course, is the essence of colonialism and the colonial mentality. Cubans and Americans alike were thus trapped in a situation with no way out except revolutionary change.

Cuba had been one, if not *the* major issue in the presidential campaign of 1960. Party politics dictated that the Democrats hammer on the Cuban issue, just as the Republicans had scored the Democrats in 1952 over China. In the later stages of the campaign, moreover, Kennedy was running hard after the conservative vote. Yet there is no reason to believe that the Democratic candidate was hiding his true feelings about the Cuban issue, or that it was not closely related to his other policy views.

At times it seemed that Kennedy had forgotten all about Richard Nixon, and was campaigning against Nikita Khrushchev.

At the University of Kentucky on October 8, 1960, the Democratic nominee declared:

We ran on the New Freedom. We ran on the New Deal. We ran on the Fair Deal and this year we run on the New Frontier.

In the 1930's Stanley Baldwin, speaking at a comparable time in the life of England, said that English frontiers were on the Rhine. Now, in 1960, American frontiers are on the Rhine and the Mekong and Tigris and the Euphrates and the Amazon. There is no place in the world that is not of concern to all of us.

Ten days later at Jacksonville, Florida, Kennedy suggested the economic aspects of this worldview:

The world economy is becoming increasingly interdependent. We cannot change this. I therefore favor expansion of our foreign trade and private investments abroad.

The "Republican Recession" of 1958-1959 was linked to the world situation on several occasions. At Canton, Ohio, Kennedy said:

Only the power and determination of the American Republic stands between the increasing menace of militant communism and world domination. History and events, as well as our own deep determination, have committed us to the defense of freedom. We cannot meet that commitment with idle plants and idle men. We cannot meet it with a stalled economy.

Then in New Orleans:

We can produce so much in the United States that the only way we can maintain our economy is to have an effective trade, not only with Europe, but also with Latin America and the Far East.

Finally, on the eve of the election, November 7, 1960:

When I began my campaign for the Presidency I said that just as the issue of the campaign 100 years ago was whether the United States would continue half slave and half free, the issue of this campaign was whether the world would continue half slave and half free, or whether it would move in the direction of freedom or the direction of slavery. . . .

But if we do respond, if we release the great untapped vitality and strength of our society, if we revive the American spirit that conquered the old frontiers, then we will cross the New Frontier to realize the unparalleled opportunities for freedom that lie ahead.

Khrushchev's appearance in New York to attend a meeting of the United Nations General Assembly at the height of the campaign gave Kennedy an opportunity to castigate Republican failures. The State Department had announced that Khrushchev, and Fidel Castro, who was also coming to the meeting, would be confined to Manhattan Island. Kennedy had a field day with that announcement, asserting that Manhattan Island was the only place where the Republicans had succeeded in containing the Communists:

In 1952 the Republicans ran on a program of rolling back the Iron Curtain in Eastern Europe. Today the Iron Curtain is 90 miles off the coast of the United States. Is there any American who feels more secure today than he did 10 years ago?

The last few years have seen a steady increase in the power and prestige of the Communist world. I think it is time we reverse it. We may be able next week to confine Mr. Khrushchev to the island of Manhattan, and Mr. Castro to the island of Manhattan, but we have not confined Mr. Khrushchev in Africa, and we have not confined Mr. Castro in Latin America. I think it is time that this country started to move again.

Throughout the Eisenhower years, Secretary of State John Foster Dulles had devoted much of his attention to what he called the dynamic independence movements in the Middle East, Africa, and the Far East. He was perfectly aware that the "containment" policies of the Truman Administration held little attraction for nations emerging from colonial status. He found it much harder, however, to fashion a policy that would be more successful. "I'm not absolutely sure that we can win this contest," Dulles once confided to an aide. "You know, it's like getting a bunch of people who are suffering from malnutrition, rickets, all sorts of congenital ailments—who are weak—and saying, 'What you ought to do is play rugby football. Come on, get in there, out on the field. Tackle each other. Be rough and tough.' Well, you know this is madness. But after all, you say to them, 'Have a free competitive system.' And they say, 'Good God, there must be a better way of doing things.' Furthermore, you say, "The way to build up your industry is to . . . become capitalists, invest—and so on. But they want a steel mill overnight. They want public utilities. They want everything. . . ." Communists were free with their promises, concluded Dulles, but that did not make it any easier for the United States. "This is a tremendous difficulty in trying to save souls for political freedom, when the devil has so much on his side."[2]

These doubts notwithstanding, Dulles continued as a preacher of the gospel of free enterprise (American style) throughout his career as Secretary of State. At times his opponents were not simply the godless Communists, but the old European colonial powers who had given capitalism such a bad name in the first place. The "Eisenhower Doctrine" for the Middle East, promulgated in the aftermath of the disastrous Suez crisis, was a good case in point.

The image of John Foster Dulles, the narrow moralist and chief prosecutor of "neutralism," must be adjusted somewhat

187

in view of the preceding statements. For all of Kennedy's sophistication, and the cleverness of the New Frontiersmen, Dulles in his private moments could see the main weakness in the American position more clearly.

American policy in the Middle East, both before and after Suez in 1956, was aimed at achieving a posture independent of that of the colonial powers.

British Prime Minister Harold MacMillan's dour comment on the Eisenhower Doctrine sums up the European view of the successor power in the Middle East:

. . . An important development was taking place in American policy. While maintaining, at least outwardly, an almost fanatical devotion to the infallibility of the United Nations in all questions great and small, whether of faith or morals, they now began to develop what was soon to become known as the "Eisenhower Doctrine." At the very beginning of the year [1957] the President, seeing the power gap which was developing in the Middle East and realising at long last the danger of growing Russian infiltration, asked Congress for authority to fill this dangerous breach in the defences of the free world. The unnatural flirtation, amounting to a liaison, if not a legal marriage, between the Russian and American representatives at the United Nations, was now beginning to cool. The State Department seemed to realise the danger, and even to reproach us, in private, for not having persisted in our military occupation of Egypt. There were two main aspects in the new doctrine as presented by the President. First, he was to have power to use the armed forces of the United States

to secure and protect the territorial integrity and political independence of any [Middle-Eastern] nation or group of nations requesting such aid against overt armed aggression from any other nation controlled by international Communism.

Secondly, a further $200 million was voted, apart from any other appropriations, as additional aid to such countries as were under pressure.

This gallant effort to shut the stable door after the horse had bolted was welcome to us, for it at least marked a return to the world of reality. The conditions were, of course, limiting. An American intervention had to follow an invitation; but with all the resources of diplomacy, overt and covert, this should not present too great a difficulty. The precise meaning of "aggression" even as interpreted by Dulles's explanations in Committees of Congress was obscure. Was the subversion of a Government by the usual Communist methods to be regarded as an act of aggression? The recent cases of Czechoslovakia in 1948 and of Hungary in 1956 were in all our minds. How would they have appeared in terms of this new theology? These questions were often asked and seldom answered. Nevertheless, as a whole, the Eisenhower Doctrine was greeted by Western Europe with a certain wry satisfaction. At least it avoided the vetoes of the Security Council or the resolutions of the Assembly. All the precious dogmas which had hitherto been sacred were now, it appeared, made subservient to the real interest of the United States and her allies. We had no objection. Yet we could not help observing that the promulgation of this new tenet on 5 January and its acceptance by the House of Representatives on 30 January and even its final endorsement, after much controversy, by the Senate at the beginning of March did not change the attitude of Washington in regard to past events or towards actions taken by their allies. Dulles, somewhat to our amazement, declared: "Unless we move quickly into the area the situation will be lost." But that applied only to American troops, navies and armies. Here a certain latitudinarianism was allowable; other nations must adhere to the full orthodox creed, first formulated at San Francisco after the war, and now enshrined in the vast glass temple of the United Nations in New York.[1]

Macmillan was right on several counts. Congress, especially the Senate, had been reluctant to give the President new authority for dealing with specific Middle-Eastern problems. The vagueness of the President's request, the domestic political ramifications of Middle Eastern questions, and the general wariness it had displayed when confronted with the complexities of Arab

[1] Harold Macmillan, *Riding the Storm, 1956–1959* (New York, Harper & Row, 1971), pp. 213–214.

world politics, all worked against the idea. Dulles was troubled by these same questions, but remained convinced that the United States must "do something," and that it must be done alone. "If I were an American boy . . . I'd rather not have a French and British soldier beside me, one on my right and one on my left." With that beginning, the Senate hearing on the proposed Eisenhower Doctrine was bound to be interesting. The setting was the post-Suez Middle East, the aftermath of a disastrous Anglo-French-Israeli invasion of Egypt aimed at forcing Nasser out of power and returning control of the Suez Canal to an international organization dominated by European interests. An enforced Soviet-American collaboration distasteful as it was had forced the invaders to withdraw their troops, and the crucial question was (as Americans saw it): Which superpower would succeed to the position once held by the colonial powers of the Ninteenth Century?

As the testimony developed, it was clear that Dulles had in mind a program that would (1) divorce American policy from the Europeans' policy and (2) maintain the internal security of friendly nations and check Nasserite ambitions. Early on, Senator Hubert Humphrey asked the question that was bothering most of the members of the Senate Foreign Relations Committee:

I am not arguing about whether or not we ought to be doing this. What I really asked about was what happened, what is the immediacy, what happened here in recent weeks that we ought to know about that made it so much more grave in light of Soviet intentions?

SECRETARY DULLES: Well, the events are, in the main, Senator, things that we all read about in the newspapers. Certainly, the events of the last 2 months, 10 weeks, have been such as to totally alter the situation in this Middle East part of the world, and it has altered it in a sense which initially, at least, is very much in favor of international communism.

It has greatly hurt the prestige and the authority of the Western peoples, the Europeans, and in much of the world, including that part of the world, the United States is colloquially known as a European. In much of Asia and Africa we are lumped in on the general term "Europeans." And I do not really think that there can be very serious doubt in the mind of anyone who follows events, as I know all of the Senators do, that there has been a cataclysmic change in the situation in the Middle East within the last few weeks.

Now, President Eisenhower thought of calling a special session of Congress to deal with this situation the latter part of December. But it seemed, in view of the Christmas holidays and the fact that the Congress would, in any event, shortly be in session, that the situation could wait over. But he obviously did not think it could wait very long because the first act he took, even before the State of the Union message, was to present this situation to the Congress just as quickly as the Congress could be organized; and I really believe that the need of the area—I have had some of these Ambassadors come to see me, and they just said unless the United States is going to do something more, make its position more clear, "We do not think that our governments can hold on in a policy which is reflective of the hopes and aspirations of the free nations of the world."

That is just the fact. Perhaps they should not be so frightened, but the fact is that they are, and the fact is that they need the kind of reassurance that would come from this kind of legislation. . . .

Then it was Senator Estes Kefauver's turn to raise a related question:

SENATOR KEFAUVER: Mr. Dulles, what worries me about this program is that we are undertaking unilaterally, by ourselves, a program for the protection of the sovereignty of the nations of the Middle East, which is primarily, of course largely, for the benefit of Western Europe, without their being a part of it, without having discussed the matter with their foreign ministers or prime ministers.

If we get in trouble there or into a war, who is obligated by alliance, by treaty, by agreement, to join us or help us in this undertaking? Who can we look forward to calling up to assist us?

SECRETARY DULLES: Well, Senator, let me say first, you say we are undertaking this for the benefit of Western Europe. That is in a sense true, but only in a sense—we are really undertaking it for the benefit of the United States—because our interest in this respect coincides with that of Western Europe.

Let me also say that if Europe, Western Europe, were, as you put it, a part of this plan, then I can say to you it would be absolutely doomed to failure from the beginning, because a plan for the Middle East of which certain of the most interested Western European nations are a part will not succeed, and I think that they would be the first to recognize that fact; indeed, are the first to recognize that.

Recent events have made it such that a plan of which they are a part, or which they appear to be the partial sponsors of, just would not succeed.

I happened to be looking last night at the scrapbook of my wife's about my first trip out to Cairo in May 1953, nearly 4 years ago, and the whole burden of the rather unfriendly reception that I got from the press there was that we were there just in the interests of the British and the French, and there was a cartoon, for instance, of Churchill putting a mask over my face and saying, "Can't you go out there and fool the Egyptians into thinking that you are independent?" And I was presented as their stooge.

It is very difficult to appreciate, perhaps, from here the strong emotion which there is on that matter. It was very strong even 4 years ago; it is much stronger today. . . .

Almost inadvertently, Senator Henry Jackson, who was probing for the answer to another question, posed the most fundamental issue of all:

SENATOR JACKSON: I am trying to get at the urgency of this situation. I want to say that I agree with the need for strong and determined policy, and I want to try to support a good, strong stand in the middle East, but we are getting a lot of mail and we have to answer our constituents.

. . . I do not want to be repetitious, but do you feel that the situation is more critical now, say, than it was in September or October [the time of the Suez crisis]?

SECRETARY DULLES: As far as the danger of the area falling under control of international communism, there is no doubt whatsoever in my mind that it is far more critical.

Since he had already testified that there seemed no likelihood of a Soviet military attack in the near future, this answer required a rather elaborate explanation. But in giving it, Dulles found himself in deep waters:

SENATOR JACKSON: How about the military threat?

SECRETARY DULLES: The Soviet military threat?

SENATOR JACKSON: International communism, that is the way you are using it. You don't use "Soviet" in the resolution?

SECRETARY DULLES: I say countries controlled by international communism.

SENATOR JACKSON: Yes. Well, they are synonymous, but for the purpose——

SECRETARY DULLES: No, it is much broader. For instance, China we consider controlled by international communism.

SENATOR JACKSON: You feel that Red China is now independent of the Soviet Union or not subject to their domination at the present time?

SECRETARY DULLES: We believe that both Russia and mainland China are subject to the control of international communism.

SENATOR JACKSON: Who controls international communism?

SECRETARY DULLES: Well——

SENATOR JACKSON: Well, is it a joint operation between Russia and China? Are they operating jointly, do you think, as copartners now?

SECRETARY DULLES: International communism, Senator, is a phrase which I assume has a meaning from the standpoint of the Congress because it uses it very frequently, and the phrase "countries controlled by international communism" is a phrase which we did not invent. We picked it out of the present Mutual Security Act as a phrase which Congress——

SENATOR JACKSON: We want to know what it means in connection with this legislation.

SECRETARY DULLES: It means the same thing here, Senator, exactly as it meant and means in the Mutual Security Act.

SENATOR JACKSON: What did it mean in the Mutual Security Act?

SECRETARY DULLES: Congress passed the act and I assume knows what it meant.

SENATOR JACKSON: You folks in the executive branch administer it. What does it mean?

SECRETARY DULLES: Well, international communism is a conspiracy composed of a certain number of people, all of whose names I do not know, and many of whom I suppose are secret. They have gotten control of one government after another. They first got control of Russia after the First World War. They have gone on getting control of one country after another until finally they were stopped. But they have not gone out of existence.

International communism is still a group which is seeking to control the world, in my opinion.

SENATOR JACKSON: I am not going to get into a long philosophical discussion on it.

SECRETARY DULLES: You can have a long discussion, Senator, on whether or not the Russian State controls international communism or international communism controls the Russian State. There are all kinds of books and theses written about it. Stalin wrote a book about it. You can argue about that one for a long time. But I think the meaning is reasonably clear because it has been used by the Congress and is a well-known phrase.

SENATOR JACKSON: Would you not agree on this: that international communism has been used to date as an instrument of Russian foreign policy since 1918?

SECRETARY DULLES: I would put it the other way around.

Russian foreign policy is an instrument of international communism. I may say the Caracas resolution which was also endorsed I think unanimously by the Congress, talks about the danger of international communism getting control of political institutions.

SENATOR JACKSON: Do you think Tito still influences Russian foreign policy?

SECRETARY DULLES: No; I do not think Tito is controlled by international communism. He is communistic but he is not controlled by international communism.

SENATOR JACKSON: Since when do you think that has been true?

SECRETARY DULLES: Since he broke with the Cominform in 1948, I believe it was. . . .*1

If this line of questioning suggested a dialogue from a James Bond thriller, the Secretary's concern was nonetheless only too real. Anti-communism might be the best way to sell a new initiative in foreign policy. But Dulles did feel the Communist threat as a very personal challenge, whether it emanated from Moscow or from some hidden Communist headquarters filled with electronic gadgetry. After all, successful revolutionaries, no matter how little aid or encouragement they had received from the Soviet Union, would link up with the Kremlin as soon as they took power, wouldn't they? Even if Nasser had put Egyptian Communists in prison, he had given the Soviets new influence

*1 U.S. Congress, Senate, Committee on Foreign Relations, *Hearings: The President's Proposal on the Middle East*, 85th Cong., 1st Sess. (Washington, D.C.: Government Printing Office, 1957), pp. 76–77, 99–100, 175–77.

and prestige in the Middle East, by his arms purchases from the Communist bloc in Eastern Europe. Still, Senator Sam Ervin was not entirely satisfied:

SENATOR ERVIN: So I come back to my original question, Mr. Secretary, and I think it is also a very simple question: The reason we do not join the Baghdad Pact and line ourselves up with the countries which have already manifested their willingness to stand by the free world at any possible Armageddon with Russia, is because we are afraid that we will anger or irritate some other countries in the Middle East which have not been willing to stand up beside the free world; is that not true?

SECRETARY DULLES: No, sir. We have announced in no uncertain terms our support for the Baghdad Pact countries. It is true that we do not want to become involved in Arab politics, which the Baghdad Pact is also involved in.

SENATOR ERVIN: Absolutely. And that is what you will get us embroiled in under this resolution.

SECRETARY DULLES: No, sir. It just keeps us out of being embroiled in it.

SENATOR ERVIN: You were asked a number of times what expenditures you proposed to make of the $200 million in the event —or in the release from restrictions, and you suggested only one, and that was this: You suggested it might partly be used, in part, to bolster the security forces of each individual nation of the Middle East, so that their government might not be overturned by internal forces; did you not? Did you not state that, make that suggestion?

SECRETARY DULLES: I said one of the purposes would be to sustain the internal security forces of these countries; yes, sir.

SENATOR ERVIN: So that their governments could be stabilized against internal forces; did you not use those terms?

SECRETARY DULLES: I think so; yes.

SENATOR ERVIN: Yes.

So that would put us having Uncle Sam sticking his nose in all of the nations of the Middle East in order to maintain the status quo; would it not? And if that would not mess us up in Arab politics, what would it do?

SECRETARY DULLES: I think that to maintain a government which is strong enough not to be overthrown by subversion is not to become involved in Arab politics.

SENATOR ERVIN: Well, it certainly is taking the side of that government against the side of the people of that country which do not want that government; is it not?

SECRETARY DULLES: I think to maintain security forces, to maintain law and order in the country, is something which is entirely appropriate for us to assist in. We are doing that all around the world.

SENATOR ERVIN: You could do that by strengthening the internal forces, that is, the security forces, of those nations, so that they could prevent their own people from overthrowing those governments; could you not?

SECRETARY DULLES: I do not believe that the kind of internal security forces we are trying to build up here would be used against the general will of the people unless it is stirred up and organized by international communism. That is the great danger, and if that is the purpose of it, then we want to have forces to resist them.

SNEATOR ERVIN: Well, still, Mr. Secretary, you tell me that you do not think you are interfering with the politics of a country, that the United States would be interfering in the politics of a country and the Arab politics, if it happened to be an Arab country, if it used money which belonged to the taxpayers of the United States to strengthen the security forces of those countries so they could prevent the people of those countries from overthrowing the government? You do not think that would be any involvement in Arab politics if it happened to be an Arab country where that was done?

SECRETARY DULLES: No, sir. Let me illustrate.

You have got pretty substantial security forces in Egypt. Those did not prevent the change of the Government of Egypt from Naguib to Nasser.

SENATOR ERVIN: Well, that is beside the point.

You are not proposing, are you, to go in there and use some of this aid to strengthen Nasser's internal forces, his internal security forces, are you? I say you do not propose to take some of this money, if this restriction is taken off, to go into Egypt to strengthen the security forces of Nasser; do you?

SECRETARY DULLES: We have no present plans to do that; no.[*1]

The Suez Crisis of October–November 1956 had seen Dulles's hopes for joining Arab nationalism to American policy interests finally come a cropper. He had even designed a regional security system based on the models for the Pacific (SEATO) and Europe (NATO), which would integrate the entire area into a solid anti-communist front.

But on October 29, 1956, the Israelis launched their attack against Egypt; two days later the British and French followed suit, under the pretext of neutralizing the Suez Canal. Their real objective, however, was nothing less than the overthrow of Nasser himself. Eisenhower was furious. He warned the British that the United States would not shrink from its obligation to go to the aid of a victim of aggression. How? asked the British *chargé d'affaires*, who had been called to the White House to receive this message. "We plan to get to the United Nations the first thing in the morning," the President replied, " . . . when the doors open, before the U.S.S.R. gets there."

American policymakers had several grievances against their European allies. First, London and Paris could not have picked a worse time to undertake this folly. It was election time in the United States, but even worse, the Russians were able to divert attention from their own embarrassments in Eastern Europe, where they were brutally suppressing a rebellion in Hungary. The

[*1] *Ibid.*, pp. 344–45.

Soviets had suddenly appeared in the Middle East as champions of Arab nationalism against a renewed imperialist menace. Soviet Premier Nikolai Bulganin even addressed a public note to Prime Minister Anthony Eden which threatened: "There are countries which need not have sent a navy or air force to the coasts of Britain but could have used other means, such as rocket techniques." It was crude rocket-rattling, but it ensured that the Russians would receive part of the credit (at least) when the Allies were forced to withdraw.

In Eisenhower's circle of advisers, a similar suggestion was blurted out, half serious, half frustrated: "I've been trying to think of what we should *do*. Well, perhaps, this is the time for a—let's call it a 'Bomb for Peace.' It's as simple as this: let's send one of Curt LeMay's gang over the Middle East, carrying an atomic bomb. And let's warn *everyone*: we'll drop it—if they *all* don't cut this nonsense out."[3] The suggestion was greeted with pained silence, but it underscored the difficulty the Administration was having with its Middle-Eastern policy.

Nasser's seizure of the Suez Canal on July 26, 1956 had set in motion the final sequence of events leading to the Anglo-French-Israeli invasion, but the background complications read like a tale from the *Arabian Nights*. To begin with, Nasser had justified his action as the direct result of Secretary Dulles' seemingly abrupt decision not to supply American money to build a high dam on the Nile River at Aswan. This decision was not an abrupt one; indeed it had been developing over several months, but it was true that Dulles had made it seem abrupt during a stormy interview with the Egyptian Ambassador on July 19, 1956 —just a week before Nasser announced the "nationalization" of the Canal. Advised by his English and French counterparts to "play it long," Dulles' indignation at a supposed Egyptian threat to accept a loan (on better terms) from the Russians had led him to cut off the Ambassador with a sharp rebuke.

The ill-fated Aswan loan project had originated in late 1955, when Egypt approached the British government seeking funds for a dam to harness the power of the Nile and convert hundreds of thousands of acres of floodlands into cultivatible territory. Russian interest in Egypt, the continuing Arab-Israeli problem, and Anglo-American rivalry further complicated the situation.

Nevertheless, Dulles seized on the project as a final effort to redirect the restless energy of the nationalist forces into an economic outlet that would contribute to the modernization of the Egyptian economy. Equally important, by putting the right strings on the money, America could check Nasser's propensity for playing the two sides—Communist and anti-Communist—off against each other. Nasser called it positive neutralism; Dulles labeled it sheer opportunism of the worst sort.

On December 17, 1955 the State Department announced that the United States and Great Britain had "assured the Egyptian Government . . . of their support in this project, which would be of inestimable importance in the development of the Egyptian economy and in the improvement of the welfare of the Egyptian people." Financial experts estimated the total cost of the dam at something over $1.3 billion, of which it was expected that the United States would put up $400 million as its share of the loan. When the Egyptian leader saw the contracts drawn up for his signature, however, he balked at stipulations that would have prevented him from purchasing arms on credit from the Soviet bloc.

After some hard bargaining sessions, Nasser said he was ready to sign on the dotted line in February of 1956. Dulles, meanwhile, had encountered new difficulties on Capitol Hill. What effect the combination of Congressional opponents to the Aswan Dam had on the Secretary's calculations of success still seems impossible to tell, but Nasser's recognition of Communist China was a big disappointment to Dulles, almost as big as the disappointment he felt at Cairo's decision to purchase arms from Czechoslovakia.

After all, the Secretary had put heavy pressure on the British to withdraw their forces from Suez. And he had gone out of his way to demonstrate his concern for the success of the Egyptian revolution. One of Dulles's first trips abroad after becoming Secretary of State in 1953 had been to the Middle East. His report to Eisenhower stressed two obvious factors: American support for the State of Israel, and the Arab belief that the United States was in league with the British and French. Both hindered American efforts to work with Middle-Eastern leaders. The whole area, he concluded, was caught up in a fanatical revolutionary spirit that led these countries to "magnify their immediate problems and depreciate the basic Soviet threat."

The situation was already at the crisis level, requiring the United States to "increase its influence in the Middle East at the earliest possible moment." The most likely spot for Communist penetration in 1953, however, was not Egypt, but Iran. Under the leadership of Premier Mohammed Mossadegh, the Iranian government had nationalized the Anglo-Iranian Oil Company in 1951, thereby creating a situation in which the United States could not help but alienate either the Iranians or the British—and very probably both. Mossadegh's local supporters, the leftist Tudeh Party, viewed the expropriation as only the first step in the reordering of Iranian society from top to bottom. Western views of the Tudeh Party and Mossadegh were, as one might expect, colored by the geographical proximity of Iran to the Soviet Union (they share a common border for 1,000 miles) and the proven oil reserves of Iran, said to total 13 per cent of the world's holdings at the time of nationalization.

For more than a year American diplomats worked on a compromise which would have granted the Iranians greater control over the development of their petroleum resources while avoiding the "serious effects of any unilateral cancelation of clear contractual relationships. . . ." Mossadegh had appealed to the United States for funds, and Eisenhower had finally given him a flat "No" for an answer. Although the following account leaves out the commonly acknowledged participation of the Central Intelligence Agency in Mossadegh's final overthrow, the President's *Memoirs* accurately describe the stakes of the confrontation:

Another troubled area that compelled our concern during 1953 was Iran—a country of 19 million people which shares a border with the Soviet Union and which holds beneath its soil a large percentage of the world's reserves of oil.[1]

In 1909 the Anglo-Persian Oil Company was formed, to take

[1] In 1947, for example, half the entire crude oil and natural gas produced in the Middle East came from Iran.

over the operation of a sixty-year concession under which it had exclusive rights to explore and exploit the oil of southern Iran. The British government controlled 52 per cent of the stock in the company. In 1949 the company negotiated an agreement with the Iranian government under which it would pay the government 25 to 30 percent of its net profits. Under the powerful pressure of members of the Moslem clergy, and members of the Tudeh (Communist [sic]) party—outlawed because of an attempt to kill the Shah in 1949—the Iranian government failed to ratify this agreement and on May 2, 1951, put the entire oil industry of the country under national ownership.

The leader of this drive was Iran's Premier, Dr. Mohammed Mossadegh, a semi-invalid who, often clad in pajamas in public, carried on a fanatical campaign, with tears and fainting fits and street mobs of followers, to throw the British out of Iran, come what might. "It is better to be independent and produce only one ton of oil a year," he said, "than to produce 32 million tons and be a slave to Britain."

In October of 1951 the British shut down Abadan, the world's largest refinery, on the Persian Gulf, and the last British employees and their families sailed for home. The British government, supported by other governments of the West, clamped a boycott on all Iranian oil. For two years the British and Iranians stayed at loggerheads. No oil flowed through the southern Iranian pipelines to the Abadan refinery and to the waiting tankers which would carry it to the homes and factories of the West. No oil royalties flowed in the opposite direction into the treasury of the government of Iran, which from this great natural resource had previously received as much as 30 per cent of its national income and 60 per cent of its foreign exchange. To most Iranians outside Teheran, living at a subsistence level off the land as in the days of Cyrus, this deadlock probably meant little. And to many Englishmen, it meant only that the oil came from Kuwait or Saudi Arabia—alternative sources under British control—rather than from Iran. But the disagreement was dangerous; it could not go on forever. . . .

Early in January of 1953, while I was still living on the Columbia University Campus, I received a cable from Premier Mossadegh, who by that time was ruling the country by decree. In his cable, three pages long, he congratulated me on the election results, and then plunged into an extended dissertation on the problems of Iran, which he feared had already been presented to me by those who did not see eye to eye with him on his country's future:

I dislike taking up with you the problems of my country even before you assume office. I do so partly because of their urgency and partly because I have reason to believe that they have already been presented to you by those who may not share my concern for the future of Iran and its people.

It is my hope that the new administration which you will head will obtain at the outset a true understanding of the significance of the vital struggle in which the Iranian people have been engaging and assist in removing the obstacles which are preventing them from realizing their aspirations for the attainment of . . . life as a politically and economically independent nation. For almost two years the Iranian people have suffered acute distress and much misery merely because a company inspired by covetousness and a desire for profit supported by the British government has been endeavoring to prevent them from obtaining their natural and elementary rights.

I immediately assured Dr. Mossadegh in an answering cable that I had in no way compromised a position of impartiality and that no one had attempted to prejudice me in the matter. I expressed the hope that our own future relationships would be completely free of any suspicion, and said I would be delighted to receive either personally and directly, or through established diplomatic channels, any communication of his views on any subject in which we might have a common interest.

In January of 1953 the Iranian parliament extended Mossadegh's dictatorial powers for another year. The following month, Mossadegh, pushing his strength, denounced the Shah, the constitutional monarch, for intrigues with "foreign interests." Pressed by Mossadegh, the Shah on February 28 announced he would abdicate "for reasons of health." This brought on serious riots;

the Shah's supporters, along with rival supporters of Mossadegh, choked the streets. As a result, in a direct challenge to Mossadegh, the Shah within hours canceled his plan of abdication.

Meanwhile, the United States ambassador in Iran, Loy Henderson, presented proposals to Mossadegh in an effort to get him and the British to cooperate in some solution to the oil problem. Under one of these proposals, a consortium of oil companies would replace the Anglo-Iranian Oil Company and buy oil from Iran's nationalized industry. Mossadegh contemptuously turned this suggestion down as a "form of plunder." On May 28 Premier Mossadegh once again wrote me a long personal message, referring back to his earlier communication:

During the few months that have elapsed since the date of that message the Iranian people have been suffering financial hardships and struggling with political intrigues carried on by the former oil company and the British government. For instance, the purchasers of Iranian oil have been dragged from one court to another, and all means of propaganda and diplomacy have been employed in order to place illegal obstacles in the way of the sale of Iranian oil. Although the Italian and Japanese courts have declared Iranian oil to be free and unencumbered, the British have not as yet abandoned their unjust and unprincipled activities.

Although it was hoped that during Your Excellency's administration attention of a more sympathetic character would be devoted to the Iranian situation, unfortunately no change seems thus far to have taken place in the position of the American government. . . .

As a result of action taken by the former company and the British government, the Iranian nation is now facing great economic and political difficulties. There can be serious consequences, from an international viewpoint as well, if this situation is permitted to continue. If prompt and effective aid is not given this country now, any steps that might be taken tomorrow to compensate for the negligence of today might well be too late. . . .

Then he made a direct appeal:

> The Iranian nation hopes that with the help and assistance of the American government the obstacles placed in the way of sale of Iranian oil can be removed, and that if the American government is not able to effect a removal of such obstacles, it can render effective economic assistance to enable Iran to utilize her other resources. This country has natural resources other than oil. The exploitation of these resources would solve the present difficulties of the country. This, however, is impossible without economic aid.
>
> In conclusion, I invite Your Excellency's sympathetic and responsive attention to the present dangerous situation of Iran, and I trust that you will ascribe to all the points contained in this message the importance due them. . . .

I refused, however, to pour more American money into a country in turmoil in order to bail Mossadegh out of troubles rooted in his refusal to work out an agreement with the British. Accordingly, on June 29, I replied:

> The failure of Iran and of the United Kingdom to reach an agreement with regard to compensation has handicapped the government of the United States in its efforts to help Iran. There is a strong feeling in the United States, even among American citizens most sympathetic to Iran and friendly to the Iranian people, that it would not be fair to the American taxpayers for the United States government to extend any considerable amount of economic aid to Iran so long as Iran could have access to funds derived from the sale of its oil and oil products if a reasonable agreement were reached with regard to compensation whereby the large-scale marketing of Iranian oil would be resumed. Similarly, many American citizens would be deeply opposed to the purchase by the United States government of Iranian oil in the absence of an oil settlement. . . .
>
> I fully understand that the government of Iran must determine for itself which foreign and domestic policies are likely to be most advantageous to Iran and to the Iranian people. In what

I have written, I am not trying to advise the Iranian government on its best interests. I am merely trying to explain why, in the circumstances, the government of the United States is not presently in a position to extend more aid to Iran or to purchase Iranian oil.

In case Iran should so desire, the United States government hopes to be able to continue to extend technical assistance and military aid on a basis comparable to that given during the past year. . . .

A crisis was approaching. Three months earlier Mossadegh had tried to get the parliament to pass legislation making him Commander-in-Chief of the Iranian Army, replacing the Shah in this position. The parliament refused. On July 19, therefore, Mossadegh called for the dissolution of the Majlis, the second house of the Iranian parliament, and for a plebiscite to be held August 2. Less than a week after this announcement, reports were coming in that Mossadegh was moving closer and closer to the Communists. More and more, he was refusing to crack down on violent Tudeh-party demonstrations in the streets. And, one report said, he was looking forward to receiving $20 million from the Soviet Union, which would keep his treasury afloat for the next two or three months. By the end of July the Tudeh party came out openly for Mossadegh, the Soviet Union sent a new and hopeful ambassador to Teheran,[*2] and the Shah, his life in danger, was forced to take refuge.

In the plebiscite three days later Mossadegh got 99.4 per cent of the votes. Iran's downhill course toward Communist-supported dictatorship was picking up momentum.

For the Shah, the time had come to check that course. As he later told an observer, Mossadegh had become "absolutely mad and insanely jealous, like a tiger who springs upon any living thing that it sees moving about him." Mossadegh, the Shah thought, be-

[*2] "Negotiations initiated by the Soviet Union are now being conducted [with Iran]," Malenkov said in a speech to the Supreme Soviet on August 8, "for the settlement of certain border problems and also mutual financial claims. We anticipate that the negotiations will be successfully concluded. Recently [June 12] a mutually advantageous agreement was reached on increasing trade between both countries."

lieved that he could form an alliance with the Tudeh party and then outwit it; but in doing so, the Shah recognized, Dr. Mossadegh would become to Iran what the ill-fated Dr. Beneš had been in Czechoslovakia—a leader whom the Communists, having gained power, would eventually destroy.

The Shah, however, decided not to conduct a military coup; instead he resolved to do what the Constitution permitted him to do—appoint Mossadegh's successor. He decided on a general named Fazlollah Zahedi.

This critical decision made, the Shah left for his palace on the Caspian Sea. From there on August 13 he sent his letter appointing Zahedi, giving it to a trusted Army colonel, who was to deliver it to Zahedi. Zahedi, in turn, sent the colonel to break the news to Mossadegh. A day went by. Nothing happened: the colonel got to Teheran too late to make the delivery. The second day was a holiday; again nothing happened. By the third day Mossadegh's spies had brought him the secret, and when the colonel showed up at his house to deliver the sad word, Mossadegh had him arrested.

The three days of delay had been disastrous. Mossadegh began arresting everybody he could get his hands on. For forty-eight hours his mobs ran through the streets rioting, smashing statues of the Shah and his father, and screaming, "Death to the Shah!" On the morning of August 16 the Shah left his Caspian Sea palace in a Beechcraft with one pilot, one palace official, and his Queen. At ten-fifteen he landed in Baghdad. On that day he obviously believed he would probably never return to his homeland.

But we did not stop trying to retrieve the situation. I conferred daily with officials of the State and Defense departments and the Central Intelligence Agency and saw reports from our representatives on the spot who were working actively with the Shah's supporters.

Then, suddenly and dramatically, the opposition to Mossadegh and the Communists—by those loyal to the Shah—began to work. The Iranian Army turned against officers whom Mossadegh had installed. The Army drove all pro-Mossadegh demonstrators off the streets, leaving them open to anti-Mossadegh rioters who swarmed through government buildings, and looted and burned Mossadegh's residence. General Zahedi rumbled through the avenues of Teheran in a tank and led in the capture of the main

Iranian radio station. Rumors spread that the Shah, by then in Italy, was coming back.

The next day, Mossadegh, in pajamas, surrendered. He was placed under arrest. Zahedi's forces rounded up and jailed the Tudeh leaders. It was all over.

Throughout this crisis the United States government had done everything it possibly could to back up the Shah. Indeed, some reports from observers on the spot in Teheran during the critical days sounded more like a dime novel than historical fact. On the Shah's return, I cabled him, as well as General Zahedi, my congratulations.

Further encouraging news reached me at the beginning of September in Colorado. There I received from Bedell Smith, Under Secretary of State, a memorandum prepared by an American in Iran, unidentified to me, who had seen General Zahedi, the new Premier, and the Shah a few days earlier.

According to the American, the Premier was particularly appreciative of the message I had sent. He believed that prompt and substantial assistance from the United States—assistance which would produce immediate and visible results—was essential to Iran.

General Zahedi, our informant wrote, had no love for the British. But he recognized the importance of establishing good relations with them and repeated over and over again his strong desire for the resumption of diplomatic contact and for an oil settlement as soon as possible.

This was good news, but what followed in the memorandum, concerning the Shah personally, was even more heartening. I reproduce this verbatim as I read it in the Colorado Mountains because it represents the kind of clear and succinct reporting by an observer that enables a recipient to evaluate a distant situation, particularly when he has some personal knowledge of the principal character himself.

The Shah is a new man. For the first time, he believes in himself because he feels that he is the king of his people's choice and not by arbitrary decision of a foreign power. The Shah is not bitter about the past, but does feel that both Britain and America—but especially Britain—have made mistakes and interfered unwisely in Iran in the past. He also feels that promises have been made to him by the United States which were not honored. He recognizes now his debt to us and hopes, as he puts it, that we have a realistic understanding of the importance of Iran to us.

Like General Zahedi he stressed the urgent need for prompt and substantial economic aid. He also spoke to me of military aid, a subject on which he has become more realistic in recent years. He no longer talks of jet planes and hundreds of tanks, but does talk of the equipment and training assistance needed to produce crack mountain troops. He is fully aware of the importance of the army to the security of his country and is also convinced—as are many members of our military mission—that with the proper help Iran can become a significant link in the Free World's defense.

The Shah was obviously determined to provide the leadership his country needed and was counting on us to give him the necessary help. He sent a message to me expressing a hope that between us we could change the whole strategic picture in the Middle East by taking advantage of the Iranian renaissance.

The same American also reported that on his way home he had discussed Iran with Winston Churchill. The Prime Minister, he said, understood the necessity for prompt economic aid to Iran without waiting for either the restoration of diplomatic relations with Britain or an oil settlement. In fact, Winston said emphatically that if it were necessary, he himself would provide economic aid to Iran before the restoration of diplomatic relations, although he did not explain how this might be accomplished. We had a wonderful and unexpected opportunity in Iran which might change the whole picture in the Middle East, he continued, and he concluded by asking our correspondent to tell me that he was feeling much better and could "hang on as long as may be necessary."

On the fourth of September, Ambassador Loy Henderson and Premier Zahedi exchanged letters to the effect that the United States could now continue its planned technical-aid program of $23.4 million for the current fiscal year. Largely as a result of a letter which I had received from Premier Zahedi on August 25, outlining the country's difficulties and need for aid and desire to align itself with the freedom-loving countries of the world, I decided that under the circumstances the technical-aid program as planned was insufficient. I announced on September 5 an additional $45 million for emergency economic assistance. In all, American aid to Iran that fiscal year came to nearly $85 million.

On October 8 I wrote in my diary:

Now, if the British will be conciliatory . . .; if the Shah and his new premier, General Zahedi, will be only a little bit flexible, and the United States will stand by to help both financially and with wise counsel, we may really give a serious defeat to Russian intentions and plans in that area.

Of course, it will not be so easy for the Iranian economy to be restored, even if her refineries again begin to operate. This is due to the fact that during the long period of shutdown of her oil fields, world buyers have gone to other sources of supply. These have been expanded to meet the need and now, literally, Iran really has no ready market for her vast oil production. However, this is a problem that we should be able to help solve.

On December 21, 1953, an Iranian court sentenced Mossadegh to three years in solitary confinement. In 1954 the country held new elections. And in August of that year the Iranian government reached an agreement with an international consortium to buy Iran's oil.

Under a special ruling by the Department of Justice, based on the national-security needs of the United States, American oil companies participated in this consortium without fear of prosecution under antitrust laws.

For the first time in three years Iran was quiet—and still free.[3]

Eisenhower's overly modest remarks about "our representatives on the spot who were working actively with the Shah's sup-

[3] Dwight D. Eisenhower, *The White House Years: Mandate For Change, 1953–1956* (Garden City, N.Y.: Doubleday & Co., 1963), pp. 159–166.

porters" should not obscure two important facts: (1) It was the United States, not Britain, which decided when and how the Shah should be supported; and, (2) the consortium which replaced the Anglo-Iranian Oil Company represented a clear triumph of American interests over *both* Russian and British interests. American money poured into Iran over the succeeding years, even though the consortium agreement provided the country's treasury with more than $300 million a year. The effort to make Iran a "significant link" in the "Free World's defense" never panned out. Dulles tried to make Cairo the site of a Middle-East defense pact, but that never worked out either. The colonial taint was still too evident.

In the midst of all the turmoil of the 1956 election campaign and Nasser's bold assertion of Egypt's right to nationalize the Suez Canal, Dulles paused to reflect on another crisis in which America had been "caught in the middle between the new nationalism and the old colonialism." The scene was Indo-China; the event the fall of the French fortress at Dienbienphu to the Vietminh guerilla army. Even with half of Vietnam now gone, Dulles told another Eisenhower aide, "We have a clean base there now, without a taint of colonialism. Dienbienphu was a blessing in disguise."

No one in Washington felt that way at the time; the Administration was filled with gloom. Since then, however, the tide of revolution had been stemmed, if not actually reversed. Much to everyone's surprise, the American-installed President of South Vietnam, Ngo Dinh Diem, had not only survived but had prospered. It took money—a whole lot of money. But Diem's government had stabilized the situation throughout South Vietnam and rebuffed Ho Chi Minh's demands for all-Vietnamese elections.

Dulles believed that his strong stand against Communist China over the tiny islands of Quemoy and Matsu in the Formosan Straits had represented the turning point. "Of course, of all the things *I* have done," Dulles told this same aide, "I think *the most brilliant* of all has been to save Quemoy and Matsu."[4] His listener was stunned: How could anyone think that "going to the brink" over two islands was anything but sheer adventurism?

Dulles saw the situation in an entirely different light. Both he and President Eisenhower were fully aware of Chiang Kai-shek's motivation in keeping large garrisons on Quemoy and Matsu to harass shipping into Amoy and Foochow, and as a staging point for guerilla raids onto the mainland. When Dulles went out to Formosa in January 1955, he went in search of an agreement that Nationalist China would not attempt to launch further offensive actions against the Communists without American approval. The Formosa Resolution, which Dulles then presented to Congress, authorized the President to employ the armed forces of the United States as he deemed necessary to defend Formosa and "closely related localities." It was, said the Secretary of State in testifying for the resolution, a "reasonable and prudent" understanding.

Thus was born the Formosa Resolution of 1955, the first of a threesome which would also include the 1957 Eisenhower Doctrine and the 1964 Gulf of Tonkin Resolution. The first crisis in the Formosan Straits soon ended when Chinese Foreign Minister Chou En-lai told the delegates to the 1955 Bandung Conference of neutrals that China did not want to go to war with the United States, and would actively seek a *détente* in the straits area. Dulles had "saved" Quemoy and Matsu by taking a strong stand against both Chinese parties.

"A great danger in Asia," the Secretary had asserted in a speech to the Foreign Policy Association of New York on February 16, 1955,

is the fear of many non-Communist peoples that the United States has no real intention of standing firmly behind them. Already that fear has mounted to the danger point.

We accepted in Korea an armistice which the Chinese Communists boisterously misrepresent as a "victory" for them. We acquiesced in an Indochina armistice which reflected the defeat of the French Union forces at Dien Bien Phu. We aided the Tachen evacuation. The reasons were compelling; nevertheless the result added a few square miles to the Communist domain.

If the non-Communist Asians ever come to feel that their Western Allies are disposed to retreat whenever communism threatens the peace, then the entire area could quickly become indefensible.

That was the real reason why the Formosa Resolution was necessary. Dulles and other American policymakers thought it significant (particularly in this light) that the Communist Chinese had begun their bombardment of the two islands on September 8, 1954, the day that the Southeast Asia Treaty Organization (SEATO) came into being. It was a bittersweet time for Dulles, however, who felt that if Britain and France had cooperated earlier, all of Vietnam might have been saved.

As it was, the SEATO pact contained a protocol which extended the treaty benefits to Cambodia, Laos "and the free territory of Vietnam." "The Indochina Armistice created obstacles to these three countries becoming parties to the Treaty at the present time," admitted the Secretary. "The Treaty will, however, to the extent practicable, throw a mantle of protection over these young nations." Dienbienphu had fallen on May 7, 1954. On July 20, the French Government signed an "Agreement on Cessation of Hostilities" with Vietminh representatives at a conference sponsored jointly by Great Britain and the Soviet Union.

The Geneva Conference, from start to finish, was regarded by American policymakers with a baleful eye. Bad enough that the French had gotten themselves into such a mess, largely by their own short-sightedness, but the spectacle of Chinese Communist Foreign Minister Chou En-lai meeting on equal terms with the Big Powers was just too much. The American delegate did not sign the armistice agreement, but pledged to do nothing to disturb its operation. Yet there was room for maneuver—at least according to American interpretations of the document. Dulles's later reference to South Vietnam as a "young nation" along with Cambodia and Laos was the American interpretation of the armistice agreement, which provided only for a "provisional" demarcation line at the 17th Parallel. All Vietnamese elections were supposed to be held not later than 1956.

The Secretary's attitude toward those (or any) Vietnamese elections had already been foreshadowed in a press conference held on May 11, 1954, only four days after the fall of Dienbienphu. The discussion was on future prospects for Vietnam and Indo-China, and a reporter asked how Dulles felt about "genuine free elections."

I would favor genuinely free elections under conditions where there would be an opportunity for the electorate to be adequately informed as to what the issues are. At the present time in a country which is politically immature, which has been the scene of civil war and disruption, we would doubt whether the immediate conditions would be conductive to a result which would really reflect the will of the people.

What if the Communist leader of the Vietminh, Ho Chi Minh, won an election?

I said that I thought that the United States should not stand passively by and see the extension of communism by any means into Southeast Asia. We are not standing passively by.

But would we recognize such a government? came another question.

I have just said that I don't think the present conditions are conducive to a free election there and I don't care now to answer the hypothetical situation of what might result if they did have elections.[*1]

Dulles wanted to talk to the reporters about another subject: his plan for a regional defense system to save Indo-China and other areas that might be threatened in the future. The essence

[*1] From a copy in the *Papers of John Foster Dulles*, Princeton University Library, Princeton, N.J.

of the plan was that the United States would supply military aid to independent States of Southeast Asia, in conjunction with England and France and the local nations themselves. The Secretary was never able to convince his European allies that the plan should be tried before accepting negotiations. There were serious discussions within the government looking toward the possibility of some other kind of intervention to prevent a French defeat in Indo-China. But there were always objections, sometimes military, sometimes political, sometimes both. Eisenhower ruled out sending troops, and air power advocates could not convince him that their proposals would really accomplish the objective of lifting the seige of Dienbienphu.

The President never underestimated the importance of Indo-China, and gave a candid explanation of the American view during a press conference on April 7, 1954.

Q. ROBERT RICHARDS, COPLEY PRESS: Mr. President, would you mind commenting on the strategic importanc of Indochina to the free world? I think there has been, across the country, some lack of understanding on just what it means to us.

THE PRESIDENT: You have, of course, both the specific and the general when you talk about such things.

First of all, you have the specific value of a locality in its production of materials that the world needs.

Then you have the possibility that many human beings pass under a dictatorship that is inimical to the free world.

Finally, you have broader considerations that might follow what you would call the "falling domino" principle. You have a row of dominoes set up, you knock over the first one, and what will happen to the last one is the certainty that it will go over very quickly. So you could have a beginning of a disintegration that would have the most profound influences.

Now, with respect to the first one, two of the items from this particular area that the world uses are tin and tungsten. They are very important. There are others, of course, the rubber plantations and so on.

Then with respect to more people passing under this domination, Asia, after all, has already lost some 450 million of its peoples to the Communist dictatorship, and we simply can't afford greater losses.

But when we come to the possible sequence of events, the loss of Indochina, of Burma, of Thailand, of the Peninsula, and Indonesia following, now you begin to talk about areas that not only multiply the disadvantages that you would suffer through loss of materials, sources of materials, but now you are talking really about millions and millions and millions of people.

Finally, the geographical position achieved thereby does many things. It turns the so-called island defensive chain of Japan, Formosa, of the Philippines and to the southward; it moves in to threaten Australia and New Zealand.

It takes away, in its economic aspects, that region that Japan must have as a trading area or Japan, in turn, will have only one place in the world to go—that is, toward the Communist areas in order to live.

So, the possible consequences of the loss are just incalculable to the free world.[*1]

Eisenhower's mind was on another domino during these months, one in Central America. President Jacobo Arbenz Guzman, who had come to power in March 1951 through perfectly legal electoral means, had set out on a land reform program which finally brought him into conflict with the United Fruit Company, owner of many thousands of acres in the countryside. He expropriated 225,000 of those acres on the Pacific slope, much to the consternation of *la Frutera*, as the company was known in Guatemala. His own political views grew more radical as a result of this experience, and he looked to Eastern Europe for support —and badly needed arms. That was too much!

The President approved a plan for the Central Intelligence Agency to find someone to lead a coup, a focal point around which anti-Arbenz Guatemalans could rally. The agency's choice

[*1] News conference of April 7, 1954, *Public Papers of the Presidents of the United States . . . Dwight D. Eisenhower, 1954* (Washington, D.C.: Government Printing Office, 1955), pp. 382–383.

was Colonel Carlos Castillo-Armas. Anti-Arbenz forces were trained by the CIA in Honduras and Nicaragua. All that remained was for Secreary Dulles to secure a resolution condemning "international communism" as incompatible with the concept of freedom in the Americas. A further provision in the resolution required all the American States to take steps to eradicate subversion within their borders. The vote was 17 to 1, with Guatemala the lone dissenter.

At a final briefing before the launching of the Castillo-Armas invasion, Eisenhower wanted some assurance that it would work. Then he added: "I'm prepared to take any steps that are necessary to see that it succeeds. For if it succeeds, it's the people of Guatemala throwing off the yoke of communism. If it fails, the flag of the United States has failed." The State Department, however, maintained that it had "no evidence . . . that this is anything other than a revolt of Guatemalans against the government." The invasion began on June 18, 1954, and with the support of some American World War II-vintage fighters for air cover, had reconquered Guatemala for the Free World by the end of the month.

Reporters David Wise and Thomas Ross described what followed:

If the CIA's coup had routed Communism in Guatemala, democracy is not what followed in its wake. As its first act, the ruling junta canceled the right of illiterates to vote, thereby disenfranchising in one stroke about 70 percent of Guatemala's population—almost all the Indians.

The junta elected Castillo-Armas as its President on July 8. In August the liberator suspended all constitutional guarantees. The ideological basis of the coup was further undercut when the chief CIA man in Guatemala quit the agency and went into the cement business there. The free election Castillo-Armas had promised when Arbenz fell turned out to be "si" or "no" vote on whether to continue Castillo-Armas as President. Castillo-Armas won.

In rapid succession, the new regime set up a Robespierre-like Committee for Defense Against Communism with sweeping police-state powers. The government took back 800,000 acres of land from the peasants, returned to United Fruit the land Arbenz had seized, and repealed amendments to a 1947 law that had guaranteed rights to workers and labor unions.

Within a week of Castillo-Armas' election as head of the junta, the new government announced it had arrested 4,000 persons on suspicion of Communist activity. By August it had passed the Preventive Penal Law Against Communism. This set up the Defense Committee, which met in secret and could declare anyone a Communist—with no right of appeal.

Those registered by the committee could be arbitrarily arrested for periods up to six months; they could not own radios or hold public office. Within four months the new government had registered 72,000 persons as Communists or sympathizers. A committee official said it was aiming for 200,000.

Castillo-Armas was generally regarded as an honest, proud and rather simple man who genuinely loved his country. But he had a covey of advisers, and some of them were less dedicated than their chief. After the 1954 coup American gambler types began drifting into Guatemala, and certain of the liberator's lieutenants were cut in. Castillo-Armas could not bring himself to realize that some of his followers were treacherous. A gambling casino was built in which various Army officers shared a heavy financial interest with the Americans.

Castillo-Armas closed down the Casino, and shortly afterwards, on July 26, 1957, he was assassinated by a member of the palace guard. The crime was first blamed on Communists, then on Castillo-Armas' enemies within the government. It has never been solved.[1]

Throughout all the Third World crises, Dulles found that the phrase "international communism" was his most reliable and most serviceable definition of the threat. On those occasions when it became necessary to give a further definition, he sometimes encountred difficulties. In the Guatemalan case, however,

[1] David Wise and Thomas Ross, *The Invisible Government* (New York: Random House, 1964), pp. 181–182.

he also had at his disposal the time-honored Monroe Doctrine and its defense. As he said in a nationwide radio and television address on June 30, 1954:

Tonight I should like to talk with you about Guatemala. It is the scene of dramatic events. They expose the evil purpose of the Kremlin to destroy the inter-American system, and they test the ability of the American states to maintain the peaceful integrity of this hemisphere.

For several years international communism has been probing here and there for nesting places in the Americas. It finally chose Guatemala as a spot which it could turn into an official base from which to breed subversion which would extend to other American republics.

This intrusion of Soviet despotism was, of course, a direct challenge to our Monroe Doctrine, the first and most fundamental of our foreign policies.

It is interesting to recall that the menace which brought that Doctrine into being was itself a menace born in Russia. It was the Russian Czar Alexander and his despotic allies in Europe who, early in the last century, sought control of South America and the western part of North America. In 1823 President Monroe confronted this challenge with his declaration that the European despots could not "extend their political system to any portion of either continent without endangering our peace and happiness. We would not," he said, "behold such interposition in any form with indifference."

These sentiments were shared by the other American republics, and they were molded into a foreign policy of us all. For 131 years that policy has well served the peace and security of this hemisphere. It serves us well today.

In Guatemala, international communism had an initial success. It began ten years ago, when a revolution occurred in Guatemala. The revolution was not without justification. But the Communists seized on it, not as an opportunity for real reforms, but as a chance to gain political power.

Communist agitators devoted themselves to infiltrating the public and private organizations of Guatemala. They sent recruits

to Russia and other Communist countries for revolutionary training and indoctrination in such institutions as the Lenin School at
Moscow. Operating in the guise of "reformers," they organized the
workers and peasants under Communist leadership. Having gained
control of what they call "mass organizations," they moved on to
take over the official press and radio of the Guatemalan government. They dominated the social security organization and ran the
agrarian reform program. Through the technique of the "popular
front" they dictated to the Congress and the President.

The judiciary made one valiant attempt to protect its integrity
and independence. But the Communists, using their control of the
legislative body, caused the Supreme Court to be dissolved when
it refused to give approval to a Communist-contrived law. Arbenz,
who until this week was President of Guatemala, was openly
manipulated by the leaders of communism.

Guatemala is a small country. But its power, standing alone,
is not a measure of the threat. The master plan of international
communism is to gain a solid political base in this hemisphere, a
base that can be used to extend Communist penetration to the
other peoples of the other American governments. It was not the
power of the Arbenz government that concerned us but the power
behind it.

If world communism captures any American state, however
small, a new and perilous front is established which will increase
the danger to the entire free world and require even greater sacrifices from the American people.

This situation in Guatemala had become so dangerous that
the American states could not ignore it. At Caracas last March
the American states held their Tenth Inter-American Conference.
They then adopted a momentous statement. They declared that
"the domination or control of the political institutions of any
American state by the international Communist movement . . .
would constitute a threat to the sovereignty and political independence of the American states, endangering the peace of America."

There was only one American state that voted against this
declaration. That state was Guatemala.

This Caracas declaration precipitated a dramatic chain of
events. From their European base the Communist leaders moved

rapidly to build up the military power of their agents in Guatemala. In May a large shipment of arms moved from behind the Iron Curtain into Guatemala. The shipment was sought to be secreted by false manifests and false clearances. Its ostensible destination was changed three times while en route.

At the same time, the agents of international communism in Guatemala intensified efforts to penetrate and subvert the neighboring Central American states. They attempted political assassinations and political strikes. They used consular agents for political warfare.

Many Guatemalan people protested against their being used by Communist dictatorship to serve the Communists' lust for power. The response was mass arrests, the suppression of constitutional guaranties, the killing of opposition leaders, and other brutal tactics normally employed by communism to secure the consolidation of its power.

In the face of these events and in accordance with the spirit of the Caracas declaration, the nations of this hemisphere laid further plans to grapple with the danger. The Arbenz government responded with an effort to disrupt the inter-American system. Because it enjoyed the full support of Soviet Russia, which is on the Security Council, it tried to bring the matter before the Security Council. It did so without first referring the matter to the American regional organization as is called for both by the United Nations Charter itself and by the treaty creating the American organization.

The Foreign Minister of Guatemala openly connived in this matter with the Foreign Minister of the Soviet Union. The two were in open correspondence and ill-concealed privity. The Security Council at first voted overwhemingly to refer the Guatemala matter to the Organization of American States. The vote was 10 to 1. But that one negative vote was a Soviet veto.

Then the Guatemalan government, with Soviet backing, redoubled its efforts to supplant the American states system by Security Council jurisdiction.

However, last Friday, the United Nations Security Council decided not to take up the Guatemalan matter but to leave it in the first instance to the American states themselves. That was a triumph for the system of balance between regional organization and world organization, which the American states had fought for when the charter was drawn up at San Francisco.

The American states then moved promptly to deal with the situation. Their peace commission left yesterday for Guatemala. Earlier the Organization of American States had voted overwhelmingly to call a meeting of their Foreign Ministers to consider the penetration of international communism in Guatemala and the measures required to eliminate it. Never before has there been so clear a call uttered with such a sense of urgency and strong resolve.

Throughout the period I have outlined, the Guatemalan government and Communist agents throughout the world have persistently attempted to obscure the real issue—that of Communist imperialism—by claiming that the United States is only interested in protecting American business. We regret that there have been disputes between the Guatemalan government and the United Fruit Company. We have urged repeatedly that these disputes be submitted for settlement to an international tribunal or to international arbitration. That is the way to dispose of problems of this sort. But this issue is relatively unimportant. All who know the temper of the United States people and government must realize that our overriding concern is that which, with others, we recorded at Caracas, namely, the endangering by international communism of the peace and security of this hemisphere.

The people of Guatemala have now been heard from. Despite the armaments piled up by the Arbenz government, it was unable to enlist the spiritual cooperation of the people.

Led by Colonel Castillo-Armas, patriots arose in Guatemala to challenge the Communist leadership—and to change it. Thus, the situation is being cured by the Guatemalans themselves.

Last Sunday, President Arbenz of Guatemala resigned and seeks asylum. Others are following his example.

Tonight, just as I speak, Colonel Castillo-Armas is in conference in El Salvador with Colonel Monzón, the head of the Council which has taken over the power in Guatemala City. It was this power that the just wrath of the Guatemalan people wrestled from President Arbenz, who then took flight.

Now the future of Guatemala lies at the disposal of the

Guatemalan people themselves. It lies also at the disposal of leaders loyal to Guatemala who have not treasonably become the agents of an alien despotism which sought to use Guatemala for its own evil ends.

The events of recent months and days add a new and glorious chapter to the already great tradition of the American states.

Each one of the American states has cause for profound gratitude. We can all be grateful that we showed at Caracas an impressive solidarity in support of our American institutions. I may add that we are prepared to do so again at the conference called for Rio. Advance knowledge of that solidarity undoubtedly shook the Guatemalan government.

We can be grateful that the Organization of American States showed that it could act quickly and vigorously in aid of peace. There was proof that our American organization is not just a paper organization, but that it has vigor and vitality to act.

We can be grateful to the United Nations Security Council, which recognized the right of regional organizations in the first instance to order their own affairs. Otherwise the Soviet Russians would have started a controversy which would have set regionalism against universality and gravely wounded both.

Above all, we can be grateful that there were loyal citizens of Guatemala who, in the face of terrorism and violence and against what seemed insuperable odds, had the courage and the will to eliminate the traitorous tools of foreign despots.

The need for vigilance is not past. Communism is still a menace everywhere. But the people of the United States and of the other American republics can feel tonight that at least one grave danger has been averted. Also an example is set which promises increased security for the future. The ambitious and unscrupulous will be less prone to feel that communism is the wave of their future.

In conclusion, let me assure the people of Guatemala. As peace and freedom are restored to that sister republic, the government of the United States will continue to support the just aspirations of the Guatemalan people. A prosperous and progressive Guatemala is vital to a healthy hemisphere. The United States pledges itself not merely to political opposition to communism but to help to alleviate conditions in Guatemala and elsewhere which might afford communism an opportunity to spread its tentacles throughout the hemisphere. Thus we shall seek in positive ways to make our Americas an example which will inspire men everywhere.*[1]

Yet ambiguities remained about Cold War crises in the Third World. At the conclusion of a SEATO Foreign Ministers' meeting in early 1955, Secretary Dulles explained how the final communique of the meeting had been written, but only after lengthy discussions with the British over the exact language to be used:

One little thing I might mention. You will find the words "international Communism" are mentioned in the communique —a hurdle which some people found a little hard to take. They were not in the communique that came out from the working group. The word Communism never found any mention at all. I called attention to the fact that it seemed rather extraordinary, when we were making all this effort to combat something, that we couldn't even give it a name. And so the words "international Communism." I think that from now on it will be respectable in this circle to talk about international Communism.†[1]

Thus the Cold War was transformed from an essentially European contest into a global struggle. The transition began during the Korean War, perhaps the most puzzling conflict in the history of American military and political decision-making.

---

*[1] Department of State *Bulletin*, XXXI (July 2, 1954), 43–45.
†[1] From a copy in the *Papers of John Foster Dulles*, Princeton University Library, Princeton, N.J.

NOTES

1 Testimony of William D. Pawley, in U.S. Senate, Sub-committee of the Internal Security Committee, *Hearings The Communist Threat Through the Caribbean*, 86th Cong., 1st Sess. (Washington, D.C.: Government Printing Office., 1960), pp. 738–740.
2 Interview with Elliot Bell, Dulles Oral History Project, Princeton University Library, Princeton, New Jersey.
3 Emmet John Hughes, *The Ordeal of Powers A Political Memoir of the Eisenhower Years* (New York: Atheneum, 1963), p. 218.
4 *Ibid.*, p. 208.

CHAPTER FOUR
★ ★ ★ ★ ★

Frame of Reference: Korea and Before

Today the Korean War is little more than a bad memory, more remote in the national consciousness than World War II. Inconclusive on the battlefield, it was fought bitterly on the domestic front by Republicans and Democrats, who sought to enlist the generals in their campaigns. Both parties wanted General Dwight D. Eisenhower; he chose the Republicans and thereby assured their victory in 1952. Many conservatives would have preferred General Douglas MacArthur, the man President Truman fired in April 1951 for insubordination, but victory with Eisenhower seemed preferable to another defeat at the polls. Besides, as the Chairman of the Joint Chiefs of Staff, General Omar N. Bradley, had testified before Congress, an all-out campaign in Korea "would involve us in the wrong war, at the wrong place, at the wrong time, and with the wrong enemy."

Four wrongs did not make a right. No one realized this more

than Eisenhower, who rejected all pleas from his old military colleagues for a last offensive in Korea. He was shrewd enough, also, to handle the 1952 Republican campaign slogan "Liberation" without committing himself to any more land confrontations with Soviet power in Asia or in Europe. Elected to liquidate an unpopular war. Eisenhower understood better than his partisans the Republican strategy of promising victory in the Cold War through "Liberation" policies while pursuing a cautious approach to the Kremlin itself. He also resisted "Containment" as a foreign policy strategy which would lead to more Koreas. At the height of the first Indo-China crisis in the spring of 1954, Eisenhower explained what he would not do to meet this new crisis, and what he hoped he could do:

Q. MERRIMAN SMITH, UNITED PRESS: I wonder if you could explore for us, sir, or amplify on Secretary Dulles' speech the other night in which he spoke of our readiness to take united action in the Far East.

THE PRESIDENT: Well, of course, the speech must stand by itself. I should say that I was over every word of it beforehand; Secretary Dulles and I, as usual, find ourselves in complete agreement.

I have forgotten the exact words that he used in respect to the question you raised, but he did point out that it is in united action of all nations and peoples and countries affected in that region that we can successfully oppose the encroachment of communism, and should be prepared to meet any kind of attack that would come in there. He pointed out the great value of the region to all the free world and what its loss would mean to us.

So, I think, aside from just the assertion that we are seeking that kind of united action among all our friends, that the speech otherwise must stand by itself.

Q. MARTIN AGRONSKY, AMERICAN BROADCASTING COMPANY: Mr. President, I wondered if I could ask one more specific question along those lines. The united action has been interpreted generally as indicating, perhaps, intervention, direct intervention or direct use, more accurately, of American troops. Can you comment on that—if necessary?

THE PRESIDENT: Well, I have said time and again that I can conceive of no greater disadvantage to America than to be employing its own ground forces, and any other kind of forces, in great numbers around the world, meeting each little situation as it arises.

What we are trying to do is to make our friends strong enough to take care of local situations by themselves, with the financial, the moral, the political and, certainly, only where our own vital interests demanded any military help.

But each of these cases is one that has its own degree, let us say, of interest for the United States, its own degree of risk and danger; consequently, each one must be met on its merits.

I could possibly give you a general rule of what the United States would do in a situation, because no one could know all of the circumstances surrounding it. I think the best answer I ever heard in diplomacy was that given by France, I believe, to Germany in late August or late July of 1914. When Germany asked her her intentions, she said, "France will do that which her best interests dictate," and that is about the only answer I believe you can give, except in terms of very great generality.*1

Eisenhower's Secretary of State, John Foster Dulles, had developed a strategy of interlocking mutual security pacts based liberally on the NATO model to meet the presumed worldwide Communist challenge emanating from Moscow: SEATO for Asia, the OAS for Latin America, and the never-realized Middle Eastern pact. After Korea this seemed the only way to police the world. Dulles had also devised a new lexicon for American foreign policy: Liberation replaced containment, massive retaliation was preferred to limited war, and neutralism became immoral. In practice, however, the Republican Administration fell into familiar Cold War patterns. As the new President recognized, the Korean War proved that America's effective options were not always between liberation and containment. One could talk a lot about a dynamic foreign policy, and one could increase the num-

*1 *Public Papers of the Presidents of the United States . . . Dwight D. Eisenhower, 1954* (Washington, D.C.: Government Printing Office, 1955), pp. 365–366.

ber of American military bases abroad—Dulles and Eisenhower did both—but the problems confronting America went deeper than semantics or firepower.

On January 12, 1954, Secretary Dulles announced the so-called "massive retaliation" doctrine, and scared the dickens out of America's critics on both sides of the Atlantic. They hopped all over the speech, forcing a series of "clarifications" from the Secretary and the President; however, read as a catalog of woes facing the nation in the aftermath of Korea, it covered the ground well:

It is now nearly a year since the Eisenhower Administration took office. During that year I have often spoken of various parts of our foreign policies. Tonight I should like to present an overall view of those policies which relate to our security.

First of all, let us recognize that many of the preceding foreign policies were good. Aid to Greece and Turkey had checked the Communist drive to the Mediterranean. The European Recovery Program had helped the peoples of Western Europe to pull out of the post-war morass. The Western powers were steadfast in Berlin and overcame the blockade with their airlift. As a loyal member of the United Nations, we had reached with force to repel the Communist attack in Korea. When that effort exposed our military weakness, we rebuilt rapidly our military establishment. We also sought a quick buildup of armed strength in Western Europe.

These were the acts of a nation which saw the danger of Soviet Communism; which realized that its own safety was tied up with that of others; which was capable of responding boldly and promptly to emergencies. These are precious values to be acclaimed. Also, we can pay tribute to Congressional bi-partisanship which puts the nation above politics.

But we need to recall that what we did was in the main emergency action, imposed on us by our enemies.

Let me illustrate.

1. We did not send our army into Korea because we judged, in advance, that it was sound military strategy to commit our

Army to fight land battles in Asia. Our decision had been to pull out of Korea. It was Soviet-inspired action that pulled us back.

2. We did not decide in advance that it was wise to grant billions annually as foreign economic aid. We adopted that policy in response to the Communist efforts to sabotage the free economies of Western Europe.

3. We did not build up our military establishment at a rate which involved huge budget deficits, a depreciating currency and a feverish economy, because this seemed, in advance, a good policy. Indeed, we decided otherwise until the Soviet military threat was clearly revealed.

We live in a world where emergencies are always possible and our survival may depend upon our capacity to meet emergencies. Let us pray that we shall always have that capacity. But, having said that, it is necessary also to say that emergency measures —however good for the emergency—do not necessarily make good permanent policies. Emergency measures are costly, they are superficial and they imply that the enemy has the initiative. They cannot be depended on to serve our long-time interests.

This "long time" factor is of critical importance. The Soviet Communists are planning for what they call "an entire historical era," and we should do the same. They seek, through many types of maneuvers, gradually to divide and weaken the free nations by overextending them in efforts which, as Lenin put it, are "beyond their strength, so that they come to practical bankruptcy." Then, said Lenin, "our victory is assured." Then, said Stalin, will be "the moment for the decisive blow."

In the face of this strategy, measures cannot be judged adequate merely because they ward off an immediate danger. It is essential to do this, but it is also essential to do so without exhausting ourselves.

When the Eisenhower Administration applied this test, we felt that some transformations were needed.

It is not sound military strategy permanently to commit U.S. land forces to Asia to a degree that leaves us no strategic reserves.

It is not sound economics, or good foreign policy, to support permanently other countries; for in the long run, that creates as much ill will as good will.

Also, it is not sound to become permanently committed to military expenditures so vast that they lead to "practical bankruptcy."

Change was imperative to assure the stamina needed for permanent security. But it was equally imperative that change should be accompanied by understanding of our true purposes. Sudden and spectacular change had to be avoided. Otherwise, there might have been a panic among our friends, and miscalculated aggression by our enemies. We can, I believe, make a good report in these respects.

We need allies and collective security. Our purpose is to make these relations more effective, less costly. This can be done by placing more reliance on deterrent power, and less dependence on local defensive power.

This is accepted practice so far as local communities are concerned. We keep locks on our doors; but we do not have an armed guard in every home. We rely principally on a community security system so well equipped to punish any who break in and steal that, in fact, would-be aggressors are generally deterred. That is the modern way of getting maximum protection at a bearable cost.

What the Eisenhower Administration seeks is a similar international security system. We want, for ourselves and the other free nations, a maximum deterrent at a bearable cost.

Local defense will always be important. But there is no local defense which alone will contain the mighty land power of the Communist world. Local defenses must be reinforced by the further deterrent of massive retaliatory power. A potential aggressor must know that he cannot always prescribe battle conditions that suit him. Otherwise, for example, a potential aggressor, who is glutted with manpower, might be tempted to attack in confidence that resistance would be confined to manpower. He might be tempted to attack in places where his superiority was decisive.

The way to deter aggression is for the free community to be willing and able to respond vigorously at places and with means of its own choosing.

So long as our basic policy concepts were unclear, our military leaders could not be selective in building our military power. If an enemy could pick his time and place and method of warfare—and if our policy was to remain the traditional one of meeting aggression by direct and local opposition—then we needed to be ready to fight in the arctic and in the tropics; in Asia, the Near East and in Europe; by sea, by land and by air; with old weapons and with new weapons.

The total cost of our security efforts, at home and abroad, was over $50,000,000,000 per annum, and involved, for 1953, a projected budgetary deficit of $9,000,000,000; and $11,000,000,000 for 1954. This was on top of taxes comparable to war-time taxes; and the dollar was depreciating in effective value. Our allies were similarly weighed down. This could not be continued for long without grave budgetary, economic and social consequences.

But before military planning could be changed, the President and his advisers, as represented by the National Security Council, had to take some basic policy decisions. This has been done. The basic decision was to depend primarily upon a great capacity to retaliate, instantly, by means and at places of our choosing. Now the Department of Defense and the Joint Chiefs of Staff can shape our military establishment to fit what is our policy, instead of having to try to be ready to meet the enemy's many choices. That permits of a selection of military means instead of a multiplication of means. As a result, it is now possible to get, and share, more basic security at less cost.

In the ways I outlined we gather strength for the long-term defense of freedom.

We do not, of course, claim to have found some magic formula that ensures against all forms of Communist successes. It is normal that at some times and at some places there may be setbacks to the cause of freedom. What we do expect to ensure is that any setbacks will have only temporary and local significance because they will leave unimpaired those free world assets which in the long run will prevail.

If we can deter such aggression as would mean general war, and that is our confident resolve, then we can let time and fundamentals work for us. We do not need self-imposed policies which sap our strength.

The fundamental, on our side, is the richness—spiritual, intellectual and material—that freedom can produce and the irresistible attraction it then sets up. That is why we do not plan ourselves to shackle freedom to preserve freedom. We intend that our conduct and example shall continue, as in the past, to show all men how good can be the fruits of freedom.

If we rely on freedom, then it follows that we must abstain from diplomatic moves which would seem to endorse captivity. That would, in effect, be a conspiracy against freedom. I can assure you that we shall never seek illusory security for ourselves by such a "deal."

We do negotiate about specific matters but only to advance the cause of human welfare.

President Eisenhower electrified the world with his proposal to lift a great weight of fear by turning atomic energy from a means of death into a source of life. Yesterday, I started procedural talks with the Soviet Government on that topic.

We have persisted, with our Allies, in seeking the unification of Germany and the liberation of Austria. Now the Soviet rulers have agreed to discuss these questions. We expect to meet them soon in Berlin. I hope they will come with a sincerity which will equal our own.

We have sought a conference to unify Korea and relieve it of foreign troops. So far, our persistence is unrewarded; but we have not given up.

These efforts at negotiation are normal initiatives that breathe the spirit of freedom. They involve no plan for a partnership division of world power with those who suppress freedom.

If we persist in the courses I outline we shall confront dictatorship with a task that is, in the long run, beyond its strength. For unless it changes, it must suppress the human desires that freedom satisfies—as we shall be demonstrating.

If the dictators persist in their present course then it is they who will be limited to superficial successes, while their foundation crumbles under the tread of their iron boots.

Human beings, for the most part, want simple things.

They want to worship God in accordance with the dictates of their conscience. But that is not easily granted by those who promote an atheistic creed.

They want to think in accordance with the dictates of their reason. But that is not easily granted by those who represent an authoritarian system.

They want to exchange views with others and to persuade and to be persuaded by what appeals to their reason and their conscience. But that is not easily granted by those who believe in a society of conformity.

They want to live in their homes without fear. But that is not easily granted by those who believe in a police state system.

They want to be able to work productively and creatively and to enjoy the fruits of their labor. But that is not easily granted by those who look upon human beings as a means to create a power-house to dominate the world.

We can be sure that there is going on, even within Russia, a silent test of strength between the powerful rulers and the multitudes of human beings. Each individual no doubt seems by himself to be helpless in this struggle. But their aspirations in the aggregate make up a mighty force.

There are signs that the rulers are bending to some of the human desires of their people. There are promises of more food, more household goods, more economic freedom.

That does not prove that the Soviet rulers have themselves been converted. It is rather that they may be dimly perceiving a basic fact, that is that there are limits to the power of any rulers indefinitely to suppress the human spirit.

In that God-given fact lies our greatest hope. It is a hope that can sustain us. For even if the path ahead be long and hard, it need not be a warlike path; and we can know that at the end may be found the blessedness of peace.[*1]

A new isolationism, the usual liberal critics said of the "massive retaliation" speech. Dulles had once been known as an isolationist, back in the 1930's. His true colors were showing again. Others feared the Secretary was really serious about "liberation" and was prepared to push to the brink of war—and over—if

---

[*1] "The Evolution of Foreign Policy," excerpted in Department of State, *American Foreign Policy, 1950–1955* (2 v. Washington, 1957), 1, 80–85.

necessary to carry out his policy. The simple truth was that Dulles was very unhappy about the truce which brought the Korean War to an end, and was anxious to make up for it. His new interest in Asian affairs (acquired when he accepted the assignment for drafting a peace treaty with Japan back in 1950) made him uneasy with anything that smacked of stalemate in the face of a dynamic Red Chinese presence just across the Yalu in Manchuria, but he also worried about a let down in Europe when the fighting stopped.

"This is the kind of time when we ought to be *doubling* our bets," he told an Eisenhower Cabinet meeting on July 10, 1953, "not reducing them—as all the Western parliaments want to do. This is the time to *crowd* the enemy—and maybe *finish* him, once and for all. But if we're dilatory, he can consolidate—and probably put us right back where we were."[1] Through various pressures and inducements, Dulles did succeed in persuading the French to abandon their opposition to German rearmament within the confines of the NATO structure. He even tried to persuade the Soviets that a rearmed Germany inside the Western alliance system was better for everybody. A "neutral" Germany, Dulles implied, would endanger both Russia and the United States. Each side would bid for German favor; and the Germans, masters of *Realpolitik*, would seize upon the first good opportunity to set the victors at one another's throat. No, it *was* better to have Germany locked into the alliance system.

The Korean War had given a final impetus to demands for German rearmament. Up until then the Truman Administration had steadfastly denied any intention of rearming Germany inside NATO or by any other means. The German resurgence was, even for Americans, a mixed blessing. On the one hand, Germany was regarded as a more stable political entity than France, a better barricade certainly against the Bolsheviks if it came to that, and certainly a greater industrial power by far than any other nation on the continent. On the other hand, of course, Germany was an ambitious nation, still not to be trusted with full responsibility for its own (and Europe's) future. American policy, under both Dean Acheson and Dulles, was designed to take advantage of the former and minimize the risks. Considered in those terms, it was a success. Eventually the Russians would have to come to terms with the new situation in Germany, which they did at much cost to themselves in 1961 with the building of the "Berlin Wall."

The Korean Truce Agreement of July 27, 1953 left Korea divided along a line which extended north of the 38th Parallel in the east, and, to a lesser extent, south of that imaginary boundary in the west. The United States also gave South Korean President Syngman Rhee assurances of support should his government come under attack again from North Korea. Rhee, however, was most unhappy at this turn of events. If any treaty arrangement was made which permitted the Chinese "volunteers" to remain on any Korean territory, north or south, he would feel justified in asking his allies to get out of his country, except those who were willing to join him in a campaign to the Yalu itself!

Eisenhower was not one to be bluffed or bullied by an enemy or an ally. He made it plain that if full-scale war resumed in Korea, he would not be bound by the tactics of his predecessors. That was for the North Koreans to consider. As to Rhee, the President was equally clear in this letter:

First, the action taken by the United Nations in Korea was to assist your valiant country in repelling the armed attack directed against it initially by the North Korean regime and subsequently by the Chinese Communists. This has successfully been accomplished.

Second, the task of repelling the armed attack having been accomplished, it would not be defensible to refuse to stop the fighting on an honorable basis as a prerequisite to working out the remaining issues by peaceful means.

Third, the United States and the United Nations have consistently supported the unification of Korea under conditions which would assure its freedom and independence. Neither the United States nor the United Nations has ever committed itself to resort to war to achieve this objective. To do so would be a complete negation of the basic tenets of this country and the United Nations.

Fourth, any agreement to stop the fighting on an honorable basis presupposes a willingness on the part of both sides to discuss the remaining issues and to make every reasonable effort to reach agreement thereon. As I said in my address of April 16 an honorable armistice "means the immediate cessation of hostilities and the prompt initiation of political discussions leading to the holding of free elections in a United Korea."[*1]

However justified by the military situation in Korea, Eisenhower's letter did reveal a change in policy. Perhaps the goal of liberating North Korea had been given up, as long ago as April 1951 when Truman removed MacArthur, but in the two years of truce talks since that decision neither side had been able to find a way to end the fighting. The talks inside the truce tents at Panmunjom, moreover, were not the only discussions about how to end the war: back in Washington high level talks between representatives of the Department of State and from the Department of Defense had also bogged down. The Chinese intervention in December 1950 had ended the dream of liberation so far as North Korea was concerned, and left the Truman Administration with a new dilemma: how to get out without suffering a serious political loss as well as military defeat. "In our regular periodic meetings with representatives of the State Department," General J. Lawton Collins wrote, "the Chiefs constantly tried to pin down at any particular time after the Chinese intervention just what our remaining political objectives were in Korea, but our diplomatic colleagues would always counter with the query 'What are your military capabilities?' The discussion would almost invariably come down to the age-old question of the chicken and the egg. The Chiefs could only deduce that our State Department co-workers, torn as they were by the often conflicting domestic and international political considerations, wanted us to attain the maximal military results within our military capabilities. But the military would have to assume all the responsibility if things went wrong."[2]

President Truman's decision to remove General Douglas MacArthur from his post as commander of all United Nations' forces in Korea was an example—the ultimate example—of the confu-

---

[*1] Dwight D. Eisenhower: *The White House Years, Mandate for Change: 1953–1956* (Garden City, N.Y.: Doubleday & Co., 1963), p. 182.

sion between political and military responsibility for the debacle then taking place in Asia. The discussions between Pentagon officials and State Department representatives, as reported by General Collins, were polite exchanges; those between Truman and MacArthur raised fundamental questions about Cold War policy, not only in Korea but on a worldwide basis. There was also the question of civilian control of the military. Indeed, it was on this issue that Truman based his decision to remove the General, specifically for violations of presidential directives against public statements of foreign or military policy without White House clearance. But Truman's radio report to the nation ranged far beyond specifics to a general defense of Cold War strategy and tactics.

My fellow Americans:

I want to talk to you plainly tonight about what we are doing in Korea and about our policy in the Far East.

In the simplest terms, what we are doing in Korea is this: We are trying to prevent a third world war.

I think most people in this country recognized that fact last June. And they warmly supported the decision of the Government to help the Republic of Korea against the Communist aggressors. Now, many persons, even some who applauded our decision to defend Korea, have forgotten the basic reason for our action.

It is right for us to be in Korea now. It was right last June. It is right today.

I want to remind you why this is true.

The Communists in the Kremlin are engaged in a monstrous conspiracy to stamp out freedom all over the world. If they were to succeed, the United States would be numbered among their principal victims. It must be clear to everyone that the United States cannot—and will not—sit idly by and await foreign conquest. The only question is: What is the best time to meet the threat and how is the best way to meet it?

The best time to meet the threat is in the beginning. It is easier to put out a fire in the beginning when it is small than after it has become a roaring blaze. And the best way to meet the threat of aggression is for the peace-loving nations to act together.

If they don't act together, they are likely to be picked off, one by one.

If they had followed the right policies in the 1930's—if the free countries had acted together to crush the aggression of the dictators, and if they had acted in the beginning when the aggression was small—there probably would have been no World War II.

If history has taught us anything, it is that aggression anywhere in the world is a threat to the peace everywhere in the world. When that aggression is supported by the cruel and selfish rulers of a powerful nation who are bent on conquest, it becomes a clear and present danger to the security and independence of every free nation.

This is a lesson that most people in this country have learned thoroughly. This is the basic reason why we joined in creating the United Nations. And, since the end of World War II, we have been putting that lesson into practice—we have been working with other free nations to check the aggressive designs of the Soviet Union before they can result in a third world war.

That is what we did in Greece, when that nation was threatened by the aggression of international communism.

The attack against Greece could have led to general war. But this country came to the aid of Greece. The United Nations supported Greek resistance. With our help, the determination and efforts of the Greek people defeated the attack on the spot.

Another big Communist threat to peace was the Berlin blockade. That too could have led to war. But again it was settled because free men would not back down in an emergency.

The aggression against Korea is the boldest and most dangerous move the Communists have yet made.

The attack on Korea was part of a greater plan for conquering all of Asia.

I would like to read to you from a secret intelligence report which came to us after the attack on Korea. It is a report of a speech a Communist army officer in North Korea gave to a group of spies and saboteurs last May, one month before South Korea was invaded. The report shows in great detail how this invasion was part of a carefully prepared plot. Here, in part, is what the Communist officer, who had been trained in Moscow, told his men:

"Our forces," he said, "are scheduled to attack South Korean forces about the middle of June. . . . The coming attack on South Korea marks the first step toward the liberation of Asia."

Notice that he used the word "liberation." This is Communist doubletalk meaning "conquest."

I have another secret intelligence report here. This one tells what another Communist officer in the Far East told his men several months before the invasion of Korea. Here is what he said: "In order to successfully undertake the long-awaited world revolution, we must first unify Asia. . . . Java, Indochina, Malaya, India, Tibet, Thailand, Philippines and Japan are our ultimate targets. . . . The United States is the only obstacle on our road for the liberation of all the countries in southeast Asia. In other words, we must unify the people of Asia and crush the United States." Again, "liberation" in "commie" language means conquest.

That is what the Communist leaders are telling their people, and that is what they have been trying to do.

They want to control all Asia from the Kremlin.

This plan of conquest is in flat contradiction to what we believe. We believe that Korea belong to the Koreans, we believe that India belongs to the Indians, we believe that all the nations of Asia should be free to work out their affairs in their own way. This is the basis of peace in the Far East, and it is the basis of peace everywhere else.

The whole Communist imperialism is back of the attack on peace in the Far East. It was the Soviet Union that trained and equipped the North Koreans for aggression. The Chinese Communists massed 44 well-trained and well-equipped divisions on the Korean frontier. There were the troops they threw into battle when the North Korean Communists were beaten.

The question we have had to face is whether the Communist plan of conquest can be stopped without a general war. Our Government and other countries associated with us in the United Nations believe that the best chance of stopping it without a general war is to meet the attack in Korea and defeat it there.

That is what we have been doing. It is a difficult and bitter task.

But so far it has been successful.

So far, we have prevented world war III.

So far, by fighting a limited war in Korea, we have prevented aggression from succeeding, and bringing on a general war. And the ability of the whole free world to resist Communist aggression has been greatly improved.

We have taught the enemy a lesson. He has found that aggression is not cheap or easy. Moreover, men all over the world who want to remain free have been given new courage and new hope. They know now that the champions of freedom can stand up and fight, and that they will stand up and fight.

Our resolute stand in Korea is helping the forces of freedom now fighting in Indo-china and other countries in that part of the world. It has already slowed down the timetable of conquest.

In Korea itself there are signs that the enemy is building up his ground forces for a new mass offensive. We also know that there have been large increases in the enemy's available air forces.

If a new attack comes, I feel confident it will be turned back. The United Nations fighting forces are tough and able and well equipped. They are fighting for a just cause. They are proving to all the world that the principle of collective security will work. We are proud of all these forces for the magnificent job they have done against heavy odds. We pray that their efforts may succeed, for upon their success may hinge the peace of the world.

The Communist side must now choose its course of action. The Communist rulers may press the attack against us. They may take further action which will spread the conflict. They have that choice, and with it the awful responsibility for what may follow. The Communists also have the choice of a peaceful settlement which could lead to a general relaxation of the tensions in the Far East. The decision is theirs, because the forces of the United Nations will strive to limit the conflict if possible.

We do not want to see the conflict in Korea extended. We are trying to prevent a world war—not to start one. And the best way to do that is to make it plain that we and the other free countries will continue to resist the attack.

But you may ask why can't we take other steps to punish the aggressor. Why don't we bomb Manchuria and China itself? Why don't we assist the Chinese Nationalist troops to land on the mainland of China?

If we were to do these things we would be running a very

grave risk of starting a general war. If that were to happen, we would have brought about the exact situation we are trying to prevent.

If we were to do these things, we would become entangled in a vast conflict on the continent of Asia and our task would become immeasurably more difficult all over the world.

What would suit the ambitions of the Kremlin better than for our military forces to be committed to a full-scale war with Red China?

It may well be that, in spite of our best efforts, the Communists may spread the war. But it would be wrong—tragically wrong—for us to take the initiative in extending the war.

The dangers are great. Make no mistake about it. Behind the North Koreans and Chinese Communists in the front lines stand additional millions of Chinese soldiers. And behind the Chinese stand the tanks, the planes, the submarines, the soldiers, and the scheming rulers of the Soviet Union.

Our aim is to avoid the spread of the conflict.

The course we have been following is the one best calculated to avoid an all-out war. It is the course consistent with our obligation to do all we can to maintain international peace and security. Our experience in Greece and Berlin shows that it is the most effective course of action we can follow.

First of all, it is clear that our efforts in Korea can blunt the will of the Chinese Communists to continue the struggle. The United Nations forces have put up a tremendous fight in Korea and have inflicted very heavy casualties on the enemy. Our forces are stronger now than they have been before. These are plain facts which may discourage the Chinese Communists from continuing their attack.

Second, the free world as a whole is growing in military strength every day. In the United States, in Western Europe, and throughout the world, free men are alert to the Soviet threat and are building their defenses. This may discourage the Communist rulers from continuing the war in Korea—and from undertaking new acts of aggression elsewhere.

If the Communist authorities realize that they cannot defeat us in Korea, if they realize it would be foolhardy to widen the hostilities beyond Korea, then they may recognize the folly of continuing their aggression. A peaceful settlement may then be possible. The door is always open.

Then we may achieve a settlement in Korea which will not compromise the principles and purposes of the United Nations.

I have thought long and hard about this question of extending the war in Asia. I have discussed it many times with the ablest military advisers in the country. I believe with all my heart that the course we are following is the best course.

I believe that we must try to limit the war to Korea for these vital reasons: to make sure that the precious lives of our fighting men are not wasted; to see that the security of our country and the free world is not needlessly jeopardized; and to prevent a third world war.

A number of events have made it evident that General MacArthur did not agree with that policy. I have therefore considered it essential to relieve General MacArthur so that there would be no doubt or confusion as to the real purpose and aim of our policy.

It was with the deepest personal regret that I found myself compelled to take this action. General MacArthur is one of our greatest military commanders. But the cause of world peace is much more important than any individual.

The change in commands in the Far East means no change whatever in the policy of the United States. We will carry on the fight in Korea with vigor and determination in an effort to bring the war to a speedy and successful conclusion. The new commander, Lt. Gen. Matthew Ridgway, has already demonstrated that he has the great qualities of military leadership needed for this task.

We are ready, at any time, to negotiate for a restoration of peace in the area. But we will not engage in appeasement. We are only interested in real peace.

Real peace can be achieved through a settlement based on the following factors:

1. The fighting must stop.

2. Concrete steps must be taken to insure that the fighting will not break out again.

3. There must be an end to the aggression.

A settlement founded upon these elements would open the way for the unification of Korea and the withdrawal of all foreign forces.

In the meantime, I want to be clear about our military objective. We are fighting to resist an outrageous aggression in Korea. We are trying to keep the Korean conflict from spreading to other areas. But at the same time we must conduct our military activities so as to insure the security of our forces. This is essential if they are to continue the fight until the enemy abandons its ruthless attempt to destroy the Republic of Korea.

That is our military objective—to repel attack and to restore peace.

In the hard fighting in Korea, we are proving that collective action among nations is not only a high principle but a workable means of resisting aggression. Defeat of aggression in Korea may be the turning point in the world's search for a practical way of achieving peace and security.

The struggle of the United Nations in Korea is a struggle for peace.

Free nations have united their strength in an effort to prevent a third world war.

That war can come if the Communist rulers want it to come. But this Nation and its allies will not be responsible for its coming.

We do not want to widen the conflict. We will use every effort to prevent that disaster. And in so doing, we know that we are following the great principles of peace, freedom, and justice.[1]

The final paragraphs of this report to the people hinted strongly that American objectives were no longer concerned with reunification of Korea by military action. This had been a particularly difficult and tricky question. There were disclaimers

---

[1] Radio report to the American people on Korea and on U.S. policy in the Far East, April 11, 1951, in *Public Papers of the Presidents of the United States . . . Harry S. Truman* (Washington, D.C.: Government Printing Office, 1965), pp. 223–227.

from Administration officials that military reunification *had ever* been a policy goal. But Secretary of State Dean Acheson had avoided a direct response when asked about Administration plans for Korea by Senator Harry Cain during the so-called MacArthur Hearings:

SECRETARY ACHESON: Well, force would have been used to round up the people who were putting on the aggression . . . unifying . . . it would have been through elections and that sort of thing.*1

The massive Chinese intervention of early November 1950 apparently came as a great surprise to Washington, partly because of MacArthur's reassurances that the Chinese would not move down from Manchuria and partly because of erroneous assumptions about the intentions and capabilities of the new Communist regime led by Mao Tse-tung. Even so, MacArthur's standing orders as of October 9, 1950, had given him great latitude in dealing with such a possibility. He was told to continue operations even if Chinese intervention occurred "as long as, in your judgment, action by forces now under your control offers a reasonable chance of success."[3]

Stories of MacArthur's disregard for Pentagon warnings and instructions flourished after the Chinese intervention. *New York Times* columnist Arthur Krock informed MacArthur on November 29, 1950, that some officials were saying that the General had turned aside all suggestions for a "stop-point" with the assertion that he would not accept responsibility for the security of his troops if such a decision were made. Officials further claimed said Krock's telegram that "this faced authorities with dilemma of taking risk replacing you with elections coming on or letting you proceed against their political and diplomatic judgment and against some high military judgments also."

The General responded to Krock with a blunt denial which he then repeated at length in a statement to Hugh Baillie, presi-

*1 David Rees, *Korea: The Limited War* (New York: St. Martin's Press, 1964), p. 101.

dent of the United Press, on December 1, 1950. In this statement, MacArthur reviewed the Korean War but also made the
case against the Truman Administration's "containment" policy
and what he presumed to be its Europe-first emphasis.

Never before has the patience of man been more sorely tried
nor high standards of human behavior been more patiently and
firmly upheld than during the course of the Korean campaigns.

From the initiation of the North Korean aggression against
the Republic of Korea until the total defeat of the North Korean
armies, support from the Communist Chinese from behind the
privileged sanctuary of neutral boundaries was open and notorious
and all-inclusive.

Long lines of supply from the international boundary to the
southern battlefront offered some opportunity for air interdiction
and proved a tortuous route, with much that entered destroyed before reaching its destination.

When the lines of battle moved northward following the
Inchon landing, however, the area of possible interdiction of such
supply movements contracted until there was left but a night's
march from the border sanctuary to the area of immediate
hostilities.

This provided the means for the Chinese Communist authorities to move troops as well as supplies forward in great force and
quantity with the ability to elude air detection and interdiction
under cover of darkness and rugged terrain.

Our general assault launched on November 20 revealed that,
availing themselves of these distinct military advantages, Chinese
Communist forces in army corps and divisional organization of an
estimated aggregate strength of over 200,000 men then confronted
our lines.

Such revelation, through the timeliness of our attack, disclosed that the tactic of the North Koreans in initially effecting
preparations for war behind the concealment of political boundaries, and then striking with overwhelming force without warning
or notice of belligerency, was followed without variation by the
Chinese Communists.

This strategic plan—which may well find repetition in future aggressions—undoubtedly envisaged a massing, under cover of concealment, of such a powerful force as to enable the complete destruction of the United Nations command and conquest of all Korea, unquestionably the Communist objective, in one invincible movement.

The premature exposure of the plan, while not denying the enemy some tactical success through force of numbers although at staggering personnel loss, resulted in a partial strategic failure.

The existing situation under which the United Nations command is confronted with a new and fresh and well-trained and equipped enemy of vastly superior and ever-increasing numbers initiating an entirely new war to cover the North Korean defeat, results largely from the acceptance of military odds without precedent in history—the odds of permitting offensive action without defensive retaliation.

These odds have been and are being cheerfully accepted in the effort to uphold the high principles and standards which have characterized guiding policy and given nobility to the cause for which we fight, and to further the universal desire that the war be localized.

Indeed, throughout the war against the North Koreans we meticulously respected and held inviolate the international boundary and I at no time even recommended that authority be granted to retaliate beyond it.

Against such odds, officers and men of all services and participating nations have fought and, if need be, will continue to fight with unexcelled gallantry.

With this background of devotion to high principles and invincible determination to achieve the stated objectives of the United Nations, it is disturbing indeed to note the irresponsible comments appearing in responsible sections of the European press. There appears to be a general failure, intentional or from misinformation, to comprehend the mission prescribed for this command by resolutions of the United Nations of which their governments were joint architects and directors, or fairly to recognize that in success or adversity this command has proceeded unerringly in compliance with controlling policies and directives.

I can only attribute this to a somewhat selfish though most shortsighted viewpoint.

To the European the welfare and security of Europe is naturally paramount. He has no fear of attack from the West, solely from the East. It is not unusual therefore that he sees in every dedication of friendly resource toward the stabilization of Asia but a substraction from that available for the betterment and security of Europe.

This is, of course, fallacious reasoning. Any breach of freedom in the East carries with it a sinister threat to freedom in the West.

The issue is a global one and failure to comprehend this fact carries the germs of freedom's ultimate destruction.

If the fight is not waged with courage and invincible determination to meet the challenge here, it will indeed be fought, and possibly lost, on the battlefields of Europe.

Every strategic and tactical movement made by the United Nations command has been in complete accordance with United Nations resolutions and in compliance with the directive under which I operate, every major step having been previously reported and fully approved.

I have received no suggestion from any authoritative source that in the execution of its mission the command should stop at the Thirty-eighth Parallel or Pyongyang, or at any other line short of the international boundary.

To have done so would have required revision of the resolutions of the United Nations and the directives received in implementation thereof.

It is historically inaccurate to attribute any degree of responsibility for the onslaught of the Chinese Communist armies to the strategic course of the campaign itself.

The decision by the Chinese Communist leaders to wage war against the United Nations could only have been a basic one, long premediated and carried into execution as a direct result of the defeat of their satellite North Korean armies.[*1]

[*1] U.S. Congress, Joint Senate Committee on Armed Services and Foreign Relations, *Hearings: Military Situation in the Far East*, 82d Cong., 1st Sess., 1951, pp. 3535–3537.

Only a few weeks before Truman and MacArthur were enjoying something of a victory celebration on Wake Island. The General believed at that time (October 15, 1950) that formal resistance in both North and South Korea would come to an end by Thanksgiving. The discussion then turned to the topic raised by Ambassador John Muccio: "This is the first time we have moved into an area that has been dominated by Communists. We have a challenging opportunity." It was clear that rehabilitation meant the installation of a pro-Rhee, pro-American regime throughout the country. The only hitch seemed to be the United Nations resolution calling for all-Korean elections, but that was easily sidetracked. Presidential adviser Averell Harriman asked Muccio about "psychological rehabilitation" and how it might be implemented:

AMBASSADOR MUCCIO: Bring in the Koreans more. They know their own people better than we do. We should provide them with radios and textbooks and also scientific guidance. We could set up a very effective system with a radio or loud-speaker in every school and village center. I had sound trucks which were very, very effective. With no newspapers and radio service, we sent them out to rural districts and village centers.

THE PRESIDENT: I believe in sound trucks. I won two elections with them. [Laughter.]

MR. HARRIMAN: What about the psychological differences between North and South Koreans?

AMBASSADOR MUCCIO: Koreans are Koreans. There is no basic difference between them. Eighty percent of them are farmers, anyway. There is no basic schism between North and South Koreans except for a few politicos and intellectuals.

MR. HARRIMAN: What about the 2,000,000 who came down south?

AMBASSADOR MUCCIO: They were, generally, people of some means. They will be going back to North Korea and will be very helpful to us.

GENERAL BRADLEY: What can you do with the 60,000 prisoners you now have?

GENERAL MACARTHUR: They are the happiest Koreans in all Korea. For the first time they are well fed and clean. They have been deloused and have good jobs for which they are being paid under the Geneva Convention. I believe there is no real split, but their attitude is due only to the banner that flies over them. There is no difference in ideology and there are no North and South Korean blocs.

THE PRESIDENT: How will Syngman Rhee take the idea of the election?

GENERAL MACARTHUR: He won't like it.

AMBASSADOR MUCCIO: The last election was an honest election, about as honest as any ever held in the Far East. How are you going to ignore that? I hope the new Commission will not interpret that as requiring a nation-wide election. How you are going to ignore members of the National Assembly is a major problem. The resolution was so worded that it could be interpreted in different ways. There have never been local elections or elections for provincial governors. These could be held.

MR. RUSK: We must not undermine the present Korean Government. I think it may be possible to have your local and byelections in the south and elections in the north, and then it will be almost time for the 1952 elections throughout the country. I think it will require a good deal of patience.

MR. HARRIMAN: How about the interim period between elections?

GENERAL MACARTHUR: North Korea will be under military control. The UN resolution calls for the maintenance of local governments wherever possible. . . . Local government will be maintained by appointing local officials recommended by ROK officials.

AMBASSADOR MUCCIO: There is also the problem of currency to use and what land reform laws to retain in North Korea.

GENERAL MACARTHUR: In the interim the military will freeze land tenure, banks, and currency. I will keep the North Korean currency in effect in North Korea without setting a rate to the dollar or ROK won until the civilian government can take over. . . .[1]

After some further discussion about the improbability of Chinese or Soviet intervention—as estimated by General Mac-Arthur—Truman asked whether or not the time was ripe to go ahead with a Japanese peace treaty and a Pacific pact similar to NATO. On the former question MacArthur was in full agreement; on the latter he suggested that it would be better to make an announcement like the Truman Doctrine. Averell Harriman then asked if MacArthur meant only direct "external aggression" or did he "mean the type of thing that has been going on in Indochina and has previously occurred in Greece to which the Truman doctrine was directed?" It was a key question, revealing how the Korean War had indeed become far more important than just a military encounter involving American troops in a far-off corner of the world. Harriman's reference to Indo China and Greece made explicit the newly developing Cold War view which took in all corners of the globe, and all revolutionary situations. Korea also brought out a potential conflict between world opinion and American policy goals, and indicated how Truman and his advisers would react in such a situation. It began with MacArthur's warning that nothing must be done to undermine Rhee's authority throughout Korea.

GENERAL MACARTHUR: I want to take all non-Korean troops out of Korea as soon as possible. They ought to move out soon after the elections. The ROK troops can handle the situation. The greatest calamity in Asia would be if the Koreans should turn against us as a result of some UN opposition to the Rhee government. They are quite capable of handling their own military affairs. It would be a pity if we turned them against us. I have been shaking

---

[1] U.S. Congress, Senate Committees on Armed Services and Foreign Relations, *Substance of Statements Made at Wake Island Conference*, 82d Cong., 1st Sess., 1951, pp. 1–8.

in my boots ever since I saw the UN resolution which would treat them exactly on the same basis as the North Koreans. As Ambassador Muccio has said, the Koreans are a sensitive people and we might easily turn them against us. It would be bad to turn out of office a government which had stood up so well and taken such a beating, and to treat them just like the North Koreans. We have supported this government and suffered 27,000 casualties in doing so. They are a government duly elected under United Nations auspices and should not be let down.

THE PRESIDENT: This cannot be done and should not be done. We must insist on supporting this government.

MR. RUSK: We have been working and explaining our point of view in the United Nations but there has been an effective propaganda campaign against the Rhee government which has infected some of the UN delegations.

THE PRESIDENT: We must make it plain that we are supporting the Rhee government and propaganda can go to hell.

No one who was not here would believe we have covered so much ground as we have been actually able to cover. We might break up to have luncheon at 12 o'clock and in the meantime a communiqué could be prepared and talks among the members of the staff can be carried on. Then I want to award a couple medals to a couple of people and we can all leave after luncheon.

GENERAL MACARTHUR: If it's all right, I am anxious to get back as soon as possible and would like to leave before luncheon if that is convenient.

THE PRESIDENT: I believe this covers the main topics. Secretary Pace, did you have anything else to take up?

SECRETARY PACE: Yes, sir, but I can take them up separately with General MacArthur, and I imagine General Bradley has some also.

THE PRESIDENT: The communiqué should be submitted as soon as it is ready and General MacArthur can return immediately. This has been a most satisfactory conference.[1]

---

[1] Senate Committees on Armed Services and Foreign Relations, *Statements Made at Wake Island Conference*, pp. 1–8.

Domestic politics were about the only question not discussed at Wake Island, but everyone there knew that, discussed or not, politics had played a part in the Korean War from the beginning. The initial decision to accept the challenge of the North Korean invasion came in the midst of Republican accusations about the Administration's failure in Asia. China was lost; Japan was in trouble economically; even the Philippines, America's protégé in Asia, were endangered by internal subversion. Of equal concern to policymakers was the European situation, where, despite the new North Atlantic Treaty Organization, it was far from clear that France and England were willing to "bite the bullet" and rearm themselves and West Germany for the duration of the Cold War. And on top of everything there was Senator Joseph McCarthy, whose attacks on the Administration for harboring Communists in sensitive positions reduced the domestic effectiveness of the Government and made it appear ridiculous in the eyes of other nations.

Stephen E. Ambrose, an historian, reviews the many considerations that came together in June of 1950 when Truman took the policy of containment to the Asian mainland.

On June 24, 1950, American foreign policy in the Pacific was remarkably close to what some of the doves of 1970 want it to be today. At its heart, the policy of 1950 was one of maintaining positions of strength on Asia's offshore islands, especially Japan, Okinawa, and the Philippines, avoiding all entanglements on the mainland, and recognizing the fundamental fact of Asian politics —the emergence of Communist China.

American troops had been withdrawn from South Korea, so there were no American combat units anywhere on the Asian mainland. Mao Tse-tung's troops were preparing an amphibious operation against Chiang Kai-shek's remnants on Formosa, and President Harry Truman and Secretary of State Dean Acheson had warned American ambassadors around the world to be prepared for the repercussions stemming from the final fall of the Chinese Nationalist government.

In Indochina, the French were struggling, without much success, to eradicate the Communist Ho Chi Minh and his Vietminh, while in the Philippines the government faced a serious challenge from the Communist Huks. The United States was giving tidbits of aid to both counterrevolutionary efforts but, in view of the budget restraints at home and what was felt to be the overwhelming need to rearm Europe (not to mention the United States itself), scarcely enough to effect the outcome in Indochina. America's overall policy remained one of holding to its offshore bases, protected by the world's most powerful navy, staying out of the Chinese civil war, and avoiding any involvement on the mainland.

There had been two recent statements by Truman Administration spokesmen making this policy clear. On January 12, 1950, at the National Press Club, Secretary Acheson had drawn a line on a map to indicate the American defensive perimeter—the line excluded South Korea and Formosa. And on May 2, Senator Tom Connally of Texas, chairman of the Senate Foreign Relations Committee, said he was afraid South Korea would have to be abandoned. He thought the Communists were going to overrun Korea when they got ready, just as they "will overrun Formosa." Connally said he did not think Korea was "very greatly important. It has been testified before us that Japan, Okinawa, and the Phillippines make the chain of defense which is absoltuely necessary."

That remained the American position until June 25, 1950, the day hostilities began in Korea. Then, after only a few hours of meetings with Acheson and a select group of top advisers, without consulting Congress or the United Nations of America's European allies, Mr. Truman announced that he was sending supplies to South Korea, immediately increasing aid to the French in Indochina and to the Philippine government, and ordering the U.S. Seventh Fleet to sail between the Chinese mainland and Formosa to prevent the expected invasion of the island by the Communists. Mr. Truman had, in short, involved the United States in four civil wars at once, and, except in the Philippines, all in areas the Americans had previously regarded as outside their sphere of influence. The United States was *on* the Asian mainland.

These were sweeping policy decisions, among the most important of the entire Cold War, carrying with them enormous long-term implications. They were hardly the kind that a government ordinarily makes without deliberation. Yet Mr. Truman later claimed that he made them solely as a result of the Korean War, the outbreak of which astonished him—as it supposedly did General Douglas MacArthur's headquarters in Tokyo—as much "as if the sun had suddenly gone out." For a man who had been surprised, Mr. Truman had recovered with amazing speed.

Actually, as I. F. Stone has shown in his book, *The Hidden History of the Korean War*, there was no surprise. The Americans had a good general idea of what was coming and had their counter-measures prepared. Intelligence reports on North Korean intentions had been specific enough to allow the U.S. State Department, days before the attack, to prepare a resolution to submit to the Security Council of the United Nations condemning North Korea for aggression.

At the time, the Soviet Union was boycotting the United Nations for its refusal to seat Red China; the State Department was prepared to take its resolution to the General Assembly if the Russians came back to the Security Council and exercised their veto. But the Soviets did not return, for they had been caught off guard. Stalin, in fact, seems to have been the most surprised by the outbreak of hostilities; certainly the Americans were much better prepared to move for U.N. action than the Russians were. The resolution the Americans pushed through the Security Council on the day of the attack branded the North Koreans as aggressors, demanded a cessation of hostilities, and requested a withdrawal behind the thirty-eighth parallel. The resolution was a brilliant stroke, for without any investigation at all it established war guilt and put the United Nations behind the official American version.

The speed and scope of the American response to the Korean War were truly impressive. So were the Cold War advantages that accrued. America eventually established a costly hegemony over non-Communist Asia, gained gigantic (and strategically invaluable) military bases for itself in South Korea, Formosa, Indochina, and Thailand, aroused public support for an enormously increased Department of Defense budget (from $13 billion in 1950 to $50 billion the next year), made possible European, including West German, rearmament, and in general put the United States on a permanent Cold War footing. In addition, the Americans saved the governments of Chiang in Formosa and Syngman Rhee in South Korea from certain extinction. After a thorough examination of these and other pieces of circumstantial evidence, Stone, and historian D. F. Fleming, in his work, *The Cold War and Its Origins*, have charged that the South Koreans—with American support—began the war.

Before that accusation can be examined, however, it is necessary to understand the basis of the Truman policy. How did it come about that the United States became committed to the containment of Communism everywhere, whatever the cost? Which is only another way of asking, "How did we get on the Asian mainland?" . . . the Republicans had not made an issue of foreign policy in the 1948 elections (only third-party Presidential candidate Henry Wallace did), and by 1950 they tended to believe that their failure to do so was a key factor in their defeat. They began, almost gleefully, to charge the Truman Administration with having "lost" China and with losing the Philippines, Formosa, South Korea, and Indochina. The Republicans, led by Senator Joseph McCarthy, began to insist that the Truman Administration, and most notably Secretary Acheson, was soft on Communism, or worse.

The Democrats were bewildered and angry. With some justice, they wondered what more they could have done to stand up to the Soviets, especially in view of the funds available, funds drastically limited by the very Republicans who now demanded blood for the State Department's shortcomings. Mr. Truman desperately wanted to extend containment to Asia, but he could not even implement it in Europe.

Mr. Truman's frustrations, in the spring of 1950, were great. Foreign and military policy were moving in opposite directions. While Acheson advocated ever greater commitments to the non-Communist world, Louis Johnson, a curious kind of Secretary of Defense was scuttling the Navy's super-carrier and doing everything he could to keep the Defense Department budget under $13 billion, all in accord with Mr. Truman's own policy of balancing the budget. Mr. Truman had commissioned a major study of America's strategic position; the final result reached his desk in early June, 1950, as National Security Council paper number 68 (thereafter known as NSC 68). Still classified and unpublished twenty years later, it was one of the key historic documents of the Cold War. NSC 68, as Senator Henry Jackson, Washington Democrat, observed, was "the first comprehensive statement of a national strategy."

NSC 68 advocated, in the words of one of its authors, "an immediate and large-scale build-up in our military and general strength and that of our allies with the intention of righting the power balance." It did so on the basis of an analysis of the Soviet Union which held that the Soviets were not only dedicated to preserving their own power and ideology but to extending and consolidating power by absorbing new satellites and weakening their enemies. Implicit in the analysis was the idea that whenever the West lost a position of strength, whether it be a military base or a colony undergoing a war of national liberation, the Kremlin was behind it. This came close to saying that all change was directed by the Communists and should be resisted. The analysis also assumed that if America were willing to try, it could stop change.

The paper was realistic in assessing what it would cost America to become the world policeman. Instead of the $13 billion the Truman Administration was planning on spending annually on defense, NSC 68 wanted to start with $35 billion in fiscal year 1951 and move up to $50 billion a year later. Politically, this was impossible. Truman recognized, as he later wrote, that NSC 68 "meant a great military effort in time of peace. It meant doubling or tripling the budget, increasing taxes heavily, and imposing various kinds of economic controls. It meant a great change in our normal peacetime way of doing things." He refused to allow any publicity about NSC 68 and indicated that he would do nothing about revising the budget until after Congressional election in November, 1950. He knew that without a major crisis there was no chance of selling the program to the Congress or to the country.

The contradictory pressures on foreign policy, meanwhile, were almost maddening. While President Truman and Acheson defended themselves from charges of having given China to Mao, they stimultaneously had to prepare for even more embarrassments, most notably the expected loss of Formosa and South Korea.

In Korea, all was tension. Postwar Soviet-American efforts to unify the country, where American troops had occupied the area south of the thirty-eighth parallel, and Russia the area to the north, had achieved nothing. In 1947 the United States had submitted the Korean question to the U.N. General Assembly for disposition. Russia, fearful of the implications, had refused to go along. The Soviets reasoned that if the question of Korea could be given to the General Assembly, where the United States controlled a voting majority, nothing would prevent the United States from giving the problem of divided Germany to the Assembly too. The Soviets therefore refused to allow the U.N. Commission on Korea to enter North Korea.

Elections were held in South Korea in May, 1948; Syngman Rhee became president. The Russians set up a government in North Korea. Both the United States and the Soviets withdrew their occupation troops; both continued to give military aid to their respective zones, although the Russians did so on a larger scale.

Rhee was a petty dictator and an embarrassment to the United States. In January, 1950, Philip C. Jessup, U.S. Ambassador-at-large, told the Korean National Assembly that the United States was dissatisfied with the severe restraints on civil liberties which it had imposed. In April, Acheson told Rhee flatly that he either had to hold previously scheduled but consistently delayed elections or lose Ameircan aid. Rhee gave in, although on the eve of the elections he arrested thirty of his leading opponents in anti-Communist raids. Still his party collected only forty-eight seats, with 120 going to other parties, mostly on the left. The new Assembly then began to indicate that it wanted to consider unification with the North. Rhee was faced with the total loss of his position.

There was a curious incident shortly after the South Korean elections, one that none of the historians of the Korean War has examined in depth. On June 9 the radio at Pyongyang, North Korea's capital, denounced the recent elections in the South as fraudulent and called for a general election throughout Korea. The North Koreans proposed an election on August 5 of a general legislative organ that would meet in Seoul, capital of South Korea. Rhee, his prime minister, and the U.N. Commission in Korea would all be barred.

Rhee scoffed at the call for elections, dismissing it as "poppy-cock propaganda" but the U.N. Commission indicated that it was interested, and on June 11, John Gaillard, an American member of the Commission, crossed the thirty-eighth parallel to talk to three North Korean representatives. They gave him copies of the appeal for an election, then crossed the parallel themselves with hundreds of copies of the appeal, which they intended to distribute to the South Koreans. Rhee's police immediately arrested them. There appears to be no evidence that Washington ever explored Pyongyang's suggestion for general elections, and this raises interesting questions about the entire U.S. policy regarding Korea.

Events everywhere in Asia were moving towards a crisis. The British were out of India, revolt was stirring in Malaya, and the Dutch had been forced to leave Indonesia. In Indochina, the French were barely able to hold on. Nearly all the independent Asian governments were hostile to the West. The substitution of native leaders, usually radical, for the white rulers in Asia carried with it terrifying implications for Washington. There was a real possibility that American corporations would lose both their access to the raw materials (especially metals) and to the markets of Southeast Asia. Strategically, none of the new governments would be able to serve as an effective counter to the Chinese, which meant an end to the balance of power in Asia. Only Rhee in South Korea and Chiang in Formosa swam against the powerful tide, and the West did not have the military means available at that time to keep either of its proxies in power. What the Americans liked to call "stability in Asia" was threatened.

This crisis was most acute in China, for if the Chinese Communists drove Chiang off Formosa they would complete their victory and eventually the United States would have to recognize the Communists as the legitimate government of China, which would mean—among other things—giving Chiang's seat on the U.N. Security Council to Mao. The United States would no longer be able to regard Chiang as head of a government or maintain the fiction that he would someday return to his rightful place as ruler of all of China. This in turn would require a new definition of the economic and political relations between China and the United States.

Since late 1949, President Truman had consistently refused to provide aid to Chiang, who had proved to be a poor investment at best. The President insisted—rather late in the game—that the United States would not be drawn into the Chinese civil war. This policy was consistent with the European orientation of the Truman Administration and, in terms of the money Congress had made available for foreign aid, it was realistic. Its only possible outcome, however, was an end to Chiang's pretensions and an American acceptance of the Chinese Communists among the family of nations.

The domestic political results for the Democrats of such a course of events were frightening to contemplate. Already former President Herbert Hoover had joined with Senator Taft in demanding that the U.S. Pacific Fleet be used to prevent an invasion of Formosa, while other Republicans advocated using the fleet to carry Chiang's forces back to the mainland for the reconquest of China. If Mr. Truman wished to quiet the McCarthyites at all, he would have to rethink his China policy.

By June, 1950, a series of desperate needs had come together. Mr. Truman had to have a crisis to sell the NSC 68 program of a huge U.S. military buildup. Chiang could not hold on, nor could Rhee, without an American commitment; the U.S. Air Force and Navy needed a justification to retain their bases in Japan; the Democrats had to prove that they could get tough with the Communists. Most of all, the Americans had to establish themselves on the mainland before the white man was driven out of Asia and its islands forever.

The needs were met on June 25, 1950. The outbreak of the Korean War came as a godsend to Chiang, Rhee, and the Truman Administration. Since it "proved" the aggressiveness of international Communism, the war enabled Mr. Truman to push through the NSC 68 program with its vastly increased military budgets, American aid for European rearmament, and an enormously expanded American military presence in Asia.

When President Truman announced that the Seventh Fleet was going to the Formosan Straits, Peiping immediately charged that the Pentagon was seeking to establish a military base on Chinese territory and asked the United Nations to order the

Americans to withdraw. Warren Austin, U.S. Ambassador to the United Nations, refuted the charge indignantly, while Mr. Truman declared that the United States "would not seek any special position or privilege on Formosa." Jakob Malik, the Russian delegate, then accused the United States of lusting for bases in Formosa and supported his charge by quoting General MacArthur's statements to the effect that America intended to establish and hold air fields on the island. Mr. Truman rejoined that MacArthur did not speak for the Administration. Yet, as everyone knows, the United States now has enormous air bases on Formosa. By the same token, the Americans declared throughout the Korean War that they had no intention of maintaining troops there once the conflict ended. Lyndon Johnson was to say the same thing about Vietnam.

For more than a decade and a half after the Korean War began, almost no one seriously questioned the Truman Administration's interpretation of the cause of the war, which held that it began because Stalin told the North Koreans to go ahead and attack South Korea. This interpretation strengthened the notion that there was an international Communist conspiracy, centered in the Kremlin, and that therefore all wars of national liberation were carried out by Russian proxies solely to serve the interests of the Soviet Union. This view in turn allowed the Americans to dash into Lebanon at President Eisenhower's orders, to attempt by force, with President Kennedy's approval, to overthrow Castro, to intervene in the Dominican Republic at President Johnson's command, and most of all to involve this country in Vietnam.

The interpretation of the causes of the Korean War, in short, has helped shape American assumptions about the nature of the world. The interpretation may conceivably be correct, but there are questions concerning it that must be asked, and answered, before it can be fully accepted. The standard explanation, for example, as to why the Russians were not in the United Nations during the critical period when the Korean War began, is that Stalin simply made a mistake. He did not think the Americans would return to the Korean peninsula, nor did he expect the United States to go to the United Nations and ask for a condemnation of aggression by North Korea. But Stalin was ordinarily a cautious man who made few mistakes.

The explanation that he was surprised by the American reaction, even if he was, is clearly unsatisfactory, for it leaves unanswered a further query: why did not Stalin send his ambassador back to the Security Council after the first U.S. resolution went through on June 25, the day war broke out, branding North Korea as the aggressor?

The importance of the second question lies in the fact that not until June 27—two days after the outbreak of hostilities—did the United States introduce the second resolution—passed that day—which recommended to the members of the United Nations that they aid South Korea in restoring peace. It was the June 27 resolution which gave the United States U.N. cover for its essentially unilateral action in Korea. Those who wish to maintain that the Russians started the North Koreans on their way south must explain why the Soviets were not in the United Nations to protect their own interests in that world body.

The second mystery about the Soviets is why they took no action elsewhere. President Truman and Acheson assumed from the start that the Korean War was a feint. They reasoned that Stalin wanted them to put America's strength into the Pacific so that he could then march against a defenseless West Europe. The Americans countered this expected strategy by concentrating their military build-up in Europe, not Korea (much to General MacArthur's disgust; indeed, this was a basic cause of the Truman-MacArthur controversy).

Administration supporters have argued that Stalin did not move in Europe only because the United States beat him to the punch. The trouble with that view is that it took months for the Americans to get any strength into Europe; in the meantime, Stalin did nothing. If he started the Korean War as part of a worldwide offensive, as Mr. Truman argued, where was the rest of the offensive?

Finally, if the Russians started the whole thing, where were they at the critical moment? The North Koreans pushed the South Koreans and the small American contingent steadily south until early August, when MacArthur's forces were pinned into a beachhead around Pusan. But the North Koreans were incapable of delivering the final blow and had to watch, more or less helplessly, as MacArthur built up his strength and made his position invulnerable.

Red Army officers must have watched from afar with anguish, for their experience against the Germans only five years earlier had made them the world's leading experts on knocking out defensive positions. If Russia did indeed urge the North Koreans to attack, and if Stalin's aim was in fact to conquer the peninsula, why were no Red Army advisers sent to the North Koreans at the decisive moment? MacArthur himself testified later that no Russians had ever been seen anywhere in the Korean peninsula during the war. Once the Americans had intervened, but before they arrived in great strength, why did not the Russians send a few "volunteer" units to Korea to insure the final push of MacArthur's forces into the sea?

The idea that Russia and China acted in concert in starting the war has, fortunately, long since disappeared. A 1960 RAND Corporation study, *China Crosses the Yalu*, by Allen S. Whiting, concluded that the Chinese were the most surprised of anyone by the outbreak of hostilities in Korea. Mao's two major priorities in June, 1950, were to use his army to reconstruct China and to invade Formosa. His troop dispositions reflected these priorities, and were about as bad as they possibly could have been to support a war in Korea. Indeed, the big losers in the war—aside from the Korean people—were the Chinese, who lost their chance to grab Formosa and who had to divert desperately needed human and material resources from reconstruction and the building of a new society to keep American troops from the Yalu River at China's southern door. The Russians lost too, for Stalin's worst fears were realized as a direct result of the war—West Germany was rearmed and integrated into an anti-Soviet military alliance, and the United States began a massive rearmament program.

The big winners were Chiang, Rhee, and the Truman Administration, which extended containment to Asia, gained additional military bases in the Far East, unilaterally wrote the Japanese peace treaty, retained American markets and access to the natural resources of Southeast Asia, proved to the public that it was not "soft on Communism," and in general reversed the tide of change—at least for a time—that had been running so strongly against the white man in the Far East.

As noted earlier, I. F. Stone and D. F. Fleming have carefully examined the problem of whose needs were met by the Korean War, and who won and who lost, and concluded that the North Koreans were merely responding to aggression by Rhee, an aggression encouraged by Chiang and the United States. But while the circumstantial evidence is strong, these charges almost certainly go too far. The North Korean offensive was too strong, too well coordinated, and too successful to be simply a counterattack.

But granting that the North Koreans were the aggressors does not automatically make the Truman Administration interpretation of the origins of the war correct. There are too many questions that must be answered before it can be accepted.

The most reasonable tentative conclusion is that the North Koreans took matters into their own hands. They decided they could over-run the peninsula before the Americans could reinforce the South Koreans—an assessment that was not far wrong —and they moved. They probably expected that the United States would not intervene at all. Certainly we have had sufficient evidence in the late 1960s of North Korean independence from the Kremlin to make this judgment reasonable.

For our time, the important point is that Mr. Truman seized the opportunity to extend containment to the Asian mainland, thereby reversing entirely—and evidently permanently—America's Pacific policy, on the basis of a highly dubious interpretation of the causes of the conflict, based in turn on a belief in an international Communist conspiracy that never existed. The irony is that of all Mr. Truman's dramatic actions in the last week of June, 1950, the least noticed turned out to be the most important—the increase in U.S. aid to the French in Indochina that demonstrated his determination to prevent Ho Chi Minh from gaining control of Vietnam.

The seeming inevitability of American foreign policy in the postwar period—the Russians act, we react to preserve freedom —rests, in its essentials, on one basic assumption. President Truman, Acheson, and the other architects of the policy of containment (which was never more than a euphemism for the expansion of American influence and dominance) believed—or at least professed to believe—that the Kremlin had a "strategy" for world conquest.

For those who demanded proof of Stalin's intentions, the Administration pointed above all to the supposed Russian influence on and support for the Greek rebels, Ho Chi Minh, and the North Koreans. Historians, however, are finding it extraordinarily difficult to come by any solid evidence of Russian involvement on a significant scale in Greece, Indochina, or even North Korea (after 1948).

The obsessive American fears, in short, not to mention the violent American reaction, were based on assumptions that were almost surely wrong. Taking into account all that flowed from those assumptions—McCarthyism, the Cold War, ABMs, Indochina, and so on—this is the major tragedy of our times.[*1]

Professor Ambrose suggests that North Korea had enough independence to carry out the attack alone, with or without the permission of the Kremlin. That may be so. Other considerations may have weighed heavily with Stalin, however, which would have allowed him to initiate the attack or acquiesce in Pyongyang's decision. Policy planner George F. Kennan has suggested that the American decision to proceed independently with the conclusion of a Japanese peace treaty involving the indefinite retention of American military bases in the Japanese Islands might have had something to do with "the Soviet decision to unleash a civil war in Korea. . . ."[4] In October 1949, moreover, Congress had appropriated $58 million for a bomber base on Okinawa from which American planes carrying atomic weapons could reach China and Asiatic Russia. It may have been also that Stalin wished to clear up his Far Eastern flank should China and Japan become involved once again. Information about the

---

[*1] Stephen E. Ambrose, "The Failure of a Policy Rooted in Fear," *The Progressive*, XXXIV (November, 1970), pp. 14–20.

background to the Sino-Soviet split of later years is still scanty, but it is known that North Korea had closer ties with Moscow than with Peking.

Truman gave different reasons for his decision to take a stand in South Korea, but it all came down to a feeling that, "If we let Korea down the Soviet will keep right on going and swallow up one piece of Asia after another." When Asia went, the Middle East would come next, and then Europe.[5] Curiously enough, however, the Joint Chiefs of Staff had recommended on at least two earlier occasions against becoming involved in the "Korean situation." The United States should not become involved, said the military men, so that an action taken by "any faction in Korea" or even by "any other power in Korea" would not be "considered a *casus belli* for the United States."[6] In other words, the Pentagon did not regard Korea as of strategic importance to the United States. Quite the opposite, in fact, for it recommended against regarding an attack by North Korea, China, or Russia as a reason for going to war.

What other conditions overrode this clear statement of military opposition in Washington? We have already noted factors which might have operated on Stalin—short of a desire for world conquest—and there was a set of considerations at work on Washington decisionmakers as well which amounted to something less than world empire. Domestic politics was one. A more intriguing, albeit problematical, combination is suggested by two memorandums by John Foster Dulles in the weeks before the North Korean invasion. Selected by the Truman Administration to undertake preliminary negotiations with the Japanese and other powers for a peace treaty to end the Pacific war, Dulles spoke with the President on April 28, 1950, about the political situation. What was needed, said the future Secretary of State, was "some early affirmative action" in foreign policy to restore the nation's confidence that the Government could and would deal with the Communist menace. The people had lost confidence in the Government because of the Far East; it was the "loss" of China that had given Senator Joe McCarthy his chance. "If we could really get going, the American people would fall in behind that leadership and attacks like McCarthy's would be forgotten." A few weeks later Dulles wrote another memorandum to himself on the Far Eastern situation. This one began with a statement that the loss of China meant a shift in the balance of power. How serious a shift depended upon several things, however, including American reactions. Above all the United States must not continue to fall back in Asia. "The situation in Japan may become untenable [if America continued to retreat] and possibly that in the Philippines. Indonesia, with its vast natural resources, may be lost and the oil of the Middle East will be in jeopardy. None of these places provide holding grounds once the people feel that Communism is the wave of the future and that even we are retreating before it."

Then came this concluding comment: "This series of disasters can probably be prevented if at some doubtful point we quickly take a dramatic and strong stand that shows our confidence and resolution. Probably this series of disasters cannot be prevented in any other way."[7] Dulles was at MacArthur's side when word came to Tokyo of the North Korean attack; his was one of the most urgent voices calling for intervention over the trans-Pacific cables. Both Dulles and the American commander in Tokyo were surprised, however, at the President's swift determination to stand firm in South Korea. The President's decision was apparently instantaneous, or nearly so, and may simply have been (as he once wrote) the product of bad memories of "appeasement" in the 1930's.

In the early spring of 1950 a group of top policy planners completed their review of American options in light of the Russian development of atomic capabilities and weapons. The document they produced, NSC-68 (National Security Council Paper No. 68), called for "virtual abandonment by the United States of trying to distinguish between national and global security." It also called for an end to "traditional budgeting restrictions" on national security needs. About this same time, Secretary of State Dean Acheson was announcing the end of another traditional distinction. There was no longer any real difference between foreign and domestic policy (if there ever had been); what the United States needed was "total diplomacy," if it was to survive the Cold War. Total diplomacy meant creating "situations of strength," said Acheson; it did not mean sitting down with the Russians to work things out.

I would like to talk to you about the need today for "total diplomacy." A few years ago, we in this country were fully acquainted with the phrase "total war" and with the implications of that phrase. We knew that we were engaged in a life and death struggle with a powerful foe and that if we were to be successful in that struggle we would not have merely to turn the problem over to the Department of Defense or to any other branch of the Government and expect that we could succeed. It was necessary for each of us to play our assigned role in our common defense, to establish controls of the most far-reaching sort, and, in other ways, to make sure that all of the forces of the country were directed in the most efficient manner possible to the winning of the war.

Today, we are engaged in a struggle—that is the word to describe it—that is just as crucial from the point of view of the continued existence of our way of life, but we clearly are not focusing our total resources on the winning of that struggle.

For one thing, we have never taken the general activities of our country—which mean governmental activities—as seriously as we should in times of peace. We have regarded them with a good-natured tolerance expressed in the phrase, "Well, politics is politics." We have thought of politics as a legitimate field for trying to promote special interests. There is a tendency to shrug our shoulders over governmental shortcomings and faults. Moreover, while we have recognized that there were foreign claims upon us which our self-interest demanded that we attend to, we have not thought of them as being in the same category of importance as our own domestic business.

Then, too, it has been hard for us to convince ourselves that human nature is not pretty much the same the world over. We hear it said that if we could only get Harry Truman to "get his feet under the same table"—that is the phrase used—with Joe Stalin, we would be able to iron out any international difficulty. Our own experience with people in our own communities has been such that it has seemed to us that good intentions must, in the long run, prevail—and if one proposition didn't meet with acceptance, all we had to do was to think up a better one.

There has been an attitude on the part of some that if things went too far we might have to "call their bluff" and possibly have a show-down.

In brief, we have felt that, somehow or other, there was an answer to our problem if only we were smart enough to figure it out.

We must realize, however, that the world situation is not one to which there is an easy answer. The only way to deal with the Soviet Union, we have found from hard experience, is to create situations of strength. Wherever the Soviet detects weakness or disunity—and it is quick to detect them—it exploits them to the full. A "show-down," in the brutal and realistic sense, of resort to a military decision is not a possible policy for a democracy. The Kremlin knows that.

We are struggling against an adversary that is deadly serious. We are in a situation where we are playing for keeps. Moreover, we are in a situation where we could lose without ever firing a shot.

It used to be said that the progress of imperialism was, first, to send out missionaries, then traders, and then colonial governors. But that is kid stuff compared to the methods that we are up against. There has never, in the history of the world, been an imperalist system that compares with what the Soviet Union has at its disposal. We have seen it in China. The Communists took over China at a ridiculously small cost. What they did was to invite some Chinese leaders who were dissatisfied with the way things were going in their country to come to Moscow. There, they thoroughly indoctrinated them so that they returned to China prepared to resort to any means whatsoever to establish Communist control. They were completely subservient to the Moscow regime. (It is, of course, because Tito has thrown off this subservience that the Tito development is regarded with such deadly seriousness by Moscow.) These agents then mingled among the people and sold them on the personal material advantages of communism. They talked to the people in their own language. They promised to turn over the land to them. (Of course, everybody knows that after the land has been turned over to them and the Communists have gotten control they immediately take the land back under a program of "collectivization.")

But the Communists don't talk only in terms of economic interest. We have all seen pictures from China of native dances out in the fields which were put on by the local Communist organization. In many cases, they provided the only fun that these peasants had, and the peasants were led to believe that the Communist organization was the only group that provided the kind of life the peasants wanted.

The arsenal of the Communists is varied. I need not describe in detail the uses which they make of force, threats, infiltration, planned chaos, despair and confusion, and the enslavement of the people they dominate by a shrewd use of informers.

Against this threat we must have a foreign policy with two interrelated branches. First, we must be prepared to meet wherever possible all thrusts of the Soviet Union. It will not always be possible to anticipate where these thrusts will take place, and we will not always be able to deal with them with equal effectiveness. In the case of Greece and Turkey, we were able to meet that thrust effectively because the Greeks and the Turks were determined to maintain their independence. There were a lot of Greeks and Turks that did not like their government. There were a lot that did. But they were united in a common belief that they preferred it to any form of government that might be imposed upon them from outside. The Greeks were able, with our assistance, to meet military force with military force. The Turks have successfully resisted the powerful Soviet pressure brought against them. It should be borne in mind that in this case we were not dealing with threats to Greece and Turkey alone. The thrust that the Soviet Union was making in this case was directed at domination of the entire Near East and, then, at all of Europe.

It has been suggested by some people that the Greek and Turkish Governments were not our kind of democracy and therefore we should not have given them our aid. Of course, they do not have exactly the same kind of institutions that we do. But we are not dealing here with the kind of situation where we can go from one country to another with a piece of litmus paper and see whether everything is true blue, whether the political, economic, and social climate is exactly, in all its details, the kind that we would like to have either for them or for us. The only question that we should ask is whether they are determined to project their independence against Communist aggression and if they are, we should recognize our basic unity with them on this point.

In the case of China, the Communist thrust succeeded because the Chinese people were not convinced that the National Government was concerned with their welfare. I do not think that this thrust could have been prevented so long as the Chinese people felt that we were supporting a government that they did not believe to be serving their interest.

The second part of our foreign policy must be to create those economic, political, social, and psychological conditions that strengthen and create confidence in the democratic way of life. In Indonesia, for instance, we have been trying to make it plain to the Indonesians that we are sympathetic with their aspirations for independence. They do not want to be ruled by the Dutch or by the Russians or by anyone else. They want to rule themselves. If we are to establish a solidarity with them, we must have Americans living among them who talk their language—I mean literally talk the Indonesian language—who understand them and are understood by them. We must do what we can to help them make the most of their natural resources. We do this not by building elaborate plants but by such things as enabling the Indonesian farmers to help themselves, to have better tools, and to use better methods than they have known before. We must see their problems from their point of view. We must help them, so far as we can, to reach their own goals.

In areas like Western Europe where there is a fully developed modern industrial economy, we must help the countries to take the measures that are necessary to put that economy on a sound basis.

One of the things that we must do is to enable other countries to buy with their own products the raw materials that they need to feed and clothe and employ their own people. This means that we must buy their goods and their services to a greater extent than at present. It is a matter of judgment as to what the level of our trade with the rest of the world should be, but probably it should be somewhere not very far from present levels. We must take that kind of action even though it requires adjustments here at home —and it will require some adjustments. Make no mistake about it, if we want to have strong allies in Europe, we have got to work out some kind of pattern of this kind. That will mean that European goods will compete with American goods and some American industries are likely to suffer. If this should prove to be the case, then means must be found to take care of any resulting adjustments.

We are going to need self-discipline in what we say and do. What we say and do has tremendous importance in strengthening or weakening this country's leadership.

It is, of course, extremely difficult to get democracies to work together. The democratic approach, by its very nature, is a varied approach. It embodies freedom of action and freedom of decision, but if we are to win against a power that has imposed complete unity on all of its members, we shall have to achieve, in our own way and by common determination, some unity of our own.

When we have reached unity and determination on the part of the free nations—when we have eliminated all of the areas of weakness that we can—we will be able to evolve working agreements with the Russians. We will not have to keep our ears to the ground in order to know when the Russians are prepared to recognize that they cannot exploit a situation to their own benefit. . . .

No good would come from our taking the initiative in calling for conversations at this point. Such an effort on our part would raise false hopes among some people and fears among others. The Russians would know that there was a public expectancy of results of some kind, and those results could only be achieved by dangerous concessions on our part. Only the Russians would benefit from such a step.

The Russians know that we are ready, always have been ready, always will be ready, to discuss with them any outstanding issue. We have discussed with them all important outstanding issues, not once, but many times. It is clear that the Russians do not want to settle those issues as long as they feel there is any possibility they can exploit them for their own objectives of world domination. It is only when they come to the conclusion that they cannot so exploit them that they will make agreements and they will let it be known when they have reached that decision.

These are some of the things that I meant when I referred to "total diplomacy." It means that all branches of the government must work closely together. Congress and the Departments of Defense, Treasury, Agriculture, and Commerce, and Interior Department, with its responsibility for our national resources, and the others, all have roles to play that are just as important in our relations with other people as the role of the Department of State.

And so it is with business, agriculture, and labor, with the press and with the radio, with all of our great national organizations. We must agree voluntarily to concert our efforts to this one overriding task. If we do that, there can be little doubt that we shall succeed. The non Communist countries together have two-thirds of the world's population, three-fourths of the world's economic productive power, and a potential preponderance of the world's military power. They have the highest standard of living and the greatest ability to help underdeveloped areas achieve higher standards of living. They have on their side the appeal of independence and of national loyalties. They have the greatest attraction of all—human freedom. With these forces on our side, provided we use them well and wisely, the chances of victory and of peace are good.[1]

Acheson's reduction of the Chinese revolution to "some Chinese leaders who were dissatisfied with the way things were going in their country," and who were willing to be "completely subservient to the Moscow regime" was nothing less than an admission that the Administration had turned its back on what it knew to be the truth about the Far East—whether from fear of Senator McCarthy and the Republicans or from reasons of wishing to oppose Communism anywhere under any circumstances.

The Secretary's statement that "no good would come from our taking the initiative in calling for conversations at this point" referred to suggestions from some quarters that the Soviet Union's development of atomic energy required the United States to re-

---

[1] "Total Diplomacy to Strengthen United States Leadership for Human Freedom," remarks to the Advertising Council at the White House, February 16, 1950, Department of State, *American Foreign Policy*, 1950–1955 (2 v. Washington, 1957), I, 5–10.

think not only its military policy and its diplomatic approach beginning with weapons control, but also political questions as well. Privately, Acheson held the position that development of hydrogen weapons was imperative for the United States—not to achieve a situation of strength *for* negotiations, but to prevent erosion of the power and will *to resist* negotiations. Negotiations meant adjustment and Acheson had no desire to adjust relationships in Europe, or to deal with revolutionary situations outside of Europe. Total diplomacy, in short, actually meant no diplomacy—until that unlikely time in the distant future when the Soviets would abandon their drive for world domination. Until such time, all wars were one war in the sense that an outbreak anywhere could be exploited by the Communists. Thus Harry S Truman declared that Korea was like Greece; and John Foster Dulles became convinced that America must respond at some unlikely point. Narrow military considerations perhaps sufficient for an earlier era no longer sufficed. Korea may have been the wrong war to the Pentagon, but not to the National Security Council which devised NSC-68.

Acheson's brief reference to "enabling . . . Indonesian farmers to help themselves" had to do with the Administration's pre-Korean plans for meeting the challenge of the underdeveloped world, specifically the series of programs known later as the Mutual Security Acts and the so-called Point IV plan for extending technological know-how to the non-European areas of the world. When Congress enacted these laws, it made sure that no element of international "do-goodism" or "New Dealism–Fair Dealism" crept in through the fine print. Enabling legislation for the Point IV program included the following:

Be it enacted by the Senate and House of Representatives of the United States of America in Congress assembled, That this Act may be cited as the "Foreign Economic Assistance Act of 1950."

Be it enacted by the Senate and House of Representatives of the United States of America in Congress assembled, That this Act may be cited as the "Foreign Economic Assistance Act of 1950."

TITLE IV

SEC. 401. This title may be cited as the "Act for International Development."

SEC. 402. The Congress hereby finds as follows:

a. The peoples of the United States and other nations have a common interest in the freedom and in the economic and social progress of all peoples. Such progress can further the secure growth of democratic ways of life, the expansion of mutually beneficial commerce, the development of international understanding and good will, and the maintenance of world peace.

b. The efforts of the peoples living in economically underdeveloped areas of the world to realize their full capabilities and to develop the resources of the lands in which they live can be furthered through the cooperative endeavor of all nations to exchange technical knowledge and skills and to encourage the flow of investment capital.

c. Technical assistance and capital investment can make maximum contribution to economic development only where there is understanding of the mutual advantages of such assistance and investment and where there is confidence of fair and reasonable treatment and due respect for the legitimate interests of the peoples of the countries to which the assistance is given and in which the investment is made and of the countries from which the assistance and investments are derived. In the case of investment this involves confidence on the part of the people of the underdeveloped areas that investors will conserve as well as develop local resources, will bear a fair share of local taxes and observe local laws, and will provide adequate wages and working conditions for local labor. It involves confidence on the part of investors, through intergovernmental agreements or otherwise, that they will not be deprived of their property without prompt, adequate, and effective compensation; that they will be given reasonable opportunity to remit their earnings and withdraw their capital; that they will have reasonable freedom to manage, operate, and control their enterprises; that they will enjoy security in the protection of their persons and property, including industrial and intellectual property, and nondiscriminatory treatment in taxation and in the conduct of their business affairs.

SEC. 403.

a. It is declared to be the policy of the United States to aid the efforts of the peoples of economically underdeveloped areas to develop their resources and improve their working and living conditions by encouraging the exchange of technical knowledge and skills and the flow of investment capital to countries which provide conditions under which such technical assistance and capital can effectively and constructively contribute to raising standards of living, creating new sources of wealth, increasing productivity and expanding purchasing power.

b. It is further declared to be the policy of the United States that in order to achieve the most effective utilization of the resources of the United States, private and public, which are or may be available for aid in the development of economically underdeveloped areas, agencies of the United States Government, in reviewing requests of foreign governments for aid for such purposes, shall take into consideration (1) whether the assistance applied for is an appropriate part of a program reasonably designed to contribute to the balanced and integrated development of the country or area concerned; (2) whether any works or facilities which may be projected are actually needed in view of similar facilities existing in the area and are otherwise economically sound; and (3) with respect to projects for which capital is requested, whether private capital is available either in the country or elsewhere upon reasonable terms and in sufficient amounts to finance such projects.*1

The first Mutual Defense Assistance Act had been enacted in 1949, making available $1.3 billion for military aid. Two months after the outbreak of war in Korea, Congress approved an additional $5.2 billion for 1951. As the State Department noted, "The Mutual Security Act of 1951 marked the end of a two-year

---

*1 Act for International Development (excerpts), Public Law 535, June 5, 1950, *American Foreign Policy, 1950–1955*, II, 3047–3048.

period during which the emphasis of United States assistance shifted gradually from economic rehabilitation to military assistance, began the effort toward integration of economic recovery and military assistance programs, and symbolized the reorientation of United States foreign policy with regard to the foreign aid programs."[8] The Mutual Security Act of 1951 and its successors included the following important clauses:

STRATEGIC MATERIALS

SEC. 514. In order to reduce the drain on United States resources and to assure the production of adequate supplies of essential raw materials for the collective defense of the free world, the Director for Mutual Security is authorized to initiate projects for, and assist in procuring and stimulating increased production of, materials in which deficiences or potential deficiencies in supply exist among nations receiving United States assistance. There is hereby authorized to be appropriated to the President for the fiscal year 1954 not to exceed $7,500,000 to carry out the provisions of this section.

ENCOURAGEMENT OF FREE ENTERPRISE

SEC. 516.*[1]

a. The Congress recognizes the vital role of free enterprise in achieving rising levels of production and standards of living essential to the economic progress and defensive strength of

*[1] Subsec. (a) was revised by sec. 710 (a) of the Mutual Security Act of 1953. It formerly read as follows:
"It is hereby declared to be the policy of the Congress that this Act shall be administered in such a way as (1) to eliminate the barriers to, and provide the incentives for, a steadily increased participation of free private enterprise in developing the resources of foreign countries consistent with the policies of this Act, (2) to the extent that it is feasible and does not interfere with the achievement of the purposes set forth in this Act, to discourage the cartel and monopolistic business practices prevailing in certain countries receiving aid under this Act which result in restricting production and increasing prices, and to encourage where suitable competition and productivity, and (3) to encourage where suitable the development and strengthening of the free labor union movements as the collective bargaining agencies of labor within such countries."

the free world. Accordingly, it is declared to be the policy of the United States, in furtherance of the objectives of this Act, to encourage the efforts of other free countries in fostering private initiative and competition, in discouraging monopolistic practices, in improving the technical efficiency of their industry, agriculture, and commerce, and in the strengthening of free labor unions; and to encourage American enterprise in contributing to the economic strength of other free countries through private investment abroad and the exchange of ideas and technical information on the matters covered by this subsection.

b. Under the coordination of the Director for Mutual Security, the Mutual Security Agency, cooperating with private business groups and governmental agencies to the fullest extent possible, shall encourage a greater participation by private capital in the guaranty program and shall develop broad criteria to facilitate such participation, including programs consistent with the purposes of the Act for International Development.

c. The Department of Commerce shall, in cooperation with such groups and agencies (including the International Bank for Reconstruction and Development), conduct a thorough study of the legal and other impediments, foreign and local, to private investment abroad, and the methods and means whereby those impediments can be removed or decreased and shall make recommendations thereon to the Director for Mutual Security.

d. The Department of State, in cooperation with other agencies of the Government concerned with private investment abroad, and taking into account the study and recommendations described in subsection (c) of this section, shall accelerate a program of negotiating treaties of commerce and trade, or other temporary arrangements where more suitable or expeditious, which shall include provisions to encourage and facilitate the flow of private investment to countries participating in programs under this Act.

e. The Technical Cooperation Administration, taking into account the study and recommendations described in subsection (c) of this section, shall encourage and facilitate a greater participation by private industrial groups or agencies in private contracts awarded by the Administration, and shall, in co-operation with the Department of Commerce and the Mutual Security Agency, find and draw the attention of private enterprise to opportunities for investment and development in underdeveloped areas.

f. The reports required by section 518 of this Act shall include detailed information on the implementation of this section.[*1]

The Mutual Security Act and the Point IV program were in fact implemented as Congress desired. Moreover, it would be a mistake to assume that there were serious divisions between Congress and the Administration on the question of encouraging free enterprise, or between the Administration and the business community. To take one more example of this basic consensus on the purpose of the foreign aid policy, the Mutual Security Agreement with Ecuador signed in early 1952 included this "Article VII."

In conformity with the principle of mutual aid, under which the two Governments have agreed as provided in Article I, to furnish assistance to each other, the Government of Ecuador agrees to facilitate the production and transfer to the Government of the United States of America for such period of time, in such quantities and upon such terms and conditions as may be agreed upon of raw and semi-processed strategic materials required by the United States of America as a result of deficiencies or potential deficiencies in its own resources, and which may be available in Ecuador. Arrangements for such transfers shall give due regard to reasonable requirements for domestic use and commercial export of Ecuador.[†1]

As we have seen, tensions developed as a result of Congressional insistence on the letter of the law, and Administration

---

[*1] A.I.D. (excerpts), Public Law 535, June 5, 1950, *American Foreign Policy, 1950–1955*, II, 3075–3076.

[†1] Department of State *Bulletin*, March 3, 1952, p. 337.

desire for flexibility, even if that meant helping friendly "socialists." In the world of NSC-68, total diplomacy also meant the integration of political and economic diplomacy. The following two documents—a memorandum on strategic areas by Averell Harriman, Truman's Director of Mutual Security, and a 1949 report by the Committee on Business Participation in Foreign Economic Development, a group which included representatives from the most powerful corporations—illustrate agreement on the ends if not perfect unity on the means.

THE NEAR EAST, SOUTH ASIA AND AFRICA

Greece, Turkey and Iran

The integrity of Greece, Turkey and Iran, countries bordering the Iron Curtain, is closely involved with the security of other nations of the free world. The fact that the membership of Greece and Turkey in NATO is under active consideration, with widespread support throughout the United States, is evidence of public acceptance of the importance of this region to the security of the United States. Our aid is required to assist these friendly countries to strengthen and maintain themselves.

Arab States and Israel: Egypt, Iraq, Israel, Jordan, Lebanon, Saudi Arabia, Syria, Yemen and the independent sheikdoms

These countries are strategically located at the nexus of world transportation routes by land, sea and air. Saudi Arabia and Iraq, and the neighboring principalities bordering on the Persian Gulf, possess substantial reserves of petroleum. A large proportion of Europe's fuel needs is met from this source, and much of this oil is transported by pipelines across the Arab States. Loss of any of these countries, by subversion or otherwise, to the Soviet orbit would have serious effects on the economy of free Europe, would undermine positions of strength in Greece and Turkey, and adversely affect the security of the United States. U.S. aid is an important factor in reducing such a possibility and in promoting the peaceful development of the area.

Independent African Countries: Libya, Ethiopia, Liberia

The land mass of Africa represents a prime source of strategic raw materials. Its area was the scene of staging operations or of active fighting in World War II, and may be of equal importance in the event of another conflict. These countries are strategically located, and Ethiopia and Liberia are important sources of raw materials. Maintenance of the independence and integrity of these countries, their peaceful and progressive development, and continued access to their raw materials are important to the security of the United States, and American aid plays a significant role in assuring that such a situation will in fact continue.

South Asia: Afghanistan, Pakistan, India, Nepal and Ceylon

These countries are of great significance to the stability and security of the free world. Their 450 million inhabitants comprise 30% of the population of the world and they are a vital source of many important commodities, the supply of which is essential for the industrial needs of the free world. Moreover, their territory forms a bridge between the free countries of the Near East and Southeast Asia, on which the security of both the Near East and Southeast Asia depend. These countries are disposed to be friendly toward the West and to resist Communist subversion and aggression. It is essential that they should continue to do so, and U.S. assistance is an important factor in giving them the will and the capability of doing so.

THE FAR EAST

Philippines, Associated States of Indochina, Thailand, Indonesia, and Burma

These countries lie on the rim of the vast Soviet-dominated land mass of Asia where they are exposed to grave risk of loss of their independence—only recently gained in most cases—through internal subversion or external aggression. In Indochina, a bitter and long drawn-out war is being fought against the Communist-dominated Viet Minh forces. Communist Huk forces are in rebellion in the Philippines. Internal disorder, largely Communist inspired, is being fomented in greater or lesser degree within the other countries of this region as well. In view of the strategic location of the area in relation to the Pacific lines of communication, its importance as a producer of rice, which is required as a basic food resource in countries from India to Japan, its vast resources of tin, rubber, and numerous other strategic materials, and likewise, its manpower resources, the loss of this area to the free world would have the most serious consequences for the security of the United States. United States military assistance is required to safeguard the internal and external defense of the Philippines; to assist the French Union forces and native forces of the Associated States of Indochina in defeating the Communist Viet Minh forces; and to maintain internal order and discourage external aggression in Thailand. In all five countries in the area United States economic and technical assistance are needed to assure the stability which United States interests require by strengthening the ability of the governments concerned to render basic services to their people, by assisting in the repair of war devastation and arresting economic deterioration, and by helping to lay a basis for economic advance and improvement. Economic assistance is also required in most of these countries in close support of United States military assistance.

Formosa

It is important to the security of the United States that Formosa should not fall into hostile hands for exploitation against the peace of the Pacific. A prerequisite for the stability and internal security of the island and for its ability to muster a sound defense against the threat of invasion is the maintenance of an economy capable of withstanding the great strains which are being placed upon it by defense requirements. United States military, economic and technical assistance to Formosa will continue to be essential for the realization of these objectives.

Korea

The provision of assistance to Korea under the Mutual Security Act will have a direct effect in strengthening the security of the United States and other nations who are demonstrating that aggression will not be accepted by the United Nations as a course of international conduct. In addition to the part which this aid is playing in the endeavor to bring the United Nations through its first great effort in collective security, it will materially strengthen the will and ability of the Korean people and the determination of other free Far Eastern nations to continue to resist Communist aggression in whatever form it takes.

LATIN AMERICA

The continuation of assistance to Latin American countries will strengthen the security of the United States and promote world peace. The geographical contiguity of these countries to the United States is such that, as long recognized in our foreign policy, a threat to their security is automatically a threat to our own security. Moreover, the industry and agriculture of the United States depends on Latin America for raw materials and markets. The assistance given these countries contributes to their economic well-being and political stability, thereby enabling them to make a more effective contribution to the common effort to maintain the peace and security of the hemisphere, including the United States. Such assistance also helps to strengthen the economic base supporting the free world's defense effort.

The Inter-American Treaty of Reciprocal Assistance provides the framework for multilateral action on a regional basis for collective self-defense against armed attack and for taking the measures necessary to meet other forms of aggression or the threat of aggression. All Latin American countries have signed this treaty and all but Guatemala have completed their ratification of it. The military assistance to be provided by the United States to the other American republics will enable such republics, in agreement with the United States, to assume responsibility for performing defense missions important to the defense of the Western Hemisphere which are essential to our security as well as to theirs and of a kind which we ourselves had to assume during the Second World War.[1]

[1] Memo, Harriman to Truman, January 5, 1952, *The Papers of Harry S. Truman*, Official File, 335-B, The Harry S. Truman Library, Independence, Mo.

Program for Implementing Point Four of
President Truman's Inaugural Address

As the fourth point of his Inaugural Address on January 20, President Truman said, "We must embark on a bold new program for making the benefits of our scientific advances and industrial progress available for the improvement and growth of underdeveloped areas."

Subsequent interpretations of the President's statement by Secretary of State Acheson and other officials of the Department of State left to future study and determination the means of carrying out the program. These official statements revealed high hopes for raising standards of living throughout the world by making available to foreign countries the technical knowledge of the United States and by providing them with the capital required to develop their resources. It was recognized that private investment, rather than government-to-government loans, must be the principal source of the needed capital. It was recognized also that American business should participate in the program on a long-term basis. Just how all of this can be brought about in practice is still to be resolved.

Many businessmen dislike seeing government go any further into programs affecting business, while many government officials are wary of giving too much support to business abroad because of the fear of charges of dollar imperialism. The problem is to devise a program based mainly on private capital and private enterprise which will avoid undue government supervision of private business, on the one hand, and any taint of exploitation under the protection of the flag, on the other hand.

In other words, what is required is a combination of government and private effort acceptable to private interests in the United States which will enlist the full cooperation of foreign countries wishing to participate in the program. If this can be achieved, private interests in the United States will be able to make a sustained contribution to the economic growth of both developed and underdeveloped areas. As in the case of all worthwhile partnerships, the benefits of a cooperative foreign investment program will be mutual and can be large.

The U.S. Associates believes that economic growth taking place anywhere in the world under conditions of individual freedom, leads, through the operation of multilateral trade, to the growth of economic activity in other areas of the world, thereby inducing rising standards of living in all the areas concerned. Our own standard of living in the United States would grow, as a result of the encouragement we would be giving elsewhere in the world. For these reasons the U.S. Associates subscribes wholeheartedly to the objectives of "Point Four" of the President's Inaugural Address. It believes these objectives can be reached by means of an integrated program along the following lines.

1. An unequivocal statement on the part of the United States Government that it does not itself intend to supply, and in fact cannot supply, foreign countries with the technology and capital which they require to develop their resources and skills; that it looks primarily to private enterprise to provide these things; and that its efforts will be concentrated on getting maximum private participation in the program.

2. The creation of a business "climate" in other countries which will be attractive to private investment.

3. Joint government and business exploration, in the light of their many pitfalls, of various government inducements to private foreign investment, especially government guaranties or insurance of investment risks.

4. Long-term government contracts for the purchase of strategic raw materials.

5. The elimination of burdensome taxation on foreign investments.

6. Statutory registration of agreements between United States business interests and foreign business interests for the exchange of methods and processes under immunity from punitive provisions of the antitrust laws.

7. Government loans for closely circumscribed types of projects under private execution in order to increase opportunities for private investment in foreign countries.

8. Technical missions to foreign countries under government auspices to advise on carefully selected development projects.

The views of U.S. Associates on each of the points outlined above are set forth below:

1. *United States Policy.* An unequivocal statement of the United States Government on foreign development policy is indispensable to any substantial participation by private business in the President's program. Such a statement must lay out both principles and practical measures designed to secure a maximum flow of technology and capital to foreign countries. It must make clear that applied technology is a scarce commodity and is generally obtainable only for a consideration. It must emphasize in particular that only private enterprise can do the job and that private enterprise will do the job only if conditions favorable to private investment are created by foreign countries seeking outside help. It must say in unmistakable terms that financial assistance from the United States Government will be available only to those countries which subscribe to a code of fair treatment for foreign investments. It should point out also that there are manifold opportunities for better methods, improved tools, and higher production in the developed as well as the underdeveloped areas of the world.

In addition, the statement must make clear that important modern technology applied by private enterprise and generated by private investment, is not an abstraction. The trained managements and technicians of private enterprise are not oblivious to the human environment in which they work. Carrying out operations connected with the economic development of a foreign land they know their enlightened self-interest and that of their foreign associates requires a partnership atmosphere of goodwill and a resulting mutual recognition of partnership obligations.

The statement must also emphasize that upon securing the cooperation of the creative forces of foreign private enterprise, capital importing countries will obtain important economic benefits; and that in the wake of higher standards of living flowing from economic growth come many social improvements. The United States Associates emphasizes that private business interests want to contribute abundantly towards the economic growth, with resulting social benefits, in both developed and undeveloped areas. Like all worthwhile partnerships, the benefits can be substantial and mutual.

To avoid raising false hopes, it should be stated however, that the process of economic development is necessarily slow, that standards of living can be raised only by raising the productivity of labor and not by mere financial expedients, and that important results can be achieved only by sustained effort over long periods of time.

2. *Climate.* In his comments on the President's Fourth Point, Secretary Acheson said, "There is also in many places a failure to understand that unless the conditions are created by which investors may fairly put their money into that country, then there is a great impediment to development."

The first task of the United States Government, after declaring its own policy, is to work with other countries for an improvement of the climate for private foreign investment. Neither the proposed I.T.O. Charter nor the Bogota Agreement, with its many reservations, will induce a flow of investment on the scale desired. These recent failures to obtain adequate assurances on a multilateral basis of fair treatment for private foreign investment suggest that, as a new approach, negotiations should be conducted bilaterally with one or a few countries. The "International Code of Fair Treatment for Foreign Investments" proposed by the International Chamber of Commerce, although intended as a multilateral convention, should be used as a model for bilateral negotiations; and businessmen of both countries concerned should actively participate. With this approach, the problem of investment in each foreign country can be dealt with in the light of the particular factors involved.

The United States Government should seek treatment for United States investors no less favorable than they accord to their own nationals or to the nationals of other countries. Countries which discriminate against United States investors should not expect financial aid from the United States Government.

The U.S. Associates believes that exchange controls and multiple rates of exchange constitute major obstacles to the international movement of capital and hence to the carrying out of the President's new program. It recognizes, however, that exchange controls are themselves the product of a generally unfavorable climate for investment characterized by unbalanced budgets, other inflationary financial practices, and a chronic tendency for the demand for foreign exchange to outrun the available supply—in other words, by a constant tendency to live beyond a country's means. The creation of a favorable climate for investment, domestic or foreign, will entail financial reform, and financial reform will make possible the elimination of exchange controls.

3. The United States Associates has directed its attention to the discussions in government and business circles of methods by which the government might stimulate an expanded flow of foreign investments. Various proposals have been made for government guaranties or for governmentally sponsored insurance against certain risks of private foreign investment. Other inducements, including tax inducements, have been put forward. The specific proposals which have been brought to the attention of the U.S. Associates are the following:

a. The United States Government might offer guaranties against certain risks of private foreign investment, in particular the risk of inconvertibility of foreign currencies and possibly also the risk of loss as the result of war, civil strife, or confiscation.

b. The United States Government might offer insurance on a voluntary basis against the above risks in consideration of the payment of suitable insurance premiums.

c. Private insurers might be invited to offer protection against specified investment risks with or without the protection of reinsurance by the United States Government up to some high percentage of the risks underwritten.

d. The United States Government might allow, for tax purposes, a very rapid depreciation of foreign plants owned by U.S. nationals.

e. The United States Government might extend loans for private foreign investment, repayment to be dependent upon profits.

f. The United States Government might assist capital importing countries in establishing guaranty funds in the United States. These funds would assure continuity of service on investments registered by the central banks or other agencies of the capital importing countries and would be in the form of escrow deposits of gold or the equivalent with the Federal Reserve Bank of New York. After being built up by agreement for several years until they come to represent three years' service on dollar investments in the countries concerned, the initial contributions to the fund by the United States Government should be supplanted within a limited period by the capital importing countries. The registration of foreign investments should apply to old and new investments alike. The annual requirements for their servicing should include the transfer of depreciation reserves as required for replacement equipment and should permit the exclusion of new investments deemed undesirable for economic or other reasons. Only registered investments should be entitled to service by drawing on the guaranty funds as necessity arises.

While the U.S. Associates would welcome any sound scheme for encouraging an expansion of private foreign investment, it sees serious hurdles which must be overcome before the above proposals or any others could become acceptable in practice. It wishes in particular to give warning as to the following pitfalls which should be guarded against:

a. United States Government guaranties or insurance should not be such as to weaken or remove the incentive to foreign countries to create conditions conducive to foreign investment.

b. It might be difficult, because of political pressures in foreign countries and in the United States, to restrict guarantied or insured investments to economically desirable projects; if not so restricted, the way would be open for all manner of ill-advised ventures at the expense of the United States taxpayer.

c. On the other hand, even if prudently administered, a government facility might well entail an undesirable intrusion by government into the affairs of private business concerns, if the government should consider itself obliged to judge the merits of each foreign investment project proposed for guaranty, to prescribe and supervise accounting methods, and, in general, to substitute its standards for business standards. The legal, technical and administrative problems involved in this relationship would be extraordinarily difficult.

d. The desire to limit the government's liability might bring about discrimination under a government system as between old and new investments. Any such discrimination would be undesirable. In many cases existing investors with their background of experience and knowledge in the field, would be the most logical source of new investments. No advantage would come from encouraging new investments and, at the same time, doing injury to existing investment which might induce the withdrawal of previous investments. Although the desire to limit the liability of the government under any such guaranty plan is understandable, such discrimination, as to economic areas, should be limited to a choice, in practice, of investments which are economically feasible and desirable.

e. Finally, despite all safeguards, a government system of aid to private foreign investment might easily result in a loss of billions of dollars to the United States Government and consequently to its taxpayers.

The U.S. Associates draws attention to the potential pitfalls set forth above not for the purpose of discouraging action favorable to the expansion of private and foreign investments but so that, by overcoming them, sound proposals can be sought. The disappointment resulting from experiences with ill-conceived guaranty or insurance schemes would, of course, do more harm than good to the objectives we hope to accomplish.

There are, finally, two principles which the U.S. Associates cannot emphasize strongly enough. One is that the responsibility for creating and maintaining favorable conditions for private foreign investment should rest primarily on foreign countries seeking outside capital. The other is that *any sharing of this responsibility by the United States Government can be justified only in the case of foreign countries which first subscribe to a code of fair treatment for foreign investments.*

The U.S. Associates fully recognizes, however, the crucial importance at the present juncture in world affairs of inducing an increased flow of private capital from the United States to foreign countries. It therefore urges that the various proposals for government aid to private investment be carefully explored by government and business jointly. It ventures the opinion that no one measure, but rather a variety of measures, will be found appropriate to a solution of the problem of foreign investment.

4. *Strategic Materials.* The United States will require a steadily increasing volume of strategic raw materials to feed a rising level of industrial production as well as to build up a stock-pile against the threat of another war. The production of strategic materials in foreign countries for export to the United States is not being stepped-up as it should be in their interest and in the interest of the United States. One requirement is clear authority and adequate funds given to an agency of the United States Government to make long-term contracts for the purchase of strategic materials with escalator clauses and reasonable anti-dumping provisions. Another requirement is a favorable climate for private investment in countries with undeveloped resources.

The development of the undeveloped natural resources of the world typically requires years of exploration and heavy investment before production on a commercial basis can be achieved. If such development is to proceed on a broad scale, it is necessary that there be an assured long-term market for primary materials. The best means to this end would be long-term contracts entered into by some agency of the United States Government for the purchase of materials classified as strategic. The benefit to foreign countries from such a program should be very great and lasting. Undeveloped raw materials are the great untapped source of dollar earnings for the underdeveloped areas of the world.

5. *Taxation.* Burdensome taxation applicable to investment abroad, including multiple taxation of earnings, should be eliminated either by treaty or legislation adopted by a foreign country and the United States. It is the view of the U.S. Associates that

earnings on investments abroad must be subject neither to discriminatory or excessive taxation nor to multiple or double taxation if foreign investment is to be encouraged. In general, earnings should be taxed by countries in which the capital is at work and not in the country in which the capital originates.

6. *Antitrust Laws.* The present interpretation and application of the antitrust laws of the United States is a serious barrier to foreign investment by United States corporations if accompanied by agreements for an exchange of methods and processes. This barrier should be removed by statutory provision for the registration with the Department of Justice of all agreements between United States business interests and foreign interests covering patent licensing, exchange of technical information, and joint investment and provision for rendering inapplicable to arrangements so registered the more punitive provisions of the antitrust laws.

7. *Government Loans.* In line with the general statement of the United States Government as advocated in (1) above, the scope for loans to foreign countries by the United States Government or its agencies should be closely circumscribed as to purpose. It should be confined to those fields which private capital cannot be expected fully to develop because of their public-utility character, low prospective returns, or extremely long pay-out periods. Generally speaking, the only appropriate fields for government loans are roads, other forms of transportation, communications, harbor development, irrigation, and, in some instances, electric power.

Even where government loans are committed for projects in these limited fields, the projects should be carried out by private business in order to insure economical use of funds and efficient installations, and the loans should cover external costs only. Government loans should be denied for purposes which would prejudice the position of existing private enterprises. They should be denied altogether to countries which are unwilling to adopt a code of fair treatment for foreign investments or which by government action tend to drive out existing private foreign investment or narrow the scope for new investment.

8. *Technical Missions.* No miracles are produced by sending technicians or technical missions abroad to advise foreign govern-

ments. This is not the way to spread industrial technology throughout the world. As a practical necessity, applied technology, or know-how, must be combined with investment. Know-how without accompanying investment is usually ineffective. Investment without adequate know-how, as in the case of many government-to-government operations, is uneconomical and wasteful. The two necessary elements are combined in the investments of United States corporations in foreign countries.

There is, nevertheless, a fruitful field for technical missions sent abroad on specific assignments and for the technical training of foreign nationals in the United States. Technical missions are especially effective in the fields of agricultural development, development of water resources, public health and sanitation, education, irrigation, and transportation and communications. Most of these are also fields, as noted above, in which government loans to foreign countries may be justified.

Missions under government or other auspices concerned with industrial development abroad should be set on foot with particular caution. Industrial technology cannot be transmitted by these means, either because it is not communicable at all or because a mission cannot give away something it does not possess. Industrial technology is ordinarily available only at a cost, financial or otherwise, and can usually be transmitted only through management and technicians actively participating in foreign enterprise. Furthermore, if plans for industrial development are to be kept within the realm of practical possibilities, industrial missions should be undertaken only by competent engineering firms.[1]

As Truman began his second term in office in January 1949, the Cold War in Europe had been stabilized. The North Atlantic Treaty Organization which came into being that year provided the necessary "backbone" for the economic rehabilitation of Western Europe. The stated purpose of NATO was to deter a Russian attack by making it plain that each of the member nations would regard an attack upon one as an attack upon all. The West's real power, of course, did not consist of new French or

[1] From a copy in the *Papers of Clark Clifford*, Truman Library.

German divisions in an all-European army, but of America's atomic arsenal. The North Atlantic Treaty Organization, then, was in effect a trip wire whose primary usefulness was to evoke American support.

In later years, however, policymakers discussed the origins of the Atlantic alliance in different terms. John J. McCloy spoke of its psychological value:

The Alliance was not exclusively or even primarily [designed] to deter an impending or threatened Soviet military attack. . . . There was a deeper and more underlying motive than the fear of a direct invasion of the West. . . . [It was the] contrast between Soviet strength and purpose on the one hand and Western European weakness and lack of concentrated direction on the other which prompted the formation of a Western security system. The system was intended at a minimum, to offset, morally and physically, the overriding, and to put it mildly, unbenign influence from the east.*1

In a 1965 lecture, another policymaker, George F. Kennan, described the Atlantic Alliance as a mistake, a "military defense against an attack no one was planning." It was born in the minds of "people capable of envisaging a favorable future for Europe only along the lines of a total military defeat of the Soviet Union or of some spectacular, inexplicable and wholly improbable collapse of the political will of its leaders." The real danger, Kennan went on, existed in the threat of revolution engineered by "the conspiratorial action of Communist-trained and inspired minorities" who hoped to seize and retain "dictatorial power *within* their respective national orbits."9

For nearly two decades Kennan had been known as the chief formulator of America's Cold War position, the father of the famous "Containment" doctrine. His disagreements with the men who applied that doctrine were also becoming famous, and had led to his retirement from government service. By his own ac-

---

*1 John J. McCloy, *The Atlantic Alliance: Its Origins and Future* (New York: Harper & Row, 1969), pp. 22–26.

count, however, he had *never* intended to write a justification for a military containment policy. Others certainly thought of containment as at least including military preparedness—Korea was by these policymakers considered a proof that containment worked—but it was much more: (1) a rationale for resisting the expansion of Communist power (not Russian power alone) and (2) a formula for the strong of heart and keen of mind for achieving "victory" in the Cold War.

NOTES

[1] Emmet John Hughes, *The Ordeal of Power* (New York: Atheneum, 1963), p. 137.
[2] J. Lawton Collins, *War in Peacetime: The History and Lessons of Korea* (Boston: Houghton Mifflin, 1969), p. 248.
[3] Harry S. Truman, *Memoirs* (2 v. New York: Doubleday, 1956), II, p. 362.
[4] George F. Kennan, *Memoirs*, 1925–1950 (Boston: Atlantic, Little, Brown, 1967), p. 395.
[5] Transcript of the President's meeting with congressional leaders, June 26, 1950, from a copy in The Harry S. Truman Library, Independence, Mo.
[6] See Lloyd C. Gardner, "From Liberation to Containment, 1945–1953," in William Appleman Williams, *From Colony to Empire* (New York: John Wiley & Sons, 1972), esp. pp. 371–384.
[7] Memoranda of April 28 and May 18, 1950, in the *John Foster Dulles Papers*, Princeton University Library, Princeton, N.J.
[8] Act for International Development (excerpts), Public Law 535, June 5, 1950, *American Foreign Policy*, 1950–1955, II, 3038.
[9] Cited in David Horowitz, ed., *Containment and Revolution* (Boston: Beacon Press, 1967), p. 11.

CHAPTER FIVE
★ ★ ★ ★ ★

In the Beginning ...

The appearance in July 1947 of an article, "The Sources of Soviet Conduct," in the journal *Foreign Affairs Quarterly* touched off a controversy—or, better said, a series of controversies—lasting down to the present day. The author's identity was supposed to be a secret, but everyone soon knew who the mysterious "Mr. X" actually was: a hitherto obscure Foreign Service officer named George Frost Kennan. The controversy over authorship was the first and easiest to resolve. The rest has proved very difficult indeed, even for Kennan himself, who now takes the position that he never meant to say what everyone (for or against containment) thought he said. And if that were not enough, containment has been both championed and attacked by advocates of all shades of the political spectrum.

In the first decade of the Cold War, containment was the liberal's policy, and his defense against attacks from right and left; in later years the policy of containment was taken over by conservatives to fend off challenges to Cold War orthodoxy. Kennan himself mused about this irony in the second volume of his *Memoirs*, recalling the somewhat embarrassing moment in 1953 when the new Secretary of State, John Foster Dulles, had to figure out what to do with the founder of the faith. If not quite on the same level as the mythical encounter between Dostoyevsky's Grand Inquisitor and the Christ, the meeting between Dulles and Kennan was tinged with the same dramatic hue—at least for the men involved. "Mr. Dulles . . . did not want to have me around. He knew very well that whatever he might say publicly, he was going to have to pursue in reality in this coming period pretty much the policy toward the Soviet Union with which my name had been often connected. But he did not at all wish things to appear this way, particularly in the eyes of the Republican right wing. He feared that if I were in the picture at all, he would be tagged as the implementer of my ideas. For this reason he wished to disembarrass himself of me, and succeeded in doing so."[1]

The fact was, however, that Mr. X was as complicated as the Cold War itself, and that containment was as simple as the man reading the article by Kennan wanted it to be. Put another way, Kennan had performed a service for the policymaking community and they expected to control the end product in much the same fashion that employers expect that inventions made on their time belong to them and not to the inventor. It was their decision, at any rate, about what to do with the product: how to package it, how to market it, and how much to charge. Dean Acheson once called Kennan a mystic of sorts, trying to persuade others by musings, wonderings, suggestions, and questions. "Mr. Kennan," he once told a journalist, "has never, in my judgment, grasped the realities of power relationships, but takes a rather mystical attitude toward them. To Mr. Kennan there is no Soviet military threat in Europe."[2]

The source of these controversies, the X article, began with a rendition of the historical background of the Bolshevik Government in Russia.

The political personality of Soviet power as we know it today is the product of ideology and circumstances: ideology inherited by the present Soviet leaders from the movement in which they had their political origin, and circumstances of the power which they now have exercised for nearly three decades in Russia. There can be few tasks of psychological analysis more difficult than to try to trace the interaction of these two forces and the relative rôle of each in the determination of official Soviet conduct. Yet the attempt must be made if that conduct is to be understood and effectively countered.

It is difficult to summarize the set of ideological concepts with which the Soviet leaders came into power. Marxian ideology, in its Russian-Communist projection, has always been in process of subtle evolution. The materials on which it bases itself are extensive and complex. But the outstanding features of Communist thought as it existed in 1916 may perhaps be summarized as follows: (a) that the central factor in the life of man, the factor which determines the character of public life and the "physiognomy of society," is the system by which material goods are produced and exchanged; (b) that the capitalist system of production is a nefarious one which inevitably leads to the exploitation of the working class by the capital-owning class and is incapable of developing adequately the economic resources of society or of distributing fairly the material goods produced by human labor; (c) that capitalism contains the seeds of its own destruction and must, in view of the inability of the capital-owning class to adjust itself to economic change, result eventually and inescapably in a revolutionary transfer of power to the working class; and (d) that imperialism, the final phase of capitalism, leads directly to war and revolution. . . .

The circumstances of the immediate post-Revolution period— the existence in Russia of civil war and foreign intervention, together with the obvious fact that the Communists represented only a tiny minority of the Russian people—made the establishment of dictatorial power a necessity. . . . Now the outstanding circumstance concerning the Soviet regime is that down to the present day this process of political consolidation has never been completed and the men in the Kremlin have continued to be predominantly absorbed with the struggle to secure and make absolute the power which they seized in November 1917. They have endeavored to secure it primarily against forces at home, within Soviet society itself. But they have also endeavored to secure it against the outside world. For ideology, as we have seen, taught them that the outside world was hostile and that it was their duty eventually to overthrow the political forces beyond their borders.

The powerful hands of Russian history and tradition reached up to sustain them in this feeling. Finally, their own aggressive intransigence with respect to the outside world began to find its own reaction; and they were soon forced, to use another Gibbonesque phrase, "to chastise the contumacy" which they themselves had provoked. It is an undeniable privilege of every man to prove himself right in the thesis that the world is his enemy; for if he reiterates it frequently enough and makes it the background of his conduct he is bound eventually to be right.

Now it lies in the nature of the mental world of the Soviet leaders, as well as in the character of their ideology, that no opposition to them can be officially recognized as having any merit or justification whatsoever. Such opposition can flow, in theory, only from the hostile and incorrigible forces of dying capitalism. As long as remnants of capitalism were officially recognized as existing in Russia, it was possible to place on them, as an internal element, part of the blame for the maintenance of a dictatorial form of society. But as these remnants were liquidated, little by little, this justification fell away; and when it was indicated officially that they had been finally destroyed, it disappeared altogether. And this fact created one of the most basic of the compulsions which came to act upon the Soviet regime: since capitalism no longer existed in Russia and since it could not be admitted that there could be serious or widespread opposition to the Kremlin springing spontaneously from the liberated masses under its authority, it became necessary to justify the retention of the dictatorship by stressing the menace of capitalism abroad. . . .

Now the maintenance of this pattern of Soviet power, namely, the pursuit of unlimited authority domestically, accompanied by the cultivation of the semi-myth of implacable foreign hostility, has gone far to shape the actual machinery of Soviet power as we know it today. Internal organs of administration which did not serve this purpose withered on the vine. Organs which did serve this purpose became vastly swollen. The security of Soviet power came to rest on the iron discipline of the Party, on the severity and ubiquity of the secret police, and on the uncompromising economic monopolism of the state. The "organs of suppression," in which the Soviet leaders had sought security from rival forces, became in large measure the masters of those whom they were designed to serve. Today the major part of the structure of Soviet power is committed to the perfection of the dictatorship and to the maintenance of the concept of Russia as in a state of siege, with the enemy lowering beyond the walls. And the millions of human beings who form that part of the structure of power must defend at all costs this concept of Russia's position, for without it they are themselves superfluous.

As things stand today, the rulers can no longer dream of parting with these organs of suppression. The quest for absolute power, pursued now for nearly three decades with a ruthlessness unparalleled (in scope at least) in modern times, has again produced internally, as it did externally, its own reaction. The excesses of the police apparatus have fanned the potential opposition to the régime into something far greater and more dangerous than it could have been before those excesses began.

But least of all can the rulers dispense with the fiction by which the maintenance of dictatorial power has been defended. For this fiction has been canonized in Soviet philosophy by the excesses already committed in its name; and it is now anchored in the Soviet structure of thought by bonds far greater than those of mere ideology.

So much for the historical background. What does it spell in terms of the political personality of Soviet power as we know it today?

Of the original ideology, nothing has been officially junked. Belief is maintained in the basic badness of capitalism, in the inevitability of its destruction, in the obligation of the proletariat to assist in that destruction and to take power into its own hands. But stress has come to be laid primarily on those concepts which relate most specifically to the Soviet régime itself: to its position as the sole truly Socialist régime in a dark and misguided world, and to the relationships of power within it.

The first of these concepts is that of the innate antagonism between capitalism and Socialism. We have seen how deeply that concept has become imbedded in foundations of Soviet power. It has profound implications for Russia's conduct as a member of international society. It means that there can never be on Moscow's side any sincere assumption of a community of aims between the Soviet Union and powers which are regarded as capitalist. It must invariably be assumed in Moscow that the aims of the capitalist world are antagonistic to the Soviet régime, and therefore to the interests of the peoples it controls. If the Soviet government occasionally sets its signature to documents which would indicate the contrary, this is to be regarded as a tactical maneuver permissible in dealing with the enemy (who is without honor) and should be taken in the spirit of *caveat emptor*. Basically, the antagonism remains. It is postulated. And from it flow many of the phenomena which we find disturbing in the Kremlin's conduct of foreign policy: the secretiveness, the lack of frankness, the duplicity, the war suspiciousness, and the basic unfriendliness of purpose. These phenomena are there to stay, for the foreseeable future. There can be variations of degree and of emphasis. When there is something the Russians want from us, one or the other of these features of their policy may be thrust temporarily into the background; and when that happens there will always be Americans who will leap forward with gleeful announcements that "the Russians have changed," and some who will even try to take credit for having brought about such "changes." But we should not be misled by tactical maneuvers. These characteristics of Soviet policy, like the postulate from which they flow, are basic to the internal nature of Soviet power, and will be with us, whether in the foreground or the background, until the internal nature of Soviet power is changed.

This means that we are going to continue for a long time to find the Russians difficult to deal with. It does not mean that they should be considered as embarked upon a do-or-die program to overthrow our society by a given date. The theory of the inevitability of the eventual fall of capitalism has the fortunate connotation that there is no hurry about it. The forces of progress can take their time in preparing the final *coup de grâce*. Meanwhile, what is vital is that the "Socialist fatherland"—that oasis of power which has been already won for Socialism in the person of the Soviet Union—should be cherished and defended by all good Communists at home and abroad, its fortunes promoted, its enemies badgered and confronted. The promotion of premature, "adventuristic" revolutionary projects abroad which might embarrass Soviet power in any way would be an inexcusable, even a counter-revolutionary act. The cause of Socialism is the support and promotion of Soviet power, as defined in Moscow.

This brings us to the second of the concepts important to contemporary Soviet outlook. That is the infallibility of the Kremlin. The Soviet concept of power, which permits no focal points of organization outside the Party itself, requires that the Party leadership remain in theory the sole repository of truth. For if truth were to be found elsewhere, there would be justification for its expression in organized activity. But it is precisely that which the Kremlin cannot and will not permit.

The leadership of the Communist Party is therefore always right, and has been always right ever since in 1929 Stalin formalized his personal power by announcing that decisions of the Politburo were being taken unanimously.

On the principle of infallibility there rests the iron discipline of the Communist Party. In fact, the two concepts are mutually self-supporting. Perfect discipline requires recognition of infallibility. Infallibility requires the observance of discipline. And the two together go far to determine the behaviorism of the entire Soviet apparatus of power. But their effect cannot be understood unless a third factor be taken into account: namely the fact that the leadership is at liberty to put foward for tactical purposes any particular thesis which it finds useful to the cause at any particular moment and to require the faithful and unquestioning acceptance of that thesis by the members of the movement as a whole. This means that truth is not a constant but is actually created, for all intents and purposes, by the Soviet leaders themselves. It may vary from week to week, from month to month. It is nothing absolute and immutable—nothing which flows from objective reality. It is only the most recent manifestation of the wisdom of those in whom the ultimate wisdom is supposed to reside, because they represent the logic of history. The accumulative effect of these factors is to give to the whole subordinate apparatus of Soviet power an unshakeable stubbornness and steadfastness in its orientation. This orientation can be changed at will by the Kremlin but by no other power. Once a given party line has been laid down on a given issue of current policy, the whole Soviet governmental machine, including the mechanism of diplomacy, moves inexorably along the prescribed path, like a persistent toy automobile wound up and headed in a given direction, stopping only when it meets with some unanswerable force. The individuals who are the components of this machine are unamenable to argument or reason which comes to them from outside sources. Their whole training has taught them to mistrust and discount the glib persuasiveness of the outside world. Like the white dog before the phonograph, they hear only the "master's voice." And if they are to be called off from the purposes last dictated to them, it is the master who must call them off.

. . .

But we have seen that the Kremlin is under no ideological compulsion to accomplish its purposes in a hurry. Like the Church, it is dealing in ideological concepts which are of long-term validity, and it can afford to be patient. It has no right to risk the existing achievements of the revolution for the sake of vain baubles of the future. The very teachings of Lenin himself require great caution and flexibility in the pursuit of Communist purposes. Again, these precepts are fortified by the lessons of Russian history: of centuries of obscure battles between nomadic forces over the stretches of a vast unfortified plain. Here caution, circumspection, flexibility and deception are the valuable qualities; and their value finds natural appreciation in the Russian or the oriental mind. Thus the Kremlin has no compunction about retreating in the face of superior force. And being under the compulsion of no timetable, it does not get panicky under the necessity for such retreat. Its political action is a fluid stream which moves constantly, wherever it is permitted to move, toward a given goal. Its main concern is to make sure that it has filled every nook and cranny available to it in the basin of world power. But if it finds unassailable barriers in its path, it accepts these philosophically and accommodates itself to them. The main thing is that there should always be pressure, increasing constant pressure, toward the desired goal. There is no trace of any feeling in Soviet psychology that that goal must be reached at any given time.

These considerations make Soviet diplomacy at once easier and more difficult to deal with than the diplomacy of individual aggressive leaders like Napoleon and Hitler. On the one hand it is more sensitive to contrary force, more ready to yield on in-dividual sectors of the diplomatic front when that force is felt to be too strong, and thus more rational in the logic and rhetoric of power. On the other hand it cannot be easily defeated or dis-couraged by a single victory on the part of its opponents. And the patient persistence by which it is animated means that it can be effectively countered not by sporadic acts which represent the momentary whims of democratic opinion but only by intelligent long-range policies on the part of Russia's adversaries—policies no less steady in their purpose, and no less variegated and resourceful in their application, than those of the Soviet Union itself.

In these circumstances it is clear that the main element of any United States policy toward the Soviet Union must be that of a long-term, patient but firm and vigilant containment of Russian expansive tendencies. It is important to note, however, that such a policy has nothing to do with outward histrionics: with threats or blustering or superfluous gestures of outward "toughness." While the Kremlin is basically flexible in its reaction to political realities, it is by no means unamenable to considerations of prestige. Like almost any other government, it can be placed by tactless and threatening gestures in a position where it cannot afford to yield even though this might be dictated by its sense of realism. The Russian leaders are keen judges of human psychology, and as such they are highly conscious that loss of temper and of self-control is never a source of strength in political affairs. They are quick to exploit such evidences of weakness. For these reasons, it is a *sine qua non* of successful dealing with Russia that the foreign government in question should remain at all times cool and collected and that its demands on Russian policy should be put forward in such a manner as to leave the way open for a compliance not too detrimental to Russian prestige.

In the light of the above, it will be clearly seen that the Soviet pressure against the free institutions of the western world is some-thing that can be contained by the adroit and vigilant application of counter-force at a series of constantly shifting geographical and political points, corresponding to the shifts and manoeuvres of Soviet policy, but which cannot be charmed or talked out of existence. The Russians look forward to a duel of infinite duration, and they see that already they have scored great successes. It must be borne in mind that there was a time when the Communist Party represented far more of a minority in the sphere of Russian national life than Soviet power today represents in the World community.

But if ideology convinces the rulers of Russia that truth is on their side and that they can therefore afford to wait, those of us on whom that ideology has no claim are free to examine objectively the validity of that premise. The Soviet thesis not only implies complete lack of control by the west over its own economic destiny, it likewise assumes Russian unity, discipline and patience over an infinite period. Let us bring this apocalyptic vision down to earth, and suppose that the Western world . . . finds the strength and resourcefulness to contain Soviet power over a period of ten to fifteen years. What does that spell for Russia itself?

The Soviet leaders, taking advantage of the contributions of modern technique to the arts of despotism, have solved the question of obedience within the confines of their power. Few challenge their authority; and even those who do are unable to make that challenge valid as against the organs of suppression of the state.

The Kremlin has also proved able to accomplish its purpose of building up in Russia, regardless of the interests of the inhabitants, an industrial foundation of heavy metallurgy, which is, to be sure, not yet complete but which is nevertheless continuing to grow and is approaching those of the other major industrial countries. All of this, however, both the maintenance of internal political security and the building of heavy industry, has been carried out at a terrible cost in human life and in human hopes and energies. It has necessitated the use of forced labor on a scale unprecedented in modern times under conditions of peace. It has involved the neglect or abuse of other phases of Soviet economic life, particularly agriculture, consumers' goods production, housing and transportation.

To all that, the war has added its tremendous toll of destruction, death and human exhaustion. In consequence of this, we have in Russia today a population which is physically and spiritually tired. The mass of the people are disillusioned, skeptical and no longer as accessible as they once were to the magical attraction which Soviet power still radiates to its followers abroad. . . .

Who can say whether, in these circumstances, the eventual rejuvenation of the higher spheres of authority (which can only be a matter of time) can take place smoothly and peacefully, or whether rivals in the quest for higher power will not eventually reach down into these politically immature and inexperienced masses in order to find support for their respective claims? If this were ever to happen, strange consequences could flow for the Communist Party: for the membership at large has been exercised only in the practices of iron discipline and obedience and not in the arts of compromise and accommodation. And if disunity were ever to seize and paralyze the Party, the chaos and weakness of Russian society would be revealed in forms beyond description. For we have seen that Soviet power is only a crust concealing an amorphous mass of human beings among whom no independent organizational structure is tolerated. In Russia there is not even such a thing as local government. The present generation of Russians have never known spontaneity of collective action. If, consequently, anything were ever to occur to disrupt the unity and efficacy of the Party as a political instrument, Soviet Russia might be changed overnight from one of the strongest to one of the weakest and most pitiable of national societies.

Thus the future of Soviet power may not be by any means as secure as Russian capacity for self-delusion would make it appear to the men in the Kremlin. That they can keep power themselves, they have demonstrated. That they can quietly and easily turn it over to others remains to be proved. Meanwhile, the hardships of their rule and the vicissitudes of international life have taken a heavy toll of the strength and hopes of the great people on whom their power rests. It is curious to note that the ideological power of Soviet authority is strongest today in areas beyond the frontiers of Russia, beyond the reach of its police power. This phenomenon brings to mind a comparison used by Thomas Mann in his novel "Buddenbrooks." Observing that human institutions often show the greatest outward brilliance at a moment when inner decay is in reality farthest advanced, he compared the Budden-brook family, in the days of its greatest glamour, to one of those stars whose light shines most brightly on this world when in reality it has long since ceased to exist. And who can say with assurance that the strong light still cast by the Kremlin on the dissatisfied peoples of the western world is not the powerful afterglow of a constellation which is in actuality on the wane? This cannot be proved. And it cannot be disproved. But the possibility remains (and in the opinion of this writer it is a strong one) that Soviet power, like the capitalist world of its conception, bears within it the seeds of its own decay, and that the sprouting of these seeds is well advanced.

It is clear that the United States cannot expect in the foreseeable future to enjoy political intimacy with the Soviet régime. It must continue to regard the Soviet Union as a rival, not a partner, in the political arena. It must continue to expect that Soviet policies will reflect no abstract love of peace and stability, no real faith in the possibility of a permanent happy coexistence of the Socialist and capitalistic worlds, but rather a cautious, persistent pressure toward the disruption and weakening of all rival influence and rival power.

Balanced against this are the facts that Russia, as opposed to the Western world in general, is still by far the weaker party, that Soviet policy is highly flexible, and that Soviet society may well contain deficiencies which will eventually weaken its own total potential. This would of itself warrant the United States entering with reasonable confidence upon a policy of firm containment, designed to confront the Russians with unalterable counter-force at every point where they show signs of encroaching upon the interests of a peaceful and stable world. . . .

It would be an exaggeration to say that American behavior unassisted and alone could exercise a power of life and death over the Communist movement and bring about the early fall of Soviet power in Russia. But the United States has it in its power to increase enormously the strains under which Soviet policy must operate, to force upon the Kremlin a far greater degree of moderation and circumspection than it has had to observe in recent years, and in this way to promote tendencies which must eventually find their outlet in either the breakup or the gradual mellowing of Soviet power. For no mystical, Messianic movement—and particularly not that of the Kremlin—can face frustration indefinitely without eventually adjusting itself in one way or another to the logic of that state of affairs.

Thus the decision will really fall in large measure in this country itself. The issue of Soviet-American relations is in essence a test of the over-all worth of the United States as a nation among nations. To avoid destruction the United States need only measure up to its own best traditions and prove itself worthy of preservation as a great nation.

Surely, there was never a fairer test of national quality than this. In the light of these circumstances, the thoughtful observer of Russian-American relations will find no cause for complaint in the Kremlin's challenge to American society. He will rather experience a certain gratitude to a Providence which, by providing the American people with this implacable challenge, has made their entire security as a nation dependent on their pulling themselves together and accepting the responsibilities of moral and political leadership that history plainly intended them to bear.[*1]

Initial interpretations of the X article were colored by its timing, which seemed to suggest a hard–soft–hard sequence in the Administration's response to the postwar challenge. A month before, in June 1947, Secretary of State George C. Marshall had unveiled a plan for economic aid to assist European recovery. Kennan had insisted that the plan be worded so as not to exclude the Soviet Union. He thought there was little likelihood of Russian participation in the Marshall Plan, but he hoped the United States would not take the initiative in dividing Europe into spheres of influence. Other State Department advisers agreed with this approach and were just as certain that the suspicious Soviets would never open up their country to economic experts as required under the terms of the American offer. Nevertheless, the announcement of the Marshall Plan did calm European fears that the United States was preparing to take on the Soviets on a global scale. The X article, on the other hand, seemed to have been penned by the same hardliners who had written the Truman Doctrine speech for the President.

[*1] "The Sources of Soviet Conduct" by George F. Kennan ("X"), *Foreign Affairs*, XXV (July, 1947), pp. 566–582.

In point of fact Kennan opposed the Truman Doctrine with its militant language and implied universalism; his opposition was smothered by arguments from presidential advisers and by Under Secretary of State Dean Acheson, who wanted the President to proclaim American responsibility for checking the advance of Communism. It was simply taken for granted that Communism everywhere was Moscow-inspired. The initial criticisms of the X article, therefore, were also shaped by the prevailing climate in Washington during the summer of 1947. The most trenchant criticism of containment from a traditional point of view came from Walter Lippmann, the nation's most popular savant. Washingtonians always read his columns, whether or not they had the slighest intention of following his advice. It was dangerous under either the Democrats or the Republicans to be caught not having read one of his "pieces" in the morning newspaper; it was often equally dangerous to argue his positions within government councils.

Lippmann is very popular today, however, especially among ex-Cold Warriors who need a strong critique of the Truman Administration's foreign policy not tainted by revisionism. Lippmann's attack was on the "strategical conception" advanced by the then unknown Mr. X, but he did venture over into the philosophical underpinnings of the author, especially the domestic change thesis which permeated the background of the containment argument. It was really this latter thesis, that a domestic change must take place in Russia before diplomacy had any real chance of success, more than the militant imagery of the X article which made containment so attractive in the 1940's to dedicated Cold Warriors like Dean Acheson, to "liberationists" like John Foster Dulles, and even to the New Frontiersmen of the next decade.

Wrote Mr. Lippmann:

We must begin with the disturbing fact . . . that Mr. X's conclusions depend upon the optimistic prediction that the "Soviet power . . . bears within itself the seeds of its own decay, and that the sprouting of these seeds is well advanced. . . ."

Of this optimistic prediction Mr. X himself says that it "cannot be proved. And it cannot be disproved." Nevertheless, he concludes that the United States should construct its policy on the assumption that the Soviet power is inherently weak and impermanent, and that this unproved assumption warrants our entering "with reasonable confidence upon a policy of firm containment. . . ."

I do not find much ground for reasonable confidence in a policy which can be successful only if the most optimistic prediction should prove to be true. Surely a sound policy must be addressed to the worst and hardest that may be judged to be probable, and not to the best and easiest that may be possible. . . .

Surely it is by no means proved that the way to lead mankind is to spend the next ten or fifteen years, as Mr. X proposes we should, in reacting at "a series of constantly shifting geographical and political points, corresponding to the shifts and maneuvers of Soviet policy." For if history has indeed intended us to bear the responsibility of leadership, then it is not leadership to adapt ourselves to the shifts and maneuvers of Soviet policy at a series of constantly shifting geographical and political points. For that would mean for ten or fifteen years Moscow, not Washington, would define the issues, would make the challenges, would select the ground where the conflict was to be waged, and would choose the weapons. And the best that Mr. X can say for his own proposal is that if for a long period of time we can prevent the Soviet power from winning, the Soviet power will eventually perish or "mellow" because it has been "frustrated." This is a dismal conclusion. . . .

Now the strength of the western world is great, and we may assume that its resourcefulness is considerable. Nevertheless there are weighty reasons for thinking that the kind of strength we have and the kind of resourcefulness we are capable of showing are peculiarly unsuited to operating a policy of containment.

How, for example, under the Constitution of the United States is Mr. X going to work out an arrangement by which the Department of State has the money and the military power always available in sufficient amounts to apply "counterforce" at constantly shifting points all over the world? Is he going to ask Congress for a blank check on the Treasury and for a blank authorization to use the armed forces? Not if the American constitutional system is to be maintained. Or is he going to ask for an appropriation and for authority each time the Russians "show signs of encroaching upon the interests of a peaceful and stable world"? If that is his plan for dealing with the maneuvers of a dictatorship, he is going to arrive at the points of encroachment with too little and he is going to arrive too late. The Russians, if they intend to encroach, will have encroached while Congress is getting ready to hold hearings.

A policy of shifts and maneuvers may be suited to the Soviet system of government, which, as Mr. X tells us, is animated by patient persistence. It is not suited to the American system of government. . . .

Thus Mr. X and the planners of policy in the State Department, and not supply and demand in the world market, must determine continually what portion of the commodities produced here may be sold in the United States, what portion is to be set aside for export, and then sold, lent, or given to this foreign country rather than to that one. The Department of State must be able to allocate the products of American industry and agriculture, to ration the goods allocated for export among the nations which are to contain the Soviet Union, and to discriminate among them, judging correctly and quickly how much each nation must be given, how much each nation can safely be squeezed, so that all shall be held in line to hold the line against the Russians. . . . [Mr. X] is proposing to meet the Soviet challenge on the ground which is most favorable to the Soviets, and with the very instruments, procedures, and weapons in which they have a manifest superiority. . . .

The policy of containment, which Mr. X recommends, demands the employment of American economic, political, and in the last analysis, American military power at "sectors" in the interior of Europe and Asia. This requires, as I have pointed out, ground forces, that is to say reserves of infantry, which we do not possess.

The United States cannot by its own military power contain the expansive pressure of the Russians "at every point where they show signs of encroaching." The United States cannot have ready "unalterable counterforce" consisting of American troops. Therefore, the counterforces which Mr. X requires have to be composed of Chinese, Afghans, Iranians, Turks, Kurds, Arabs, Greeks, Italians, Austrians, of anti-Soviet Poles, Czechoslovaks, Bulgars, Yugoslavs, Albanians, Hungarians, Finns and Germans.

The policy can be implemented only by recruiting, subsidizing and supporting a heterogeneous array of satellites, clients, dependents and puppets. The instrument of the policy of containment is therefore a coalition of disorganized, disunited, feeble or disorderly nations, tribes and factions around the perimeter of the Soviet Union....

It would require, however much the real name for it were disavowed, continual and complicated intervention by the United States in the affairs of all the members of the coalition which we were proposing to organize, to protect, to lead and to use. Our diplomatic agents abroad would have to have an almost unerring capacity to judge correctly and quickly which men and which parties were reliable containers. Here at home Congress and the people would have to stand ready to back their judgments as to who should be nominated, who should be subsidized, who should be white-washed, who should be seen through rose-colored spectacles, who should be made our clients and our allies. . . .

In the complicated contest over this great heterogeneous array of unstable states, the odds are heavily in favor of the Soviets. For if we are to succeed, we must organize our satellites as unified, orderly and reasonably contented nations. The Russians can defeat us by disorganizing states that are already disorganized, by disuniting peoples that are torn with civil strife, and by inciting their discontent which is already very great. . . .

These weak states are vulnerable. Yet the effort to defend them brings us no nearer to a decision or to a settlement of the main conflict. Worst of all, the effort to develop such an unnatural alliance of backward states must alienate the natural allies of the United States.

The natural allies of the United States are the nations of the Atlantic community: that is to say, the nations of western Europe and of the Americas. The Atlantic Ocean and the Mediterranean Sea, which is an arm of the Atlantic Ocean, unite them in a common strategic, economic and cultural system. The chief components of the Atlantic community are the British Commonwealth of nations, the Latin states on both sides of the Atlantic, the Low

Countries and Switzerland, Scandinavia and the United States. . . .

By forcing us to expend our energies and our substance upon . . . dubious and unnatural allies on the perimeter of the Soviet Union, the effect of the policy is to neglect our natural allies in the Atlantic community, and to alienate them.

They are alienated also by the fact that they do not wish to become, like the nations of the perimeter, the clients of the United States in whose affairs we intervene, asking as the price of our support that they take the directives of their own policy from Washington. They are alienated above all by the prospect of war, which could break out by design or accident, by miscalculation or provocation, if at any of these constantly shifting geographical and political points the Russians or Americans became so deeply engaged that no retreat or compromise was possible. In this war their lands would be the battlefield. Their peoples would be divided by civil conflict. Their cities and their fields would be the bases and the bridgeheads in a total war which, because it would emerge into a general civil war, would be as indecisive as it was savage.

We may now ask why the official diagnosis of Soviet conduct, as disclosed by Mr. X's article, has led to such an unworkable policy for dealing with Russia. It is, I believe, because Mr. X has neglected even to mention the fact that the Soviet Union is the successor of the Russian Empire and that Stalin is not only the heir of Marx and of Lenin but of Peter the Great, and the Czars of all the Russias.

For reasons which I do not understand, Mr. X decided not to consider the men in the Kremlin as the rulers of the Russian State and Empire, and has limited his analysis to the interaction of "two forces": "the ideology inherited by the present Soviet leaders from the movement in which they had their political origin" and the "circumstances of the power which they have now exercised for nearly three decades in Russia". . . .

But with these two observations alone he cannot, and does not, explain the conduct of the Soviet government in this postwar era—that is to say its aims and claims to territory and to the sphere of influence which it dominates. The Soviet government has been run by Marxian revolutionists for thirty years; what has to be explained by a planner of American foreign policy is why

313

in 1945 the Soviet government expanded its frontiers and its orbit, and what was the plan and pattern of its expansion. That can be done only by remembering that the Soviet government is a Russian government and that this Russian government has emerged victorious over Germany and Japan. . . .

The westward expansion of the Russian frontier and of the Russian sphere of influence, though always a Russian aim, was accomplished when, as, and because the Red Army defeated the German army and advanced to the center of Europe. It was the mighty power of the Red Army, not the ideology of Karl Marx, which enabled the Russian government to expand its frontiers. It is the pressure of that army far beyond the new frontiers which makes the will of the Kremlin irresistible within the Russian sphere of influence. It is the threat that the Red Army may advance still farther west—into Italy, into western Germany, into Scandinavia—that gives the Kremlin and the native communist parties of western Europe an abnormal and intolerable influence in the affairs of the European continent.

Therefore, the immediate and the decisive problem of our relations with the Soviet Union is whether, when, on what conditions the Red Army can be prevailed upon to evacuate Europe.

I am contending that the American diplomatic effort should be concentrated on the problem created by the armistice—which is on how the continent of Europe can be evacuated by the three non-European armies [Russian, American, and British] which are now inside Europe. This is the problem which will have to be solved if the independence of the European nations is to be restored. Without that there is no possibility of a tolerable peace. . . .

We may now examine a question which must be answered before the policy, which I contend is preferable to the Truman Doctrine, can be accepted with conviction. What about the communist parties which are also the instruments of Soviet power? If the Red Army withdrew behind the frontiers of the Soviet Union, the communist parties would remain—to put it bluntly, as a Soviet fifth column. They will be assisted, we may take it, by Soviet agents and by Soviet funds and Soviet contraband weapons and by Soviet propaganda and by Soviet diplomacy.

That is true. There will still be the problem of communism.

Nevertheless, the heart of our problem is, I contend, the presence of the Red Army in Europe. The communist party in any country is the *fifth column*. It is, however, only a fifth column. There are the *other four columns*, and they are the Red Army. The policy which I suggest is designed to separate the first four columns from the fifth, to divide the Red Army from the Red International. For the Soviet power is most formidable where they are able to work together, that is to say, where the communist party has the support and protection of the Red Army. . . .

The evacuation of Europe can be accomplished only if we can negotiate, sign, and ratify a treaty of peace for Germany and for Austria to which the Soviet government is a party. For the peace treaties about eastern Europe, which is between Germany and Russia, cannot become effective until there are German and Austrian treaties. The Red Army will remain in eastern Europe as long as it remains in Germany and in Austria. . . .

In its approach to the German problem, which is crucial in a world settlement, we come upon the most dangerous and destructive consequences of what Mr. X calls a policy of firm containment and what the world knows as the Truman Doctrine. . . .

The underlying assumption, which is implicit though unavowed, has been that since Germany has lost the eastern provinces to the Russians and to a Russian satellite, Poland, German national feeling will naturally be directed against the Soviet Union. Historical experience and the logic of the situation indicate, I believe, that this is a profound miscalculation. For we are encouraging the Germans to want something—namely, national unity—which we cannot give them except by going to war with Russia. Germany cannot have unity, as all Germans must understand unity, except by recovering the lost provinces of eastern Germany. We would have to conquer Russia and Poland in order to restore the eastern provinces to Germany.

But Russia can return them to Germany whenever she decides than an alliance with Germany is a vital Russian interest. This can be done by performing another partition of Poland, an act which the men who signed the Molotov-Ribbentrop pact of 1939 [between Russia and Germany] could carry out if they deemed it expedient and necessary. . . .

The truncated area [of Germany] will have to be decentralized, not unified, and the German states which are in it will have to take their places within a larger European system and a European economy. Not German unity but European unity, not German self-sufficiency but European self-sufficiency, not a Germany to contain Russia but a Germany neutralized as between Russia and the west, not the Truman Doctrine but the Marshall Plan, purged of the Truman Doctrine, should be the aims of our German policy. . . .

If, nevertheless, the Soviet government will not negotiate an agreement, if the price of a settlement is impossibly high, if the ransom is deliberately set in terms which mean that Russia does not intend to evacuate Europe, the situation will be no more dangerous than it is today. But our energies will be concentrated, not dispersed all over the globe, and the real issues will be much clearer. . . .

We may now consider how we are to relate our role in the United Nations to our policy in the conflict with Russia. Mr. X does not deal with this question. But the State Department, in its attempt to operate under the Truman Doctrine, has shown where that doctrine would take us. It would take us to the destruction of the U.N.

The Charter and the organization of the United Nations are designed to maintain peace *after* a settlement of the Second World War has been arrived at. Until there is a settlement of that war, the United Nations does not come of age. . . .

[But] the policy of containment, as Mr. X has exposed it to the world, does not have as its objective a settlement of the conflict with Russia. It is therefore implicit in the policy that the U.N. has no future as a universal society, and that either the U.N. will be cast aside like the League of Nations, or it will be transformed into an anti-Soviet coalition. In either event the U.N. will have been destroyed. . . .

Mr. X has reached the conclusion that all we can do is to "contain" Russia until Russia changes, ceases to be our rival, and becomes our partner.

The conclusion is, it seems to me, quite unwarranted. . . .

The method by which diplomacy deals with a world where there are rival powers is to organize a balance of power which deprives the rivals, however lacking in intimacy and however unresponsive to common appeals, of a good prospect of successful aggression. That is what a diplomat means by the settlement of a conflict among rival powers. He does not mean that they will cease to be rivals. He does not mean that they will all be converted to thinking and wanting the same things. He means that, whatever they think, whatever they want, whatever their ideological purposes, the balance of power is such that they cannot afford to commit aggression. . . .*1

Lippmann's running commentary on the Administration's Cold War policy antedated his remarks on the X article. A member of the Senate Foreign Relations Committee cited an earlier critique of the Truman Doctrine speech during secret hearings on the President's request for $500 million to help Greece and Turkey resist communism. The Chairman, Senator Arthur Vandenberg, had asked Navy Secretary James V. Forrestal to outline the strategic reasons for accepting this responsibility:

SECRETARY FORRESTAL: . . . From a naval point of view . . . this involves the Mediterranean area. There are two ends to that battle. One is at Gibralter and Spain and the other, of course, is the eastern end of it, and if our people were faced with the closing of the Mediterranean, which is what the demolition of Greece as an active power means, and the accession by Turkey to Russia's demand for the Dardanelles, you have cut the world in half. That is the naval interest.

I think . . . it may be wise to point out that American interest in the Mediterranean is not a new thing. The earliest history of the American Navy dealt with the Mediterranean. In fact, we were more active there than we have ever been anywhere since we have had merchant shipping. The actions of the pirates of the Barbary Coast in connection with that shipping brought it home to us very sharply. . . .

*1 Walter Lippmann, *The Cold War: A Study in U.S. Foreign Policy* (New York: Harper & Row, 1947), pp. 10–17, 21–24, 30–31, 33–35, 40, 46–47, 50, 51, 58–59, 60–61.

It might be well for us to show that line. Take that so-called Iron Curtain, running right down here and across, and through the Black Sea. The Russians, you remember, were asking for a trusteeship in Tripolitania, which would be an extension over the sea of that same curtain.

Turkey and Greece are each a function of the other. If Greece goes it is on the flank; if Turkey goes, you have an impossible military situation.

SENATOR VANDENBERG: What is the answer to this question—and with great respect I think this was the chief weakness in the President's message, that at no point did he bring this hazard home to the United States as an American hazard in any aspect. He left it rather in the ideological field, of interest in freedom. Does not this come back to the United States and its own intelligent self-interest in very realistic fashion?

SECRETARY FORRESTAL: Absolutely.

SENATOR VANDENBERG: How can you prove that to the American people? What can you say to them? What dare you say to them on that subject?

SENATOR [H. ALEXANDER] SMITH: Mr. Chairman, if I may ask one other question of the Secretary, Mr. Lippmann, in an editorial a few days ago, pointed out that if we got into the business of spreading our financial resources too thin, we would accomplish nothing by it, we might get ourselves into trouble, the dollar go off, and so on, and he raised the interesting suggestion that possibly it was our job, as a matter of foreign policy, to seek certain strategic areas that we could bolster, and limit our policy to that, instead of being caught with a lot of things we cannot keep up with. That is what troubles me.

[UNDER-SECRETARY OF STATE] ACHESON: I read that article of Walter Lippmann. One of the interesting things is that in prior articles of Mr. Lippmann, Greece and Turkey have always been the strategic area in which he was most interested. Now he talks about other strategic areas as though this were not one. I do not know whether he is still interested in Greece and Turkey, but he is interested in some other places.

It is true that there are parts of the world to which we have no access. It would be silly to believe that we can do anything effective in Rumania, Bulgaria, or Poland. You cannot do that. That is within the Russian area of physical force. We are excluded from that. There are other places where we can be effective. One of them is Korea, and I think that is another place where the line has been clearly drawn between the Russians and ourselves.

SENATOR SMITH: Then we have come to this place in our policy: We are saying, "You have come this far. Now you have to stop or you are running head on into us." Is that what the President's message means?

SECRETARY ACHESON: In these areas where our help can be effective in resisting this penetration.

Forrestal and Acheson had made a powerful strategic argument, and had successfully reduced one of Lippmann's counter-arguments. It was indeed hard to say where to draw the line, but clearly if strategy was an issue there was certainly reason enough to draw it at Greece and Turkey. The question really was, therefore, what *was* American strategy—and what was the threat? Acheson spoke of penetration, not direct aggression. The issue was raised later in the hearings with the American Ambassador to Greece, Lincoln MacVeagh:

SENATOR [ALEXANDER] WILEY: As I see it, Mr. Ambassador, we feel that in our own self-interest—and I want that amplified on the record—we are going to do what will benefit our self-interest. In other words, we are going all out to stop Russia at the Bosphorus, and stop communism. Yet we had a former Ambassador, [Joseph] Kennedy, who said, "Let communism go. It will wear itself out," or what not. There you have two ideas clashing. That is what you have in America today. You have two Ambassadors clashing here, Kennedy and you, on that theory.

I could not help but be very much impressed the other day by former Mayor [Fiorello] LaGuardia, when he told very dramatically how once we put ourselves into the Balkans, what it means in years, in lives, and in expenditures. He said it was like the old Irish tale of a man coming around a corner in Dublin and seeing a man and woman fighting. He interfered, and they turned on him and licked hell out of him. The Balkans are a family of nations. They fight among themselves, probably. To me this is such a tremendous change in our policy that I want to be very clear in my own thinking, and that is why I asked you, sir, to put them down, as many as you can, and show that it is to the self-interest of our own country that we take this very important step. . . . The world interprets it as our interfering deliberately in the Near East, and we can only justify that on good, sound self-interest. . . .

AMBASSADOR MACVEAGH: We in Greece are right up against these fellows, and just for your interest I will read you a few lines of Mr. Stalin's own statement made twenty years ago. People do not seem to read what Mr. Stalin says. Here it is:

> The essential task of the victorious revolution in one country is to develop and support the revolution in others, so the victorious revolution in a victorious country ought not consider itself as a victory self-contained, but as a means of hastening the victory in another country.

What is going on in Greece now is the efforts of the successful revolution in the bordering countries to bring about a successful revolution in the next country. When that is successful in the next country, it is the doctrine of international communism to breed into the next country as it goes along. The same line has to be drawn, and Greece and Turkey are a strategic line. If they break that down, the whole Near East falls and they pick the lock of world dominion. Every one of these revolutionists has been turned back in the Near East. Hitler was turned back at El Alemain; the fellow before him, the Kaiser, was turned back at Jerusalem. They always go down to that region. If they ever go through that area, we will have to fight our battle against this spreading movement somewhere along another line further back—Dakar or Casablanca. That is where our interest comes in, not in the beautiful hills of Greece. In our own interests the thing to do is to hold them before they get to a critical line which weakens our position when the time comes when they wish to communize the Western Hemisphere. . . . Communism is never at peace with Capitalism. . . .

Thus the final answer to Vandenberg's complaint that the President had spent too much time in his speech on ideology and not enough on self-interest was that the two were inextricably linked. At least that was the only way to read Ambassador Mac-Veagh's comment to Senator Wiley. Wiley and others remained unconvinced. Senator Vandenberg then added another key point:

SENATOR VANDENBERG: Well, I think the President . . . frankly asserted that the fall of Greece, followed by the fall of Turkey, would establish a chain reaction around the world which could very easily leave us isolated in a Communist-dominated earth. That is about what he said.

That is my view. . . . Here we sit, not as free agents, because we have no power to initiate foreign policy. It is like, or almost like, a Presidential request for a declaration of war. When that reaches us there is precious little we can do except say "Yes." . . . I think that if we failed within a reasonable time to support the attitude of the President of the United States we would have lost any chance whatsoever to find a peaceful basis of settlement with the Soviet Union. . . . I think they have never gotten it out of their heads that if they press us hard enough we will finally yield. I think we have started to get that out of their heads during the last year or two, and I think with a considerable degree of success. I think we would throw that all away if we were to indicate a divisive attitude between the executive and the legislative in respect of the main objective to which the President's message was dedicated.

Senator Tom Connally took a position alongside Vandenberg, thus assuring bi-partisan support for the President and success within the Committee:

SENATOR CONNALLY: . . . Since the President has taken this position it is known all over the world. If we hesitate or surrender in any wise, we will be nullifying the purpose that we have in view. . . . For those reasons I do not see how we can do anything else except to go along or to forget the whole business, and that would put us in a ridiculous attitude before the world. We would then be regarded as having been bluffed out of it by Russia, and we had better never have started. . . .

SENATOR VANDENBERG: Let me add this. . . . I spent the evening last night with a very wise old man whom I shall not identify, but at whose feet I have often sat when I was in doubt. And he said one thing which I shall never forget. We were discussing what would happen if the United States did not follow through in the present instance, and he said:

> Well, that is a very simple question to answer. Put yourself in Athens or in Ankara. If you were a responsible Greek in Athens and you got word that the United States had said "No," what would you do? Would you not immediately say, "There is no course left for us except to make the best terms we can with Moscow"?
>
> And if you were in Ankara, and a responsible government official and had been bravely standing up against this war of nerves for two years, and you got word that Congress had said "No" to the President's program, would you not say to yourself, "Well, the jig is up. I had better go to Moscow and see how good a deal I can make"?

It just seems to me that this is the inevitable result, and I do not believe we can afford to get within a thousand miles of any such situation for the sake of peace.[*1]

Here was the answer also to Lippmann's assertion concerning the Constitutional question posed by the Truman Doctrine and

[*1] U.S. Congress, Senate Committee on Foreign Relations, *Hearings Held in Executive Session on S. 938: A Bill to Provide for Assistance to Greece and Turkey* (80th Cong., 1st Sess., Washington, 1973), pp. 20–21, 66–67, 128–129, 132–133, 198.

containment. Lippmann had stated that the President could not ask Congress for a blank check to meet all threats in all parts of the world without abandoning the Constitution with its checks and balances. Vandenberg and Connally had it right: Congress could not refuse a presidential initiative without risking the danger that the Soviets would see the situation as a symptom of American weakness, and (whether or not they had originally planned aggression) would move in to help themselves. Here, it should be added finally, was the beginning of the central dilemma for Americans in the Cold War. There was no way to wage a successful Cold War without surrendering to the executive almost all power in the area of foreign affairs, and eventually much in the area of domestic affairs as well, in the era of total diplomacy.

From the secret hearings, finally released twenty-five years after the fact, it is now clear that the Senators were deeply troubled about all these problems. The most eloquent (and prophetic) statement came from Walter George of Georgia:

I do not think I have to defend myself here. I carried the burden in large part—Senator [Alben] Barkley and myself did—of the Lend-Lease proposal. I have never had any apologies to make for that. But I could then see the shadows of war lengthening all over the earth, and I thought it was absolutely necessary to move.

This is not that situation. Nobody thinks Russia is going to attack us. Nobody thinks Russia is going to make any war now on anybody. Certainly not. That she will keep up the same aggravating aggressiveness that she has had in the past, and infiltrations and the pressures and war of nerves, I guess few of us doubt, few of us question. But there is not, it seems to me, the necessity for doing more than passing this act, making your Section 4 immediately effective and giving a chance to the amendment [invoking United Nations intervention] which we have put in this bill this morning to really have some life and some vitality.

Once the fact is accomplished and we are into it, the United Nations of course will have no incentive and it will have no proper motive, at least, to make any inquiry about it. They will say, "The United States has taken this burden. Let them carry it." And they will let it run, and that will be the situation. And we will have it on our hands.

I do not know that we will have to go anywhere else in this world, and I do not say that at the moment. I do not see how we are going to escape going into Manchuria, North China, and Korea and doing things in that area of the world. But at the same time that is another question, and we have got the right to exercise common sense. But I know that when we make a policy of this kind we are irrevocably committing ourselves to a course of action, and there is no way to get out of it next week or next year. You go down to the end of the road. . . .*1

Despite such qualms, Senator George and other doubters voted for the funds Truman requested. And kept on voting for similar appropriations for the next twenty years, through the Korean war and to pay for doing other things "in that area of the world." The road did not end until Vietnam.

Secretary Acheson had testified at both secret hearings and public sessions that the United States was not undertaking an obligation to intervene anywhere in the world, but only where strategy dictated and where intervention could be effective. The trouble with that explanation was that (just as Acheson had pointed out about Lippmann's critique concerning Turkey and Greece) what seemed unimportant or nonstrategic yesterday became so when viewed through doctrinal lenses. Tomorrow everywhere would become integral to national security; every place was a strategic outpost, or bordered on one, or was next to an area that bordered on one, and so on.

Truman had even found the State Department draft of his proposed speech to Congress on Greece and Turkey too weak. "The drafting of the actual message which I would deliver to the Congress," he wrote later,

had meanwhile been started in the State Department. The first version was not at all to my liking. The writers had filled the

*1 Senate Committee on Foreign Relations, A *Bill to Provide for Assistance to Greece and Turkey,* pp. 20–21, 66–67, 128–129, 132–133, 198.

speech with all sorts of background data and statistical figures about Greece and made the whole thing sound like an investment prospectus. I returned this draft to Acheson with a note asking for more emphasis on a declaration of general policy. The department's draftsmen then rewrote the speech to include a general policy statement, but it seemed to me half-hearted. The key sentence, for instance, read, "I believe that it should be the policy of the United States . . ." I took my pencil, scratched out "should" and wrote in "must." In several other places I did the same thing. I wanted no hedging in this speech. This was America's answer to the surge of expansion of Communist tyranny. It had to be clear and free of hesitation or double talk.*1

Clear and free of hesitation it certainly was:

MR. PRESIDENT, MR. SPEAKER, MEMBERS OF THE CONGRESS OF THE UNITED STATES: The gravity of the situation which confronts the world today necessitates my appearance before a joint session of the Congress.

The foreign policy and the national security of this country are involved.

One aspect of the present situation, which I wish to present to you at this time for your consideration and decision, concerns Greece and Turkey.

The United States has received from the Greek Government an urgent appeal for financial and economic assistance. Preliminary reports from the American Economic Mission now in Greece and reports from the American Ambassador in Greece corroborate the statement of the Greek Government that assistance is imperative if Greece is to survive as a free nation.

I do not believe that the American people and the Congress wish to turn a deaf ear to the appeal of the Greek Government.

Greece is not a rich country. Lack of sufficient natural resources has always forced the Greek people to work hard to make both ends meet. Since 1940, this industrious and peace-

*1 Harry S. Truman, *Memoirs* (2 vols. Garden City, N.Y.: Doubleday & Co., 1956), II, 105.

loving country has suffered invasion, 4 years of cruel enemy occupation, and bitter internal strife.

When forces of liberation entered Greece they found that the retreating Germans had destroyed virtually all the railways, roads, port facilities, communications, and merchant marine. More than a thousand villages had been burned. Eighty-five percent of the children were tubercular. Livestock, poultry, and draft animals had almost disappeared. Inflation had wiped out practically all savings.

As a result of these tragic conditions, a militant minority, exploiting human want and misery, was able to create political chaos which, until now, has made economic recovery impossible.

Greece is today without funds to finance the importation of those goods which are essential to bare subsistence. Under these circumstances the people of Greece cannot make progress in solving their problems of reconstruction. Greece is in desperate need of financial and economic assistance to enable it to resume purchases of food, clothing, fuel, and seeds. These are indispensable for the subsistence of its people and are obtainable only from abroad. Greece must have help to import the goods necessary to restore internal order and security so essential for economic and political recovery.

The Greek Government has also asked for the assistance of experienced American administrators, economists, and technicians to insure that the financial and other aid given to Greece shall be used effectively in creating a stable and self-sustaining economy and in improving its public administration.

The very existence of the Greek State is today threatened by the terrorist activities of several thousand armed men, led by Communists, who defy the Government's authority at a number of points, particularly along the northern boundaries. A Commission appointed by the United Nations Security Council is at present investigating disturbed conditions in northern Greece, and alleged border violations along the frontier between Greece on the one hand and Albania, Bulgaria, and Yugoslavia on the other.

Meanwhile, the Greek Government is unable to cope with the situation. The Greek Army is small and poorly equipped. It needs supplies and equipment if it is to restore the authority of the Government throughout Greek territory.

Greece must have assistance if it is to become a self-supporting and self-respecting democracy.

The United States must supply that assistance. We have already extended to Greece certain types of relief and economic aid, but these are inadequate.

There is no other country to which democratic Greece can turn.

No other nation is willing and able to provide the necessary support for a democratic Greek Government.

The British Government, which has been helping Greece, can give no further financial or economic aid after March 31. Great Britain finds itself under the necessity of reducing or liquidating its commitments in several parts of the world, including Greece.

We have considered how the United Nations might assist in this crisis. But the situation is an urgent one requiring immediate action, and the United Nations and its related organizations are not in a position to extend help of the kind that is required.

It is important to note that the Greek Government has asked for our aid in utilizing effectively the financial and other assistance we may give to Greece, and in improving its public administration. It is of the utmost importance that we supervise the use of any funds made available to Greece, in such a manner that each dollar spent will count toward making Greece self-supporting, and will help to build an economy in which a healthy democracy can flourish.

No government is perfect. One of the chief virtues of a democracy, however, is that its defects are always visible and under democratic processes can be pointed out and corrected. The government of Greece is not perfect. Nevertheless it represents 85 percent of the members of the Greek Parliament who were chosen in an election last year. Foreign observers, including 692 Americans, considered this election to be a fair expression of the views of the Greek people.

The Greek Government has been operating in an atmosphere of chaos and extremism. It has made mistakes. The extension of aid by this country does not mean that the United States condones everything that the Greek Government has done or will do. We have condemned in the past, and we condemn now, extremist measures of the right or the left. We have in the past advised tolerance, and we advise tolerance now.

Greece's neighbor, Turkey, also deserves our attention.

The future of Turkey as an independent and economically sound state is clearly no less important to the freedom-loving peoples of the world than the future of Greece. The circumstances in which Turkey finds itself today are considerably different from those of Greece. Turkey has been spared the disasters that have beset Greece; and, during the war, the United States and Great Britain furnished Turkey with material aid. Nevertheless, Turkey now needs our support.

Since the war Turkey has sought financial assistance from Great Britain and the United States for the purpose of effecting that modernization necessary for the maintenance of its national integrity.

That integrity is essential to the preservation of order in the Middle East.

The British Government has informed us that, owing to its own difficulties, it can no longer extend financial or economic aid to Turkey.

As in the case of Greece, if Turkey is to have the assistance it needs, the United States must supply it. We are the only country able to provide that help.

I am fully aware of the broad implications involved if the United States extends assistance to Greece and Turkey, and I shall discuss these implications with you at this time.

One of the primary objectives of the foreign policy of the United States is the creation of conditions in which we and other nations will be able to work out a way of life free from coercion. This was a fundamental issue in the war with Germany and Japan. Our victory was won over countries which sought to impose their will, and their way of life, upon other nations.

To insure the peaceful development of nations, free from coercion, the United States has taken a leading part in establishing the United Nations. The United Nations is designed to make possible lasting freedom and independence for all its members. We shall not realize our objectives, however, unless we are willing to help free peoples to maintain their free institutions and their national integrity against aggressive movements that seek to impose upon them totalitarian regimes. This is no more than a frank recognition that totalitarian regimes imposed on free peoples, by direct or indirect aggression, undermine the foundations of international peace and hence the security of the United States.

The peoples of a number of countries of the world have recently had totalitarian regimes forced upon them against their will. The Government of the United States has made frequent protests against coercion and intimidation, in violation of the Yalta agreement, in Poland, Rumania, and Bulgaria. I must also state that in a number of other countries there have been similar developments.

At the present moment in world history nearly every nation must choose between alternative ways of life. The choice is too often not a free one.

One way of life is based upon the will of the majority, and is distinguished by free institutions, representative government, free elections, guaranties of individual liberty, freedom of speech and religion, and freedom from political oppression.

The second way of life is based upon the will of a minority forcibly imposed upon the majority. It relies upon terror and oppression, a controlled press and radio, fixed elections, and the suppression of personal freedoms.

I believe that it must be the policy of the United States to support free peoples who are resisting attempted subjugation by armed minorities or by outside pressures.

I believe that we must assist free peoples to work out their own destinies in their own way.

I believe that our help should be primarily through economic and financial aid which is essential to economic stability and orderly political processes.

The world is not static, and the status quo is not sacred. But we cannot allow changes in the status quo in violation of the Charter of the United Nations by such methods as coercion, or by such subterfuges as political infiltration. In helping free and independent nations to maintain their freedom, the United States will be giving effect to the principles of the Charter of the United Nations.

329

It is necessary only to glance at a map to realize that the survival and integrity of the Greek nation are of grave importance in a much wider situation. If Greece should fall under the control of an armed minority, the effect upon its neighbor Turkey, would be immediate and serious. Confusion and disorder might well spread throughout the entire Middle East.

Moreover, the disappearance of Greece as an independent state would have a profound effect upon those countries in Europe whose peoples are struggling against great difficulties to maintain their freedoms and their independence while they repair the damages of war.

It would be an unspeakable tragedy if these countries, which have struggled so long against overwhelming odds, should lose that victory for which they sacrificed so much. Collapse of free institutions and loss of independence would be disastrous not only for them but for the world. Discouragement and possibly failure would quickly be the lot of neighboring peoles striving to maintain their freedom and independence.

Should we fail to aid Greece and Turkey in this fateful hour, the effect will be far reaching to the West as well as to the East.

We must take immediate and resolute action.

I, therefore, ask the Congress to provide authority for assistance to Greece and Turkey in the amount of $400,000,000 for the period ending June 30, 1948. In requesting these funds, I have taken into consideration the maximum amount of relief assistance which would be furnished to Greece out of the $350,000,000 which I recently requested that the Congress authorize for the prevention of starvation and suffering in countries devastated by the war.

In addition to funds, I ask the Congress to authorize the detail of American civilian and military personnel to Greece and Turkey, at the request of those countries, to assist in the tasks of reconstruction, and for the purpose of supervising the use of such financial and material assistance as may be furnished. I recommend that authority also be provided for the instruction and training of selected Greek and Turkish personnel.

Finally, I ask that the Congress provide authority which will permit the speediest and most effective use, in terms of needed commodities, supplies, and equipment, of such funds as may be authorized.

If further funds, or further authority, should be needed for purposes indicated in this message, I shall not hesitate to bring the situation before the Congress. On this subject the executive and legislative branches of the Government must work together.

This is a serious course upon which we embark.

I would not recommend it except that the alternative is much more serious.

The United States contributed $341,000,000,000 toward winning World War II. This is an investment in world freedom and world peace.

The assistance that I am recommending for Greece and Turkey amounts to little more than one-tenth of 1 percent of this investment. It is only common sense that we should safeguard this investment and make sure that it was not in vain.

The seeds of totalitarian regimes are nurtured by misery and want. They spread and grow in the evil soil of poverty and strife. They reach their full growth when the hope of a people for a better life has died.

We must keep that hope alive.

The free peoples of the world look to us for support in maintaining their freedoms.

If we falter in our leadership, we may endanger the peace of the world—and we shall surely endanger the welfare of our own Nation.

Great responsibilities have been placed upon us by the swift movement of events.

I am confident that the Congress will face these responsibilities squarely.

HARRY S. TRUMAN.

THE WHITE HOUSE, *March 12, 1947.*[1]

Truman did not like making an "investment prospectus" out of the Greek-Turkish situation. "A few days earlier, at Baylor University in Waco, Texas, I had expressed my belief that free

[1] *Public Papers of the Presidents of the United States . . . Harry S. Truman, 1947* (Washington, D.C.: Government Printing Office, 1963), pp. 176–180.

world trade was an inseparable part of the peaceful world," he explained in his *Memoirs*. "I said, 'Our foreign relations, political and economic, are indivisible. We cannot say that we are willing to cooperate in the one field and are unwilling to cooperate in the other.' I cited the economic war of the thirties, when nations strangled normal trade, depositors lost their savings, and farmers lost their lands. The lesson in history, I said, was plain: Freedom of international trade would provide the atmosphere necessary to the preservation of peace. My advisers were already at work seeking further practical ways to strengthen international cooperation in economic matters."[3]

A comprehensive statement of the developing struggle over trade ideologies came from a former State Department planner, Herbert Feis, in another article in *Foreign Affairs Quarterly*.

When a dispute erupts in the realms of action and of doctrine at the same time it is ominous. An eruption of this type is occuring now over commercial policy. The lava of argument is pouring over the surfaces where national wills clash and shooting into the skies where doctrines spend their angry eternity. I will begin with the dispute over doctrine as the better way of defining the issues uncomplicated by particular local circumstances.

The American Government is sponsoring at an international conference now meeting [January, 1947] in London a suggested Charter for an International Trade Organization. This proposal is the outcome of sustained searching by American and foreign experts for an agreed statement of principles to govern the trade policy of nations. Its terms express a stubborn will to draw countries into a joint program for the reduction of trade restrictions; and they reflect a dogged judgment that the most satisfactory basis for trade is world-wide and unmanaged competition.

It is impossible to condense the detailed prescriptions of the many articles of this Charter satisfactorily. But the basic economic conceptions which shaped them all are easily identified. They are: (1) that governments should reduce all types of restriction imposed on imports and exports; (2) that each should abstain from actions which would cause products produced within their territories to be offered in foreign markets at prices out of correspondence with domestic prices; (3) that each should permit products from every foreign land to compete within its markets on equal terms, and thereby leave the origin of imports to be settled by universal competition; (4) that each should accord all foreign buyers equal opportunity to secure its products on the same terms; (5) that each should abstain from bilateral agreements for the exchange of goods that would or might lessen the opportunity of others to compete for the trade. This is a broad but, I believe, correct interpretation of the conceptions embodied in the many articles of the Charter.

I will not try to trace the intricate ways in which the attempt is made to apply these rules to the medley of restrictions and forms of trading systems—private, part-private and part state, wholly state. For one thing, the technical details are voluminous; and to omit some is to distort the rest. For another, there seems to be an unsettled difference of judgment even among officials who composed the Charter as to whether or how some of the provisions apply to countries that conduct *all* their trade through a state monopoly.

But the foregoing recitation of governing standards is enough to indicate that the proposed rules of behavior are less natural for Socialist or managed systems than for private competitive ones. Still, if they are given a common-sense interpretation they might not prove too confining a garment of principle even for the former. It would be by no means easy for competitive private economics to observe them either. Freedom to be arbitrary is a great convenience to them as well. It should be possible to shape most of the provisions by further discussion into a mutually acceptable program. But only if good will exists; and only if the way is left open for exceptions that can be well justified. There are, and there will be, countries that cannot get along satisfactorily without the benefit of some favored trade relationships. We have recently recognized this in the case of the Philippines. These rules, if they are to be tolerable, must not stubbornly block bilateral arrangements that promise healthy growth without plain and needless injury to others.

The specific provisions in the Charter having to do with the conduct of a complete state trading monopoly, such as that maintained by the U.S.S.R., is apt to prove the most stubborn cause of dispute. They seemed designed to assure that the behavior of such monopolies will be akin to that of private trade and to establish a parity of advantage between the two types of systems. I believe the authors have been too much swayed by the judgment that this could be done only by having all trade open to uncircumscribed competition.

Let me illustrate. Article 26 specifies that state trading enterprises should be operated on a non-discriminatory basis; that is, that in their buying and selling they should accord the commerce of all other countries most-favored-nation advantages. The U.S.S.R. has customarily been ready so to pledge itself in general terms. A promise of this kind was contained in the trade agreements negotiated with the United States before the war. It is to be found also, for example, in the commercial agreement recently negotiated with France. But in the Charter this idea is given a more precise and confining interpretation than the U.S.S.R. has ever been asked to observe. It is provided that in order to give effect to a non-discriminatory policy any state trading enterprise "shall, in making its external purchases or sales of any product or service, be influenced solely by commercial considerations, such as price, quality, marketability, transportation and terms of purchase or sale."

The reasons for seeking agreement upon the rules of behavior for state trading organizations are grave. For if this method of trading is used ruthlessly and greedily it can disturb the economic life of other countries greatly. It can be more easily directed than private trading arrangements to dispossess established trade, to acquire a monopoly of resources, and to extort unfair advantage in the exchange of goods. It can also, as German behavior before the war so bitterly illustrated, be intently directed towards the accomplishment of an aggressive political purpose. These are reasons for seeking assurance against the abuse of state systems.

But it is best not to insist upon formulas which seem too deeply dyed by the values of private competitive practice such as the one cited. And in this instance the impulse to evade might be bolstered by knowledge that privately conducted trade is not entirely determined by commercial considerations. It is sometimes affected by governmental measures taken for political reasons—domestic or foreign. Thus, for example, our foreign loan program and the trade resulting therefrom is subject to reckonings that are not wholly commercial. And the impulse to treat such a formula cynically may be encouraged by the knowledge that private trade is not always competitive; that private monopolies sometimes discriminate. There are in fact students of the Charter who argue that this provision will be accepted without question, because it can be twisted to mean anything.

I do not know, and it is not necessary now to guess, what position the U.S.S.R. and countries closely allied to it or under its control will ultimately take towards the Charter proposals. They may be much modified before a decision is required. The U.S.S.R. alone of all countries did not respond to American invitations to confer about measures to make effective Article VII of the Lend-Lease Agreements; it is supposed, in fact, not even to have acknowledged the invitation. After an earlier show of willingness to become a member of the International Fund and the International Bank, it has remained outside. The fact that the text of these agreements contained provisions having to do with trade policy may well have been one of the reasons. And now the U.S.S.R. is absent from the discussions being conducted in London. In short, its responses in the recent past do not encourage the belief that it will join.

This possibility gives more than theoretical importance to the provisions of the Charter proposals having to do with the relations between the members of the International Trade Organizations and non-members. I will state them in full despite their cumbrous clauses. The proposed text (Article 31) stipulates first that no member shall seek exclusive or preferential advantages for its trade in the territory of any non-member which would result, directly or indirectly, in discrimination against the trade of any other member. Construed by standards defined in other sections of the text, this stipulation would mean that members could not enter into agreement with the U.S.S.R. which provided for specific exchanges of goods unless the exchanges fitted into quotas allotted by reference to a previous representative period. This would require modification of most, if not all, the agreements to which the U.S.S.R. is now a party. It was quite possibly this provision of the Charter that the Deputy Minister of Finance of Czechoslovakia had in mind when he remarked that the chief obstacle to a new trade understanding with the United States was our desire to include a clause providing for membership in a world trade body. He explained that Czechoslovakia could not pledge itself to join a trade arrangement that might in effect exclude the Soviet Union and the eastern bloc of states with which Czechoslovakia is closely linked economically.*¹ Article 31 of the Charter further provides that no member shall be a party to any agreement with a non-member under which the latter becomes contractually entitled to *any* of the benefits under this Charter. And also that members shall not, except with the concurrence of the Organization, apply tariff reductions made in pursurance of the Charter to the trade of non-members.

This group of provisions should be reconsidered, if they already have not been by the time this article appears. It is probable they are intended merely to provide a basis of joint defense against any member that threatened the unity of the organization or took advantage of its weaker members. But they may be construed as a threat. A serious attempt to apply them would result either in the demoralization of the International Trade Organization, or open economic warfare between members on the one side and the U.S.S.R. and its allies on the other. Either would be a sorry outcome of a good impulse, valiantly pursued, to restore and bring order into international trade relations.

This conclusion is not meant as a dismissal of the need of obtaining proofs and promises of reasonable behavior from the U.S.S.R.—whether or not it joins the International Trade Organization. These should be definite enough to testify to its willingness to abstain from using its trading system unfairly, or as a means of forcing other countries to join it in a bloc, separated from, if not actively hostile to, the rest of the world. That the U.S.S.R. may now be attempting to do just that is suggested by the agreements negotiated with the former satellites of Germany and other neigh-

*¹ *The New York Times,* November 1, 1946.

boring countries. The agreements with Bulgaria, Rumania and Hungary in particular have caused anxiety and resentment on the part of the American Government. They were completed in secrecy. Unless I am mistaken, their texts have not been published. The Soviet Government is reported to have refused to supply even foreign governments with copies. So any account of their contents is subject to error in detail.

The agreements seem to fall into two groups. One may be called trade agreements; these contain arrangements for the exchange of products, specifying quantity, prices, payment methods and other related matters. The others have become known as economic collaboration agreements; these provide for 50 percent participation by the Soviet Government in various branches of the economic life of the former satellite countries. Any appraisal of the significance of these two sets of agreements must take into account as well the claims on production acquired by the U.S.S.R. as restitution and reparations.

The student of the history of these agreements gets the impression that the U.S.S.R. first sought to put itself in a position to claim control of all the trade and production of these smaller countries that desperate need or grasping desire could identify. After all, these countries were defeated enemies which had taken part in an attempt to destroy the Soviet Union; and most of the former directors of their industrial life had close ties with Berlin. Then, the general claim having been established, the U.S.S.R. seems to have proceeded to adjust its demands to actual possibilities and to the protests encountered.

The first trade agreement with Rumania (May 1945) contemplated an exchange of goods to the value of $20,000,000 in each direction. The total scheduled Rumanian deliveries were in excess of the country's immediate capacity. This is proven by the fact that during the first year of the agreement's operation Rumanian exports to the U.S.S.R. were only 33 percent of the scheduled total; and, contrary to intention, less than Soviet deliveries to Rumania. Under the economic collaboration agreement negotiated simultaneously, joint Soviet-Rumanian companies were to be established for the development of Rumanian resources. It is reported that such joint companies have been created for oil production, navigation, civil aviation, banking and lumber.

Whether or not these are as yet on a full operating basis is not known. The capital of these joint companies is divided equally between the appropriate Soviet state enterprises and private Rumanian companies. The Soviet contribution has consisted mainly of former German assets acquired by the U.S.S.R. under the Potsdam Agreement, or under the war booty clause (Article VII) of the Armistice agreement. In each of the fields in which these joint companies are to operate they appear to have been accorded a preferential or almost monopolistic position—in fact, if not in form. Rumania is also obligated under the Armistice arrangements to make extensive deliveries as restitution and reparations. The expected result of a perpetuation of these arrangements, in combination, would be that Rumania would not be in a position to trade on a satisfactory scale with other countries.

The Bulgarian trade agreements (March 1945 and April 1946) are similarly comprehensive. It is reported that the cash value of the trade arrangement included within its scope about one-half of the total value of Bulgarian trade in 1939. But here again the actual trade up to the present has been less than the specified amounts. The only economic collaboration agreement known to have been concluded between the two countries is the mining field ; under the nationalization program it was apparently planned that this joint company would acquire control of all important mining enterprises in Bulgaria.

The trade agreement between the U.S.S.R. and Hungary (August 1945) provided for an exchange of goods of $30,000,000 in each direction. This would be only about 19 percent of Hungarian trade in 1939, and much less than the prewar trade between Germany and Hungary. It is reported that the agreement operated unsatisfactorily and that deliveries were much smaller than those set forth in its text. There is reason to believe it is in process of re-negotiation. The economic collaboration agreement with Hungary (August 1945) has been carried out by the formation of joint companies for aviation, navigation, oil and bauxite production. The navigation and aviation companies would be placed in dominant, if not exclusive, positions. The bauxite company would possess a preferential position, and the oil company a favored one in regard to future opportunity. It is understood that these agreements do not seriously jeopardize the operation of existing American properties in Hungary; but they would curtail the possibility of expansion or entry into new fields.

It is unsafe to draw final conclusions regarding the economic consequences of these arrangements, for the actual outcome thus far seems to have been quite different from that scheduled. But it is easy to appreciate why the American and other governments have suspected that these arrangements might result in bringing the economic life of the small countries in question under Russian domination. It has been estimated that the value of imports into the U.S.S.R. specified in the trade agreements concluded in 1945 with Rumania, Hungary, Bulgaria and Finland was approximately $60,000,000, while reparations deliveries from the same countries were scheduled at about $130,000,000. This, combined with the arrangements for joint control of basic branches of economic activity in the case of Rumania and Hungary, might well have left the smaller countries unable to resume outside trade relationships on a satisfactory scale. Or at least they would have made that possibility subject to Russian tolerance. Thus our opposition up to the present has been justified. This opposition has been more directly addressed to the economic collaboration accords than to the trade agreements. And our criticism of the latter has not been unique; it is part of our general show of dislike for all bilateral agreements of this kind. But we have not usually pushed our protests so vigorously and dramatically. Or is it that the press and radio have selected them for noisy demonstration?

But a basic question of policy remains to be settled. How far shall we carry our objections? Shall we merely try to satisfy some broad purposes by rough compromise, sufficient to assure that these arrangements do not deprive us of our main natural opportunities to trade with these countries and do not ban American enterprises from fields like oil production and aviation in which they are competitively well qualified? Or shall we go further? Shall we insist that these countries and the U.S.S.R. abstain from any accord that may supplant previous trade flows, and might interfere with the full operation of international competition? Shall we contend against any arrangements which may result in granting the U.S.S.R. a greater or more privileged place in the trade and economic life of these countries than it would obtain if all opportunity was left open to competition? It is the latter course that the American Government seems now inclined to take—if I interpret correctly the meaning of some of the contentions we have advanced. Inclined to take, let me make clear again, not only in connection with this set of accords, but whenever two countries arrange for an exchange of products in channels not clearly etched by past competition or bounded by future competition.

The American Government had made several direct attempts to halt and bring about a revision of the agreements to which objection has been taken. As early as July 1945 it informed the U.S.S.R. that it judged the economic collaboration agreements with Rumania, particularly those concerned with oil, were discriminatory. It repeatedly presented objections to both the Soviet and Hungarian Governments regarding their agreements. In both cases it urged that all such arrangements be deferred until the peace treaties had been concluded; and it asserted that the only satisfactory and fair approach to the problem of economic reconstruction in these countries was a comprehensive, tripartite arrangement that would provide a framework for the reintegration of their economies with the general economy of Europe. It advanced the same view in the course of discussions of a possible loan from the United States to the U.S.S.R., proposing joint negotiations for the establishment of concerted policies to assist former Axis satellite states to solve their economic difficulties. All these American proposals were denied and the suggestions for joint discussions have been evaded. The Soviet Government has refused to accede to the American conception of equality in its trade agreements; and it has claimed that the arrangements for economic collaboration were not discriminatory. It has cited the dominant place obtained by private American enterprise in some of the countries of this hemisphere; and it has noted the fact that American private enterprise abroad has sometimes acquired exclusive opportunity.

And now this issue has become the subject of a harsh public quarrel in the Council of Foreign Ministers, engaged in framing peace treaties with Rumania, Hungary, Bulgaria and Italy. The American and other Governments proposed that the following clauses be put in the treaties:

1. Pending the conclusion of commercial treaties or agreements between . . . . and the United Nations, the . . . . Government shall, during the . . . . months following the coming into force of the present Treaty, grant the following treatment to each of the United Nations, which, in fact, reciprocally grants similar treatment in like matters to . . . . :

a. In all that concerns duties and charges on importation and exportation, the internal taxation of imported goods and all regulations pertaining thereto, the United Nations shall be granted unconditional most favoured treatment.

b. In all other respects, to make no arbitrary discrimination against goods originating in or destined for any territory of any of the United Nations as compared with like goods originating in or destined for any other territory of the United Nations or any other foreign country.

c. Natural and legal persons who are nationals of any of the United Nations shall be granted national and most-favoured-nation treatment in all matters pertaining to commerce, industry, shipping and other forms of business activities within . . . .

The U.S.S.R. has denied both the necessity and the equity of these provisions; and it has sought to destroy their clinching meaning by various amendments. Their representatives have inserted in bitter phrases the opinion that the United States and other countries were trying to force abandonment of their type of state trading arrangement. They have said particularly that we were doing this in order to keep the economies of the smaller states of central Europe subject to capitalist control. Thus Molotov avowed before the Peace Conference in Paris, on August 15, that "Nobody can say that the unlimited application of 'equality of opportunity' is equally suitable for powerful and for weak states, for great and small Powers. Nobody could prove this. . . . It is obvious that the unlimited application of this principle is something which is convenient for those who have the power and the wealth, for those who are trying to use their capital to subjugate those who are weaker."

It is not likely that either side will completely yield on this question. It may be necessary to exclude any economic provisions from these treaties to avoid indefinite postponement of their signature. That the U.S.S.R. is determined to secure a greatly extended, if not dominant, place in the economies of these countries is clear. That it intends to supervise their political and social development seems no less clear. And in this matter the United States cannot compromise happily or too far. For it is not striving merely to obtain a few extra million dollars of trade or profit. It is seeking to assure that these small countries have a genuine chance to follow their independent judgment in economic and political spheres. And it is seeking to protect American trade relations throughout the world against a possible assault of a combined bloc of countries under the leadership of the U.S.S.R.

The line of settlement—if any is to be reached—would appear to be a loosening of the formulas we have been propounding. We can accept arrangements between the U.S.S.R. and these countries that permit them to develop trade and economic relations not confined by theoretical calculations of competitive opportunity. But these should be well defined and so limited as to enable the smaller countries to take advantage of opportunities to deal with the outside world. For we cannot freely consent to arbitrary exclusion from their economic life or to have our entry decisively subject to the will of the U.S.S.R.

The dilemma we face over the matter of how strictly to insist upon application of a theoretical principle of equality of opportunity will not be restricted to the geographical area that is the present field of dispute. It is almost certain to arise, and with great tension, in connection with the German peace settlement. Here both the rights and the interests of the United States would justify insistence on terms that place no country in an advantageous position as compared with others. If foreign governments are to join with a central German Government in the administration of any branch or enterprise in that country, the participation should be joint and equal, or in accord with agreed principles. But if the American Government intends to obtain and retain an equal place in the economy of Germany, it must be prepared to have more positive instruments of policy than formulas. It will have to be willing to undertake or underwrite trading operations.

And what if the same issue spreads even further? What if the Soviet Government should negotiate economic collaboration agreements with the countries of western Europe or of this hemisphere of the kind it has with Hungary and Rumania? The chief source of trade and financial advantages for most foreign countries is clearly outside of the U.S.S.R. They will be hesitant to risk these—as they would be doing—for fulfillment of any very objectional accord with the U.S.S.R. The accord with Sweden was a warning incident. This was a combined loan and "goods delivery" agreement, not an economic collaboration accord. American refusal to countenance the very form of these agreements is not likely to prevent their negotiation. And American attempts to confine them by rigid formula are likely to be evaded. All that we can successfully hope to do, I think, is to insist that they remain within the realm of easy justification on economic grounds; and if they do not, withhold the advantages that we have the power to bestow.

The most promising safeguard against harsh train of argument would be universal participation in the International Trade Organization. Within its web of mutual obligations, equities could be debated and defined, rivalries adjusted, compromises conceived and benefits exchanged. If this cannot be realized, a direct understanding should be sought with the U.S.S.R. Failing either, the question may prove to be one of the most troublesome in the realm of Great Power politics. The sponsors of the Charter effort should be given the utmost of support—and be "aided" by criticism.

The various lines of compromise I have suggested may be ridiculed as pointless. For it may be argued that the positions of nations in this field represent only strategic steps in a long struggle regarding the political and social destinies of central Europe, and perhaps of the whole world. But it would be desperate defeatism now to be deterred by this conjecture from making the utmost effort to find out whether reconcilation in the trade field—as in others—is not possible.[2]

*2 "The Conflict Over Trade Ideologies," *Foreign Affairs Quarterly*, XXV (January, 1947), 218–228.

With the Feis reading we have reached all the way back to the origins of the Cold War in the dispute over Eastern Europe. The main point of his article, and of Truman's statement that political and economic foreign policy were indivisible, was not that the United States had to have access to Eastern Europe to avoid a postwar depression. If the issue had been that simple policymakers would have had a much easier time of it. The problem confronting American policymakers at the end of the War was nothing less than the reconstruction of a functioning world system, an inheritance, if you like, from the British. Americans did not hope to follow in the footsteps of the British *raj* in India, or of British government in any other colony or protectorate; what they hoped to do was to construct a new world system based on democratic liberalism. They did feel, however, that a reformed capitalism was the economic system most compatible with democratic liberalism and with American interests. They defined the world in their image; the Soviets did the same, perhaps, but their economic ability to influence world affairs was considerably less in power terms. On the other hand, Soviet ability to influence postwar Europe and the rest of the world through the propagation of Marxism was another matter.

The existence of a Soviet sphere of influence in Eastern Europe posed several dangers to the United States. On the most basic level, there was the danger to the next "tier" of states in Europe. As Averell Harriman explained to the American delegation to the first United Nations Conference on April 25, 1945, " Russia is building a tier of friendly states there [in Eastern Europe] and our task is to make it difficult for her to do so, since to build one tier of states implies the possibility of further tiers, layer on layer."[4] On a somewhat more abstract level, it was felt that Stalin's control of Eastern Europe would lead him to believe that he could withhold the resources of the area in the hope of making economic recovery in the West impossibly difficult. As George Kennan explained to the National War College in 1947, the Soviets apparently believed they need only "continue to deny those resources for a while longer in order to put themselves in a position where they will be able practically to name the political price at which they will make them available."[5] On the most abstract level, the ideological plane, Russian presence in Eastern Europe promoted socialist thinking in all countries.

Speaking in mid-summer 1946, Under Secretary Acheson spoke of the necessity of sustaining "the continued moral, military, and economic power of the United States," and warned against those who mouthed the slogans "Bring the boys home!" and "Don't be Santa Claus!" "They lie at the root . . . of the difficulty which we have in using our great economic power, in our own interest, to hasten recovery in other countries *along lines which are essential to our own system.*"[6] [Author's emphasis] Only one member of Truman's Cabinet attempted to separate economic and political issues, Commerce Secretary Henry A. Wallace. A former Vice-President under Franklin Delano Roosevelt, Wallace was regarded by his supporters as that President's only true heir. Truman was considered little better than a usurper, foisted on the Democratic faithful by a conservative claque within the Party at the 1944 convention. Wallace may not have felt quite so strongly about Truman as did his liberal friends, but certainly he did see the need to speak out on foreign policy as the Cold War began, and regarded himself as qualified to do so.

Hence on September 12, 1946, he appeared before a rally in Madison Square Garden. Sponsored by three liberal groups, the meeting was a form of protest against both domestic and foreign policies of the Administration. Interestingly, however, Wallace declared during the speech that Truman had seen his prepared statement and had agreed with "these words" and said "they represented the policy of his Administration." Wallace began:

Tonight I want to talk about peace—and how to get peace. Never have the common people of all lands so longed for peace. Yet, never in a time of comparative peace have they feared war so much.

Up till now peace has been negative and unexciting. War has been positive and exciting. Far too often, hatred and fear, intolerance and deceit have had the upper hand over love and confidence, trust and joy. Far too often, the law of nations has been the law of the jungle; and the constructive spiritual forces of the Lord have bowed to the destructive forces of Satan.

During the past year or so, the significance of peace has been increased immeasurably by the atom bomb, guided missiles and airplanes which soon will travel as fast as sound. Make no mistake about it—another war would hurt the United States many times as much as the last war. We cannot rest in the assurance that we invented the atom bomb—and therefore that this agent of destruction will work best for us. He who trusts in the atom bomb will sooner or later perish by the atom bomb—or something worse.

I say this as one who steadfastly backed preparedness throughout the '30s. We have no use for namby-pamby pacifism. But we must realize that modern inventions have now made peace the most exciting thing in the world—and we should be willing to pay a just price for peace. If modern war can cost us $400,000,-000,000, we should be willing and happy to pay much more for peace. But certainly, the cost of peace is to be measured not in dollars, but in the hearts and minds of men.

The price of peace—for us and for every nation in the world—is the price of giving up prejudice, hatred, fear and ignorance. . . .

I plead for an America vigorously dedicated to peace—just as I plead for opportunities for the next generation throughout the world to enjoy the abundance which now, more than ever before, is the birthright of man.

To achieve lasting peace, we must study in detail just how the Russian character was formed—by invasions of Tartars, Mongols, Germans, Poles, Swedes, and French; by the czarist rule based on ignorance, fear and force; by the intervention of the British, French and Americans in Russian affairs from 1919 to 1921; by the geography of the huge Russian land mass situated strategically between Europe and Asia; and by the vitality received from the rich Russian soil and the strenuous Russian climate. Add to all this the tremendous emotional power which Marxism and Leninism gives to the Russian leaders—and then we can realize that we are reckoning with a force which cannot be handled successfully by a "get tough with Russia" policy. "Getting tough" never bought anything real and lasting—whether for schoolyard bullies or businessmen or world powers. The tougher we get, the tougher the Russians will get.

Throughout the world there are numerous reactionary elements which had hoped for Axis victory—and now profess great friendship for the United States. Yet, these enemies of yesterday and false friends of today continually try to provoke war between the United States and Russia. They have no real love of the United States. They only long for the day when the United States and Russia will destroy each other.

We must not let our Russian policy be guided or influenced by those inside or outside the United States who want war with Russia. This does not mean appeasement.

We most earnestly want peace with Russia—but we want to be met halfway. We want co-operation. And I believe that we can get co-operation once Russia understands that our primary objective is neither saving the British Empire nor purchasing oil in the Near East with the lives of American soldiers. We cannot allow national oil rivalries to force us into war. All of the nations producing oil, whether inside or outside of their own boundaries, must fulfill the provisions of the United Nations Charter and encourage the development of world petroleum reserves so as to make the maximum amount of oil available to all nations of the world on an equitable peaceful basis—and not on the basis of fighting the next war.

For her part, Russia can retain our respect by co-operating with the United Nations in a spirit of open-minded and flexible give and take.

The real peace treaty we now need is between the United States and Russia. On our part, we should recognize that we have no more business in the *political* affairs of Eastern Europe than Russia has in the *political* affairs of Latin America, Western Europe and the United States. We may not like what Russia does in Eastern Europe. Her type of land reform, industrial expropriation, and suppression of basic liberties offends the great majority of the people of the United States. But whether we like it or not, the Russians will try to socialize their sphere of influence just as we try to democratize our sphere of influence. This applies also to

Germany and Japan. We are striving to democratize Japan and our area of control in Germany, while Russia strives to socialize Eastern Germany.

As for Germany, we all must recognize that an equitable settlement, based on a unified German nation, is absolutely essential to any lasting European settlement. This means that Russia must be assured that never again can German industry be converted into military might to be used against her—and Britain, Western Europe and the United States must be certain that Russia's German policy will not become a tool of Russian design against Western Europe.

The Russians have no more business in stirring up native Communists to political activity in Western Europe, Latin America and the United States than we have in interfering in the politics of Eastern Europe and Russia. We know what Russia is up to in Eastern Europe, for example, and Russia knows what we are up to. We cannot permit the door to be closed against our trade in Eastern Europe any more than we can in China. But at the same time we have to recognize that the Balkans are closer to Russia than to us—and that Russia cannot permit either England or the United States to dominate the politics of that area.

China is a special case, and, although she holds the longest frontier in the world with Russia, the interests of world peace demand that China remain free from any sphere of influence, either politically or economically. We insist that the door to trade and economic development opportunities be left wide open in China as in all the world. However, the open door to trade and opportunities for economic development in China are meaningless unless there is a unified and peaceful China—built on the co-operation of the various groups in that country and based on a hands-off policy of the outside powers.

We are still arming to the hilt. Our excessive expenses for military purposes are the chief cause of our unbalanced budget. If taxes are to be lightened we must have the basis of a real peace with Russia—a peace that cannot be broken by extremist propagandists. We do not want our course determined for us by master minds operating out of London, Moscow or Nanking.

Russian ideas of social-economic justice are going to govern nearly a third of the world. Our ideas of free-enterprise democracy will govern much of the rest. The two ideas will endeavor to prove which can deliver the most satisfaction to the common man in their respective areas of political dominance. But by mutual agreement, this competition should be put on a friendly basis and the Russians should stop conniving against us in certain areas of the world, just as we should stop scheming against them in other parts of the world. Let the results of the two systems speak for themselves.

Meanwhile, the Russians should stop teaching that their form of communism must, by force if necessary, ultimately triumph over democratic capitalism—while we should close our ears to those among us who would have us believe that Russian communism and our free-enterprise system cannot live, one with another, in a profitable and productive peace.

Under friendly, peaceful competition the Russian world and the American world will gradually become more alike. The Russians will be forced to grant more and more of the personal freedoms; and we shall become more and more absorbed with the problems of social-economic justice.

Russia must be convinced that we are not planning for war against her, and we must be certain that Russia is not carrying on territorial expansion or world domination through native Communists faithfully following every twist and turn in the Moscow party line. But in this competition, we must insist on an open door for trade throughout the world. There will always be an ideological conflict—but that is no reason why diplomats cannot work out a basis for both systems to live safely in the world side by side.

Once the fears of Russia and the United States Senate have been allayed by practical regional political reservations, I am sure that concern over the veto power would be greatly diminished. Then the United Nations would have a really great power in those areas which are truly international and not regional. In the world-wide, as distinguished from the regional, field, the armed might of the United Nations should be so great as to make opposition useless. Only the United Nations should have atomic bombs, and its military establishment should give special emphasis to air power. It should have control of the strategically located air bases with which the United States and Britain have encircled the world. And not only should individual nations be prohibited from manufacturing atomic bombs, guided missiles and military aircraft for bombing purposes, but no nation should be allowed to spend on its military establishment more than perhaps 15 per cent of its budget.

Practically and immediately, we must recognize that we are not yet ready for world federation. Realistically, the most we can hope for now is a safe reduction in military expense and a long period of peace based on mutual trust between the Big Three.

During this period, every effort should be made to develop as rapidly as possible a body of international law based on moral principles and not on the Machiavellian principles of deceit, force and distrust—which, if continued, will lead the modern world to rapid disintegration.

In brief, as I see it today, the world order is bankrupt—and the United States, Russia and England are the receivers. These are the hard facts of power politics on which we have to build a functioning, powerful United Nations and a body of international law. And as we build, we must develop fully the doctrine of the rights of small peoples as contained in the United Nations Charter. This law should ideally apply as much to Indonesians and Greeks as to Bulgarians and Poles—but practically, the application may be delayed until both British and Russians discover the futility of their methods.

In the full development of the rights of small nations, the British and Russians can learn a lesson from the Good Neighbor policy of Franklin Roosevelt. For under Roosevelt, we in the Western Hemisphere built a workable system of regional internationalism that fully protected the sovereign rights of every nation—a system of multilateral action that immeasurbly strengthened the whole or world order.

In the United States an informed public opinion will be all-powerful. Our people are peace-minded. But they often express themselves too late—for events today move much faster than public opinion. The people here, as everywhere in the world, must be convinced that another war is not inevitable, and through mass meetings such as this, and through persistent pamphleteering, the people can be organized for peace—even though a large segment of our press is propagandizing our people for war in the hope of scaring Russia. And we who look on this war-with-Russia talk as criminal foolishness must carry our message direct to the people—even though we may be called Communists because we dare to speak out.

I believe that peace—the kind of peace I have outlined tonight —is the basic issue, both in the congressional campaign this fall and right on through the presidential election in 1948. How we meet this issue will determine whether we live not in "one world" or "two worlds"—but whether we live at all.[*1]

Banished from the Cabinet, Wallace led a Progressive Party crusade in 1948 to unseat Truman. It failed, as did a conservative revolt in the form of a "Dixiecrat" Party. Truman's advisers had recommended that he deal with Wallace by isolating and identifying "him in the public mind with the Communists." Communists did "infiltrate" the Wallace campaign, but the real tragedy of the former Vice-President was seen (from a Cold War point of view) as one of those "who adhered to . . . obsolete concepts."

Three decades earlier, another liberal, William Jennings Bryan, had sought to distinguish political from economic questions and to sort out the good from the bad. Dollar diplomacy was bad, but increased economic expansion was good; special privilege was bad, encouragement of foreign investment good, and so on. Byran spelled it all out in an interview with a reporter from the St. Louis *Post-Dispatch*. The headline read: SECRETARY OF STATE TELLS THE POST-DISPATCH HOW THE WILSON ADMINISTRATION HAS BROKEN THE PARTNERSHIP BETWEEN GOVERNMENT AND SPECIAL INTERESTS.

[*1] *Vital Speeches*, XII (October 1, 1946), p. 738–741.

Premier of President Wilson's Cabinet Declares in a Notable Interview That the Day When a Gunboat Goes With Each Foreign Bond Bought by a Citizen of This Country Is at an End, and Henceforth We Shall Deal With Other Peoples According to the Same Standards of Honor We Observe in Dealing With Each Other.

Also, There Is to Be an End of the Custom of Accrediting to Latin-American Republics As Representatives of This Nation, Men Who Are Largely Interested in Concerns That Hold Big Concessions From Those Governments and Are Trying to Get Additional Grants and Privileges.

By Henry Hall,

WASHINGTON, April 19. [1913] A Special Correspondent of the Post-Dispatch.

William Jennings Bryan, Secretary of State, looks just like what he is, a prosperous, professional man. The responsibilities of his high office have added dignity to his strength. Cautious he always was, but now he cloaks himself in a mantle of reserve which he had no occasion to wear when a candidate for office, or as an orator on the stump. For years, by patient labor and despite discouragement, he led his followers into untrodden paths and conjured up new—some people think, better—forms of political life; today the sobering effect of great authority is making itself felt and Bryan satisfies himself that the policies and the reforms he advocates are practical as well as beneficial and will work for the greatest good of the greatest number.

Versatility, accuracy, executive ability and commanding power are the traits which most impress one when facing the rather heavy, middleaged man who, thrice an unsuccessful candidate for the presidency, now first takes office as the senior member of President Wilson's Cabinet. His bearing is that of a leader of men.

The face, somewhat angular yet full is a very human and attractive face. The cheek bones are still prominent, albeit the cheeks are heavy. The forehead is square. A deep line cleaves the eyebrows and two other lines diverge to right and left of his nostrils. The top of his head is almost bald, but a wealth of locks, once raven, now turning to an iron gray, still forms a halo around that, when all is said, is a very noble head.

The lips are thin, the mouth tight closed. Large ears, a prominent nose and a generous mouth, add to the character of unusual strength. But the impression made by Mr. Bryan's appearance is but a fleeing, flimsy fantasy, compared to the deep conviction of honesty which even a few hours' intercourse with him forces upon one's mind.

He is an ideal companion, a delightful talker—the kind of man who can be friends with a book and give to others the advantage of his reading without a trace of pedantry—but, above all, he is a really religious man, a true follower of Christ, pure in mind and strong in body, whose sole aim is to do what is right for righteousness' sake regardless of whom it may hurt.

HIS ADVENT MARKS AN EPOCH IN OUR INTERNATIONAL RELATIONS

His advent in the State Department marks the beginning of a new era in the international relations of the United States, because his conception of the uses of diplomacy is radically different from that which for the past 16 years has directed this country's foreign policy. Mr. Bryan had been discussing with me what is known as "Dollar Diplomacy" and its effects. There was nothing of the emotional orator about him. His talk was as calmly reasoned as a court decision, but it radiated heartfelt faith in the American people, in their principles, their morality and their form of Government. He was rugged, brave, studious and sincere. He epitomized all our talk in one of those short, expressive sentences he is so fond of using when he said:

The preceding administration attempted to till the field of foreign investment with a pen knife; President Wilson intends to cultivate it with a spade.

We were traveling together from Washington to Philadelhpia, the drawing room car was close and stuffy, and before he settled down to express his view Mr. Bryan threw off his well-tailored frock coat, tucked a big white handkerchief inside his collar and, after making himself thoroughly comfortable, began speaking in a very even voice, the rich fullness of which added to the charm of his delightfully melodious English.

Dollar diplomacy . . . is a phrase coined to describe a policy of government under which the State Department has been used to coerce smaller nations into recognizing claims of American citizens which did not rest upon a legitimate basis, claims that either were founded in injustice or which were exaggerated until they represented an unfair demand.

When a great nation like ours deals with one comparatively smaller, as for instance the republics of Central and South America, the larger nation must be even more scrupulous as to the methods employed then when it is dealing with a nation that can defend itself.

If, for instance, an American corporation, or an American promoter, goes into a country waiting development and obtains a concession or makes a contract, questions may arise—they actually have arisen—as to the performance of the contract by the American corporation. The corporation, when its rights are affected, turns to the State Department for assistance, and it is proper that the State Department should render such assistance as can be legitimately rendered.

But what assistance is legitimate? I asked.

TELL HOW COUNTRY HAS PULLED PROMOTERS' CHESTNUTS FROM FIRE

Bryan, who makes very few gestures in speaking, gives a little pull to his white shirt sleeve and looked for a moment at the old-fashioned flat cuff button he was wearing. Then he went on:

Everything depends upon the definition of the word 'legitimate.' Some of the American promoters have acted upon the supposition that 'a gunboat goes with each bond,' to quote language that has been actually employed. They demand of the Government that the diplomatic representative of the

United States accredited to the country they are interested in shall require that country to meet any and every demand that the promoting company may make, and some seem to think it right that these demands be supported without regard to their character—unjust ones as well as just ones.

Sometimes the contract entered into between the Latin-American and the American promoter provides for the arbitration of controversies, the President of the United States to appoint the American representatives on the Arbitration Board.

It has even been the opinion of some—trained to the ways of dollar diplomacy—that this American representative should be not a judicial officer, but the special representative of the corporation engaged in the controversy. The corporation has even been allowed to name the American arbiter and the Government has been expected to support him and his findings just as if he were representing the honor of the nation instead of the interests of the corporation.

There was a shade of indignation in Mr. Bryan's voice as he spoke, and it was plain that he would never for a moment consider the placing of his country's interest before its honor. His manliness is attractive. He is a man of medium height and splendid physique, graceful and snappy in poise and gesture. With a simple dignity worthy of a great statesman, he continued to outline the future policy of the administration. He said:

The change that has taken place in the conception of the nation's obligation in such matters was clearly set forth in the President's admirable statement on the Chinese loan. The preceding administration, acting in perfect good faith and in accordance with the former President's ideas of American interests, asked a group of American bankers to join similar groups in five other countries and negotiate a loan to the Chinese Government. The American group was to have a monopoly of this nation's part in the loan, not only a monopoly of the nation's part in the present, but a preference in certain loans contemplated in the future.

The American group joined with the groups in the other

countries to arrange the details of the loan, one of the details being a provision for the appointment of foreigners to supervise the collection of certain custom duties as a matter of security.

President Wilson, after a careful investigation of the subject, and after the American bankers had had a hearing, refused to renew the request, setting forth his reasons therefor. While the statement related but to this Chinese loan the reasons given for a reversal of the policy of this country on the subject applied and apply to the entire subject of diplomacy as it relates to American investments abroad, and marks an era.

Bryan took the white handkerchief from around his neck, and rising, thrust it into his trousers pocket. He put on his frock coat and changing his seat, resumed the conversation:

NATIONS, LIKE INDIVIDUALS, MUST APPLY THE GOLDEN RULE

The country has endorsed the President's course with unanimity and it can hardly be doubted that this approval will be extended to the subsequent development of this policy as it is applied to similar cases.

The President believes—and what disinterested citizen does not?—that this nation's obligation to urge fairness on the part of Americans dealing with foreigners is as binding as its obligation to ask fairness on the part of foreigners dealing with Americans.

And then, a somewhat stern expression in his dark eyes, he looked me full in the face and, raising his voice gradually until it swelled into an organ-toned tumult of sound, declared:

The change that has taken place cannot honestly be regarded as the inauguration of a new diplomacy; it is simply a return to the diplomacy of earlier years.

It is the application of common sense, of common honesty and of plain everyday morality to our international affairs. It is a recognition of that sound philosophy which teaches that national ethics cannot differ from individual ethics.

President Wilson believes, and I believe, that there are no moral principles binding upon an individual that are not binding upon a nation. The attempt to formulate a moral code for nations different from that which governs us as individuals is the fruitful cause of much of the injustice that strong nations attempt to perpetuate upon weak ones.

The Golden Rule is just as useful in international affairs as it is among neighbors, and it is just as dangerous to ignore it.

Resuming his argument, Mr. Bryan continued:

In a suit between two individuals in this country we are careful to insist upon the impartiality of the judge and jury. Any suitor can disqualify a judge if he can show that the judge is interested, either pecuniarily or because of relations which would bias him. We carefully exclude from a jury every person who for any reason can be suspected of partiality to either litigant.

Is there any good reason why we should be less insistent in our demand for fairness when the United States engages in a controversy with a foreign government over the claims of one of its citizens? Can we in good conscience ask that any other nation shall consent to arbitration before a board if the American representative is tainted with an interest or biased in favor of a party to the suit? Does not our country's sense of honor require that its representative shall be above suspicion?

DOLLAR DIPLOMACY REPUDIATION OF FUNDAMENTAL PRINCIPLES OF MORALITY

Dollar diplomacy was a repudiation of the fundamental principles of morality as universally understood and accepted, and it offended that sense of justice which is equally universal. THE POLICY INAUGURATED BY PRESIDENT WILSON SEEKS TO BRING INTERNATIONAL DEALING INTO HARMONY WITH THE UNIVERSAL CONSCIENCE.

"What effect will this have on Americn business investments abroad?" I asked. There was confidence in Mr. Bryan's voice as he replied:

I have no doubt that the effect will be most beneficial. To doubt it would be to distrust the economic value of righteousness.

Justice is to the economic world what the law of gravitation is to the material world, and the suspension of justice is as disastrous as would be the suspension of the natural law that draws each particle of matter on the earth's surface toward the center of it.

The attempt to enforce the claims of Americans by methods repugnant alike to conscience and to established usage has always resulted and will always result in an irritation that imperils our trade relations and diminishes that opportunity.

When the people of other countries understand that the United States will investigate claims before it puts its moral force behind them, and that when it does approve a claim it will support that claim not by methods consistent with the nation's honor and the traditions of fair dealing— when the people of all other nations understand this, they will welcome American capital and American capitalists.

Many rich fields are awaiting development—the development of Central and South America is still in its infancy—and our nation is the nation to which our sister republics to the south of the United States naturally look for such assistance as they need. They followed our example in winning their independence, with a gallantry no less than that of our own heroes, they modeled their constitutions after ours; their school systems are increasingly borrowing from ours, they are sending to us for instructors and for experts in various lines of material development. Why should they not be encouraged to avail themselves of our rich experience, of our advanced system of instruction and of our widespread prosperity? Why should they not look upon the United States as the great clearing house of their natural wealth? It would be mutually advantageous. We need each other. Why not put our relationship upon an enduring basis of mutual confidence?

The President's policy means extension, expansion and multiplication of American interests.

We have, so to speak, been busy watching the spigot and neglecting the bung hole, and we have been doing it because of the short-sighted policy that allowed the man at the spigot to dictate the policy. The effort to get a few dollars by the employment of unfair and offensive methods has prevented our industries from securing that large and lucrative business which would have come with a more liberal policy—for a just policy is a liberal policy.

NEW GOLDEN RULE POLICY SOON
WILL HEAL WOUND OF THE PAST

And then I asked him a question which for some time has been uppermost in my mind:

"How are you going to win back the lost confidence of South America?" He answered in straight-flung words and few, and with an honesty so obvious and plainly apparent that it won my heart.

That matter will take care of itself. A splinter in the hand will make a sore and the sore will continue as long as the splinter remains. But when the splinter is withdrawn, nature heals and heals quickly. Dollar diplomacy was a foreign substance; irritation was a natural consequence. THE WOUNDS OF THE PAST WILL SOON BE HEALED NOW THAT DOLLAR DIPLOMACY IS DEAD. . . ."[*1]

Bryan soon found difficulty in applying the "Golden Rule Policy," especially in the Caribbean where the Secretary of State pursued much the same approach as his predecessors, the much-criticized Dollar Diplomats. Haitian officials continued to resist the imposition of American financial control by responding to Bryan's overtures with counteroffers of concessions and special preferences for American capitalists. These were beneath

[*1] St. Louis *Post-Dispatch*, April 20, 1913.

the Department's dignity, declared Bryan, who went on to stipulate American desires:

> While we desire to encourage in every proper way American investments in Haiti, we believe that this can be better done by contributing the stability and order than by favoring special concessions to Americans. American capital will gladly avail itself of business opportunities in Haiti when assured of peace and quiet necessary for profitable production.[*1]

After nearly two years of continued frustration, Bryan finally recommended to President Wilson "a plan similar to that which the Netherlands adopts in Java—namely, having a resident Advisor." He believed the plan was also used by the British "in some of the provinces of India." And when it came time, the Secretary of State did not hestitate to recommend military intervention and occupation. The intervention was justified, in part, by fears of German intervention in the Caribbean, but the Bryan plan (in one form or another) antedated those concerns. Nor was it that Americans had to have Haitian markets and investment opportunities to survive. The idea was to bring about a lasting resolution of issues disturbing the American nation in its relations with a much larger surrounding underdeveloped area—which was essential to the continued progress and prosperity of the nation. Or, as Dean Acheson would put it in 1946, the problem was to find a way to make use of "our great economic power, in our own interest, to hasten recovery [and, one would add, development] in other countries along lines which are essential to our own system."

Bryan resigned a few months later in protest over Wilson's decision to take a hard line with Germany on submarine warfare. Like Henry Wallace in 1946, he had found it impossible to square his own position and interpretation with the President's determination to condemn German actions on the seas while seeming to accept British restrictions on neutral trade. And like Wallace, Bryan soon found himself isolated within the Cabinet

---

[*1] Gardner, LaFeber, and McCormick, *Creation of the American Empire* (Chicago: Rand McNally & Co., 1973), p. 304.

and the Democratic Party. Unlike Wallace, however, he led no crusade in the next presidential election. Even so, Wilson campaigned as the centrist candidate who had kept America out of war.

Foreign policies, these readings and documents make clear, are not made up out of neat abstractions. Nor is it easy to distinguish between "Dollar Diplomacy" and the "Golden Rule Policy"—as Bryan found out. Similarly, later policy makers learned that "containment" was not divisible into strategic and nonstrategic areas—or separable from "liberation" as John Foster Dulles would have liked. Again, it was Dean Acheson who put it best: a foreign policy problem usually cannot be "separated in the intellectual equivalent of a cream separator" into military, political, and economic components.

Convinced that "imperialism" was something certain people did wrong, like robbing a bank or cheating the poor, Americans went about constructing a world order in which their freedoms could flourish. They made the world safe for democracy as they knew it. American diplomats did not run around the world thirsting after new markets; nor was the nation's foreign policy determined by the trade balance with each country of an alphabetical list of states. Very real fears of military weakness in the face of a powerful adversary determined many decisions. But an understanding of the sources of American foreign policy requires more than an identification of the external stimulus and determinants, or the drive to power all men share. Hopefully, these readings have provided the readers with questions for developing such an insight.

NOTES

[1] George F. Kennan, *Memoirs, 1950–1963* (Boston: Atlantic, Little, Brown, 1972), p. 178.
[2] Cited in Walter LaFeber, *America, Russia, and the Cold War* (New York: John Wiley & Sons, 1967), p. 209.
[3] Harry S. Truman, *Memoirs* (Garden City, N.Y.: Doubleday & Co., 1956), II, 111–112.
[4] Cited in Lloyd C. Gardner, Walter LaFeber, and Thomas McCormick, *Creation of the American Empire* (Chicago: Rand-McNally Co., 1973), p. 444.
[5] Kennan, *Memoirs*, I, p. 330.
[6] See *Vital Speeches*, XII (August 1, 1946), p. 634.

Index

Africa: foreign aid to, 138, 142; total diplomacy in, 281; type of investments in, 126

Alliance for Progress: in Brazil, 74–78; design of program, 78; Dominican crisis and, 64, 66, 68; Dominican Republic as showcase for, 73–74; funding, 74; as instrument of change, 38

Arms sales: see Military aid

Asia: establishing U.S. hegemony over, 255–64; total diplomacy in, 281–83; type of investments in, 126

Aswan dam project (1950s), 199–200

Baghdad Pact (1955), 196

Berlin problem, 162–65, 229, 239

Brazil: Alliance for Progress in, 74–78; arms for, 115

Capitalism: see Economy

China: change in policy toward (1970s), ix, x, xiv–xvi, 3–6; Cuba and (1959–1960), 171, 173–74; Egypt recognizes (1956), 200; free from spheres of influence, 348; international communism controlling, 193–94; intervention in Korean War, 236, 237, 240–42, 245–48,

263, 265; philosophy of, 5, 6; Quemoy and Matsu confrontation, 211–13; recognizing emergence of (1950), 253; total diplomacy and, 267–73; U.S. "loss" of, 256, 257, 266, 267; in Vietnam War, 35–38, 42–43

Clay Report (1963), 138–43

Communism: international, defined, 193–95; international, as useful threat, 218–19, 224; revolution and, 64–66

Congress: growth of executive power and, 323–24; reassertion of responsibility of, 101–102

Containment doctrine, 10, 187, 294–323; criticized, 246–48, 308–17; described, 297–308; as euphemism for expansion, 265; expressions of, 324–31; justified, 317–23; see also Korean War

Cuba: anti-American campaign in (1959, 1960), 175; intervention in (1898), 91; intervention in Dominican crisis and fear of, 67, 68, 70–73; protection of U.S. interests in, 183–84; seizure of U.S.-owned businesses in, 77; U.S.–Cuban relations (1959–1960), 169–74; U.S. investments in (1959), 167, 168; U.S. investments in public utilities

in, 175–78; U.S. investments in
sugar of, 178–82; U.S. investments
and U.S. foreign policy toward,
182–83; U.S. labor movement and,
80; U.S. presence in, 166
Cuban missile crisis (1962), 56–57,
144–66; effects of, 145–46; evaluation of, 146–48; October 22
(1962) address on, 147–54; overthrow of Castro as purpose of,
161–65; Russian intentions in,
154–61

Defense, Department of: criticism of,
96–101; military aid and, *see* Military aid; popular support for increased budget for (1950s), 255;
social responsibilities of, 91–96
Dollar diplomacy, 351, 357–59
Dominican crisis (1965), 41, 63–74;
defense of intervention in, 70–73;
faulty basis for intervention in, 63–
68; Vietnam War and, 69–70
Dominoes, theory of falling, 54–55,
215–16, 266

Economy: attempts to disassociate
political and economic questions,
345–60; bases of imperial, 123–31;
expansion of, 185; national interest,
defined, 130–31; new economic
power centers and, xii–xvii; raw
materials and development of,
126–30; 1960 Cuban and U.S.,
174–83; Point IV program and,
274–76, 279, 284–93; political
problems of expanding, 344–45; total diplomacy for, 280–93; U.S. interests and reformed, 344; violence
and stagnation of, 93; *see also*
Containment doctrine; Exports; Investments; Military aid; Trade;
World order
Egypt: foreign aid to, 142; invasion
of (1950s), 190; Iran and, 104–
106; Suez crisis, 198, 199; total
dipomacy and, 290
Eisenhower administration, 97; Cuba
and, 172, 174; Indochina and, 211
(*see also* Indochina); intervention
in Guatemala under, 216–24; intervention in Iran under, 201–11;

massive retaliation doctrine under,
228–34; U.S. entry into Middle
East under (1950s), 188–201
Eisenhower Doctrine (1957), 187–
90, 212
England: arms sale and, 116, 119;
attacks Egypt (1956), 198, 199;
military aid to Indochina (1950s),
215; as part of new economic
power center, xiii; and U.S. intervention in Iran (1950s), 201–11
Establishment, the: "strange sickness"
in, 6–8, 15; Vietnam War and
limits imposed by, 18
Europe, *see* Western Europe
Executive power, growth of, 323–24
Exports, 135–38; concentration of,
136, 138

Foreign aid: strategy for, 138–43; *see
also* Military aid
Foreign Assistance Act (1961), 116,
117
Foreign Assistance Act (1963), 141
Foreign Assistance Act (1966), 119
Foreign Economic Assistance Act
(1950), 274
Formosa, *see* Taiwan
Formosa Resolution (1955), 212–13
France: attacks Egypt (1956), 198,
199; Indochina war of, 211–14,
253–54; military aid to Indochina
(1950s), 215

Geneva Conference (1954), 213–14
Germany, *see* West Germany
Greece: justifying aid to, 317–21,
324–31; preventing takeover of,
229, 239, 251, 265, 270; total
diplomacy and, 280
Guatemala: intervention in, 216–24
Guerrilla war, 11; bodycount ratio in,
34; counter-insurgency measures,
96; Dominican (1963), 71; spread
of, 92–94; underdeveloped world
and, 37–40; *see also* Vietnam War

Hungary: trade with, 337–39; uprising in (1956), 189, 198, 340

Imperialism: bases for, 123–31; *see
also* Military aid

Indochina, 215; importance of, in U.S. view, 215–16; French war in, 211–14, 253–54; military aid to (1950s), 214–15; Russian involvement in, 265; total displomacy in, 281; U.S. bases in (1950s), 255; U.S. intervention in (1950s), 211

Investments: Alliance for Progress as aid to, 78–79; Clay Report and, 141; Cuban revolution and protection of, 183–84 (see also Cuba); direct foreign (1957), 125, 126; flows of (1950–1965), 130; gross private (1968), 132–33; growth of foreign (1960–1969), 132; intervention in Guatemala and, 216, 218; in Latin America (1945–1969; 1959), 77, 167, 168; national interest as business, 130–31; protecting Latin American, 74–78; rate of return on (1960–1970), 134; in raw materials (1969), 134; rejection of economic argument as influence on foreign policy, 132–37; U.S. labor movement, U.S.-style institutions in Latin America and, 79–91

Iran: intervention in (1950s), 201–11; military aid to, 102–106, 109; nationalizes oil, 201; total diplomacy and, 280

Isolationism, 234; neoisolationism, 1, 5

Japan: democratizing, 347–48; exports to (1968), 136; investments in, 133; and loss of Indochina, 216; as new economic power center, xiii, xvi; peace treaty with, 263, 265; in U.S. defense perimeter (1950), 254

Johnson administration: Dominican crisis under, see Dominican crisis; Johnson's decision not to run again (1968), 32–33; Vietnam War policy reversal under (1968), 16–33 (see also Vietnam War)

Kennedy administration: foreign aid under, 138–43; see also Cuban missile crisis

Korean Truce Agreement (1953), 236

Korean War (1949–1953), 224, 226–67; armistice in, 212; as civil war, 36; containment policy in, 295 (see also Containment doctrine); critical review of, 248–58; domestic political questions in, 253–65; and establishing U.S. hegemony over Asia, 255–64; MacArthur's removal, 237–38; total diplomacy and, 274; unification of Korea as aim of, 249–52; U.S. Far East policy and, 238–44; who started, 255–56, 261–65

Labor movement: U.S.-style institutions in Latin America and U.S., 79–91

Latin America: exports of, 129; investments in, see Investments; military aid to, 105–108; military aid and deficits in, 119; support for oligarchies in, 66–67; total diplomacy in, 283; U.S. arms sales and guerrillas in, 119; U.S. labor movement and U.S.-style institutions in, 79–91; in U.S. sphere of influence, 347–48

Liberation policy, 10

Mansfield Report (1962), 140

Marshall Plan (1947), 309

Massive retaliation doctrine, 228–34

Middle East: entry into (1950s), 188–201; military aid to, 196–97; responsibilities in (1970s), 3–6

Military, the: as major instrument of U.S. leadership, 100–101

Military aid, 100–23; to Cuba, 182; to developing nations, 101–107; Eximbank in, 116–17; to Indochina (1950s), 214–15; justified, 102–108; to Middle East (1950s), 196–97; military assistance credit account for, 117–20; 1952–1966, 110, 116; 1962–1966, 115; potential sales (1965–1975), 114; private banking in, 117; purposes of, 107–108, 110–14; shortcomings of, 120–23

Military-industrial complex, 120, 123

Monroe Doctrine (1823), 216
Mutual Defense Assistance Act (1949), 108–109, 277
Mutual Security Act (1951), 276–79; encouragement of free enterprise and, 277–79; strategic material and, 277
Mutual Security Act (1957), 117, 194
Mutual Security Agreement (1952) with Ecuador, 279

National liberation wars, 37–40; Vietnam as test case of, 55; see also Guerrilla war; Vietnam War
Neoisolationism, 1, 5
Nixon administration: changes in policy inaugurated by, ix–xviii; effects of Vietnam War on foreign policy and, 1–7; Vietnam War under, 7–16
Nixon Doctrine, 5
North Atlantic Treaty Organization (NATO; 1949), 293–94
North Korea, 236
Nuclear weapons: political effects of Russian development of, 273–74; U.S. control of, 349–50

Pax Americana research project, 98–102
Point IV program, 274–76, 279; implementing, 284–93
Potsdam Agreement (1945), 338
Power: expansion prompted by, 136–37

Raw materials: capitalist development and, 126–30; percent investment in (1969), 134
Russia: Arab nationalism and, 198–99; change in policy toward (1970s), ix–x, xiii–xv, xvi, 3–6; containment of, see Containment doctrine; Cuba and (1959–1960), 171, 173–74 (see also Cuban missile crisis); and developing struggle over trade, 331–44; and German rearmament, 235–36; goal to control Asia, 240, 242; international communism controlling, 193–94; Iran and, 103–105; military aid from, 109; massive retaliation doctrine and aims of, 230 (see also Massive retaliation doctrine); Monroe Doctrine and, 219–21; philosophy of, 5, 6; political effects of development of nuclear weapons by, 273–74; possibility for peace and competition with, 345–51; sphere of influence of, 344–45; start of Korean War and, 261–63, 265 (see also Korean War); total diplomacy and, 267–73; and U.S. intervention in Iran (1950s), 201–11

Sino–Soviet split, 265–66
Social sciences, 95–98
South East Asia Treaty Organization (SEATO; 1954), 213
South Korea, 236–37; government of, saved from extinction (1950s), 255–57, 260; military aid to, 102; total diplomacy and, 282–83; see also Korean War
South Vietnam: proposed elections in (1956), 213–14; SEATO and, 213; U.S. intervention in, 211; see also Vietnam War,
Soviet Union, see Russia
Suez Crisis (1956), 198, 199

Taiwan, 60; assuming loss of (1950), 253–57, 259, 260, 263; support for (1950s), 211–12; total diplomacy and, 282; U.S. bases in, 255
Tonkin Gulf Resolution (1964), 36, 48–49, 212; contingency plans and, 54–56; disagreements over, 40–41
Total diplomacy, 267–73, 280–93
Trade: developing struggle over, 331–44; as tool of stability, 271–72; see also Exports; Raw materials
Truman administration: criticism of foreign policy of, 245–48; Far East policy of, 238–44; total diplomacy in, 267–73; see also Containment doctrine; Korean War
Truman Doctrine (1947): opposition to, 308–309; support for, 317–23
Turkey: justifying aid to, 317–21, 324–31; preventing takeover of, 229, 270; total diplomacy and, 280

Vietnam War, 1–62; bodycount ratio in, 34; bombing started, 46; bombing halted, 16–18, 23–33; Chinese national interests in, 35–38, 42–43; cost of, 8–9; domestic opposition to, 48; Dominican crisis and, 69–70; Johns Hopkins speech and Hanoi's four point for settling (1965), 41–48; policy reversal in (1968), 16–33; problems of negotiations in, 11–15; process of escalation of (1961–1965), 48–62; prospects for negotiations (1967–1968), 26; U.S. disengagement from, ix, x, xi, xii, 3–6; wars of national liberation and, 37–40; *see also* Tonkin Gulf Resolution
Vietnamization, 9–10, 15, 17–18

West Germany: arms sales to, 111–13, 116, 119; democratizing, 347–48; as part of new economic power center, xiii; rearmament of, 235, 263
Western Europe: arms sales to (1962–1966), 115; arms sales and relations with, 118–19; exports to (1968), 136; interests of U.S. and, in Middle East, 188–98; investments in, 126, 130, 133; Korean War and security of, 248; as new economic power center, xiii, xvi; U.S. responsibilities in (1970s), 3–6; in U.S. sphere of influence, 347–48
World order: defense of, 43; essence of security and, 91–95; expansion and security of, 137; foreign aid as vital to security of, 139–40; maintaining Middle East (1950s) security and, 196–98; U.S. leadership and new, xvii–xviii